Farm Management Pocketbook

by

JOHN NIX

THIRTY-SEVENTH EDITION
(2007)

SEPTEMBER 2006

Copies of this book may be obtained from:

The Pocketbook, 2 Nottingham Street,
Melton Mowbray, Leicestershire LE13 1NW.

(Tel: 01664 564508 Fax: 01664 410505)

PRICE £17.00 +**£1.50 p&p**
5 to 19 copies: £16.00
20 to 99 copies: £15.00
100 to 999 copies: £14.00
Postage & Packaging free for 5 or more copies

ISBN 0-9541201-5-9
ISBN 978-0-9541201-5-3

FOREWORD TO THE FIRST EDITION

This booklet is intended for farmers, advisers, students and everyone else who, frequently or infrequently, find themselves hunting for data relating to farm management - whether it is for blunt pencil calculations on the back of an envelope or for feeding into a computer. The material contained is based upon the sort of information which the author finds himself frequently having to look up in his twin roles as adviser and teacher in farm management. There are several excellent handbooks already in existence, but this pocketbook endeavours to cover a wider field and thus to be substantially more comprehensive. It is intended that most of the data herein contained will have a national application, although there is inevitably some bias towards conditions in the south-eastern half of the country.

The development of farm planning techniques in recent years has outstripped the quality and quantity of data available. It is hoped that this booklet will go a little further in supplying the type of information required. It cannot, however, claim to be the ultimate in this respect. For example, there are many variations in labour requirements according to farm conditions and sizes and types of machine used and there are many more variations in sheep and beef systems than are dealt with here. More detailed data on these lines are gradually becoming available from various sources. It is hoped further to refine the material in this booklet and to keep it up to date in subsequent editions, as the information becomes available. As a help towards this end, any comments or criticisms will be gratefully received.

The author wishes to thank his many friends and colleagues who have given him so much time and help in compiling this information.

John Nix
October, 1966

First published October 1966

Thirty-seventh Edition   September 2006

FOREWORD TO THE THIRTY-SEVENTH EDITION

The Pocketbook continues to evolve as agriculture and agricultural policy change. No references to area or headage payments are included – all having been swept away by the introduction of the Single Payment Scheme. The latest sector to face CAP reform is sugar. The margin for this crop has changed markedly from the last Pocketbook with the reduction in guaranteed prices.

Prices for combinable crops look somewhat better for the next harvest – with much of the firming on the back of the perceived positive outlook for biofuels. Higher grain prices can be a double-edged sword as they mean higher feed costs for livestock farmers. All sectors are having to cope with input cost rises driven by continuing high energy costs.

Most of the figures are predicted forward one year, i.e. to 2007. *Thus the crops data relate to the 2007 harvest, i.e. the 2007/2008 marketing year. The livestock data relate either to the 2007 calendar year (e.g. for milk production) or to 2007/2008 (e.g. for winter finished beef), as appropriate.* In a few cases current (i.e. mid-2006) figures are given, where it seemed particularly difficult to try to forecast ahead. The year to which the figures relate is normally stated.

The figures for yields and prices assume a 'normal', or average, season, based on trends, e.g. for potatoes, looking 18-24 months ahead to 2007/2008, no one can predict what the actual average yield and price for that particular year will be.

The data in this book should always be used with caution. *The figures should be adjusted as appropriate according to circumstances and price and cost differences.* As far as possible the assumptions in the tables are set out so as to enable this to be done fairly readily.

As ever, all the enterprises have been reviewed and revised for this edition. I would like to thank the Andersons' Business Research team, who have assisted greatly in its production.

Both Paul Hill and Angela Edwards decided to retire from contributing to the book after the previous edition. I wish to thank them considerably for their invaluable help over many years – since the very early editions in the case of Paul Hill.

John Nix

August, 2006

CONTENTS

I GENERAL

1. THE USE OF GROSS MARGINS

DEFINITION

The Gross Margin of an enterprise is its enterprise output less its variable costs. Enterprise output includes the market value of production retained on the farm. The variable costs must (a) be specific to the enterprise and (b) vary in proportion to the size of the enterprise, i.e. number of hectares or head of stock. The main items of variable costs are: Crops: fertilizer, seed, sprays, casual labour and contract work specific to the crop. Non-Grazing Livestock: concentrate feed, vet. and med., marketing expenses. Grazing Livestock: as for non-grazing livestock, plus forage crop variable costs.

POINTS TO NOTE

1. The gross margin is in no sense a profit figure. The so-called 'fixed costs' (rent, labour, machinery, general overheads - see pages 172-176) have to be covered by the total farm gross margin before arriving at a profit.

2. The gross margin of an enterprise will differ from season to season, partly because of yield and price differences affecting output and partly because variable costs may vary, e.g. the number and type of sprays required. Different soils and other natural factors, as well as level of management, will also cause differences between farms.

3. Items of variable cost may vary from farm to farm, e.g. some farmers use casual labour (a variable cost) to plant and pick their potatoes, others use only regular labour (a fixed cost); some farmers employ a contractor to combine their cereals (a variable cost), others employ their own equipment (a fixed cost); some employ a contractor to cart their sugar beet to the factory (a variable cost), others have their own lorry (a fixed cost). These differences must be borne in mind in making inter-farm comparisons.

4. Provided points 2 and 3 are borne in mind, comparison of gross margins (particularly averages over several seasons) with standards can be a useful check on technical efficiency.

5. The other main usefulness of gross margins lies in farm planning. This is not simply a matter of substituting high gross margin enterprises for low gross margin enterprises. The gross margin is only one relevant feature of an enterprise, although an important one. It says nothing about the call the enterprise makes on the basic farm resources - labour at different times of the year, machinery,

buildings, working capital requirements, etc. All these factors and more have to be taken into account in the planning process.

6. This is not to argue that these other costs should be allocated. Complete allocation of many farm expenses is only possible on an arbitrary basis, since they are shared by two or more, possibly all, farm enterprises. Allocation can therefore be completely misleading when making planning decisions. The same is true even when regular labour and machinery are employed specifically on certain enterprises, if such costs are calculated on a per hectare or per head basis. This is because when enterprises are substituted, expanded, contracted or deleted the variable costs for each enterprise will vary roughly in proportion to the size of that enterprise, but other costs will not, except possibly for fuel and some repair costs. Most 'fixed' costs may stay the same, others will change - but not smoothly in small amounts at a time. Either the same regular labour force will cope with a revised plan or a smaller or larger number of men will be needed. The same is true of tractors, other machines and buildings. Such cost changes must of course be taken into account, but allocating these costs on a per hectare or per head basis will not aid, and may positively confuse, planning decisions. The only point of making such calculations is for efficiency comparisons, e.g. labour costs per cow.

7. Allocating fixed costs at a flat rate (e.g. per hectare) for all enterprises, deducting this from the gross margin and hence calculating a 'net profit' from each enterprise can also be misleading. It ignores the whole problem of enterprise inter-relationships, differences between enterprises in total and seasonal requirements for labour, machinery and capital, and other factors such as different quality land on the same farm.

8. Changes in the scale of an enterprise may well affect its gross margin per unit, e.g. increasing the area of winter wheat from 30% to 50% on a farm will mean more second and third crop wheats being grown and a smaller proportion of the crop being drilled under the best conditions; hence yields will in all probability fall. Even if yields remain the same, variable costs (e.g. fertilizer use) will probably increase.

9. Gross margins used for planning future changes should also take account of possible changes in price, and the effect of changes in production techniques.

LOW, AVERAGE AND HIGH LEVELS

The three performance and production levels given for most crop and livestock enterprises are meant for the most part to indicate differences in natural factors, soil productivity, and/or managerial skill, *given the level of variable cost inputs.* They refer, at each level, to *an average over several years* taking *trends* into account. The evidence on the effect of significantly higher or lower levels of variable inputs on gross margins is conflicting and highly uncertain, depending on many factors, including soil type, and will vary from season to season.

2. COMPLETE ENTERPRISE COSTINGS

Requests are occasionally made for this book to include 'complete' enterprise costings, by which is meant the allocation of all costs to each individual enterprise, not only the variable costs as in the calculation of gross margins.

In the early days of farm business management teaching and research this was the preoccupation of most of those specialising in the subject. The system was, however, abandoned by nearly all practising farm economists in the 1950s. The main reasons are given in item 6 of the previous section explaining gross margins. Much meaningless and arbitrary allocation of 'joint costs' is required, (attempting 'to allocate the unallocatable'), and the results are often misleading in making farm decisions. Furthermore, it requires a considerable amount of record-keeping - in allocating labour on a mixed farm, tractor and machinery costs, telephone bills and so on. Few farmers are prepared to spend the required time and money to do this, nor do they need to.

Another problem in 'complete enterprise costing' is where to stop. Should interest on capital be included, whether borrowed or not? Further problems of asset valuation and allocation are involved if so. What of management and marketing supplied by the farmer? Should these be for free, as is usually assumed in such cases?

Variations between farms in their financial situations are considerable as, for instance, between the farmer who owns all his land without any mortgage and has no other borrowings and the one with both a rent to pay for all his land and heavy borrowings in addition.

In some situations, e.g. in some company-owned farms, farm managers are obliged to supply such data to their employers, whether they want to or not. Also, if enterprise costs are used for price fixing purposes governments, or price negotiators, usually require some such attempt to be made, whatever the difficulties and shortcomings of the methodology employed.

The above problems arise when 'costs per tonne' or 'costs per litre' are calculated. Wheat can be calculated to cost anything between £50 and £150 a tonne according to just what costs are included, how they are calculated (allocated) and the yield level assumed.

This is not to decry the efforts that are sometimes made in this direction. Particularly when product prices are falling it seems a natural thing to want to do - to calculate 'unit costs' to compare with prices received. Sometimes they do make clearer particular costs that need investigating and by that means economies that might be made, and they always attract interest. For these reasons costs per litre of milk are included, although the calculation of some of the 'fixed cost' items is difficult. If a farm has only one enterprise such calculations on that farm are obviously straightforward. However, even on solely dairy farms followers are usually reared, which is a second enterprise to milk production.

If required a cost per tonne of wheat (and other combinable crops) can be readily calculated by adding the fixed costs per hectare of mainly cereals farms (according to size range, given on page 174) to the variable costs per hectare given in the enterprise gross margin data and dividing by the selected yield.

The allocation of specific labour (e.g. a full-time cowman), machinery (e.g. a potato harvester) and buildings (e.g. a grain store) is relatively simple and can provide useful information both for purposes of efficiency comparisons and partial budgeting. For some enterprises on many mixed farms, however, there are few, if any, such specific items and the question of the other so-called fixed cost items remains if a full costing is attempted.

3. TOTAL FARM GROSS MARGIN

No attempt is made in this book to compile total gross margins for the whole farm, based on the forecasts made for individual enterprises for 2007, since the possible permutations in terms of enterprise combinations and performance levels are endless. Nor has it ever been the intention in the Pocketbook to include 'historical data', except for some of the material in the Agristats section. Hence total farm survey results, which are inevitably a year or two old by the time they are collated, analysed and published, are not included. Their usefulness for any particular farm is bound to be limited, particularly if the farm systems are broadly defined and cover much of the United Kingdom.

Furthermore, such data are published annually on a regional basis, covering the wide range of farm types and size ranges in each particular part of the country.

Easily the main source in the United Kingdom is the Farm Business Survey, carried out for and financed by DEFRA in England, the National Assembly for Wales ARAD, the Scottish Executive ERAD and the Department of Agriculture and Rural Development in Northern Ireland. The annual reports are readily available from the departments that do the work. The names of the publications and the relevant University, College or Department are given below. The addresses and telephone numbers are given on page 249.

North:	Farming in Northern England (University of Newcastle-upon-Tyne).
Yorkshire:	Farming in Yorkshire (Askham Bryan College).
North-West:	*The University of Manchester has discontinued its survey and no longer publishes* An Economic Review of Farming in the North West. *Survey work in this region has been taken on by a consortium of other institutions led by the University of Nottingham. The University of Nottingham is collecting results for Staffordshire. Askam Bryan is responsible for Lancashire, Cheshire, Merseyside and Greater Manchester. Shropshire is now surveyed by Reading University.*
East Midlands:	Farming in the East Midlands (University of Nottingham).
Eastern Counties:	Report on Farming in the Eastern Counties (University of Cambridge).
South-East	Farm Business Statistics for South East England (Imperial College London, Wye Campus).
South:	Farm Business Data (University of Reading).
South-West:	Farm Management Handbook (University of Exeter).
Wales:	Farm Business Survey in Wales (University of Wales, Aberystwyth).

Data for Scotland and Northern Ireland are available from the Scottish Agricultural College and Department of Agriculture and Rural Development, Northern Ireland respectively. Their addresses too are given on page 250.

II. SINGLE PAYMENT SCHEME

Major reforms of the Common Agricultural Policy were agreed in 2003. They came into effect, for the most part, on the 1st January 2005. Then in November 2005 a major reform of the Sugar Regime was agreed including price cuts and compensation to farmers starting with the 2006 sugar beet crop.

The following account of the new regime(s) is deliberately restricted to the main features. Points of detail, including exceptions that are likely to arise in few cases, are omitted so as not to confound the main aspects; they are available in full in other publications, if required. Some details still remain to be clarified (as at July 2006).

1. THE BASICS

The major, essential change is *decoupling*. This means that farm support is no longer linked to what is being produced on the farm during the year, i.e. to the crops being grown or the livestock kept. The 'Single Payment' (still often referred to as the 'Single Farm Payment') will be made according to what was being produced, by each individual farmer who made the claims, during the three years 2000-2002, expressed on a £ per hectare basis. While it was originally conceived (by most people at least) that these would be paid directly to the individuals who originally made the claims ('historic entitlements') an alternative method of distributing the total entitlements gained increasing support during the later months of 2003: paying it as a flat-rate regional average payment per hectare. Various 'hybrids' – combinations of the two methods – were also advocated.

The governments in the various EU member states finally made widely different decisions regarding the distribution of the payment: often varying in different regions within their countries. Differences even occurred within the UK. Essentially (with some relatively small variations), Scotland and Wales decided to adopt an individual historic entitlements basis, Northern Ireland a hybrid.

For England the government opted for what may be regarded as a complex 'sophisticated' method: generally referred to as a 'dynamic hybrid' or 'delayed flat-rate'. It consists of some of each, historic and regional average, with the proportions changing over an eight-year period: starting mainly historic and changing in annual steps to become entirely regional average, as follows:

Year	2005	2006	2007	2008	2009	2010	2011	2012
% historic	90	85	70	55	40	25	10	0
% regional	10	15	30	45	60	75	90	100

The regional payments in England will differ according to topography, with three types: lowland (or non SDA), non-moorland severely disadvantaged areas (SDAs) and moorland SDA. Payments for the second of these will be approximately 80% of those in the lowland and those for moorland about 12% (i.e. about a seventh of those in non-moorland SDAs).

In order to receive payment recipients will have to be farming 'eligible' land (see below). They must also satisfy 'cross-compliance' rules, which are in two parts: 'Statutory Management Requirements' (directives, largely already in force, on public and plant health, animal welfare and the environment) and keeping the land in 'Good Agricultural and Environmental Condition'. They apply to the entire holding. The rules in England include no cultivating, fertilising or spraying within two metres of the centre line of any hedge or ditch (after July 2005), no hedge cutting between 1st March and 31st July and providing a soil management plan. The area of permanent pasture in each region must be maintained (this is a government responsibility to monitor not an individual farmer responsibility).

A claimant's total reference amount will be calculated by multiplying the area and headage claims by the 2005 aid rates in euros per hectare, per head or per litre. These are as follows:

Arable Area: €/ha		*Livestock*: €/head	
England	371.07	Suckler Cow Premium	237.5
Scotland non-LFA	357.21	Beef Special Premium (steers)	150
Scotland LFA	328.23	Beef Special Premium (bulls)	210
Wales non-LFA	325.71	Slaughter Premium	80
Wales LFA	318.15	Extensification (lower rate)	40
N.Ireland non-LFA	328.86	Extensification (higher rate)	80
N.Ireland LFA	316.89	Sheep Annual Premium (SAP)	21.79
Other Crops:		SAP LFA Supplement	7
Hops	480.00	*Dairy: (€/litre)*	
Dried Fodder Aid (€/tonne)	68.83	2005	0.02435
		2006	0.03654

Sugar: no final decision on how sugar compensation will be distributed had been announced by the UK government at the time of going to print. The expectation is that farmers' reference amounts will be increased on the basis of their contract tonnage for the 2005 crop. For 2006 the whole amount of approximately £6.90 per tonne will be added to single payments, but subject to modulation and financial discipline deductions. For 2007 onwards the amount could increase to £8.40 per tonne if all the compensation is again paid to 2005 sugar beet grower rather than included in the 70%/30% historic/regional split for that year. If it is included in the usual split the payment for 2007 could be approximately £7.40 or £5.80 per tonne depending on which compensation options the government chooses.

2. OTHER POINTS

The other important points are as follows:

- As the payments are calculated in euros the £: euro exchange rate remains important, as pre-2005. The rate will be that prevailing on 30th September each year.

- The entitlements were awarded to the IACS claimant of agricultural land in 2005. They will be transferable/tradable: sold with or without land, or if leased, only with an equivalent area of land.

- Most farmland is 'eligible', comprising arable land and permanent pasture but excluding 'permanent crops' (essentially orchards and vineyards), woodland and land in non-agricultural use. Thus 'eligible land' is not the same as under the old arable area Payment Scheme (AAPS). The land has to be 'at the farmer's disposal' for at least ten months of the year; farmers can choose which ten months, within certain limits.

- Soft fruit, vegetables and potatoes are labelled 'negative list' crops. Land in such crops cannot be used to validate SFP entitlements in that year under historic systems, but such land can validate payments under the regional average system, though only up to a maximum reference area per farmer. This is to discourage producers from starting to grow, or increasing their area of, these crops.

- *Set-aside:* In Scotland and Wales 10% of the Arable area Payment claims in the years 2000-02 will give 'set-aside entitlements', which must be validated annually by eligible land in set-aside; these entitlements must be claimed before any others. They can be validated also by the land being part of an agri-environmental scheme or in the Farm Woodland Premium Scheme. They will be transferable. A big difference to pre-2005 set-aside is that under the regional system all land except permanent pasture will generate set-aside entitlements including temporary grass and root crops; consequently set-aside entitlements were based on 8% in English lowland (1.3% in non-moorland SDA) of arable land in 2005. In England the payment will be only at the regional average rate and so will be very low in the early years. The set-aside land can be rotated and non-food cropping is allowed, as are 6 metre strips. Fully organic holdings are exempt from set-aside rules. See further pages 73-75.

- In 2005 only, farmers could opt for the historic payments to which they were entitled to be paid in full on a smaller area of land than that previously farmed. This provision applied in England, and to a much lesser extent elsewhere.

- A *Dairy Premium* is being paid to milk producers as compensation for price cuts (15% in skim milk powder over three years and 25% in butter over four) which started in July 2004 and restrictions in butter intervention. They were decoupled in 2005, based on quota held at 31st March 2005, and converted into per hectare Single Payment entitlements: the value before any deductions is approximately 1.65ppl in 2005, rising to around 2.48ppl in 2006 and thereafter. In England, as with all other payments, the annual historic element will be calculated by multiplying by the relevant annual percentage.

- There are supplements (euros/ha) for protein corps (55.57) and energy crops (45).

- *Sugar Reform*: the main consequence of the reforms for sugar beet growers is savage cuts in minimum beet price over four years. British Sugar has agreed with the NFU to pay farmers close to the minimum beet price plus delivery allowance. If one euro = 68p minimum beet price would be £22.34 per tonne in 2006/07, £20.25 in 2007/08, £18.92 in 2008/09 and £17.87 in 2009/10 onwards. Average delivery allowance is about £3.30 per tonne. For 2009/10 the agreed price should not drop below £18.50 and will be linked to wheat price, and could reach almost £20 per tonne if wheat was £95. The compensation to growers for these cuts is explained on page 7. The ongoing payments are fully decoupled. Other elements of the reform include merging of A & B quota, with the quota system retained until 2014/15. There is a voluntary restructuring scheme for sugar factories with compensation if quota is given up. British Sugar does not intend to give up quota although it has announced the closure of the York and Allscott factories after processing the 2006 crop.

- A number of *deductions* will be made to the payments, most of them increasing over time. A 'National Ceiling', based on past subsidy receipts led to a 0.17% reduction in England only. Across the UK 4.2% was deducted for the *'National Reserve'*, to provide payments for special cases, e.g. new entrants since the end of 2002 and purchasers of extra land. Up to 10% of direct aids from each sector can be deducted to set up a 'National Envelope' to support specific types of farming or improve product quality/marketing; in the UK this is only being used in Scotland (for beef). There will be compulsory *'Modulation'* (for all EU member states) to fund EU-wide Rural Development projects; this is 3% in 2005 , 4% in 2006 and 5% in 2007 and thereafter; member states will keep 1%

themselves and each will get back at least 80% of its own total; the first 5,000 euros of aid on every farm will be exempt. Member states may add 'voluntary' modulation to the above. In England this will be 2% in 2005 and 6% in 2006; in Scotland 3.5% and 4.5% respectively; in Wales 1.5% and 0.5%. Finally, after 2007 there is EU 'Financial Discipline': EU Farm Ministers will decide annually what percentage reductions are needed to keep spending within stipulated budget thresholds; as with EU modulation the first 5,000 euros of aid per farm will be exempt.

Even by 2008 the total of the above deductions could be as much as 25%, by 2012 35%.

3. WINNERS AND LOSERS

The gradual change to a flat-rate area payment in England will clearly create winners and losers. By 2012 a farm in 100% combinable crops will lose around £20/ha (from approximately £235/ha to £215/ha), probably increasing to around £74/ha after deductions. Growers of unsupported crops, such as potatoes and soft fruit, will gain the whole of the payment, though at the cost of having to incur set-aside and cross-compliance rules. Sugar beet growers will see their single payments increase in 2006 and probably again in 2007, but then as the sugar compensation becomes subject to the relevant annual percentage most growers will find their single payments declining steeply to the regional average rate in 2012. In the case of dairy farmers the higher their milk yields and the higher their stocking rate the more they will lose, especially if they have a flying herd, i.e. no followers; a low-yielding, extensively stocked dairy farm with many followers may lose little or even gain. Intensive beef producers could lose considerably; a low stocking rate suckler herd could be no worse off. Lowland sheep would have to be stocked at a very high rate to lose from the new system; most should gain, some significantly.

4. TOTAL PAYMENTS PER FARM

It is obvious from the above that every farm will have a different total payment per hectare each year as far as the historic payments are concerned. In Wales and Scotland these differences will persist unless they decide later to change from the wholly historic system. In England the differences will gradually iron out as a higher and higher proportion becomes a flat-rate per hectare across all 'lowland' (or all non-moorland SDA or all moorland SDA in the case of the other two areas).

The following are estimates of the flat-rate area payments in 2012 in the three areas (or sub-regions) of England, with one euro = 68p. 'Lowland' covers all non-SDA (Severely Disadvantaged Area) land, which is more than 84% of farmed land. The estimates are made by Andersons and include allowance for the inclusion of Dairy Premium and Sugar Beet compensation in the flat-rate area payments.

The deductions (25% from modulation and financial discipline by 2012, i.e. 7 years ahead) can obviously only be assumed; they may well be higher, for several reasons: the future entry into the EU of more, poorer member states, increasing demands for a faster transference of funds to rural/environmental expenditure, increasing demands by certain member states for budgetary cuts. The figures are per hectare (with per acre in brackets).

	Lowland £	Non-Moorland SDA £	Moorland SDA £
Payments before deductions	215 (87)	175 (71)	24 (10)
Payments after deductions	161 (65)	131 (53)	18 (8)

As a first example, let us take a 100% combinable cropping farm in England. Assuming one euro = 68p the change in average payments per hectare over time is as follows. The annual % deductions assumed for modulation and financial discipline are: 2005, 5; 2006, 10; 2007, 20; 2008, 21; 2009, 22' 2010, 23; 2011, 24; 2012, 25.

	A. Before Deductions			B. After Deductions
	Historic Part	Flat-rate Part	Total	Total
Year	£	£	£	£
2005	216	19	235	223
2006	203	30	233	210
2007	167	63	230	184
2008	131	95	226	179
2009	96	127	223	174
2010	60	160	220	169
2011	24	193	217	165
2012	0	215	215	161

As a second example, let us assume a lowland farm with a considerable amount of intensive or semi-intensive beef, giving a gross historic payment of approximately £400/ha. The example could also apply to a very intensive dairy farm (i.e. high yield and high stocking rate), except that the figures would be higher in year 2006 than 2005 (because the dairy premium rises, before levelling off). Clearly the rate of the loss compared with pre 2005 increases over time – more quickly than the first example.

	A. Before Deductions			B. After Deductions
Year	Historic Part £	Flat-rate Part £	Total £	Total £
2005	349	19	368	350
2006	329	30	359	323
2007	270	63	333	267
2008	213	95	308	243
2009	155	127	282	220
2010	97	160	257	198
2011	39	193	232	176
2012	0	215	215	161

Finally, as a third example, let us assume a lowland sheep farm extensively stocked, giving an historic payment of only £100/ha.

	A. Before Deductions			B. After Deductions
Year	Historic Part £	Flat-rate Part £	Total £	Total £
2005	90	19	109	103
2006	84	30	114	103
2007	69	63	132	106
2008	55	95	150	118
2009	40	127	167	130
2010	25	160	185	142
2011	10	193	203	154
2012	0	215	215	161

In this example the farmer gains from the new system increasingly over time.

5. IMPLICATIONS FOR PRODUCTION

1. Despite the enormity of the change made in the gross margins – and even more so in net margins, or profits – of the major enterprises affected, the impact on production (areas planted and number of livestock reared) would appear to be small in 2005 and 2006. They may be greater in subsequent years.

   There are a number of reasons for the likely small impact in the short term:

   i)   The changes, though considerable, will take time to 'register' for many producers. The instinct to 'wait and see' will be strong. Simple inertia will also play a part. Also in England the continued delay in completing the 2005 application process has contributed to the inertia.

ii) Many will continue to sow and to rear as in the past because 'it is what they do': it is what their farm life (which is often the major part of their life) is about. The single farm payment, in many (perhaps most) cases at least will enable this to be done – even if it could be regarded as subsidising unprofitable production.

iii) There will be continuing uncertainty about some of the details of the new policy. How strictly will cross-compliance be enforced, for example? There must be no risk of losing the single farm payments.

iv) There are penalties/restrictions on making some changes that might otherwise be contemplated, e.g. growing more potatoes. In any case, new enterprises often mean more capital, more know-how, risk of overproduction and hence reduced prices. This goes for many diversification, as well as farm, enterprises.

v) If ones own labour, whether manual or managerial, capital and land is charged at 'the going rate', or opportunity cost, most enterprises that might previously have shown a profit, with an area and headage payment, will no longer do so. However, if one stays farming (or even if one does not) many of these costs will still have to be borne, i.e. they are unavoidable, or inescapable by reducing, or even stopping, production. On many farms, especially small and medium sized ones, little would be saved in the way of 'fixed' costs: they really *are* largely, 'fixed'. Hence even a low gross margin may still be leaving an addition to the net income that one would otherwise not have.

vi) The same point as above needs also to be remembered when considering leaving poorer fields fallow while still cropping the rest. The only actual costs saved on those fields may be the variable costs (primarily seed, fertilizer and sprays) and some fuel and repairs, a total for cereals of around £350/ha (£142/acre), which would be covered by a wheat yield of only 4.7 tonnes/ha (1.9/acre) at £75/tonne. However, there would be benefits of greater timeliness on the rest in difficult seasons and casual labour and 'catch up' contract work may be saved on some farms.

vii) Many arable farmers made heavy investments in expensive new machinery following the high prices for the 2003 harvest crops, many of them with a view to farming more land, particularly in contract farming arrangements; they are unlikely to want to see such investments wasted.

viii) If the equipment is allowed to run down it will be expensive to re-equip if prices suddenly improve markedly in the future, which could well happen. Similarly, well established farmers will not want to lose their skilled workers.

2) However, an increasing number of farmers, particularly those who are older, with no obvious successors, or others simply tired of the work involved, the uncertainties and the paperwork, will no doubt opt for a simpler system of farming, with very low inputs, taking care to abide by cross-compliance rules.

3) Those with a rent to pay on most or all of their land, or who have most of their farm operations done by contractors, will be in different positions than those described above (under1v). Clearly the contractor's cost is saved if one ceases production, which could be crucial, especially where yields are only average or below.

4) The higher the crop yields, or present levels of enterprise profitability, the more clearly it will pay to continue to farm similarly as in the past. Those in the opposite situation who are still farming either have very low (escapable) fixed costs or another source of income. These will be among those likely to turn to more extensive farming, as described above.

5) Also relevant is the level of ex-farm prices. Obviously more are likely to stay in production at 2003 harvest prices than at 2004 and 2005 levels. At the time of going to print (August 2006) the price prospects for the 2006 and 2007 harvests have improved. Beef and sheep prices are also higher, but milk prices are falling.

6) More farmers are expected to introduce, or expand existing, diversification enterprises, partly, even entirely in some cases, replacing farm enterprises. For many, however, this is easier said than done.

7) With regard to the so called 'variable' costs, primarily seed, fertilizer and sprays, the initial thought might be to reduce them. However, if the right (economic) level of these was being applied before (where, as an economist would put it, marginal cost roughly equates to marginal revenue) then it remains the right amount. Reducing these costs will reduce the net margin (or remaining gross margin) from the crop, with or without an aid payment. The exception might be some economies, cutting out waste, but these should already have been attended to, regardless of policy changes.

8) However, there is no doubting one possibly major exception to the general tenor of the above, suggesting comparatively little change on many farms. That regards beef production. This is commented on separately below, at the start of the beef section (page 88). Here

was quite the strongest case for leaving an enterprise 'coupled': no doubt partly the reason for Scotland using the 'national envelope' option for beef – a per head payment is made on 'beef' calves. Lower calf or store prices would help some beef enterprises, but obviously not others. Higher end prices, i.e. for the finished animal, would/will obviously help, but this will be limited by the ready availability of imports. Cuts in production could still be severe, once the full impact of decoupling has become clear.

9) Another exception to the general 'little change' tenor above will be sugar beet production. Many of the growers' delivering to Allscott and York factories in 2006 will have little option but to abandon beet growing in 2007 or at the latest 2008: a complex compensation package has been agreed for most of these growers. To encourage restructuring of where beet is grown (British Sugar would like full quota to be produced close to the remaining four factories, and indeed it plans to purchase additional quota), Contract Tonnage Entitlements (CTE) will become fully tradable from Autumn 2006. This is likely to result in far fewer growers and an expansion of beet close to the three East Anglian factories – the Newark factory will become full taking on some of the York and Allscott tonnage. Farmers in the East, who can see a future at the lower prices, have the opportunity to increase the scale of their beet growing operations, or indeed become new entrants to beet growing by buying CTEs.

III ENTERPRISE DATA

1. CASH CROPS

WINTER WHEAT

Production level..............................	Low	Average	High
Yield: tonnes per ha (tons per acre)			
Feed...	6.75 (2.7)	8.25 (3.3)	9.75 (3.9)
Milling.......................................	6.15 (2.5)	7.5 (3.0)	8.85 (3.5)
	£	£	£
Output:...	505 (202)	620 (250)	730 (295)
Variable Costs:			
Seed...		43 (17.5)	
Fertilizer....................................		100 (40.5)	
Sprays..		118.5 (48)	
Total Variable Costs....................		261 (106)	
Gross Margin per ha (acre)	244 (96)	359 (144)	469 (189)

1. *Prices.* The average feed wheat price for the 2007 harvest crop (i.e. 2007/08 marketing year) is taken to be £75 tonne (£70.00 for harvest sale and delivery). The average milling price is taken to be £82.50/tonne after allowing for a proportion of rejections; this is simply the 'break-even' price that gives the same output/ha as feed wheat at the price assumed for the latter and the assumed yield differential; the average premium achieved varies widely according to quality and season: see further comments below (note 3).

   Intervention. For the 2007 harvest the intervention price is €101.77/tonne delivered to centre (£69.20 at 68p/euro) in November, rising by €0.46 (31.3p) a month to €104.53 (£71.08) in May, but this excludes most feed wheat on specification issues. The EU Commission is presently negotiating reform of the cereal intervention system for likely implementation before the 2007 harvest. Transport and merchant charges are likely to total at least £6/tonne.

2. *Yields.* The overall average yield, for all winter wheat, i.e. all varieties, is taken as approximately 8.0 tonnes/ha (3.2 tons (64 cwt.)/acre).

3. *Milling v. Feed.* It is assumed that the yield of milling wheat averages 9% below that of feed wheat (the difference could be greater on high-yielding land and less on moderate quality land and also tends to be greater on second than on first wheats). Although slightly higher costs for seed, fertilizer and sprays might be expected for milling wheats such survey data as exists indicates little difference in variable costs in practice. Obviously different relative yields and premiums will give different gross margins: these can be readily calculated. The actual premium in any one season varies according to quality and scarcity. The average premium for breadmaking quality exceeds the £7.50/tonne (10%) assumed; however, that for other milling wheat is below and not all deliveries achieve 'full specification'. Grade 2 varieties normally achieve a premium of only a few pounds a tonne but their average yields are higher than grade 1 varieties. Overall, the milling premium averaged approximately £8.50/tonne (12% over feed) for the five harvest years 2001-2005. Not all wheat grown for milling achieves a premium and more care is required. The proportion of the UK wheat area sown with milling varieties has risen from a fifth several years ago to approximately a third (grade 1 and 2 varieties combined) for recent harvests and a HGCA publication suggested that for 2006 harvest, this had risen further to 42%.

4. *First v. Second (Feed) Wheats.* The evidence concerning the effect of different types and lengths of rotational breaks on subsequent cereal yields is inevitably variable given the differences between seasons (weather effects), soils, varieties etc. The table below (for feed wheat only) assumes a yield reduction of approximately 10% for second wheats compared with first and higher fertilizer and seed costs as shown; (the later the sowing date the less the yield gap tends to be). The same price is assumed as in the initial table. Only average and high levels are shown. Third wheats could yield 10-15% below second wheats; variable costs are likely to be similar. Large scale NIAB trials from 1996 to 2000 showed second wheats yielding an average of just under 1 tonne/ha less than first wheats; the yield difference varied between varieties. Heavy, well-structured, well-drained clay soils appear to be best suited to second wheats; lighter, silty soils usually have a greater risk of take-all; a firm seedbed is needed. A seven year Arable Research Centres project gave the average yield of first wheats as being approximately 20% above continuous wheats.

Production level	Average		High	
Year (after break)	First	Second	First	Second
Yield: tonnes per ha (tons per acre)	8.75 (3.5)	7.9 (3.15)	10.0 (4.0)	9.00 (3.6)
	£	£	£	£
Output...	655 (265)	590 (240)	750 (300)	675 (270)
Variable Costs...............................	250 (101)	270 (109)	250 (101)	270 (109)
Gross Margin per ha (acre)...........	405 (164)	320 (130)	500 (202)	405 (164)

5. *Straw* is not included above. Average yield is approx. 3·5 tonnes per hectare (range 2·5 to 5); value £10 to £50 per tonne according to region and season but mainly £20 to £25 (£5 less in big bales); (average sale value approx. £85/ha); variable costs (string) approx. £2 per tonne. Standing straw (sold for baling): anything from no value to £150/ha (£60/acre), according to type of crop, season and area of the country/local demand: national average around £30/ha (£12/acre), double this in the West, at least treble in a season when straw is in short supply.

6. *Seed and Fertilizer.* From survey data, updated. Seed rates and fertilizer applications vary according to soil, season, variety, farm policy, etc. Seed: main range £215-265/tonne (C2); 175kg/ha in good conditions, but more is often applied; 40-50% farm-saved: dressed etc. and BSPB levy of £31.72/tonne for autumn 2006 and spring 2007 for most varieties.

7. *Sprays.* Amounts variable according to season, variety, policy, etc. Typical breakdown: herbicides 43%, fungicides 45%, insecticides 5%, growth regulators 5%, slug pellets 2%.

8. If a *Contractor* is employed, extra variable costs (£ per hectare) will be approximately as follows (see further, pages 156-159):

Spraying:	£11-£15 (LV-HV; material included above)
Drilling:	£27
Combining:	£75 (excluding carting)
	£90 (including carting)
Drying:	£60 to £100 (according to yield and moisture content; transport one way is included; this assumes that two thirds of the crop needs to be dried in an average season).
Baling Straw:	£50 (including string).

9. *Fuel and Repairs* (per hectare): grain £100, straw £35.

10. *Specialized Equipment Prices*: see pages 151-155.

11. *Labour*: see pages 134-137.

Use Excluding exports, just under half the UK 2005 harvest wheat crop was used for animal feed, a third for milling and the remainder for seed, starch and distilling (approx. 5% for each). Some 15% of the total crop was exported.

SPRING WHEAT

Production level..............................	Low	Average	High
Yield: tonnes per ha (tons per acre):	4.75 (1.9)	5.75 (2.3)	6.75 (2.7)
	£	**£**	**£**
Output:...	385 (155)	465 (190)	545 (220)
Variable Costs:			
Seed..		55 (22)	
Fertilizer.....................................		71 (29)	
Sprays...		75 (30.5)	
Total Variable Costs....................		201 (81)	
Gross Margin per ha (acre)	184 (75)	264 (107)	344 (140)

1. *Price*: In general, see Winter Wheat (page 16). A higher proportion of spring wheat is sold for milling compared with winter wheat. The average price taken above (£81), for the 2007 harvest, assumes approximately 80% is sold for milling and 20% for feed.

2. *Straw*: See Winter Wheat, Page 17.

3. If a *contractor* is employed, extra variable costs (£/ha) will be shown as for Winter Wheat above.

4. *Fuel and repairs* (per hectare): grain £95, straw £35.

5. *Specialised Equipment Prices*: see pages 151-155.

6. *Labour*: see pages 134-137.

N.B. Normally, only about 1% of the UK wheat area is spring sown; the percentage is naturally higher after a particularly wet autumn. The percentage is even lower in Scotland (1% or less) than in England or Wales.

WINTER BARLEY

Production level............................	Low	Average	High
Yield: tonnes per ha (tons per acre)			
Feed..	5.4 (2.15)	6.6 (2.6)	7.8 (3.1)
Malting......................................	4.7 (1.85)	5.75 (2.3)	6.8 (2.7)
	£	£	£
Output (Feed and Malting)............	378 (153)	460 (187)	546 (220)

Variable Costs:	Feed	Malting
Seed..	37.5 (15)	42.5 (17)
Fertilizer......................................	89 (36)	76 (30.75)
Sprays...	85.5 (34.5)	93 (37.5)
Total Variable Costs.....................	212 (85)	212 (86)

| **Gross Margin** per ha (acre)........... | 166 (67) | 248 (100) | 334 (135) |

1. *Prices.* The average feed barley price for the 2007 harvest crop (i.e. 2007/08 marketing year) is taken to be £70/tonne (£65 to £70.00 for sale and delivery at harvest). The malting price (£80/tonne) assumes a premium over feed of £10/tonne (14%), which is what is required to equate the output and hence the gross margin for feed barley given the same total variable costs per hectare and the assumed yield difference. This allows for malting varieties sown that do not reach malting standards. The actual premium obtained over feed barley varies according to season and quality: for the best malting barleys the premium in the past has usually been at least £25 and in some years has even reached £50 plus; however, in the five harvest years 23001-2005 the overall premium has in fact averaged approximately £11/tonne (17% over feed). See page 16 for intervention prices.

2. *Straw* is not included. Average yield is approx. 2·75 tonnes per hectare, value £12·50 to £55 per tonne according to region and season but mainly £25 to £30 (£5 less in big bales); (average sale value approx. £100/ha), variable cost (string) approximately £1·50 per tonne. Standing straw (sold for baling): anything from no value to £150/ha (£60/acre) according to crop, season and area of the country (local demand): average around £35/ha (£14/acre), double this or more in the West.

3. *Fertilizer and Seed.* Fertilizer costs on continuous barley will be approximately £15 higher. Seed includes 25 to 35% farm-saved; amounts average 175-180kg/ha, varying according to soil, conditions etc. and BSPB levy of. £30.55/tonne for autumn 2006 and £32.89 for spring 2007.

4. *Sprays.* Amounts variable according to season, variety, policy, etc. Typical breakdown: herbicides 47%, fungicides 44%, growth regulators 6%, other 3%.

5. If *Contractor* employed, extra variable costs as shown for Winter Wheat (p.17, note 8).

6. *Fuel and Repairs* (per hectare): grain £100, straw £35.

7. *Specialized Equipment Prices*: see pages 151-155.

8. *Labour*: see pages 134-137.

SPRING BARLEY

Production level	Low		Average		High	
Yield: tonnes per ha (tons per acre)						
Feed	5.0	(2.0)	6.0	(2.4)	7.0	(2.8)
Malting	4.4	(1.75)	5.25	(2.1)	6.1	(2.4)
	£		£		£	
Output (Feed and Malting)	350	(142)	420	(170)	490	(200)

Variable Costs:	**Feed**	**Malting**
Seed	40 (16)	45 (18)
Fertilizer	68 (27.5)	58 (23.5)
Sprays	63.0 (25.5)	68.0 (27.5)
Total Variable Costs	171 (69)	171 (69)

Gross Margin per ha (acre)	179 (72.5)	235 (95)	319 (129)

The notes re. prices, variable costs, straw etc. are as for Winter Barley above except sprays, which consist typically of: herbicides 54%, fungicides 41%, other 5%. The average malting premiums for spring barleys are normally significantly higher than those for winter varieties.

Areas and Use of Winter and Spring Barley. The UK percentage of winter barley averaged 45% in the five harvest years 2001-2005, ranging from 52% in 2000 falling towards 40% in more recent years. It had been as high as 62% in 1997 and 1998. In general the percentage is higher than the UK average in England (e.g. 47%) but only around 20% in Scotland and Northern Ireland.

Excluding exports, just over 50% of the UK 2005 harvest barley crop was used for feed and 30% for malting. Some 11% of the total crop was exported. The balance represents a rise in commercial and intervention stocks.

WINTER OATS

Production level............................	Low	Average	High
Yield: tonnes per ha (tons per acre)	5.25 (2.1)	6.5 (2.6)	7.75 (3.1)
	£	**£**	**£**
Output Feed.................................	367 (149)	455 (184)	542 (220)
Milling.............................	383 (155)	475 (192)	555 (230)

Variable Costs:			
Seed...		40 (16)	
Fertilizer......................................		81.0 (33)	
Sprays..		60.5 (24.5)	
Total Variable Costs....................		181 (73.5)	

Gross Margin per ha (acre)			
Feed	186 (75)	274 (111)	361 (146)
Milling	202 (82)	294 (119)	374 (151)

1. *Prices.* Prices are the assumed averages for the 2007 harvest crop, i.e. the whole 2007/08 marketing year, at £70 and £73 per tonne for feed and milling respectively. Roughly half the UK oat crop goes for milling and half for feed. Conservation grade milling oats may obtain a premium of £10/tonne.

2. BSPB levy of. £24.68/tonne for autumn 2006 and spring 2007.

3. Straw is not included above. Average yield is 3.5 tonnes per hectare; value £10 to £50 per tonne according to region and season; variable costs (string) approximately £1.50 per tonne.

4. If a Contractor is employed, extra variable costs will be as shown for Winter Wheat (p.17, note 8).

5. For Naked Oats refer to page 37.

5. Fuel and Repairs (per hectare): grain £95, straw £35.

6. Labour: see pages 134-137.

SPRING OATS

Production level............................	Low	Average	High
Yield: tonnes per ha (tons per acre)	4.5 (1.8)	5.5 (2.2)	6.5 (2.6)
	£	**£**	**£**
Output Feed.................................	315 (127)	385 (155)	455 (184)
Milling...............................	328 (133)	400 (163)	474 (192)

Variable Costs:			
Seed...		42.5 (17)	
Fertilizer......................................		52.5 (21.25)	
Sprays..		50.5 (20)	
Total Variable Costs....................		145 (59)	

Gross Margin Per ha (acre)			
Feed	170 (69)	240 (97)	310 (125)
Milling	183 (74)	255 (103)	329 (133)

The notes re. prices, straw etc. are as for winter oats above.

N.B. Around 75% of the oats in Great Britain are winter crops; the proportion increases from north to south; it is normally 90% or more in England and Wales but only 25% to 35% in Scotland. Oats now account for only about 4% of the total UK cereals area. The risk of lodging and thus difficult harvesting remains a drawback.

OILSEED RAPE

Winter Rape

Production level..............................	**Low**	**Average**	**High**
Yield: tonnes per ha (tons per acre)	2.5 (1.0)	3.25 (1.3)	4.0 (1.6)
	£	**£**	**£**
Output..	375 (152)	487 (197)	600 (243)
Variable Costs:			
Seed..		30 (12)	
Fertilizer.....................................		113 (45.75)	
Sprays...		96 (39)	
Total Variable Costs...................		239 (97)	
Gross Margin per ha (acre)...........	136 (55)	248 (100)	361 (146)

Spring Rape

Production level..............................	**Low**	**Average**	**High**
Yield: tonnes per ha (tons per acre)	1.5 (0.6)	2.0 (0.8)	2.5 (1.0)
	£	**£**	**£**
Output..	225 (91)	300 (121)	375 (152)
Variable Costs:			
Seed..		35 (14)	
Fertilizer.....................................		81.25 (33)	
Sprays...		61.5 (25.0)	
Total Variable Costs...................		170 (69)	
Gross Margin per ha (acre)...........	55 (22)	130 (53)	205 (83)

1. *Prices.* The price assumed for the 2007 crop is £150/tonne, including oil bonuses.

2. *Varieties.* Winter crops are mainly sown between 10th August and 10th September (before the end of August if possible). Spring-sown crops are best sown between late March and mid-April. Winter crops normally are harvested between late July and mid-August, spring-sown crops in the first half of September. With spring-sown crops inputs are lower, pigeons are less trouble and the late summer/autumn workload is eased; however, the later harvesting tends to clash with the winter wheat harvest, there is less time to prepare the ground for, and drill, the following winter cereal crop, and spring droughts are a potential hazard to establishment; above all, yields average only 60% of those of winter rape; hence normally less than 10% of the total oilseed rape crop is spring-sown except when a higher proportion of spring crops than usual is grown following a very wet autumn and early winter. The proportion of the total area sown with hybrid winter rape is increasing rapidly; the seed is more expensive but an average increase in yield of 0·5 tonnes/ha is claimed by its plant breeders.

3. *Seed.* Approximately 35% farm-saved. BSPB levy of. £1544.76/tonne for autumn 2006 and spring 2007.

4. *Sprays.* Variable with season, etc. Typically: herbicides 65%, fungicides 25%, insecticides 10%.

5. Labour: see page 142.

LINSEED

Production level...........................	Low	Average	High
Yield: tonnes per ha (tons per acre):	1.0 (0.4)	1.5 (0.6)	2.0 (0.8)
	£	£	£
Output..	160 (65)	240 (97)	320 (130)
Variable Costs:			
Seed..		55 (22)	
Fertilizer....................................		34 (13.8)	
Sprays..		42 (17)	
Total Variable Costs.....................		131 (53)	
Gross Margin per ha (acre)...........	29 (12)	109 (44)	189 (77)

The price assumed for the 2007 crop is £160/tonne. Contract prices are normally tied to a standard 38% oil content and 9% moisture content. Open market prices are usually lower. Some specialist contracts for specific varieties such as Yellow Linseed can be worth more.

Mainly spring-sown, drilling mid-March to mid-April (best mid-March to end March). Susceptible to frost. Should not be grown more than 1 year in 5. Care needed re level of nitrogen use: too much (over 75 kg/ha) can cause severe lodging, delayed maturity and excessive weed growth – and hence difficult harvesting, poor quality and lower yields; it should be applied early.

Harvesting: normally not before September and can even be after mid-October in a late season. Does not shed. Moisture content most likely 12-16%: must be dried to 9% for storage.

Winter Linseed

There was a big surge in plantings of winter linseed for the 1997 harvest: around 30,000 ha, but this fell to about 20,000 the following year, when crops were again disappointing; there has been little sustained interest since – which has been true of all linseed since 2001. The main attractions are easier establishment and earlier harvesting (about a month before the spring varieties). Higher yields than the spring-sown crop were expected but trials indicated little difference. Yield affected by frost heave, disease and thrips, with most varieties susceptible to lodging; pigeons and rabbits can also be troublesome. Early sowing (early to mid-September) appears best, with higher seed rates; otherwise variable costs similar to spring.

Linola

Edible linseed: the oil contains more linoleic and less linolenic acid than conventional linseed, like sunflower oil. It is difficult to see much future for the crop, because its gross margin is very low. It is grown on contract, with the price based on the oilseed rape price. Spring-sown: agronomy and yield similar to conventional linseed; good weed control is essential.

INDUSTRIAL OILSEED RAPE

Rape for non-food uses may be grown on set-aside land, provided a direct contract with a buyer or collector is obtained. The non-food product must be worth more than the total value of any food by-products. Only approved varieties may be grown, or high erucic rapeseed.

Growers must deliver the entire crop from their set-aside land to their processor. Penalties are imposed if stipulated minimum yields are not delivered. Refer to the table in the set-aside section on page 75 for the minimum representative yields.

Two types of industrial rape are grown: high erucic acid (HEAR) and, mainly, double low, which is primarily spring-sown. The former usually has a lower yield, reckoned to be around 10% for winter-sown and up to 20% for spring-sown; the price is consequently £15 to £30/tonne higher.

The following are estimated gross margins for double low industrial rape for the 2007 harvest, given a price of £145/tonne and slightly lower variable costs (lower seed cost).

	Winter-sown		Spring-sown	
Production level............................	Average	High	Average	High
Yield (tonnes per ha (tons per acre))	3.0 (1.2)	3.75 (1.5)	1.8 (0.7)	2.25 (0.9)
	£	£	£	£
Output...	435 (176)	543 (220)	260 (105)	326 (132)
Variable Costs..............................	230 (93)	230 (93)	160 (65)	160 (65)
Gross Margin per ha (acre)...........	205 (83)	313 (127)	100 (40)	166 (67)

It is widely believed that subsequent crops benefit more from following oilseed rape than from following a (virtual) fallow.

Other industrial crops including linseed can also be grown on set-aside land but the area is very small compared with industrial oilseed rape.

FIELD BEANS

Winter Beans

Production level	Low	Average	High
Yield: tonnes per ha (tons per acre)	3.0 (1.2)	4.0 (1.6)	5.0 (2.0)
	£	£	£
Output	296 (120)	383 (155)	470 (190)
Variable Costs: (3)			
Seed		45 (18.5)	
Fertilizer		15 (6)	
Sprays		69 (28)	
Total Variable Costs		129 (52)	
Gross Margin per ha (acre)	167 (68)	254 (103)	341 (138)

1. *Price.* The 2007 harvest (2007/08 marketing year) price assumed is £87.00 per tonne. Tannin-free varieties usually fetch about £8 a tonne more but yield some 5% less. Beans for human consumption normally fetch a premium of around £12/tonne.

2. *Support.* EU Protein Supplement. Under the Mid-Term Review agreement there is a supplement of €55.57/ha for beans, peas and lupins harvested dry. The output figure above includes the value of this supplement, worth around £35/ha in 2007 at a euro value of 68p, after deducting modulation, assuming a stipulated maximum EU guaranteed area of 1.4 million ha is not exceeded.

3. *Physical input.* Seed: 185-220 kg per hectare, about 60% farm-saved. Fertilizer: 200 kg of no (or low) nitrogen compound where applied, but some crops receive no fertilizer.

4. *Labour:* see page 141.

Spring Beans

Production level	Low	Average	High
Yield: tonnes per ha (tons per acre)	2.8 (1.15)	3.7 (1.5)	4.6(1.85)
	£	£	£
Output	280 (113)	357 (144)	435 (176)
Variable Costs:			
Seed		50 (20)	
Fertilizer		15 (6)	
Sprays		58.5 (23.75)	
Total Variable Costs		123 (50)	
Gross Margin per ha (acre)	157 (64)	234 (95)	312 (126)

1. Price. As for winter beans above. Spring beans contain more protein than winter beans (except for tannin-free varieties), but large-scale compounders appear to make no distinction between them.

2. *Winter versus Spring Beans.* It used to be assumed that the yield of winter beans was about 0·5 tonnes per hectare above spring beans provided a full crop was obtained, that is, where there was no exceptional damage from frost and birds and, in particular, where there was no severe attack of chocolate spot. Thus, whether the average yield over a period of years was higher or lower than spring beans depended mainly upon the incidence of attacks of chocolate spot, which can write off the crop completely. In drier parts of the Eastern Counties this may be only one year in six or eight but in south-eastern counties the frequency may be substantially higher. NIAB data have shown an average 8% yield advantage for winter over spring beans.

Other points in favour of spring beans are that: cold, wet seedbeds and winter kill can lead to poor establishment of winter beans; the yield difference between autumn- and spring-sown crops is less than for other crops, especially cereals; there is a longer 'near-optimal' period during which they can be sown; and there have been substantial genetic improvements in recent years for spring beans but little for winter beans. However, spring beans are vulnerable to droughts in spring and early summer, especially on light land.

The relative area of winter and spring beans is largely determined by the autumn rainfall and recent comparative yields.

DRIED PEAS

Production level	Low	Average	High
Yield: tonnes per ha (tons per acre)	3.0 (1.2)	3.75 (1.5)	4.5 (1.8)
	£	£	£
Output (feed)	296 (120)	360 (146)	426 (172)
Variable Costs:			
Seed		80 (32)	
Fertilizer		15 (6)	
Sprays		99.5 (40)	
Total Variable Costs		194 (79)	
Gross Margin per ha (acre)	102 (41)	166 (67)	232 (94)

1. Dried peas are combine harvested and include peas (especially marrowfats) for human consumption (after processing) and protein peas, for animal feed. About 75% of the crop goes for feed compounding.

2. *Price.* The 2007 harvest year (2007/08 marketing year) price assumed above (which is for feed peas) is £87.00 per tonne. Feed peas sold on the open market are subject to wide price variations, particularly as poor samples can fetch very low prices. Human consumption premiums vary mainly between £10 and £20/tonne for blue varieties while those for marrowfats are generally £25 to £50/tonne (even £70 for the very best) according to quality (size and colour) and the percentage of wastage, but marrowfat yields are generally around 10% lower than feed varieties; most peas for human consumption are grown on contract. The premium for peas for the pigeon trade is usually around £10/tonne.

    EU Protein Supplement. See Winter Beans (page 25). Included in output above.

3. *Physical Inputs.* Seed: 210 to 250 kg, about 40% farm-saved. Fertilizer: 250 kg of no nitrogen compound where applied, but some crops receive no fertilizer.

4. *Harvesting* (normally in late July – early August) can be a difficult operation. Most crops are direct combined, although there is a high risk of loss and poor quality, as well as heavy wear and tear on the combine. Drying and handling the crop can be very difficult, much care being needed. Sometimes the crop is desiccated before direct combining, using diquat, to even out maturity and kill green weeds.

5. *Winter Peas.* Lots of interest in the mid-1990's, because of the ability to cope better with an early summer drought, earlier harvesting and potentially higher yields. This culminated in some 4,000 ha being grown in 1996/97. However, wet Junes in 1997 and 1998 caused disease and flat crops, difficult harvesting and reduced yields; also at risk in a severe winter and highly vulnerable to pigeons. Only a small area is grown currently.

    Labour: see page 141.

Peas versus Beans (for feed). On average, yields of peas are slightly above those for beans nationally. Peas are normally spring-sown and spring beans are easier to manage than peas. Peas are unsuited to heavier soils and are more vulnerable if the weather is wet during flowering and harvest. They are more sensitive to soil compaction and waterlogging. Their yields are thus more variable than for beans. Their seed costs are also much higher. On the other hand, peas for human consumption fetch higher prices than beans and the same used to be true of feed peas also; however the average prices of field beans and feed peas has been very similar in recent years. Peas are less sensitive to drought and are normally ready to harvest well before spring beans. In 1998 the area of field beans was 20% above that of dried peas but the difference has widened substantially since then: the area of field beans was more than double that of peas for harvesting dry in 2001 and 2002 . By 2005 beans outstripped pea area more than 4 fold.

VINING PEAS

Production level	Low £	Average £	High £
Output (1)	800 (324)	1000 (405)	1200 (485)
Variable Costs:			
Seed (1)		170 (69)	
Fertilizer (2)		20 (8)	
Sprays (3)		61 (25)	
Total Variable Costs		250 (101)	
Gross Margin per ha (per acre)	550 (223)	750 (304)	950 (384)

1. The table above relates to vining peas grown on contract where harvesting (approx. £48/tonne) and haulage (approx. £20/tonne) are paid for separately; the average price in this situation is taken as approximately £210/tonne. The price will clearly be higher if 'all-inclusive'. The average yield is taken as 4.75 tonne/ha; the national average (fresh weight) for the last five years has ranged between 4.3 and 5.4. The price varies with the quality: high quality crops (which can have an all-inclusive price up to £270/tonne) will normally have a lower yield than low quality crops (where the price can be as low as £170/tonne) but the latter (which include "long haul" peas) can average 6 tonnes/ha. Top quality ("150 minute") peas have to be grown within 40 miles of the factory. A pea viner costs about £250,000.

   The average yield of petit pois is lower but the price averages 12 to 15% more.

2. Fertilizer: many growers use no fertilizer; it is more often used on light land.

3. Sprays: both herbicide and aphicides. There are large seasonal variations according to weather conditions and the need for midge control.

4. Labour: see page 140.

5. Around 34,000 ha are grown in the UK annually.

Note:

For full details (yields, prices, variable costs) of actual average past Cash Crop Gross Margins in different parts of the country, see the following annual reports:

   Report on Farming in The Eastern Counties of England: University of Cambridge, Rural Business Unit, Department of Land Economy.

   An Economic Review of Farming in the North West: University of Manchester,

   Centre for Agricultural, Food and Resource Economics, School of Economic Studies.

   Farm Management Handbook: University of Exeter, Centre for Rural Research.

   (Full addresses on page 249).

LUPINS

The following table refers to spring sown *white lupins*. Differences in yield and price for yellow and blue lupins are given in the accompanying notes:

Production level............................	Low	Average	High
Yield: tonnes per ha (tons per acre):	2.25 (0.9)	3.0 (1.2)	3.75 (1.5)
	£	£	£
Output*:..	305 (123)	395 (160)	485 (196)
Variable Costs:			
Seed..		140	
Fertilizer.....................................		25	
Sprays..		40	
Total Variable Costs....................		205 (83)	
Gross Margin per ha (acre)	100 (40)	190 (77)	280 (158)

* price assumed £120 plus estimated £35/ha protein supplement (net of modulation)

A leguminous crop traditionally associated with light land. Their protein content is about 40 to 50% higher than peas and beans, making lupins a good substitute for soya beans in livestock feed compounds. Some 30,000 tonnes of lupin products are imported into the UK from Australia each year.

In 1985 1,300 ha of lupins were grown in the UK but the results were so poor that few were grown for more than a decade. There is now renewed interest in the crop following the development of fully- and semi- determinant varieties that are suitable for cultivation in the UK. In 2001 2,500ha were grown and the area expanded to 4,500ha in 2002, 6,500ha in 2004 and 8,000ha in 2006, virtually all spring lupins. Winter-sown varieties, although potentially they mature earlier and yield better than spring varieties, have not been successful in practice and few if any are now being grown. Lupins are a useful nitrogen-fixing break crop. They have the further advantage in being a non-GM source of high quality digestible protein. The crop can be cut whole for silage, crimped or milled and fed directly to stock or the grain traded as a cash crop.

Lupins can be grown on all but the heaviest land but are not tolerant of alkaline soils. A free draining soil with a pH of 5-7 is ideal but there are new varieties that are more tolerant of soils outside this range. Lupins need a good cereal seedbed and pre-emergence weed control. A specific seed inoculant is required for soil nitrogen fixation. Sowing is from mid-March to early April and harvest from mid-August onwards. If the crop is to be cut for silage, sowing can be as late as mid-May using an appropriate variety. No nitrogen fertiliser is necessary but P and K at 50-55kg/ha should be replaced later. There are no serious pests of the crop. Anthracnose is a potentially serious threat but plant health measures have so far kept it under control. Other diseases are not yet a problem. Determinant varieties do not generally need pre-harvest desiccants.

What is crucial is the choice of an appropriate species and variety. This will depend on area of the country, soil pH, intended end use and growth habit required. There are three distinct species of spring lupins, white (lupinus albus), blue (lupinus angustifolus) and yellow (lupinus luteus) and all are suitable for grain or to be fed on-farm. White lupins have a higher protein content and potentially greater yield than blue lupins but require a longer growing season. Yellow lupins fall somewhere between blue and white; they have a rather shorter growing season than white lupins and a higher protein content than blue lupins. They are more tolerant of acidic soils while white lupins are suitable for more alkaline soils. Spring lupin varieties have no northern limit but blue lupins are most suitable as a grain crop in northern and western areas, where white lupins are best grown for whole crop silage or crimped for feed. White and yellow varieties have palmate leaves and are generally semi-determinate (with some branching) and compete well with weeds. Blue lupins have thinner stems and strip-like leaves and can be semi-determinate or full-determinate (growing in a single spike), which makes the crop early but less competitive with weed growth. All three species do well as a grain crop in southern and eastern England.

Currently 60% of the national lupin area is white, 25% blue and 15% yellow. In the South-East and East Anglia 90% of lupins are white. In Scotland 60% are blue 30% white and 10% yellow, with blue and yellow grown for combining or crimping and white for whole crop. In Northern Ireland, where almost all lupins are wholecrop, 90% are white.

It is estimated that about half of the UK lupin crop is for grain and half for wholecrop forage. However, only a third of the grain, 20% of the total crop, is traded, although there is a ready market for grain lupins from both feed compounders and the growing farm to farm trade. There is also an export market primarily to Egypt for white lupins which has contributed to setting a floor price for the crop. The grain should receive a premium over peas and beans and approach the value of soya beans. Blue lupins should have a value of £95-100/tonne and white or yellow lupins £110/tonne or even more, reflecting their different feed value. There is also a valuable market for white lupins for human consumption in the Middle East. Traditionally, this has been supplied by Australia, but disease and purity issues there have provided an opportunity for the British crop. Cleaned and dried to 15% moisture, they can make £130 to £140/tonne

Lupins harvested dry are eligible for the EU protein supplement of €55.57/ha, worth about £35/ha in 2007 after deducting modulation; this is included in the output figures given. Overwintered stubbles are worth 70 points per hectare in the Entry Level Scheme.

Lupin characteristics

	White *Lupinus Albus*	Yellow *lupinus luteus*	Blue *lupinus angustifolius*
Flower Colour	white or blue	yellow	white or blue
Growth habit	semi-determinate	semi-determinate	fully or semi-determinate
pH tolerance	5 to 7.6	<5 to 6.8	5 to 6.8
Protein	36-40%	34-42%	31-35%
Oil content	10%	4%	6%
Main use	Combining in the Southern half of England on acidic land Forage in all areas	Combining in Southern England	Combining in the North (fully determinate) Forage in the very North (semi-determinate)
Yield	3-3.5 t/ha	2-2.5 t/ha	2-2.5t/ha

MAINCROP POTATOES

Production level	Low	Average	High
Yield: tonnes per ha (tons per acre)	36.5 (14.75)	44.5 (18.0)	53 (21.5)
	£	£	£
Output	3066 (1239)	3738 (1512)	4452 (1806)
Variable Costs:			
Seed		600 (243)	
Fertilizer		210 (85)	
Sprays		430 (175)	
Casual Labour for harvesting and grading (3)	584 (237)	712 (288)	848 (343)
Sundries (levy, sacks, etc.)	355 (144)	405 (142)	460 (186)
Total Variable Costs	2179 (882)	2357 (955)	2548 (1032)
Gross Margin per hectare (acre)	887 (357)	1381 (557)	1904 (774)

1. *Prices.* The price assumed above is £90 per tonne for ware and £10 for stockfeed (assumed to be 7½ per cent), which is £84 per tonne for the whole crop. The actual price in any one season will depend mainly on the national average yield. Variations according to quality and market (as well as season) are now considerable. The six-year average GB price for maincrops between 1999/2000 and 2005/06 was approximately £97 per tonne but the average annual price varied from around £65 (2002/03) to £140 (2003/04) per tonne.

   The average seasonal monthly price indices between 1999/00 and 2003/04 (with each annual price = 100) were as follows: August 109, September 97, October 88, November 91, December 96, January 98, February 97, March 100, April 105, May 113, June 115. The variation between years is substantial, particularly at the beginning and end of the season.

2. *Physical Inputs.* Seed: 60% planted with certified seed: 2.8 tonnes per hectare at £185-250 per tonne (the price varies widely from season to season); 40% with once-grown seed: 2.6 tonnes per hectare at £160 per tonne. Sprays: herbicide, blight control, and haulm destruction.

3. *Casual Labour.* The figure in the table above is for assistance during (machine) harvesting and for grading/riddling (approx. £16.00/tonne); it is assumed that most of the labour for the latter is supplied by casuals.

4. *Contract mechanical harvesting:* approximately £250/hectare (excl. pickers, carting, etc.). Other contract work see page 159.

5. *British Potato Council levy:* £39/ha (£15.78/acre) for growers in 2006, £44/ha for late payers; exempt from levy if less than 3ha grown.

6. *Potato Land Rentals.* Have been falling, from an average of around £750/ha (£300/acre) several years ago to around £500/ha (£200/acre) in recent years.

7. *Sacks.* Approx. £7.50 per tonne.

8. *Fuel and Repairs* (per hectare): £250.

9. *Specialised Equipment Prices:* see page 154.

10. *Potato Store Costs:* see page 189.

11. *Labour:* see page 138-139.

EARLY POTATOES

Production level............................	**Low**	**Average**	**High**
Yield: tonnes per ha (tons per acre):	15 (6)	20 (8)	25 (10)
	£	**£**	**£**
Output...	2250 (910)	3000 (1210)	3750 (1520)
Variable Costs:			
Seed..		700 (285)	
Fertilizer....................................		183 (74)	
Sprays...		216 (87.5)	
Casual labour		335 (135)	
Sundries, levy, sacks etc		255 (103)	
Total Variable Costs.....................		1689 (684)	
Gross Margin per ha (acre)...........	561 (227)	1311 (531)	2061 (835)

1. *Prices and Yields.* The price assumed above is an average of £150 per tonne for a 20 tonne/ha yield. However, yields increase and prices fall as the season progresses. Thus both depend on the date of lifting, e.g. late May to early June, 7 to 12 tonnes per hectare; July, 20 to 30 tonnes per hectare. Prices in late May to mid June are typically three times those in July; the very earliest crops (early May) can even fetch more than £1,000 per tonne, but the price could be down to £500 by mid May and to £250 or even £200 by the end of May. Thus the average output of £3000 given above could be obtained from 10 tonnes at £300 per tonne, 15 at £200, 20 at £150 or 30 at £100.

2. *Casual labour for planting*: £118 per hectare, plus help with harvesting/grading.

3. *Fuel and Repairs* (£ per hectare): £220.

4. *Labour*: see page 139.

SECOND EARLY POTATOES

Output (average): 42 tonnes/ha (16.75 tons/acre) @ £75/tonne = £3150 (1275) (lifting July to early September).

Variable Costs: Seed £525 (225), fertilizer £225 (91), sprays £325 (132), casual labour £625 (253), miscellaneous £400 (162); total £2100 (850).

Gross Margin: £1050 (425).

Labour: see page 139.

In 2005/6, the percentages of the total potato area in Great Britain planted in maincrop, early and seed crops respectively were 84, 5 and 11; in England and Wales: 91, 5 and 4; in Scotland: 57, 2 and 41%. 21% of the total GB potato area was in Scotland.

SUGAR BEET

Production level............................. Yield: tonnes per ha (tons per acre)*	Low 46 (19)	Average 58 (23)	High 70 (28)
	£	£	£
Output..	1043 (422)	1315 (533)	1587 (643)
Variable Costs:			
Seed..		140 (57)	
Fertilizer.....................................		130 (53)	
Sprays...		130 (53)	
Transport (Contract)......................	193 (78)	243 (99)	294 (119)
Total Variable Costs....................	593 (240)	643 (260)	694 (28)
Gross Margin per ha (acre)...........	450 (182)	672 (272)	893 (362)

* *'Adjusted tonnes' at standard 16% sugar content (DEFRA)*

1. *Prices.* The 'all in' delivered price for the 2007 crop is expected to be £22.67 per adjusted tonne, based upon £19.99/tonne contract price (at 1€ = 68p) and £11.00/tonne surplus beet for bio-butanol. To the contract tonnage price is added an average transport allowance of £3.30/tonne. The 2007 harvest will be the second year of price cuts following the reform of the sugar policy. Refer to page 9 for details.

   At assumed proportions of beet are 95% within contract and 5% surplus. This is not a reflection of what has happened in the past, but the change in contract and lower prices will encourage growers to focus on achieving the tonnage within contract with minimal tonnage exceeding it. Historically, production has exceeded contracted tonnage by as much as 17%. This 95:5 split gives an average delivered price of £22.67/tonne. All the above prices are per adjusted (contract) tonne and are based upon the British Sugar letter to growers dated 11 August 2006.

   The price is varied by approximately 1.1% of the contract price for each 0.1 per cent difference in sugar.

   Early and late delivery allowances are paid as follows. Early delivery: this starts at 0.5% of the UK minimum beet price on September 30th and increases by 0.5% for each day prior to September 30th on which deliveries are made. Late delivery: 26th December — 7th January: 0.8% of UK minimum price; thereafter, the rate rises by 0.2% per day.

2. *Effect of Harvesting Date.* As the season progresses, changes occur in the crop before lifting, approximately as follows, on average:

	early Sept to early Oct.	early Oct. to early Nov.	early Nov. to early Dec.	early Dec to early Jan.
Yield (tons of washed beet /ha)	up 3.75	up 1.9	up 1.25	up 1.25
Sugar Content (%)	up 1%	up ¼%	down ¼%	up ¾%
Yield of Sugar (kg / ha)	up 1000	up 375	up 190	down 60

3. *Sprays.* Herbicides normally comprise between 85% and 92.5% of the total cost of spray materials.

4. *Contract.* Contract mechanical harvesting costs approx. £180 per hectare excluding carting or £215 per hectare including carting.

5. *Transport.* Contract haulage charges vary widely according to distance from the factory. The figure assumed above is approximately £4.50 per (unadjusted) tonne of unwashed beet including loading and cleaning (dirt & top tare assumed to total 14%).

6. *Fuel and Repairs* (per hectare): £220.

7. *Specialized Equipment Prices*: see page 151-155.

8. *Labour*: see page 140.

HERBAGE SEEDS

	Italian Ryegrass		Early Perennial Ryegrass	
	Average	High	Average	High
Yield (tonnes/ha)	1.3	1.7	1.25	1.6
Price per 50 kg (£)		25		27
Output	650	850	675	864
Variable costs:				
Seed		60		45
Fertilizer		100		100
Sprays		65		65
Cleaning	210	260	195	245
Total Variable Costs	435	485	405	455
Gross Margin per ha.	**215**	**365**	**270**	**409**
Gross Margin per acre	87	148	109	166

	Intermediate Perennial Ryegrass		Late Perennial Ryegrass	
	Average	High	Average	High
Yield (tonnes/ha)	1.25	1.6	1.25	1.6
Price per 50 kg (£)		30		32
Output	750	960	800	1024
Variable Costs:				
Seed		60		45
Fertilizer		100		100
Sprays		65		65
Cleaning, etc	195	245	180	230
Total Variable Costs	420	470	390	440
Gross Margin per ha.	**330**	**490**	**410**	**584**
Gross Margin per acre	133	198	166	236

	Hybrid Ryegrass		Kent Wild White Clover & Kent Indig. Peren. Ryegrass	
	Average	High	Average	High
Yield (tonnes/ha)	1.2	1.55	0.09 (Clover)	0.11 (C)
			0.6 (R'grass)	0.8 (R)
Price per 50 kg (£)		27	200(C); 30(R)	
Output	648	837	720	920
Variable Costs:				
Seed		60		40
Fertilizer		95		45
Sprays		65		40
Cleaning, etc	190	240	130	170
Total Variable Costs	410	460	255	295
Gross Margin per ha.	**238**	**377**	**465**	**625**
Gross Margin per acre.	96	153	188	253

Notes

1. The following were the number of hectares entered for certified seed production for the main grasses and clovers in the UK for the 2005 harvest:

Italian/Westerwold Ryegrass .	208	Cocksfoot	212
Early Perennial Ryegrass	222	Timothy	310
Inter. Perennial Ryegrass	1,495	Red Fescue	418
Late Perennial Ryegrass	2,185	White Clover	101
Amenity Perennial Ryegrass . .	829	Red Clover	54
Hybrid Ryegrass	539	Vetch	69

   The ryegrasses total 5,478 ha (13,536 acres).

   All herbage seeds total 6,642 ha (16,412 acres).

2. Average *yields* are approximate NIAB recorded averages for cleaned certified seed. The crop is very risky, i.e. yields are highly variable, depending especially on the weather at, and precise timeliness of, harvesting. A considerable amount of skill is necessary to average the 'high' levels over a number of years. Most grasses give their highest yield in their first harvest year, assuming good establishment. Yields can be increased by up to 0.2 tonnes per ha with a combination of higher Nitrogen applications along with a growth regulator.

3. Prices in the table are estimated prices for certified seed for the 2007 year. The figures relate to Diploid varieties. Tetraploid prices are lower (intermediate and late varieties achieving around £25 per 50kg). However, tetraploid yields should be higher. High sugar varieties should command a small premium over the values seen in the tables. *There is no longer any specific Seed Production Aid as this was decoupled and became part of the Single Payment as from 2005.*

4. No allowance has been made above for by-products. Some crops produce 4 to 5 tonnes of threshed hay, which is, however, of low feeding value. This could be worth £150 or more per hectare. Some grasses, especially spring-sown ryegrass, also provide substantial quantities of autumn and winter grazing. Clovers can be either grazed or cut for hay or silage and do not have to be 'shut up' until mid or late May, or, in some cases and seasons, even early June. More grazing (until end of May) and better quality threshed hay is provided with a combination of ryegrass and white clover than with the specialist herbage seed grasses.

5. If the seed crop is to be undersown, specialist growers often reduce the seed rate for the cover crop by up to half and restrict nitrogen dressing: the cereal yield may thus be reduced by up to 0.6 tonnes per hectare. If this is not done the grass seed yield is usually lower in the first year compared with direct drilling, except for ryegrass.

6. Labour: see page 142.

Acknowledgments: *NIAB*, Tel: 01223 342200, www.niab.com; *Herbage Seed Services*, Tel: 01962 774432

RYE

Production level	Low	Average	High
Yield: tonnes per ha (tons per acre)	4.5 (1.8)	5.8 (2.35)	7.1 (2.9)
	£	£	£
Output: (Contract price)	342 (138)	440 (178)	540 (219)
Variable Costs:			
Seed		80 (32.5)	
Fertilizer		80 (32.5)	
Sprays		80 (32.5)	
Total Variable Costs		240 (97.5)	
Gross Margin per ha (acre)	**102 (41)**	**200 (81)**	**300 (122)**

Largely grown on light, infertile, sandy or stony soils, where yields are poor for other cereals. Yields would clearly be higher on better soils, but then rye has difficulty in competing with wheat and barley; it could never do so on good wheat land. The average yield in England and Wales in the six years 2000 to 2005 was 5.85 tonnes/ha.

The area grown in England and Wales increased steadily from 5,700 ha in 1993 to 9,700 ha in 1998, mainly in the south, south-east and East Anglia. It has subsequently fallen back to between 5,500 – 6,000 Ha in the last few years (5,600 in 2005). Rye crispbread is a major outlet. It is also milled into flour, used in mixed-grain bread and muesli. About two-thirds of UK requirements are imported, mainly from Canada (which produces the highest quality), Denmark, Germany and Spain. The demand for UK-grown rye has been falling in recent years, owing to increased competition in the crispbread market.

The price assumed above (£76 a tonne) is an estimated 2007 price at harvest. It assumes a milling specification is achieved which produces a price £4-£6 above that for feed wheat. Deductions are made for low quality, particularly if it is only of feed grade (price then between feed wheat and feed barley price). Only a small percentage of the crop is grown for the free market, which is risky.

Rye, which is autumn-sown, is drought tolerant and very hardy, can withstand low temperatures and starts growing early in the spring. It has all-round resistance to wheat and barley diseases, e.g. eyespot, and suffers less from take-all than wheat – hence it is a possible replacement for third or fourth wheat. Its vigour keeps weeds down. Its herbicide, fungicide and fertilizer requirements are lower than for other cereals, except for growth regulators. Harvested earlier than winter wheat (useful for following with oilseed rape).

Drawbacks: it sprouts in a wet harvest: must thus harvest early, at relatively high moisture content. It grows very tall and lodges easily: hence high levels of nitrogen are not possible; but growth regulators help. Its heavy straw crop means very slow combining (takes about twice as long per hectare as wheat and barley), and difficult straw incorporation. New hybrid varieties, with shorter, stiffer straw, are being developed; these would improve the comparative profitability of rye on better soils.

Drilling: 2nd and 3rd weeks September.

Harvesting: by mid-August at relatively high moisture content, then dry to 14-15% (no drying costs include in margin).

TRITICALE

Production level	Low	Average	High
Yield: tonnes per ha (tons per acre)	4.35 (1.75)	5.8 (2.3)	7.2 (2.9)
	£	£	£
Output: (Contract price)	305 (123)	406 (161)	504 (203)
Variable Costs:			
Seed		45 (18)	
Fertilizer		85 (34.5)	
Sprays		55 (22.5)	
Total Variable Costs		185 (75)	
Gross Margin per ha (acre)	**120 (48)**	**221 (86)**	**319 (128)**

A 'man-made' cross between rye and hard wheat. Combines the hardiness of rye and the marketability of feed wheat. It is favoured in livestock feed, particularly pig and poultry rations, due to its high levels of lysine. However, due to the relatively low quantities available it is not widely used by feed compounders. The area grown in England and Wales has risen steadily since the mid-1990's. In 2005, between 11-12,000 hectares were grown. However, the areas grown on the Continent are considerably greater.

The price is usually £3 or £4 a tonne below the price for feed wheat, but this tends to vary from season to season; £70 per tonne is assumed above for the 2007 harvest crop.

The average yield in England and Wales in the five years 2001-06 was only 4.4 tonnes per ha, but in the previous 5 years it had been 5.9 tonnes per ha. The low yields are a result of it mainly being grown on light land, especially thin, drought-prone, poorish, marginal cereal-growing soils. In these circumstances, it can frequently out yield wheat or barley, especially the former, and it has lower input requirements. Its yields tend to be more consistent on such soil than those of barley. Triticale tends to do well compared with second and subsequent wheats owing to its resistance to drought and fungal diseases.

Lower levels of fungicide are needed because of its good disease resistance, except for ergot, but including take-all (making it a possible replacement for a third or fourth wheat, as indicated above). It is a tall crop, which helps to suppress weeds, but it is susceptible to lodging; growth regulators are beneficial. New semi-dwarf varieties are being developed, to overcome straw strength weakness and susceptibility to rust infections.

The crop is best drilled early (September) on very light, drought-prone soils; otherwise October is satisfactory. Harvesting is at approximately the same time as wheat. There is more straw, which slows combining, and incorporation is difficult; this is less of a problem on poor soils as there is less straw.

Spring Triticale

New spring varieties of this crop have been introduced in the last few years. These have been taken up strongly in livestock areas – the north and west of England, as well as western Scotland, Wales and N. Ireland. Being a spring crop means that winter waterlogging is not an issue, and it can be grown on a wider range of soils. In total over 4,000 ha of spring triticale may well now be grown in the UK.

It has lower yields than winter triticale if it is harvested for grain in the conventional way. However, most is whole-cropped to produce an 'arable forage'. Often it is grown in a mixture with a proteins crop – peas or lupins for example. Inputs for spring triticale will be lower than those for winter varieties.

NAKED OATS

Production level	Low	Average	High
Yield: tonnes per ha (tons per acre)	4.5 (1.8)	5.5 (2.2)	6.5 (2.6)
	£	£	£
Output: (Contract price)	450 (182)	550 (223)	650 (263)
Variable Costs:			
Seed		55 (22.5)	
Fertilizer		85 (34.4)	
Sprays		70 (28.3)	
Total Variable Costs		210 (85.2)	
Gross Margin per ha (acre)	240 (97)	340 (138)	440 (178)

Naked oats have a higher protein, energy and oil content than 'traditional' oats, but the fibre content is lower – as the husk falls off during harvesting. Because of the high oil content it can go rancid if stored too moist, hence contracts require a maximum moisture content of 14% and 12% is recommended for long-term storage. The crop needs priority treatment at harvest. It is a very dusty crop and attracts mites.

The area being grown has increased steadily over the last few years with now around 12,000 ha grown in the UK at present. The traditional markets such as racehorse feed, dog food, and bird feed markets are all increasing. Over recent years the human consumption market has developed so that at least half the crop is now sold for health foods, fancy breads and breakfast cereals. In future, a further growth area is likely to be from demand for inclusion of the crop in monogastric animal feeds. The poultry industry in particular is setting up supply chains.

The 2007 harvest crop price assumed is £100 per tonne. Contracts offering premiums 35% above the average feed wheat price are standard. The premium can be reduced according to husk content.

Over 90% of the crop is winter sown, which is assumed above. NIAB has suggested that yields average 25%-30% less than conventional oats, but survey data over several years is not available. Spring varieties are likely to yield around 20% less than winter.

The agronomy of naked oats is similar to that of husked oat varieties. Variable inputs are lower than for wheat or barley – high nitrogen use is not possible due to the risk of lodging. Oats provide a break in the take-all cycle.

Naked Barley

Naked barley, suitable for roasting, flaking or milling as pearl barley, is now rarely heard of. It is grown like normal barley, but yields are reckoned to be some 15% lower. It could be either autumn or spring sown.

DURUM WHEAT

Production level	Low	Average	High
Yield: tonnes per ha (tons per acre)	4.5 (1.8)	5.5 (2.2)	6.5 (2.6)
	£	£	£
Output: (Contract price)	473 (189)	578 (231)	683 (273)
Variable Costs:			
Seed		75 (30)	
Fertilizer		95 (38.5)	
Sprays		85 (34.5)	
Total Variable Costs		255 (103)	
Gross Margin per ha (acre)	**218 (86)**	**323 (128)**	**428 (170)**

N.B. Extra drying costs estimated at £10 per tonne.

A Mediterranean crop. As well as pasta, it is used to produce ethnic foods, semolina, biscuits, etc. Must be grown under contract to the one processor in the UK. Domestic demand is relatively small, but expanding; UK consumption per head is approx. 4% that of Italy and 10% that of France but total UK use nevertheless amounts to about 60,000 tonnes a year.

The crop started to be grown in England in the late 1970s and built up to 11,000 ha (27,000 acres) in 1984. A series of years of poor yields reduced this to a few hundred hectares by the mid-1990s. It has now well recovered, to around 3,000 ha (7,500 acres) in recent years.

Yields well above the average given above are often quoted (typically 75%-80% of conventional feed wheat, which would mean an average of nearly 6.5 tonnes/ha), but average yields obtained from farm surveys have been found to be far lower than this in practice.

Contracts are based on a premium over the feed wheat price. For the 2007 harvest this will be £42 per tonne for 'Grade A' durum. However this is a delivered price to East Anglian mills and will be reduced if the crop does not fully meet quality specifications. In the table above an average premium of £30 per tonne after haulage is assumed, giving an ex-farm price of £105 per tonne. *There is no longer any specific EU area supplement for growing durum in England.*

As with milling wheat, there is a risk of rejection if contaminated with excess foreign seeds, especially self-set cereals from previous crop; thus safer as a first cereal crop. A poor price is obtained if quality is too poor for pasta and thus has to go for feed.

The crop is likely to be grown only in the driest parts of the east/south east, where it can best compete with second and third wheats. It may be either autumn or spring sown; around two-thirds is currently autumn sown and this is assumed in the table. The crop is very sensitive to stress and frost-kill in severe winters; the spring-sown crop is more reliable, and cheaper to grow, but the yield is usually substantially lower. The crop has a higher disease resistance than other wheats, except for eyespot and ergot.

Harvesting is a critical operation; it needs to be done as soon as the crop reaches 20% moisture content, or at most 18%: it is very prone to sprouting and the quality for semolina is reduced if harvest is delayed. Must be dried (slowly) to 15%. It is easier and quicker to dry than normal wheat. The straw is of poorer quality and lesser quantity than conventional wheat straw and is therefore rarely baled.

MINORITY CROPS

Borage

Indigenous to Britain (or at least here since Roman times); grown wild and cultivated for centuries. Produced principally for use as a dietary supplement but it may be used in cosmetics and pharmaceuticals. The oil has a high gamma linolenic acid (GLA) content – more than twice that of evening primrose. It was first grown as a field crop in the UK in 1983, mainly in Suffolk, Essex and Yorkshire.

In the late 1990's there was possibly 2,000-3,000 ha being grown but planting fell significantly as competition from overseas, and domestic over-production, caused a marked fall in prices. The area has probably now recovered to a couple of thousand hectares. It is essential for a grower to have a buy-back contract with a reputable company, and the crop should not be grown speculatively.

Compared with evening primrose it has the advantages of larger seeds, faster growth and earlier harvesting (late July/early August). Its aggressive growth gives good weed control with a high plant density. Low rainfall areas are preferred owing to harvesting difficulties in wet conditions. There are no significant pests and diseases, except for powdery mildew. It is combinable, after swathing and drying, which takes a minimum of two weeks. Harvesting can be difficult and seed shedding at maturity is a problem. Seed should be promptly dried to 10% for safe storage. Cleaning may be necessary. Borage should only be considered by those prepared to invest sufficient time in the crop's husbandry, harvest and storage. Borage is a low yield / high risk crop.

Yields: from virtually nothing to 0.75 tonnes/ha (6 cwt./acre); average 0.4 (3.2).

Price: Around £2,000 a tonne (there is a premium for an organic crop). Output at assumed average yield and price, £800/ha (£324/acre).

Variable costs (approximately) (£ per ha [acre]): seed 110 (45); fertilizer 45 (18); sprays 20 (8); total £175 (71).

Gross margin: £625/ha (253/acre).

Camelina Sativa

Camelina, or Gold of Pleasure, or False Flax is a fast growing spring (or occasionally winter) sown crop. It is easily grown and harvested and is drought tolerant. The oil contains a range of essential fatty acids. It can be used as a food supplement or in industry as a drying oil. A few hundred hectares are being grown at present including 100 ha of organic production. It is thought that current requirements could support around 1,000 ha of the crop. Yields are in the 2.5tonne/ha range. Price is variable depending on the end use but the minimum for 2007 is likely to be £250/tonne.

Crambe - Abyssinian Mustard

Crambe is an industrial oilseed that contains high levels of erucic acid. Converted into erucamide it is used as a slip agent in plastics and is a constituent of heat sensitive dyes. The area of crambe in the UK is around 5,000 ha and more growers are being recruited. It is suggested that another 15,000 ha could be needed to meet demand. As an industrial crop it can be grown on set-aside.

Crambe is a cruciferous non-GM spring crop well suited to growing in UK conditions on a wide range of soils. The crop can be managed like spring oilseed rape but needs some care and attention to achieve a good yield and oil content. It requires a fine firm seedbed and can be sown from April till the end of May. Good weed control is essential. The crop has a short growing season, requiring only 100-120 days to reach maturity after emergence. As with oilseed rape timely harvesting is important. Crambe can be combined direct, desiccated and combined or swathed depending on weather, uniformity of maturity and cleanliness of the crop. The crop should be stored and marketed at a moisture content of 9% or less.

Under fixed price buy back contracts, prices for 2007 are £180/tonne for commercial crops, and £230/tonne for seed. Contract requirements stipulate that the crop must be 98% pure with 35% oil content. There is a bonus/deduction of £2.70/tonne per 1% oil above/below that level. Seed contracts are not available on set-aside land.

Yield 2.5t/ha (1t/acre), Price £180/t ex-farm	£/ha	(£/ac)
Output	450	(182)
Variable costs:		
Seed	60	(24.5)
Fertilizer	85	(35)
Sprays*	50	(20)
Total Variable Costs	195	(79.5)
Gross Margin	255	(102.5)

* No desiccant included. Could be less depending on grass weeds and low risk of pollen beetle.

Echium

Echium is a relatively new commercial plant to the UK. It has been cultivated on contract only for the last 6-8 years. Currently there is less than 1,000 ha or so grown in the UK but the area is steadily increasing. It is a member of the Boraginacea family and is rich in stearidonic acid, which is used in cosmetic creams to reduce skin wrinkling and the effects of sunburn. It is essential for a grower to have a buy-back contract with a reputable company, and the crop should not be grown speculatively. In the past prices have collapsed to almost nothing due to over-supply in the market.

The crop can be grown as far north as Yorkshire. It has a husbandry programme similar to that of borage but does not shed its seed as readily as borage. The seed is relatively small in size. Echium is suitable for light to medium land whereas borage performs better on a wider range of soil types.

The crop is sown in April and should come to harvest in July/August. There appear to be no significant pests of the crop. Harvesting is carried out with the use of a swather.

Yield approximately: 250kg/ha (100kg/acre).

Price £3,500/tonne of clean seed.

Gross margin: £520/ha (£210/acre).

Evening Primrose

This crop is still an important source of gamma linolenic acid (GLA), but it is no longer grown in the UK and very little is cultivated elsewhere in Western Europe – it has been largely superseded by borage, which is easier to grow. The crop is still widely grown in China where the climate is more suitable, and labour costs are lower. Previous editions have given details of the crop and possible gross margin data.

Hemp

Approved for growing in the UK for industrial purposes. Production is co-ordinated by Hemcore of Essex under licence from the Home Office - growers no longer need individual licences. The area expanded to 3,000 ha in 2001 but has now stabilised at around 1,500 ha. With better yields this covers the existing Hemcore processing capacity. The majority of the crop is still grown in the eastern counties, near to the processing facility. However, a certain proportion is being grown in the south-west, where the yield is good although haulage costs are greater.

It is drilled in late April/May and the fibre crop grows 3 to 3.5m (10-12 feet) tall. Hemcore suggests a minimum area of 10ha. A well-grown crop should have no weed or pest problems. The crop is cut in August and left to rett in the field for 2-4 weeks, baled and immediately stored under cover. These operations are critical to the quality and hence the success of the crop. Average yields are around 6 tonnes/ha (2.4t/acre), target yields are 7.5t/ha (3t/acre). The price of the delivered crop £90/tonne in September. This increases to £100/tonne in October, and there is then an increment of £1.50/tonne/month (giving a price of £115 in August). An average delivered price of £105/tonne is assumed in the table below.

The outlook for hemp is good, as new markets have opened up. 80% of the fibre now goes into industrial textiles used for insulation for the automotive trade and demand is strong. Although this has been helped by European legislation directing the automotive industry to use a minimum percentage of recyclable materials, the quality and consistency of the fibre has finally convinced the motor trade. Some is also used for clothing. The core or pith of the plant is used for horse or poultry bedding, for which there is a strong demand.

Yield 6t/ha (2.4t/acre), Price £105/t	£/ha	(£/ac)
Output	630	(255)
Variable costs:		
Seed	125	(51)
Fertilizer	87	(35)
Sprays	nil	(-)
Contract cutting, turning and baling*	90	(36.5)
Haulage to factory (£13/tonne)	78	(32)
Total Variable Costs	380	(154)
Gross Margin	250	(101)

* less if the grower does some or all of these operations; more if the yield is higher.

Dual Hemp
Hemp may also be grown as a dual-purpose crop. By using an early variety, Finola, which is slightly shorter, the top can be combined for the seed before the straw is mown and retted. A yield of 1.25 tonne/ha of seed is possible, with a contract price of up to £350/tonne. However, the yield of straw is only about 1.5 tonne/ha, and the price is at a discount to 'conventional' hemp at £70/tonne. The seed is used for bird feed, fishing bait and the oil for nutritional supplements and cosmetics.

Flax (cut flax for industrial fibre)
Flax was re-introduced into the UK during the 1990s, not as the traditional, pulled, long fibre variety used for linen textiles but as a cut, combinable crop producing shorter fibres for industrial uses – 'short-fibre flax'. As a natural, biodegradable fibre and a renewable resource it was promoted as a 'green' alternative to synthetic fibres and plastics. New markets were developed and several processing plants set up. It could be grown on IACS or non-IACS land and attracted a generous subsidy. The area of flax expanded to 20,200 ha in 1996 but after several years of poor fibre prices the area fell to 11,000 ha in 2000. After reform of the subsidy regime in 2000, which removed most of the advantages of the crop, the area fell to less than 2,000 ha by 2003, and the one remaining processing facility in Wales was closed. Little, if any, is currently grown.

The agronomy of flax is similar to that of linseed but it is harvested earlier. It is spring sown, suitable for most soil types although lighter soil is preferred. It is a low input crop but weed control is essential. It grows best in areas of high rainfall such as Wales and the South-west. There are several harvesting options (described in earlier editions). Currently the preferred option is desiccation followed by combining. The straw is left to rett in the field and then baled. Retting takes 10-21 days, depending on weather conditions. The price paid for straw will reflect quality. The fibre content of a reasonable crop is 20-30%.

Grain Maize

Maize is one of the major global grains – with world output being higher than that for wheat. However, the climate of the UK has made it difficult to ripen the crop and most maize is grown for forage rather than grain. A combination of earlier varieties, the development of machinery that copes with wet conditions, and even possibly the effects of warmer summers has improved the prospects of this crop.

There is market potential, as over 1.1 million tonnes of grain maize are imported annually. It is used in animal rations, human foods, and in industrial processes. Marketing the UK crop is a problem at present as consignments are generally not big enough to interest the major buyers. The animal feed market is the likeliest outlet for domestic production - a specialised or local market can be developed, for example feed for pigeons or corn-fed chickens. The basis of pricing in the cost of imported (French) maize. A price premium of £20-30/tonne may be available for GM-free crops.

There is no fundamental difference between forage and grain maize – the same varieties are simply left in the field for 3-6 weeks longer to let the cobs mature. It is difficult to know how much of the total UK maize area is taken for grain but it could be around 3,000 ha. The crop can be grown south of a line from Bristol to East Anglia, excluding the far south-west. Fields should be below 500ft in elevation and south-facing. To maximise heat units, the crop should be drilled as soon as soil temperatures are above 8°c – usually late April/May. Harvest by conventional combine with an adapted header in November or December. In UK conditions grain maize seldom drops below 30% moisture. The crop needs to be dried to 15% for storage which can be expensive and time-consuming. On good land the crop can yield 8-10 t/ha but the average is not likely to be so high.

The majority of grain maize is currently stored as a crimped product. This sees the crop cut at 30-35% moisture at the end of October/early November with the 'wet' grain being processed, and an additive added (usually an organic acid). The overall cost of crimping and preservative is around £12/tonne. The grain is clamped or put into large bales or bags. It provides a very digestible dairy feed of high nutrition content. Yields can be 11-13t/ha and it sells of £80-£90/tonne ex-farm.

Yield 7.0t/ha (2.8t/acre), Price £90/t	£/ha	(£/ac)
Output	630	(255)
Variable costs:		
Seed	100	(41)
Fertilizer	80	(32)
Spray	30	(12)
Total Variable Costs	210	(85)
Gross Margin	420	(170)
But note high drying costs:		
£12-16/t done on farm; £15-18/t off farm	85-125	(34-51)

Contact: *Maize Growers Association*: Town Barton Farm, Sandford, Crediton, Devon. EX17 4LS. www.maizegrowersassociation.co.uk

Navy Beans

Used for baked beans, for which the UK imports 110,000 tonnes annually from North America. A few years ago there was some interest in the crop, as varieties adapted to the soil types and climate of the UK were introduced. However, disappointing prices, and the lack of area aid discouraged growers. Under the Single Payment navy beans are no longer at a disadvantage and growing contracts are available along the south coast, Kent, and some areas of East Anglia. The crop requires good fertile land and some care in growing. Sowing is in mid-May when there is no further frost risk. Harvesting is late August/early September.

Yields: target yield is 3.0t/ha but the average is likely to be substantially less; average 2.0t/ha (0.8t/acre) assumed.

Price: very little market information is available, but likely to be in the region of £220/tonne. Output at assumed average yield and price, £440/ha (£178/acre).

Variable costs (approximately) (£ per ha [acre]): seed 75 (30.5); fertilizer 80 (32.5); sprays 110 (44); total £265 (£107).

Gross margin: £175/ha (£71/acre).

Soya Beans

Soya is a sub-tropical crop in origin, grown mainly in North and South America, but also to a small extent in southern Europe. The UK imports 1 million tonnes each year as beans and a further 1 million tonnes as meal, all for animal feed, so there would appear to be a ready market for the home grown product.

Various attempts have been made to commercialise the crop to the UK. In the late 1990's new varieties, developed from a conventional plant breeding programme, were introduced which could be grown in latitudes up to 52° North, which includes southern Britain. In 1999 380 ha were grown in the UK; and the area subsequently expanded to 1,700 ha. But after several difficult years the planted area has declined. Currently, less than 100 ha are being grown. No significant expansion is expected until more reliable varieties are available to growers. However, the plant breeding process continues and the introduction of types more suited to the UK climate could see the viability of the crop improve. As a legume, soya is a good alternative break crop.

Sown from mid-April, depending on soil temperature, altitude should not exceed 70m above sea level. The crop is combine harvested in September. The crop should be cleaned and dried to 14% moisture and 2% admixture. Fertilizer and spray costs are low. Target yield is 3t/ha but the average achieved is likely to be less, particularly in early years as producers become familiar with the crop.

Yields: target yield is 3.0t/ha but the average is likely to be less; average 2.5t/ha (1.0t/acre) assumed

Price: is largely determined by the price of imported crop. The UK crop is GM free, for which a premium is paid. A further premium may be paid for Identity Preserved UK crop which goes into human consumption or for organically grown soya. The average price is £160/tonne. Output at assumed average yield and price, £400/ha (£162/acre).

Variable costs (approximately) (£ per ha [acre]): seed 130 (53); fertilizer (including seed innoculant) 50 (20); sprays 70 (28); total £250 (£101).

Gross margin: £150/ha (£61/acre).

Sunflower

The UK imports the equivalent of about 400,000 tonnes of sunflower seed each year, mainly as sunflower oil. Currently none is commercially crushed in the UK. There has been continued interest in sunflower, but late harvests and low yields have restricted the development of the crop. Currently only about 500 to 600 ha are grown, producing some 1,000 tonnes of seed. Almost all UK production goes into the pet-food or bird seed market; with good demand, but only in localised areas. Producers should satisfy themselves of the end-market before planting the crop. The birdseed market takes 20,000 tonnes of sunflower seed annually, so there is scope for import substitution. Some attempts have been made to cold-press sunflowers to produce a UK-sunflower oil, but this market is still in its infancy.

Extra-early maturing semi-dwarf hybrid varieties are the most suitable to conditions in the UK. This should allow harvesting by mid-September without significant yield reduction. Yields of up to 2.5t/ha with oil content of 44% are possible. However, the crop still needs a relatively mild climate and is best grown south-east of a line from the Wash to east Dorset. Although sunflower will grow on a broad range of soil types its capacity to do well in dry and sandy soils and areas of low rainfall is a recommendation. Sowing is from April to early May when the soil temperature is 7-8°C. Pre-emergence weed control may be necessary; at the right plant density weeds should not subsequently be a problem. As it is a broad row crop, chemical or mechanical weed control is possible. Sclerotina and botrytis, in a wet season, may affect the crop; on areas of less than 6 ha bird damage can be serious. The crop is dried to 8 or 9% for safe storage (costs average £60/ha). Sunflower has a low nitrogen requirement, which may offer benefits in areas of restricted nitrogen use and in organic production.

The price is usually based on a premium over the price of oilseed rape, but other pricing mechanisms may be used in specialist markets.

Yield 2.0t/ha (0.8t/acre), Price £170/t	£/ha	(£/ac)
Output	340	(138)
Variable costs:		
Seed	110	(45)
Fertilizer	45	(18)
Spray	35	(14)
Total Variable Costs	190	(77)
Gross Margin*	150	(61)

*   Note: drying costs can be very high.

Contact: *United Kingdom Sunflower Association* (UKSA): www.uksunflowers.org.uk

Others

Other crops that have been in the news in recent years as possible new crops for the future (or present crops capable of substantial development) include the following: chickpeas and lentils, fenugreek, meadowfoam, cuphea, peppermint, poppies (for cooking oils and pharmaceutical uses), quinoa, buckwheat, honesty and herbs for their essential oils. At present there are no reliable data for these crops on average yield expectations and little on prices or variable costs, when grown on a commercial scale in this country. A number of them are either for the health food market or are sources of oil for industry as replacements for whale oil and light mineral oil. Research continues on many of them. More details may be available from the contact listed below;

Contact: *National Non-Food Crops Centre* (NNFCC): www.nnfcc.co.uk

HOPS

1. *Output data*

   Average Yield: per ha, 2000-2005: 28.1 zentners (1 zentner = 50 kg); range 26.8 (2003) to 31.6 (2004).

Average Price (£ per zenter)	Contract	Spot	Overall
2000	204	140	193
2001	191	131	178
2002	177	114	142
2003	160	104	155
2004	164	67	134
2005	191	136	186

Main Varieties	ha 2005	av. yield 2000-2005 (z. per ha)	prices (£ per zentner)					
			2004			2005		
			contract	spot	overall	contract	spot	overall
Target	124	32.1	113	43	87	130	70	116
Challenger . .	84	31.7	197	185	194	228	219	228
Goldings . . .	247	33.2	205	215	205	224	228	224
Fuggles	154	33.2	205	210	205	225	221	224
First Gold . .	169	21.0	105	0	105	161	147	161
Phoenix	22	34.4	84	49	67	85	77	81
Admiral	48	39.5	132	66	111	130	116	127
Others	77	(includes Northdown (25), Progress (28) and WGV (24))						

Total area of hops (ha): 1984: 5,091; 1997: 3,067; 2005: 1,071. Early last century over 28,000 ha (70,000 acres) were grown.

There is no longer any separate Hops Income Aid scheme, as aid has been subsumed into the Single Payment.

2. *Variable Costs* per mature hectare (acre) (materials only)

	£/ha	(£/ac)
Fertilisers and Manure	140	(57)
Insecticide / Fungicide	520	(210)
Herbicide	110	(45)
String	170	(69)
Pockets / Bales	35	(14)
Drying Fuel	300	(121)
Total	1275	(516)

3. *Average Direct Labour Costs* per mature hectare (acre)

	£/ha	(£/ac)
Growing	750	(304)
Picking	875	(354)
Drying	150	(61)
Total	1775	(718)

N.B. The above costs are the author's approximations for 2006-07 based on a limited sample of crops for the three years 2002-2004.

A new hop garden (erecting the poles, wiring and planting) could cost in the order of £16,000 to £20,000 per hectare (£6,475 to £8,095 per acre).

Acknowledgement: T. W. Smith, Grower Liaison Manager, English Hops and Herbs.

VINEYARDS

As at August 2005 there were 353 registered vineyards in England and Wales, covering 793 hectares. The largest vineyard is over 100 hectares but the average in production is only 2.25 hectares. The five largest vineyards (over 15 ha) represent around a quarter of the UK area; half the vineyards are below 1ha. The South East predominates with 32% of vineyards and 48% of the area. Any vineyard over 0.1 hectare must be registered with the Wine Standards Board, though many of the smaller vineyards are run purely as a hobby. There has been a steady fall in the number of vineyards and the area planted since the mid-1990s (425 vineyards, 1,015 ha in 1995), although numbers have recovered in more recent years. Most of the vineyards that have gone out of production are thought to be smaller non-commercial ones.

In 2005 1.28m litres (1,770 litres per productive hectare) were produced. Around 80% of production is white wine and 20% red. Red wine production had been increasing up to 2004 as a red grape variety more suitable to the English climate had been introduced. This trend has now reversed somewhat. There is also a very significant increase in the production of English sparkling wine.

There is no EU ban on planting vines in the UK and there will not be until annual production exceeds 2.5 million litres on a five-year average. A Quality Wine Scheme for England and Wales was introduced in 1991 and a Regional Wine Scheme in 1997. Hybrid varieties may be planted in the UK but may not currently be made into quality wine. They may be used for quality sparkling wine and regional wine. All wines sold in the UK bear the same VAT and duty, irrespective of origin. A significant proportion of home-produced wine is sold at the farm gate but supermarkets and off-licences are increasingly stocking it. It supplies only 0.3% of the home market. UKVA has recently set up a marketing arm, English Wine Producers, to promote all English wine. From 2003, to conform with EU legislation, English table wine will be called United Kingdom table wine unless it qualifies for a description of regional origin, which could amount to 80% of the crop. From the 2003 vintage, regional wines have been allowed to carry details of vintage, vineyard and varieties on their labels. Since then there has been a marked increase in successful applications for Quality and Regional wine labelling.

Vineyards ideally need south facing, well-drained and sheltered land, less than 100 metres (330 ft.) above sea level, in the southern half of England and Wales. A high level of management and marketing is essential, as is expert advice. There is no minimum area for profitable production. A small enterprise selling wine at the farm gate and to local hotels and restaurants may be more profitable than one with 10 hectares selling only grapes. Some vineyards have associated gift shops and restaurants and are involved with corporate entertaining, which provide extra income. It is now possible to grow grapes under contract for several successful vineyards that have run out of suitable land of their own. Contracts vary, but prices are in the order of £1000/tonne for grapes for still wine and £1500/tonne for sparkling. Help with finance for establishment may be provided.

There are various growing systems: the intensive Double Guyot, the most common in France and Germany, and now 60% of British vineyards, and the more extensive Geneva Double Curtain. However, growers are moving to the Scott-Henry system, with planting density somewhat less than the Double Guyot but giving significantly higher yields and reduced disease pressure. Both Scott-Henry and Double Guyot are cultivated in divided canopies; this helps control vigour, which can be a problem in fertile UK soils. Each vine does twice the work, and the lower density provides better air movement and easier spraying. Scott-Henry is more labour intensive than Geneva Double Curtain, but mechanisation is easier. In any frost-prone area Geneva Double Curtain with its higher fruiting wires can reduce damage.

The Double Guyot system will yield little until year 3 and be in full production in year 4. Geneva Double Curtain will not have a full yield until year 5 or 6 but crops more heavily. The Scott-Henry system crops fully in year 4 or 5. Investment capital (to include materials and labour for planting) of £14,000 to £19,000/ha (£5,665-£7,690/acre) is typically required for the vineyard. Equipment for a winery costs £50,000-£60,000 and a suitable building is needed. Contract winemaking is, however, generally considered better for smaller vineyards of less than 4ha as it gives them access to state of the art equipment and techniques.

Yields and quality are very variable, according to the variety of grape and the year. In a reasonable year a well-managed vineyard should yield 7.5-10 tonnes/hectare (3-4 tonnes/acre). Varieties for more specialised wine styles such as sparkling wines will yield less, at 6-7.5 tonnes/ha (2.5-3.0 tonnes/acre). One tonne of grapes will produce a maximum of 900 75cl bottles of wine.

The following costs refer to a commercial enterprise on a suitable site with a broad variety range. Establishment costs could be double if the site has to be drained and provided with windbreaks and rabbit fencing. Annual growing costs can also be significantly greater, depending on planting density, variety, yield and management.

	Double Guyot		*Geneva Double Curtain*	
	per ha	(per acre)	per ha	(per acre)
Number of Vines.	2,600-3,450*	(1,050-1,400)	1,785**	(725)
	£ per ha	£ per ac	£per ha	£ per ac
Establishment Costs:	over 2 years		over 3 years	
Materials	10,000	(4,045)	7,500	(3,035)
Labour	8,000	(3,240)	7,000	(2,835)
Total Establishment Costs	18,000	(7,285)	14,500	(5,870)
Subsequent Annual Costs:				
Materials	850	(345)	850	(345)
Labour (growing) . . .	3,640	(1,475)	3,640	(1,475)
Harvesting	450	(180)	450	(180)
Total Annual Costs	4,940	(2,000)	4,940	(2,000)

*   Lower density is advised to allow some of the more vigorous verities space to grow without causing excessive shading within the canopy.

** The Scott-Henry System uses a lower planting density, but the extra trellis work means that establishment costs are typically some 5-10% higher.

Prices: Grape prices will vary according to the variety and the vintage. They range from £400 to £1,000 per tonne delivered to a winery. Pinot Noir or Chardonnay for sparkling wine may be £1,200 to £1,500 per tonne. Transport as well as picking costs has therefore to be deducted. Wine prices vary widely but are likely to be in the range £5 to £6.50 a bottle and up to £10 for red wine at retail. English sparkling wine may retail at £15 to £20 a bottle but is more costly to produce. A retail price of at least £4.28 per bottle is necessary to break even for most enterprises.

e.g.   £4.28 less 17.5% vat and £1.26 duty = £2.28*

      Less own winery costs (materials and labour) £1.20 per bottle** = £1.08.

      At 7.5 tonne per ha and 900 bottles per tonne = £7,290 per ha (£2,950/acre).

*   An allowance may also have to be made for a retail mark up of 25%.

** Having wine made under contract costs about £1.85 a bottle.

Acknowledgements: *United Kingdom Vineyards Association* (UKVA); Simon Day, *Vine and Wine Ltd.*, www.vineandwine.co.uk; *Wine Standards Board.*

FRUIT

Established crops: per hectare (per acre in brackets)

Note: The *wide range* of yields, prices and costs, both from farm to farm and season to season, has to be stressed. Thus these figures (which are deliberately rounded) can only be considered to be broad guidelines, i.e. yields and prices in any particular year may differ markedly. Similarly, labour requirements, both regular and casual, vary considerably. *Prices are net of marketing and commission* and assume sales in the open market unless otherwise stated and exclude pick-your-own crops. **Yields** *refer to marketed yields only, of established crops.* The figures relate to *average* levels; 'high' outputs may be about 50% above those shown; naturally the top producers will achieve still better results, especially in good years.

	Dessert Apples	Culinary Apples	Pears	Plums
Yield: tonnes/ha (tons/acre)...	15 (6.1)	20 (8.1)	14 (5.7)	11 (4.5)
Net Price (£/tonne)	400	275	350	675
	£	£	£	£
Output.................	6000 (2430)	5500 (2230)	4900 (1980)	7425 (3000)
Variable Costs:*				
Fertilizer.............	90 (40)	90 (40)	120 (50)	90 (40)
Sprays................	400 (160)	400 (160)	350 (140)	325 (130)
Packaging............	500 (200)	660 (270)	525 (210)	1100 (450)
Casual Labour (picking)	1600 (650)	1485 (600)	1485 (600)	2200 (890)
Total Variable Costs*.......	2590 (1050)	2635 (1070)	2480 (1000)	3715 (1500)
Gross Margin.............	3410 (1380)	2865 (1160)	2420 (980)	3710 (1500)
Regular Labour (hours)......	185 (75)	185 (75)	185 (75)	135 (55)

* excluding establishment, storage and transport.

	Strawberries	Raspberries	Blackcurrants
Yield: tonnes/ha (tons/acre)...	13 (5.3)	5 (2)	6 (2.4)
Net Price (£/tonne)	1700	2650	650
	£	£	£
Output...................	22100 (8940)	13250 (5000)	3900 (1580)
Variable Costs:*			
Fertilizer.............	90 (40)	120 (50)	150 (60)
Sprays................	725 (290)	475 (190)	425 (170)
Packaging............	4125 (1670)	1925 (780)	– –
Casual Labour	8800 (3560)	4680 (1890)	575 (230)
Total Variable Costs*.......	13740 (5560)	7200 (2910)	1150 (470)
Gross Margin.............	8360 (3380)	6050 (2450)	2750 (1110)
Regular Labour (hours)......	200 (80)	300 (120)	125 (50)

* excluding establishment, storage and transport.

Sources: In particular, for yields and prices, the annual 'Basic Horticultural Statistics' published by DEFRA. Data on costs is limited – figures are based on updates of previous rate. Costs are likely to vary widely in practice.

FRUIT ESTABLISHMENT

It is important to appreciate that the figures on pages 49 refer only to established crops. In previous years establishment costs have to be borne, with no (or, later, low) returns.

Apples and Pears: Trees, stake, etc., approximately £5.50/tree. Total establishment costs £4,000-£20,000/ha depending especially on planting density, which varies from 750 to 3,500/ha.

First picking for apples is commonly in year 3 at 30% of full crop. For pears first picking is likely to be in year 4 at 20% of the full crop. Full picking for apples generally arrives in years 6 to 9; for pears years 7 to 12.

Orchard duration: traditional, apples 20 years, pears 30 years plus; denser bed systems 15 years.

Strawberries: Costs in establishment year approximately £5,500/ha for traditional system, £12,500/ha for intensive systems; 60% of the cost is for plants. 35% pick in year 1 in intensive systems, none in traditional systems, full pick in year 2; generally 3 years cropping.

Raspberries: Establishment costs approximately £3,500/ha, including wirework. 50% pick in year 2, full pick in year 3; 10 years cropping.

Blackcurrants: Establishment costs approximately £6,750/ha using bushes, £3,400/ha using cuttings. Takes 1.5 years to establish from 1 year old bushes (i.e. planting November 2006 gives first crop in July 2008), 2.5 years from cuttings. approximately one-third of full crop in first picking year, 75% in second, peak in third, levelling out at slightly lower yield thereafter; 8 or 9 years cropping.

Acknowledgements: *Farm Advisory Services Team Ltd.* and *SmithKline Beecham.*

FIELD-SCALE VEGETABLES

Per hectare (per acre in brackets)

Note: The same comments regarding variability apply as to fruit (page 48). The same main source has been used, for most of the crops. The 'other' variable cost figures are intended only as a general indication of their level; survey data on many of these crops is rarely available and, when it is, particularly variable between farms and seasons. *Prices are net of marketing expenses.*

	Carrots (maincrop)	*Dry Bulb Onions*	*Dwarf Beans (for Processing)*
Yield: tonnes/ha (tons/acre)...	58 (24)	38 (15)	6.5 (2.6)
Net Price (£/tonne)	125	115	320
	£	£	£
Output...................	7250 (2930)	4370 (1770)	2080 (840)
Variable Costs:			
Seed	500 (202)	350 (140)	275 (110)
Fertilizer..............	120 (50)	150 (60)	145 (60)
Sprays	450 (180)	375 (150)	140 (60)
Other*	4130 (1670)	1650 (670)	70 (30)
Total Variable Costs........	5200 (2100)	2525 (1020)	630 (250)
Gross Margin.............	2050 (830)	1845 (750)	1450 (590)
Regular Labour (hours)......	50-150	40-60	n/a

	Brussels Sprouts	Cabbage	Spring Greens
Yield: tonnes/ha (tons/acre)...	14 (5.7)	32.5 (13)	11 (4.5)
Net Price (£/tonne)	400	230	300
	£	£	£
Output...................	5600 (2270)	7475 (3030)	3300 (1340)
Variable Costs:			
Seed	450 (180)	550 (220)	400 (160)
Fertilizer..............	150 (60)	210 (80)	210 (80)
Sprays	225 (90)	275 (110)	275 (110)
Other*	1100 (450)	3025 (1220)	1155 (470)
Total Variable Costs.......	1925 (780)	4060 (1640)	2040 (830)
Gross Margin.............	3675 (1490)	3415 (1380)	1260 (510)
Regular Labour (hours)......	75 (30)	75 (30)	60 (24)

	Cauliflower	Broccoli	Calabrese	Sweetcorn
Yield: tonnes/ha (tons/acre)...	14 (5.7)	14 (5.7)	9.5 (3.8)	12.5 (5)
Net Price (£/tonne)	300	300	650	120
	£	£	£	£
Output...................	4200 (1700)	4200 (1700)	6175 (2500)	1500 (605)
Variable Costs:				
Seed	800 (320)	725 (290)	650 (260)	125 (50)
Fertilizer..............	210 (80)	180 (70)	180 (70)	120 (50)
Sprays	150 (60)	150 (60)	175 (70)	50 (20)
Other*	1320 (530)	1375 (560)	3400 (1380)	275 (110)
Total Variable Costs.......	2480 (1000)	2430 (980)	4405 (1780)	570 (230)
Gross Margin.............	1720 (700)	1770 (720)	1770 (720)	930 (380)

	Lettuce (Outdoor)	Parsnips	Leeks	Rhubarb
Yield: tonnes/ha (tons/acre)...	24 (9.5)	25 (10.1)	20 (8.1)	45 (18.2)
Net Price (£/tonne)	500	450	650	600
	£	£	£	£
Output...................	12000 (4860)	11125 (4550)	13000 (2560)	27000 (10930)
Variable Costs:				
Seed	1275 (520)	150 (60)	600 (240)	150 (61)
Fertilizer..............	210 (80)	120 (50)	150 (00)	90 (40)
Sprays	325 (130)	350 (140)	400 (160)	75 (30)
Other*	5200 (2100)	3800 (1540)	8250 (3340)	n/a
Total Variable Costs.......	7010 (2840)	4420 (1790)	9400 (3800)	n/a
Gross Margin.............	4990 (2020)	6830 (2760)	3600 (1460)	n/a

* Other = Casual Labour, Packaging, etc.

HORTICULTURE – WHOLE FARM DATA

Comparative whole farm data is less generally available for horticultural holdings than for various types of farm in different regions of the country (see sources of reports listed on page 5). Data from across a wide area of England is presented below. Because the results vary so much from year to year two-year averages are presented: for 2003 and 2004 harvest/cropping years. The data are collected by seven College/University centres: Askham Bryan, Cambridge, Exeter, Newcastle, Nottingham, Reading and Wye.

All financial figures are per hectare. The averages cover a wide range.

| Type of Holding | Specialist Glass | | Specialist Outdoor | |
	Mainly edible crops	Flowers & nursery stock	Fruit	Hortic.
No. of Farms in Sample......	33	65	37	30
Average Size (ha [acres])	1.08 (2.7)	0.74 (1.8)	33 (82)	37 (91)
	£	£	£	£
Gross Output	253,530	461,048	4,962	7,619
Less:				
Bought Seed and Plants......	12,952	111,087	24	973
Market Charges	22,233	12,060	634	315
Packing Materials	12,914	21,261	670	539
Net Output................	205,431	316,640	3,634	5,792
Other Costs:				
Labour (inc. Unpaid Manual)	84,133	147,562	1,693	2,412
Glasshouse Fuel............	28,997	14,852	3	28
Manures..................	6,201	16,737	46	172
Sprays and Fumigants	2,313	3,638	274	197
Horticultural Sundries	14,246	20,262	287	678
Power and Machinery	19,964	29,989	586	832
Land Rent, Glass Deprecn. ...	16,143	20,458	340	508
Other Fixed Costs	16,276	30,257	634	442
Total Other Costs	188,270	283,752	3,860	5,267
Management and Inv. Inc.....	17,162	32,888	-266	526
Grower and Spouse Labour (+)	15,965	26,912	318	413
Net Income	33,126	59,799	92	938
Tenant's Valuation	129,040	210,918	4,235	3,033

Source: *Horticultural Business Data*, compiled by R. L. Vaughan and R. T. Crane, Department of Agricultural and Food Economics, The University of Reading, 2006.

Glasshouse Crop Outputs (at 5-year average yields (2001-2005) and 5-year average prices (same period); all figures rounded):

	Yield t/ha (t/acre)	Price £/tonne	Output £/ha (acre)
Tomatoes, heated...........	423 (171)	830	353,200 (142,900)
Tomatoes, cold	127 (52)	1,000	129,800 (52,500)
Cucumbers	470 (190)	510	240,500 (97,300)
Lettuce	37 (15)	1,230	45,500 (18,400)

MUSHROOMS

The mushroom industry has changed considerably during the past 5 years or so. A significant number of businesses of all sizes and in different parts of the country have ceased production and few if any new growers have entered the business. Less than 75 firms remain in production. Those that remain are either highly efficient enterprises with strong links to supermarkets or small low cost family-run businesses selling largely to wholesalers. The reasons for this are static consumption levels and competition from cheap imports. There are a few organic mushroom producers who sell at a premium.

Among the firms that remain there have also been changes in the method of production. Traditionally, the majority of UK growers employed Phase 1 compost, which they pasteurised and spawn-ran on the premises, to fill moveable trays or shelves in their growing rooms. Currently, the most prevalent system (perhaps 70% of all growers) uses purchased Phase 2 compost (pasteurised, with spawn added). This is supplied in shrink-wrapped blocks but it is also available in plastic bags as well as in bulk. Phase 3 compost (fully spawn-run) in blocks or bags is used by some growers. Organic Phase 3 and Phase 3 compost is also available.

Type of compost used	*Phase 2*	*Phase 3*
	per tonne compost	
Mushroom Yield/tonne compost	250kg	300kg
	£	£
Mushroom Price/kg....................	1.80	1.80
Spent compost	2	2
Output	452.0	542.0
Variable costs:*		
Compost (incl. delivery)	95.0	135.0
Casing............................	12.5	12.5
Growing labour at 4p/kg.............	10.0	12.0
Picking labour at 35p/kg.............	87.5	105.0
Packing materials at 17.5kg...........	44.0	52.5
Packing labour at 4.5p/kg	11.3	13.5
Energy costs at 5p/kg	12.5	15.0
Other costs at 5p/kg	12.5	15.0
Total Variable Costs	285.3	360.5
Margin/tonne compost.................	166.7	181.5
Variable cost/kg mushrooms	1.14	1.20
Margin/kg mushrooms	0.67	0.60

N.B. All labour is included but labour for growing, if not picking and packing, could well be regular.

Output: Growers using Phase 2 compost will fill on an 8-week cycle and produce 6.5 crops per year. Phase 3 compost can be filled on a 6-week cycle and allows 8.5 crops per year. Yields are expressed as kg per square metre of bed or kg per tonne of compost. Commercial yields are 25-35kg/sq m of bed area per crop (250-350kg per tonne of compost) using Phase 2 or 3 compost, but only 18-20kg/sq metre (180-200kg/tonne of compost) using Phase 1. Phase 1 compost costs £25/tonne, Phase 2 £85/tonne and Phase 3 £125/tonne plus delivery which can add £6-15/tonne, depending on distance and size of load.

Labour costs: If Phase 2 or 3 compost is used, labour for growing amounts to 10% of all labour costs while picking is 80% and packing 10%. Using Phase 1 compost labour cost for growing is significantly greater, perhaps 25p/kg or 40% of total labour, but the initial compost is cheaper.

Prices: Mushroom prices are in the range of £2.00/kg supplied to a supermarket to £1.00 or less sold on the wholesale market. Small growers marketing through a producer organisation would get around £1.60/kg delivered. At present 60% of the crop is sold by growers direct to supermarkets. Prices can be volatile and oversupply can lead to mushrooms being sold at a loss. Imports now account for 65% of all mushrooms sold in the UK, and 60% of the value of sales. Almost all imports are from the Netherlands and the Republic of Ireland.

Returns: The data suggest that ex-farm it costs £1.14 to produce 1kg of mushrooms using Phase 2 compost and £1.20 using Phase 3 compost. This does not take into account management or finance costs. The yield of the crop and the number of cycles each year are, of course, crucial.

Establishment Costs: A mushroom farm using Phase 2 compost on an 8-week cycle would require 8 rooms each with a 200sq m capacity. A farm using Phase 3 compost on a 6-week cycle would need 6 rooms of 200sq m capacity. In both cases one growing room would be filled each week using 20 tonnes of compost. To set up such a production system would require a capital investment of £200,000-£300,000 for the rooms, trays or shelves, heating and cooling systems, packing area, hard standings and equipment. If Phase 1 compost is used then buildings and equipment for composting, peak heating and spawning are also required.

Acknowledgement*: Mushroom Growers Association*, Box 192, Ketton, Stamford, Lincs PE9 3ZT: www.mushroomgrowers.org.

ORGANIC FARMING

The Organic Sector:

4.1% of UK agricultural land (excluding common grazing) is in organic production: more than 4,000 holdings. The percentage in England is 2.8%. In January 2005 the area (in hectares) devoted to organic production was as follows:

	Fully Organic	In conversion	Total	% of Agric. Area	of UK Organic Area	% of UK Organic Producers
England	230,377	28,995	259,372	2.8	37.6	63.8
Wales	55,558	8,973	64,531	4.4	9.3	16.0
Scotland	344,416	15,199	359,615	7.3	52.1	15.8
N. Ireland	5,146	1,604	6,705	0.7	1.0	4.4
UK	**635,497**	**54,771**	**690,269**	**4.1**	**100**	**100**

The amount has risen significantly in recent years for a number of reasons: poor prices for conventionally produced crops and livestock, good premium price levels, increasing demand - owing largely to health concerns (e.g. BSE/CJD and the introduction of genetically modified crops) and the introduction and augmentation of the aid scheme covering the required conversion period (see next page). The market potential is shown by the fact that around 55% of UK consumption of organic produce is currently imported (down from 70% in 2000). Demand has risen considerably in recent years. The Soil Association's Organic Food and Farming Report 2004, the value of UK retail sales was £1.12 billion in 2003, which compares with £384 million five years before. This is about 2% of total food sales. The Government's aim is to increase the UK share of the total domestic market to at least 70%. However, some organic farmers have reverted to conventional production primarily because of declining premiums (see next page). Imports of organic fruit and vegetables are especially high.

Approximately 22.5% of organic land in England is in crops, just under 10% in the UK as a whole. Most conversion has been taking place on hill and upland livestock farms. It is reported that nearly 98% of Scotland's registered organic land is extensive hill grazing, where management changes need only be small. Thus in January 2006 England had 64% of the UK's organic producers compared with 18% in Scotland, 15% in Wales and 3% in Northern Ireland.

Organic Systems:

The benefits to the nation claimed for organic farming are as follows:

(i)   lower yields = less surpluses = less national and EU expenditure on storage and disposal; additionally, less need for set-aside

(ii) environmental (including wildlife and water pollution) benefits of non-use of inorganic fertilizers and agrochemical sprays

(iii) reduction in use of fossil energy

(iv) increasing concern over health means a rising demand and thus an expanding market (as noted above)

(v)   a saving in imported produce (again as noted above).

Against these points critics argue that:

(i)   it is unproven that inorganic fertilizers and (tested and approved) agrochemicals harm the environment;

(ii) it is unproven that organically produced foods are more nutritious, healthier or tastier;

(iii) there is insufficient land available to feed the present population adequately if all farming were organic;

(iv) since organic farming requires more land than conventional farming to produce a given amount of food, less land would be available for environmental purposes, recreation and woodland;

(v)   if organic production became widespread in the UK compared with other countries our competitive position in terms of production costs per tonne would become increasingly eroded.

The economics to the farmer (though this is of secondary interest to many organic farmers) depend primarily upon:

(i)   relative yield compared with conventional farming;

(ii) the price premium compared with conventional farming.

In the case of cereals both research and experience suggests that yields of organic crops are typically between 60% and two-thirds of those of conventionally produced crops, but the much higher prices obtained have easily compensated for this to date, with cereals and feed peas and beans £150 to £200 a tonne and there is also the obvious saving in fertilizer and spray costs. Hence the gross margin is normally much higher. However, there are also the wider whole farm effects to be considered, e.g., unless the farm already has a substantial percentage of its area down to leys this will probably have to be increased in order to maintain yields and this extra grass has to be utilised profitably – which is far from easy, and the extra capital requirements could be heavy.

Furthermore, there is a two year 'conversion period' to undergo before full price premiums can be claimed. In the case of vegetable crops, quality (in the sense of appearance) can be badly affected by pests and diseases.

As regards relative cultivation costs, in one ADAS monitored study these were reported to be 15% higher on the organically grown wheat (approximately £20 more per ha (£8 per acre) at present costs). However no spraying is required. Survey data have indicated overall labour requirements to be 10-30% higher than on conventional farms, with machinery costs generally similar.

In the case of livestock, premiums have been highly attractive. In some sectors, such as milk, this led to many producers converting to organic, creating an excess of supply over demand. This then collapsed the organic premium. A steady increase in demand has since re-balanced the milk market and average prices have returned to around 29.5p/litre. It is a demonstration of the need to consider markets fully in a 'niche' market like organic. Organic production of grazing livestock is generally speaking of greater value to the larger farm, especially on land that favours grass rather than cash crops, where the reduction in stocking rate caused by the lack of nitrogen fertilizer is less important. Concentrate feed costs per tonne are much higher.

As already stated, the big questions are the relative yields and the price difference. Future price premiums will depend on how much the consumption of organic produce increases compared with increases in supply.

Aid for Organic Farmers:

The Organic Farming Scheme for England has now closed for new applications following the introduction of the Organic Entry Level Stewardship (OELS) (see page 216). Existing agreements will continue until the end of their term. There were two options, as follows.

The *conversion option* aimed to encourage producers to convert to organic production by providing payments over a five year conversion period. Participants must have registered their proposed land for conversion with one of the organic sector bodies and provided a conversion plan. There was a minimum eligible area of 1 ha; there was no maximum limit. Rates of aid (£/ha) are given in the table below.

The second option was a *maintenance option* extending over five years. It was intended to support organic production on registered land beyond the conversion period by providing flat rate annual payments as given below.

| Year | Conversion Option | | | | | Maintce. |
	1	2	3	4/5	Total	
Top fruit orchards (pears, plums, cherries and apples (not cider))	600	600	600	30	1,860	30
AAPS eligible land and land in permanent crops (not top fruit)	225	135	30	30	450	30
Ineligible arable land and grassland	175	105	23	23	349	23
Unimproved grassland or rough grazing	25	10	5	5	50	5

Similar schemes, but with different categories and payment rates, are available in Wales and in Scotland.

Under the CAP Reform (Mid-Term Review) holdings that are totally organic will be exempt from the requirement to set land aside in order to activate set-aside entitlements.

Further Information:

No gross margin data for organic enterprises are included in this section because a specialist publication is available on the subject: the '2006 Organic Farm Management Handbook', (7th Ed - Sept 2006) by Nic Lampkin, Mark Measures and Susanne Padel, University of Wales, Aberystwyth. Tel: 01970 622248.

Additional information may be available from the following organisations:

DEFRA (Organic Food and Industrial Crops Division)
Nobel House, 17 Smith Square, London, SW1P 3JR.   020 7238 5605

Organic Farmers and Growers Limited
The Elim Centre, Lancaster Road, Shrewsbury, Shropshire, SY1 3LE.   01743 440512

Soil Association
Bristol House, 40-56 Victoria Street, Bristol, BS1 6BY.   0117 929 0661

Elm Farm Research Centre
Hamstead Marshall, Newbury, Berkshire, RG20 0HR.   01488 658298

Biodynamic Agricultural Association
The Secretary, Painswick Inn, Stroud, Glos. GL5 1QG.   01453 759501

Organic Food Federation
1 Turbine Way, EcoTech Business Park, Swaffham, Norfolk, PE37 7XD. 01760 720444

Organic Centre Wales
University of Wales, Aberystwyth, Ceredigion, SY23 3AL.   01970 622248

Tesco Centre for Organic Agriculture
Nafferton Farm, Stocksfield, Northumberland, NE47 7XD.   01661 830222

Scottish Agricultural College
Organic Farming Unit, Craibstone Estate, Bucksburn, Aberdeen,
AB21 9YA   01224 711293

TURF

The market for turf continues to be good but competition within the sector is strong, particularly among the producers of general contract grade turf. The market is now predominantly supplied with seed sown turf or 'turfgrass'. Pasture turf is still available in certain areas, but overall its importance is small and declining. Suitable pasture for turf lifting is hard to find and it can now be cheaper to grow cultivated turf than treat and prepare existing pasture. Special seed mixtures and cultivation techniques produce a range of types of turfgrass that can be matched to particular sites and uses. In some cases special soil mixes are provided for the site as well as the turf. The Turfgrass Growers Association (TGA) has introduced quality standards and buyers are increasingly specifying the precise type of turf they require. It is estimated that there are around 16,000 ha (40,000 acres) of turfgrass grown in the UK. Although several turfgrass companies were originally set up by farmers, the business has moved away from mainstream farming. However, farms may be involved in the following ways:

1. *Selling existing pasture turf to a turf company*

This is the traditional option but it now represents very little of the turf market and its share will continue to decline. The opportunity will be open to very few farmers indeed. The approach may be by the farmer to the company or vice-versa. Minimum 5-6 year ley/pasture generally needed for spring or autumn lifting, 8-10 year grass is better for summer cutting.

Important features: good root structure, number and type of weeds, level, well-drained, stone-free land; good access; timing (farmer wants lifting completed in time to drill next crop).

Payment varies between £750-£1,500 per hectare (£300-£600 per acre), but mainly £900-£1,200 per ha (£360-£480 per acre). There is usually an initial payment plus further payments as turf is lifted. There may be a penalty clause if lifting delays prevent subsequent timely drilling. Lifting can take from two months to even a year. It can be done at any time of year except when there is snow on the ground. The turf company usually sprays against broadleaved weeds, fertilizes and mows before lifting; the farmer may do these tasks, for payment. He may graze the land, for a rent, if lifting is delayed.

Apparently the effect on the land is not detrimental; some say there are benefits (removal of accumulated pests, etc. in the top inch of grass, roots and topsoil).

Some local authorities require planning consent for turf stripping. In some instances it has been refused on the grounds that pasture turf is not an agricultural crop.

Cultivated turf, however, is deemed to be an agricultural crop. On tenanted land landlord's permission is necessary to cut pasture turf.

2. Farmer cutting, lifting and selling pasture turf himself

Extremely uncommon. The turf must be treated, as in option 1. A small turf cutting machine can be hired for about £60 a day. This slices off the turf which must then be cut into lengths and picked up by hand. Two or three workers are required. It is slow going even in good conditions. The wastage figure is commonly 10-20% of the area, perhaps more. To hire a machine which cuts and picks up the turf may be possible but the charge will be considerably more.

Turf has a short life once cut and stacked - a maximum 2 to 3 days in summer, 7 days in winter, depending on temperature.

3. Renting land to a turf company for production of cultivated turf

Turf companies rent land for turfgrass production in addition to using their own land. As before, well-drained, stone-free land with good access is required. Typically the land is rented on a per crop basis and one or two crops grown. A turf crop usually takes 10 to 15 months from preparation to harvest but autumn sown crops may be harvested within 9 months. Rent levels depend on the quality of the land, the provision of irrigation and the profitability of competing agricultural enterprises. Currently rents are in the order of £900-£1,500 per hectare per crop (£365-£525 per acre) or £700-£1,000 per ha per year (£285-£405 per acre).

4. Cultivated turf production

On their own land turf producers can grow turf continuously, taking a crop every 18 months to two years on average. On rented land (as in option 3), they take one or two crops and move on. Usually they produce a quick growing type of turf which sells quickly on rented land and cultivate more specialist and slower growing turf on their own land. A high level of agronomic expertise and considerable investment in machinery are needed and labour requirements are heavy. As the business is very competitive a high degree of marketing expertise is essential. While the bulk of the trade goes into general landscaping or garden centres there is an increase in the number of contracts where the quality and type of turf is specified. It is estimated that a turf farm would need to be 150-200 hectares (400-500 acres) or more in size to be viable – in order to justify the machinery and equipment necessary and to produce a succession of turf for the market. There are significant economies of scale. The cost of specialist machinery for turf production can be £350,000. The new one-man harvesting machine costs in the order of £120,000-£200,000 but significantly reduces labour costs.

Costs and Returns

Variable Costs plus Rent:	£/ha	(£/ac)
Seed	375-525	(150-215)
Fertilizer	140-300	(57-120)
Herbicide	70-150	(28-60)
Fungicide	0-150	(0-60)
Rent (for 15 months)	900-1,300	(365-525)
Total Costs	1,485-2,425	(600-980)

It may be necessary to irrigate and on occasions use netting to grow the grass through for certain sites.

Labour

Special seed bed preparation (including subsoiling and stone burying), regular mowing (twice a week May/June), picking up clippings, harvesting (2 men on harvester plus one loading lorry) between 0.2-0.4 hectares per day (0.5-1.0 acre). The new one-man harvester can do 2 ha (5 acres) a day.

Total costs of the order of £4,725-£6,825 per ha (£1,910-£2,760 per acre), approximately 53-76p per sq.m. (43-63p per sq.yd.)

Value of Turf (on the field)

	per sq. m	per sq. yd.	per ha*	per acre*
Pasture turf	38-43p	32-36p	£3,420-£3,850	£1,380-£1,570
Hardwearing, domestic general contract	75-95p	65-80p	£6,840-£8,550	£2,755-£3,470
Football, hockey, prestige landscape	115-145p	95-120p	£10,260-£12,825	£4,150-£5,200
High quality/specialist** ...	190-475p	160-405p	£17,100-£42,750	£6,910-£17,290

* assuming 90% recovery, but some producers work on 85%.

** for some contracts the price may be higher.

Delivery charges 45-55p per sq.m.

Acknowledgements: *Turfgrass Growers Association*, 133 Eastgate, Louth, Lincolnshire, LN11 9QG. Telephone: 01507 607722. www.turfgrass.co.uk. *Sports Turf Research Institute*, Bingley, West Yorkshire BD16 1AU. Telephone: 01274 565131.

GOLF

The boom in golf course construction that was seen in the early 1990s, when almost 70 a year were being built, is long over. Golf is still very popular in the UK but the supply of courses comfortably exceeds demand in most areas. The traditional membership clubs and municipal courses have been joined by proprietary golf, where courses are owned by business corporations and developers and are run largely on a 'pay and play' basis. Currently there are only a few courses under construction. These are what may be described as resort or 'lifestyle' courses involving a very high level of investment in accommodation and other facilities as well as the golf course itself. The opportunity for farmers to be involved in golf course development is now extremely limited. However, there are other facilities such as driving ranges or 6-hole courses that could well offer opportunities – but location is crucial.

It is important that any new golf facility is near a substantial centre of population that can support the course. A rule of thumb measure is that a population of 25,000 within a 20-minute drive will support an 18-hole course. The proposed course will need good road access, an attractive free-draining site and good staff and management. Golf ranges and 6-hole courses need to be located even closer to centres of population, retail parks, or other leisure facilities to meet planning requirements and to be economically viable. Any new development needs to have a concept that will make it special and hence attractive. Planning legislation is complex and the cost of preparing an application, which requires a full Environmental Impact Assessment, can be prohibitive. With the above in mind, the followings options are available for landowners in the right situation;

Type of facility

- 18-hole course: 60-70 ha (150-180 acres) with Clubhouse and Pro Shop (600 sq. metres), parking, proper access and maintenance buildings. It takes between 1 and 2 years to construct.
- 9-hole course: 30-40 ha (79-95 acres).
- 9-hole Par 3 course: 6 ha (15 acres).
- 6-hole Par 3 or 4 course: 12 ha (30 acres).
- Driving range: 4 ha (10 acres).
- Pitch and putt course: 1.5 ha (4 acres).

- 'Compac Golf': 4-10 ha (10-25 acres). This is a new concept which allows 18-hole golf to be played on a relatively small area using a cleverly designed combination of 4 greens and 7-9 tees; played by the hour.

Type of business organisation
- To sell land with planning permission. The cost of development of an average new course can be significantly more than the value of the facility when it is complete. Thus little or no premium over agricultural value can be expected unless the situation or planning consent offers something exceptional.
- To let land to a developer/operator. Assuming the latter pays for constructing the course, a long lease will be required. Rental levels will depend on the expected profitability of the facility.
- To form a joint company with a developer/operator. This obviously means the farmer shares in the success or failure. The land would be all or part of the farmer's equity. A well constructed agreement is essential.
- To develop and operate the course himself. The farmer would need good knowledge of golf and exceptional management ability besides access to substantial capital. In the present circumstances it is not to be recommended.

Construction methods and cost
- Specialist golf course constructor:
  18-hole course (60-75 ha): £1,000,000-£3,000,000 according to drainage, earthmoving and irrigation, but excluding green keepers building and machinery.
  9-hole course (30-40 ha): £400,000-750,000.
  9-hole par 3 course (6 ha): £200,000-£350,000.
  6-hole par 3 or 4 course (12 ha): £200,000-£300,000.
  Driving range (4 ha): £150,000-£300,000, to include offices, storage, equipment, fencing and floodlighting.
  'Compac Golf' (4-10 ha): £200,000-£400,000, depending on site and size.
  Green keeper's building: £120,000-£200,000.
  Full inventory of new machinery for 18-hole course: £360,000.
  Clubhouse (600 sq. metres): from £600,000 to £1,500,000 fitted out.
- Direct labour may reduce costs by a third.
- Using own farm labour it is possible to reduce costs but it is very risky in terms of resultant course quality.

It is crucial to obtain professional advice at the outset for investment appraisal, feasibility study and a business plan. Only when planning approval and finance are in place should a specialist course designer be employed. Advice should also be sought on the management of the business.

Returns
A successful well-run golf business should achieve more than a 15% return on capital employed by the fourth year after a gradual build up: year 1 loss, year 2 break even, year 3 a small profit (5-8%). Thus an 18-hole course could produce over £300,000 annually; however, a significant number of new clubs are currently making a loss.

Acknowledgement: *PGA Design Consulting Ltd.*, The Old Church, Neath Road, Bristol BS5 9AP. Telephone: 0117 952 7585. www.pgadc.com

BED AND BREAKFAST

It is estimated that around 2,000 farms across the UK offer B&B. Some are seasonal and informally run but many are open for much of the year, inspected under the auspices of VisitBritain, and are members of a Regional Tourist Board and/or an organisation such as Farm Stay UK.

A bed and breakfast enterprise can be rewarding in both financial and social terms. However, the person running the business should enjoy meeting people, have good social skills and be prepared to work long hours. Other members of the family must be willing to share their home with visitors and to lose a certain amount of privacy. In a crowded market, and with rising customer expectations, the standard of the product is increasingly important. The aim must be to provide a standard of accommodation equal to that found in hotels. This is likely to involve some refurbishment of the farmhouse; either before starting the enterprise, to upgrade an existing B&B to modern standards, or just ongoing repair of wear and tear. Very little grant assistance is available to cover capital costs in setting-up a B&B. Any support is likely to be on a regional basis. The relevant Regional Development Agency (RDA) should be contacted as a first step. As with all new ventures, it is good practice, and essential if seeking additional finance, to create a well-thought-out business plan containing realistic projections.

Although they are not necessarily onerous for smaller operations, it is vital to know the planning, legislative and financial requirements involved in B&B provision. '*The Pink Booklet - a practical guide to legislation for accommodation providers*' produced by VisitBritain covers all the points which have to be addressed. In addition a great deal of help and advice is provided by both VisitBritain, the Regional Tourist Boards and the Regional Development Agencies. A series of information pamphlets is available and one-day tourism training courses are run.

Marketing is very important. It can be done through a national organisation, in local Tourist Information Centres, in newspapers and magazines, and by word of mouth. Some establishments produce an attractive brochure or card giving details of the B&B, its location, facilities, and quality standards rating. Copies are left at tourist information centres etc and sent to prospective visitors. The internet is becoming an important tool for the promotion of farmhouse B&Bs; either through a stand-alone site, or via a website grouping together many providers. Presenting an attractive online presence, including photographs and descriptions, is likely to result in more interest.

As there is considerable competition it is useful if the enterprise can offer something special or different such as accommodation for visitors' horses, a welcome for pets or use of a tennis court or pool. Establishments that can accommodate bigger parties are gaining in popularity. The number of B&Bs offering an evening meal has tended to decline in recent years, but providing locally grown produce can also be a draw. If evening meals are not offered it helps to have good local restaurants and pubs that customers can be directed to.

To join a marketing organisation it is important for the B&B to have a Quality Assurance Standard rating, awarded by Quality in Tourism.. The rating is at one of five levels, at present expressed as diamonds in England and stars in Scotland and Wales. It is based on guest care and the quality of what is provided following an unannounced overnight inspection visit. The inspection fee depends on the number of bedrooms and the level of charges. The rated establishment gets a listing in the VisitBritain guides and on their internet site. In some areas membership of a Regional Tourist Board is an option; this confers additional benefits including a reduction in inspection fees, access to legal advice, and discounted rates for promotional activities and training courses.

Prices charged will reflect the quality of accommodation and location but cannot be far out of line with other local B&Bs and small hotels. Prices can also vary depending on length of stay and time of year. The price range for one person per night at a farmhouse B&B is £20-£35 with the average for 2006 being about £27 on the basis of two adults sharing a room. A higher rate usually applies for single occupancy of a double room.

The receipts from the enterprise can be calculated as follows: If the B&B is open for 40 weeks of the year at £27 per person per night, given a 60% occupancy rate the gross return per bed will be just over £4,500. Most farmhouse B&Bs have 4-6 bed spaces, which would generate a gross return of £18,000 to £27,000.

As every farmhouse B&B is different and some costs are difficult to apportion between guests and family, it is hard to provide realistic average costings. The following provides some pointers. Variable costs are food, electricity and heating, laundry, cleaning materials and additional help. There will also be regular redecoration costs, repairs, and replacement and renewal of glassware, china, cutlery, towels and bedlinen. Variable costs if no non-family labour is used might average about 20% of the nightly charge. If casual labour has to be included variable costs could amount to 30-35% of the nightly charge. Fixed costs will include insurance, business rates (if they apply), membership of a marketing organisation, regular advertising, repayments on any loans taken out for building and equipment to start the business and regular labour; they are likely to average 30-35% of charges.

Contact: *VisitBritain* (formerly English Tourism Council), Thames Tower, Black's Road, Hammersmith, London W6 9EL. Tel: 020 8563 3000. www.visitbritain.com. *Quality in Tourism*, Farncombe House, Braodway, Worcs. WR12 7LJ. Tel: 0845 300 6996. www.qualityintourism.com. *Farm Stay UK*, NAC, Stoneleigh Park, Warwickshire, CV8 2LG. Tel: 02476 696909. www.farmstayuk.co.uk

CHRISTMAS TREES

About 7 million trees are sold a year in the UK: 5.5 million of them home-grown. Five years ago 80% were Norway Spruce, but this is now down to less than 30%, with Nordman Fir, which retains its needles longer, at 50% (95% in urban areas) and Fraser Fir, a US favourite, 12%. The most popular size has been increasing and is now 5 to 7 feet. Only 5% are sold rooted.

Imported trees have accounted for 1.5 million (21%) of total sales, but imports for Christmas 2005 fell to a few hundred thousand, putting pressure on supplies and raising prices by 10%. Christmas trees are not eligible for the Single Payment, and as a result, many growers throughout the EU have grubbed-up trees, or note replanted in order to grow crops or pasture that is eligible for support. The supply of trees in mainland Europe has therefore been substantially reduced. UK Christmas tree growers, unlike those in other countries, have never received subsidies and have not cut back production significantly.

There are some 400 British growers, with plantations ranging from less than one hectare to 1,000 ha, all across the country. It is estimated that there are 60 million trees being grown, on some 10,000 ha. The average grower sells 6 to 7,000 a year from about 20 ha. The majority of sales are through the big garden centres, which require a uniform tree, netted and palletised, but there are successful 'choose and cut' operations and the enterprise works well on a farm with a farm shop. Producers need to sell 10 to 15,000 a year to justify the required machinery.

The enterprise is slow to make a return. Norway Spruce is harvested in years 5 to 7, Nordman and Fraser Firs in years 7 to 9, making the enterprise vulnerable to changing market conditions. About 30% of the crop is harvested in the first harvest year, 40% in the second, 30% in the third. All species need a well-drained site free from late frosts, with good access. As with any crop the better the land the better the crop.

Rabbit fencing (£2 per m) and possibly deer fencing (£5.50 per m) are pre-requisites. Spacing is possible from 60cm x 60cm to 1.8m x 1.8m, but 1.2m x 1.2m is recommended. This gives 5,500 plants per ha allowing for 80% land loss for headlands, access, etc. Losses of 5 to 10% in the first year means 300-500 replacements are needed in second year. Norway Spruce transplants 12-14p each, Nordman Fir 25-35p. Planting, by hand or machine, 8-12p/per plant.

Variable Inputs: Fertiliser in a split top dressing of 350 kg/ha 12: 11:18 + Mg and TE in late March and mid-September. Herbicides for weed control: residual herbicide, as cereals, in first year; subsequently an over-spray in October/November plus spot weeding until the canopy closes over. Weed control costs 26p/plant over the life of the tree.

Pesticides: aphicide three times a year for Norway Spruce, once for Nordman Fir at £16 per ha per application. Acaricide from year 3 to harvest: £126 per ha per year for Norway Spruce, £63 for Nordman Fir.

Pruning and Shaping: This is essential to produce the shape of tree the market demands. Norway Spruce: shaping 15p per tree per year from year 3 or 4. Nordman Fir: basal pruning in year 3 or 4 at 15p-20p per tree plus shaping in the same year at 15p per tree and bud-rubbing every year except harvest at 5-10p per tree per year.

Harvesting: Done over 3 to 6 weeks, for dispatch Nov. 20 - Dec. 12. A full-time person is needed per 3,000 trees sold, or one person per week per 400-500 trees. Cost: Norway Spruce 60-80p per tree, Nordman Fir 70-90p; Norway Spruce may be dipped or sprayed to reduce needle drop. Marketing costs around 10% of output.

Machinery: Inter-row plantation tractors £15,000-£65,000; stump clearing machines £7,000-£25,000; palletiser £13,000-£14,000; mist blowers £8,000-£10,000; hydraulic netting funnel £8,000-£10,000; manual netting funnel £175.

Labour: Planting and pruning can be done in January/February and tagging for height and quality in October/November. Thus it fits in well with combinable cropping.

Whilst the gross margins given are high, these will only be achieved by a high level of expertise and commitment, and the long period before any return is obtained must also be stressed, together with the risk this entails.

	Norway Spruce		Nordman Fir	
	£/ha	(£/ac)	£/ha	(£/ac)
4,000 5-7 foot trees per Ha @ price of. . . .	75p per ft		£1.20-£1.30 per ft	
Output (average)	18,000	(7,285)	30,000	(12,140)
Variable costs:*				
Plants	850	(345)	2,150	(870)
Planting	625	(255)	625	(255)
Fertiliser	625	(255)	800	(325)
Weed Control	1,450	(585)	1,450	(585)
Pesticides	850	(345)	550	(220)
Pruning and Shaping	2,250	(910)	2,250	(910)
Harvesting	3,000	(1,215)	3,400	(1,375)
Total Variable Costs	9,650	(3,910)	11,225	(4,540)
Gross Margin (whole period)	8,350	(3,380)	18,775	(7,600)
Gross Margin per Year (over 7 & 9 years)	1,195	(485)	2,085	(845)

* Labour assumed to be casuals.

Acknowledgements: British Christmas Tree Growers Association, 13 Wolridge Road, Edinburgh, EH16 6HX. Tel: 0131 664 1100 www.bctga.co.uk. *Snowbird Christmas Tree Specialists* (A. T. Morgan), Plantation Lodge Farm, Grantham NG33 4SP. Tel: 01780 410101.

FORESTRY

(Estimated for 2007)

A. Establishment Costs (before grant)

1. *Unit Cost of Operations*

Year/s	Operation	Estimated Cost (£)
1.	Trees for planting	
	(i) Bare rooted:	
	Conifers	125-200 per 1,000
	Broadleaves	250-350 per 1,000
	(ii) Rooted in small peat blocks:	
	Conifers	150-200 per 1,000
	Broadleaves	300-360 per 1,000
1.	Tree Protection	
	(i) Fencing (materials and erection)	
	Rabbit......................	3·00-3·50 per metre
	Stock	3·00-3·75 per metre
	Deer	5·00-7·00 per metre
	Deer and Rabbit	7·00-9·00 per metre
	Split post and rail	6·00-7·00 per metre
	(ii) Tree guards/shelters	
	Spiral and canes (450mm)	30-40 per 100
	Plastic tubes (1,200mm)	60-70 per 100
	Stakes	40-50 per 100
1.	Spot spraying	100 per 1,000 trees
1.	Hand planting at approximately 2m spacing	
	Conifers	150-180 per ha
	Broadleaves*	450-650 per ha
	Machine planting (loams and sand)	130-150 per ha
2-3.	Replacing dead trees**	
	Operation	50-100 per ha
	Plant supply	35-45 per ha
1-4.	Weeding per operation	
	Herbicide***......................	80-120 per ha weeded
2.	Inter-row mowing	80-120 per ha

Costs specific to location		Upland	Lowland
1. Ground Preparation:	ploughing	100-150 per ha	50- 80 per ha
	mounding	250-300 per ha	250-300 per ha
1. Drainage		60- 80 per ha	—
1. Fertilizing		90-190 per ha	—

*   Includes cost of erecting guards/shelters.

**   Replacing dead trees (beating up) may be necessary, once in the second year and again in the third year. Costs depend on number of trees.

***   Up to 2 weeding operations may be necessary in each of the first 4 years in extreme situations. Costs are inclusive of materials.

Access roads may need to be constructed and can typically cost between £6,000 and £22,000 per kilometre (£9,600 to £35,000 per mile) depending on availability of roadstone and the number of culverts and bridges required.

2. Total Establishment Costs up to Year 3.

(i) Conifer—Lowland Sites

On a fairly typical lowland site, requiring little or no clearing or draining, the approximate cost before grant of establishing a conifer plantation would be in the range £1,200-£1,800 per hectare. Up to 8 separate weeding operations may be required.

(ii) Conifer—Upland Sites

Establishing a similar conifer plantation on an upland site could cost £1,100 to £1,600 per hectare. Normally some form of site preparation and drainage is required but only one weeding operation may be necessary. Overall costs tend to be £100-£200 per ha less than on lowland sites.

(iii) Hardwoods

Costs of establishing hardwood plantations are highly dependent on the fencing and/or tree protection required. If tubes are needed the overall costs will be influenced by the number of plants per hectare. Costs could be in the range £1,600-£2,500 per ha. Site conditions normally mean that hardwoods being grown for timber production are restricted to lowland sites.

(iv) Farm Woodlands

Establishment costs for farm woodlands may be lower than those indicated for hardwoods in (iii) above if lower planting densities are used. Initial establishment costs in the first year of the order of £1,800 per ha for woods under 3 ha and £1,600 per ha for woods of 3 to 10 ha would be typical.

(v) Size Factor

Savings in fencing and other economies of scale may reduce average costs per ha by 10 to 20% where large plantations are being established; conversely costs for small woods may easily be 25% higher per ha established.

(vi) Method of Establishment

A range of organisations and individuals undertake forestry contracting work and competitive tendering can help to control costs.

3. Re-Stocking Costs

Once trees on a site have been felled the Forestry Commission usually requires the site to be restocked as one of the conditions of awarding a felling licence. Re-stocking can either be done by planting or through natural regeneration by leaving a proportion of the existing trees standing and using seed from these trees to re-stock the site. Only minimum site preparation is usually required if using natural regeneration and grant aid is available (see Grant section).

The costs of establishment given above, and those for maintenance given below in section B, are estimates for England. Costs in Scotland tend to be lower, for a variety of reasons, but some indication of costs there can be obtained from the Forestry Commission Scotland publication "Standard Costs and Specification Booklet", which is accessible on www.forestry.gov.uk and is called 'SFGS Applicant's Booklet online'

B. Maintenance Costs

Once trees have been established they will normally require some maintenance and management work each year. For trees being grown primarily for timber production on a large scale, operations required may include ride maintenance, fence maintenance, pest control, fire protection, management fee and insurance premiums. Costs will normally fall within the range £10-£50 per ha per annum depending upon the size of the plantation and the complexity of management. In upland areas one or more fertilizing operations may be needed in the first 20 years in the life of a tree depending on the quality of the site. Estimated cost £90-£150 per ha, depending on elements applied. For trees being grown for sporting and amenity purposes, annual maintenance costs are likely to be less and may range up to about £10 per ha.

A brashing operation which involves removing branches up to two metres may be required for access reasons as the crop matures. Opening up inspection racks over 5-10% of the crop may cost £30-£60 per ha. Brashing 40-50% of the crop could cost £150-£300 per ha.

C. Production

Production is usually measured in terms of cubic metres (m3) of marketable timber per hectare and will vary according to the quality of the site, species planted and thinning policy. Sites in lowland Britain planted to conifers typically produce an average of 12 to 18 m3 of timber per ha per year over the rotation as a whole and would accordingly be assessed as falling in yield classes 12 to 18. Under traditional management systems thinning begins 18 to 25 years after planting and is repeated at intervals of approximately 5 years until the wood is clearfelled at between 40 and 60 years. Approximately 40-45% of total production will be from thinnings. Broadleaves typically produce an average of between 4 and 8 m3 of timber per hectare per year and fall in yield classes 4 to 8. A felling licence must be obtained from the Forestry Commission before any felling takes place.

Prior to a thinning sale the trees normally have to be marked and measured at an estimated cost of 35p per m3, which is equivalent to £100-£125 per hectare depending on species, crop density and age. For a clearfelling sale the cost can range from £250 to £350 per ha, or about £1 per m3 where a full tariff applies, i.e. where each tree is counted and sample measurements of individual trees are taken.

D. Prices

Prices for standing timber are extremely variable, depending on species, tree size and quality, ease of extraction from site, geographical location (nearness to end user), quantity being sold, world market prices and effectiveness of marketing method used. The use of wood for energy generation is beginning to open up a new market for poorer quality hardwood and conifer logs and forest residues.

Conifers

Average prices paid for standing coniferous timber sold from Forest Enterprise areas in the year to 31st March, 2006, were:

Harvesting stage	Average tree size (m3)	Price (£ per m3) England	Wales	Scotland
1st Thinning	Up to 0.074	4.97	1.01	7.63
	0.075-0.124	5.21	0.47	4.05
Subsequent Thinnings	0.125-0.174	6.28	7.15	2.66
	0.175-0.224	7.54	5.47	2.90
	0.225-0.274	7.98	3.91	8.19
	0.275-0.424	8.71	7.72	6.26
	0.425-0.499	10.09	7.27	5.50
Clearfelling	0.500-0.599	10.09	7.73	8.55
	0.600-0.699	12.47	5.72	4.25
	0.700-0.799	12.48	6.19	11.24
	0.800-0.899	14.76	7.06	8.37
	0.900-0.999	13.20	5.98	8.10
	1.000 and over	19.62	7.20	11.05

Source: Forest Enterprise, July 2006.

Hardwoods

The hardwood trade is very complex. Merchants normally assess and value all but the smallest trees on a stem by stem basis. Actual prices fetched can show considerable variation depending on species, size, form, quality and marketing expertise of the seller. Felling usually takes place in the winter months.

Some indicative prices for hardwoods are given below, but it is important to note that actual prices fetched can vary quite widely. Wood quality is particularly important in determining prices.

Harvesting stage	Tree size range (m3)	Price range £ per m3	Possible use
First thinnings	<0.13	0-12	Firewood, board products and pulp wood. Poles for refineries and turnery.
Subsequent Thinnings	0.13-0.3 0.3 -0.6 0.6 -1.0	5- 20 8- 22 10- 40	Smaller sizes and lower quality material may go for fencing or for use in the mining industry.
Clearfellings	1.0 -2.0 2+	15- 80 25-150	Trees over 30 cm in diameter and of better quality may go for planking, furniture or joinery. High quality material may go for veneers and can fetch between £150 and £300 per m3 depending on species and specifications.

Prices for Oak, Ash, Sycamore, Cherry and Elm tend to be significantly higher than for Beech, which seldom exceeds about £45 per m3 standing even for stands containing significant volumes of first quality planking.

E. Timber Marketing

In-house marketing by the owner or agent can be cost effective but only if they have detailed, up-to-date knowledge of timber buyers in the market place. The alternative is marketing through a forestry manager or management company, but this can be expensive and is not guaranteed to test the open market fully.

Nationwide electronic sales of timber by auction and tender are now available for all types and quantities of timber. This cost effective, no-sale-no-fee (1·5 to 2·3% sales commission) method offers full exposure to the trade and should realise the correct market value. (Beacon Forestry: www.beaconforestry.co.uk). For small, unusual or low value timber parcels free advertising is available on the Ecolots website and in a free magazine (www.ecolots.co.uk or tel: 01721 724 788).

F. Market Value of Established Plantations and Woods

The value of woods depends on many factors, such as location, access, species, age and soil type. The table on the following page gives an indication of the range of current (2006) market values of commercial woodlands of different ages, based on recent market sales.

From years 20 to 25 onwards prices of commercial woods will also be increasingly influenced by the quantity of merchantable timber they contain. Depending on the time of clearfelling, the timber may be worth between £900 to £6,000 per hectare (£360 to £2,500 per acre).

Woods with high amenity or Ancient Woodland status can often command a premium over prices fetched for commercial woodlands and also those which are freehold including minerals and sporting rights. Conversely conservation designation can restrict value by preventing economic forest management.

The value of woods containing mature hardwoods will depend on the quality and value of the timber they contain and the quality of access.

Market Value of Commercial Sitka Spruce Woodlands

Age of Commercial Woods and Plantations	Price Range for crop and land	
	£/ha	£/acre
0-5 years	125- 625	(50- 250)
6-10 years	625-1000	(250- 400)
11-15 years	875-1125	(350- 450)
16-20 years	1000-1500	(400- 600)
21-25 years	1250-2375	(500- 950)

G. Grants

With devolution, each part of the United Kingdom has introduced new schemes that replace the previous Woodland Grant Scheme (WGS) and the Farm Woodland Premium Scheme (FWPS). In England, the English Woodland Grant Scheme (EWGS) opened in July 2005 (with some elements becoming later that year). The Scottish Forestry Grant Scheme (SFGS) was introduced in June 2002. In Wales, the Better Woodlands for Wales (BWW) programme began in April 2006. Planting grants will be brought under the BWW umbrella sometime in 2007.

English Woodland Grant Scheme

Initially this scheme will operate in a similar manner across the whole of England. However, it is envisaged that in time variations in levels of support will be introduced on a regional basis to meet the needs of each region. The EWGS will comprise six components and applications can be made for combinations of these components where appropriate.

1. *Woodland Management Planning Grant:* available as a contribution towards the cost of producing plans for existing woodlands, and which meet the UK Woodland Assurance Standard. Rates of grant contribution are £10 per hectare for the first 100 hectares and £5 thereafter. There is a minimum payment of £300 for plans covering more than 3 hectares but less than 30 hectares.

2. *Woodland Assessment Grant:* available as a contribution towards the costs of obtaining additional information about the woodland in relation to ecology, landscape, historic and heritage assessments, and to determine stakeholder interests. A fixed hourly rate of £35 is payable plus a contribution at 80% of a set range of standard assessment costs.

3. *Woodland Management Grant:* aid for providing public benefits and to undertake sustainable woodland management. Potentially eligible activities include public access, maintaining boundaries, protecting archaeological features, management of old wood habitat and open space, soil and ground water protection, controlling non-native species, pest control, woodland health and monitoring sustainability. The rate of grant is in line with ELS payments at £30 per hectare per year.

4. *Woodland Regeneration Grant:* a contribution towards the cost of regenerating woodland after felling. The aim is to promote the replacement of felled woodland whilst changing woodland types for increased public benefit. Grant rates depend on the type of wood being felled and the type of wood which replaces it:

Type of woodland felled	Type of woodland being regenerated	Grant (£/ha)
Conifer plantation	Native species	1,100
	Broadleaved species	950
	Conifer species	360
Broadleaved plantation	Native species	1,100
	Broadleaved species	950
Conifer plantation on	Native species	1,760
Ancient Woodland Site	Broadleaved species	950
	Conifer species....................	0
Broadleaved plantation	Native species	1,760
on Ancient Woodland Site	Broadleaved species	950
Ancient and other	Native species	1,100
semi-natural woodland		

5. *Woodland Improvement Grant:* a contribution towards the cost of work improve the quality of woodland for social, environmental, and economic benefits. Initially the rate of grant is set at 50% of agreed costs in a five-year plan. The focus is on improving access, biodiversity, and protecting SSSIs. In the course of time regions may choose to vary the rate of contributions or priority areas to reflect regional differences. There will be a maximum grant contribution of £100,000.

6. *Woodland Creation Grants:* aids the establishment of new woodlands. This element of the EWGS is competitive and will be assessed on a points scoring system with the applications that giving the greatest benefits being selected. Woodland creation may be by natural regeneration or by direct seeding. The rates of grant will depend on the type of woodland; Standard (3 ha or more), Small Standard (less than 3 ha), Native Species Only, Community (designed for public access), or Special Broadleaved (species appropriate for growth at wide spacing). Planting density requirements, percentage open space and percentage of shrub element are set for each woodland type. Rates of grant are as follows:

Woodland category	Broadleaves £/ha	Conifers £/ha
Standard, Native and Community.........	1,800	1,200
Special Broadleaved..................	700	n/a

In addition to the above grant an extra £500 per ha is paid for woodland established within five miles of 100,000 people or within the National Forest Area, OR where there is an agreement to provide for public access and there is an identified need. Woodland meeting both of these requirements will be eligible to claim £1000 per ha.

Payment is made 80% on the completion of the work, with the final 20% payable after 5 years as long as the plantation is maintained. Applications usually have to be made in the summer prior to the winter/spring when the planting will take place. In 2006 the deadline was 31st August.

Planting on Agricultural Land: Annual payments are available under the EWGS for converting agricultural land to woodland (similar to the old FWPS). Payments will continue for 15 years when new woodlands comprise more than 50% broadleaved species, and 10 years when the percentage broadleaves is less than 50% (or fast growing broadleaved species such as poplar). Payment rates will depend on the agricultural land use category being converted to woodland. Current rates are set out below, although they may be subject to revision in future years;

Agricultural Land Category	Annual payment (£/ha)		
	Non-Less Favoured Area (LFA)	LFA: Disadvantaged Areas	LFA: Severely Disadvantaged
Arable Land*	300	230	160
Improved Grassland	260	200	140
Other Cropped Land	260	200	140
Unimproved Land	ineligible	60	60

* defined as land that used to be eligible for AAPS under the old IACS system

More details of the EWGS are available on the Forestry Commission website (www.forestry.gov.uk). There are deadlines for the submission of application forms for the different components of the scheme as funding is limited. Early discussions with one of Forestry Commission England' Conservancy offices is advised. Help and advice can also be obtained from the EWGS helpline Tel: 01223 346004.

H. Woodland and the Single Payment

In general, land being used to grow trees is not eligible to activate Single Payment entitlements. However, farm woodland planted on arable land under the English Woodland Grant Scheme (EWGS) and the previous Woodland Grant Scheme / Farm Woodland Premium Scheme (FWPS) can be counted towards a farmer's set-aside obligation under the Single Payment Scheme. Farmers receive the annual payments under the FWPS / Woodland Creation Grant payments, not set-aside payments. Short-rotation coppice is not eligible for entry into woodland grant schemes but where it is planted on set-aside land, such land will remain eligible for the Single Payment.

I. Taxation

Income from commercial woodlands is no longer subject to income tax, and tax relief cannot be claimed for the cost of establishing new woodlands.

In general EWGS grants are tax free but annual payments under the Farm Woodland Premium Scheme (and now Woodland Creation Grants) are regarded as compensation for agricultural income forgone and are liable to income tax.

The sale of timber does not attract Capital Gains Tax, although the disposal of the underlying land may give rise to an assessment.

Woodlands which are managed commercially or which are ancillary to a farming business may be eligible for either Business Property Relief or Agricultural Relief for Inheritance Tax purposes.

Acknowledgement: The above estimates are based in part on information supplied by *John Clegg Consulting Ltd.*

A magazine, 'Forestry and British Timber', is published monthly (Miller Freeman, Telephone 01732-377651).

ENERGY CROPS

A. General

Energy crops are those grown to be used for generating heat and electricity or to produce transport fuels. They are considered 'carbon neutral' which means the carbon released on burning is only what they (recently) took up into the plant when growing, thereby not releasing additional carbon from fossil reserves beyond the requirements for mechanical cultivation, harvest and transport to end-use location.

The UK has a legally binding target under the Kyoto Protocol to reduce its greenhouse gas emissions by 12.5% below 1990 levels between 2008 and 2012. It also has a further domestic goal to reduce carbon dioxide emissions (one of the main greenhouse gases) by 20% below 1990 levels by 2010. Developing the use of energy crops is seen as one of the ways to help to achieve these targets.

B. Support and Grants

Under the Single Payment Scheme, an Energy Aid Payment is available to growers of €45 per hectare. This is subject to a Maximum Guaranteed Area throughout the EU-15 (those countries participating in the Single Payment Scheme) of 1.5 million hectares. It is likely this will be exceeded in 2006/7. If so, the payment will be reduced pro rata. Having administration to cover and guarantees to finance, the grant is normally split between the grower and processor.

The Energy Crops Scheme which has been running since 2000 to finance the crop establishment and infrastructure of both SRC and miscanthus crops is now closed pending the development of the new Rural Development schemes for 2007-2013 (See page 217 for details). Any new scheme will not be available before 2007. Likewise, the Bio-energy Infrastructure Scheme, whilst not part of the Rural Development fund is also temporarily closed, having completed its first round and is awaiting a second round, probably to open in 2007.

Further support for energy crops comes via UK legislation that encourages the use of renewable-derived energy. These 'Renewable Obligations' are covered in the following biomass and biofuel sections.

C. Biomass for Power

This area covers crops that are grown to be burnt directly to produce heat and/or electricity. The plant material is chopped, chipped, or baled and is generally either used in boilers in dedicated biomass power stations, or mixed with coal for co-firing in conventional power stations.

Biomass includes short rotation coppice, miscanthus, straw, canary reed grass and switch grass as well as forest residues. It could form a significant part of renewable resources.

The European Union's Renewable's Directive that came into force in 2001 encourages Member States to adopt national targets of deriving energy from renewable sources. The UK government has introduced legislation requiring 10% of UK electricity to be generated from renewable resources by 2010 (subject to the cost to consumers being acceptable) and an aspiration to reach 20% by 2020. The mechanisms for achieving this in the UK are:

- The Non Fossil Fuel Obligation (NFFO) covering England, Wales and N. Ireland
- Scottish Renewables Obligation (SRO)

They are monitored by the Office of Gas and Electricity Markets (OFGEM) through a system of certification. Renewables Obligation Certificates (ROCs) are issued to power generators for providing electricity from renewable sources. Generators failing to meet targets for renewable generation are 'fined'. However, it is possible to fulfil the renewables obligation by purchasing surplus ROCs from other generators. Thus ROCs have a market value.

Originally a number of large power projects were planned that would use biomass as fuel. The first power station, built by ARBRE, reached the commissioning stage before it went into receivership in 2002. A number of other power generation projects failed, some with financial or technical problems, others because they were unable to obtain planning consent. At present the only significant biomass-only plant is the Ely straw burning facility consuming 200,000 tonnes of feedstock annually (now also using some miscanthus and oilseed rape).

Other dedicated plants are still planned. But the greatest current demand for biomass is for co-firing existing coal power stations. There are also small local markets.

Short Rotation Coppice

Short Rotation Coppice (SRC) is a fast growing species of willow or poplar that when harvested, chipped and dried can be used as a fuel for heat or power generation.

SRC willow needs access to moisture but will otherwise grow on any cultivable land. It requires a seedbed similar to that of a conventional arable crop, with particular attention to weed control. Planting is carried out in the spring using unrooted cuttings at a rate of 15,000/ha. Rabbit fencing may be necessary. Pest and weed control is essential when the plants are young, until canopy closure is achieved in the second year. In the autumn after planting the willow is cut back to encourage coppicing. After 3 years the crop is harvested and then harvested every 3 years throughout its life which can be as long as 30 years but is generally put at 16 years. Fertilizer is applied after each harvest. The harvested crop can be stored on-farm, normally as billets. It is then processed according to the needs of the end processor. Some generators require the wood to be processed into granules which, with transport charges can add substantially to production costs. The first harvest should yield 25-30odt/ha (oven dried tonnes), subsequent ones 32-35odt/ha. DEFRA suggests that in the longer term the value of the crop should be £35 to £45/odt.

The following gives a very broad indication of likely costs and net annual returns:

Establishment Costs:	£/ha
Fencing (optional)	200
Pre-planting spraying	80
Fertiliser	25
Cultivations	50
Planting	300
Cuttings	750
Post-planting spraying	90
Cut-back	35
Total Establishment	1,530

No account has been taken here of planting grants that may become available with the new Rural Development Scheme in 2007.

Annual Net Returns: Output 27 odt @ £45 every third year; £405/year plus Energy Aid Payment net of deductions of approximately £15/ha. Variable costs per year including fertiliser and sprays £50, Harvesting £100, transport and handling £100, processing making a total of £350. Note, this equates to harvesting etc, each costing £300 every 3 years.

Miscanthus (Elephant Grass)

Miscanthus is a perennial energy and fibre crop, indigenous to Africa and Asia, now being grown commercially in the UK. As an energy crop it differs from short-rotation coppice as it is harvested annually using existing farm machinery. The crop has a useful life of 15-20 years.

There is a range of other uses for miscanthus. After suitable treatment it makes valuable animal bedding, for which there is a ready market. It can go into paper making and biopolymer manufacture or be used to produce a number of bio-degradable products, such as flowerpots.

Potential cropping zones in the UK are reasonably widespread but the crop is vulnerable to late spring frosts and is best grown south of a line from Chester to Lincoln. It can be grown successfully further north but yields may be reduced. Trials have performed well in Scotland and the area in Yorkshire is growing to supply a local power generator. It is suitable for a wide range of soil types and pH values but is not recommended for drought prone soils where again yield can be reduced.

The crop is propagated from rhizomes or by micro-propagation. Rhizome cuttings are now produced from specifically planted nursery beds with cuttings taken after about 2 years by lifting and processing the crop using specialised miscanthus equipment. This has improved the uniformity and quality of planting material which has reduced the planting rate needed for a successful stand. Muck spreaders or modified potato planters have been replaced by fully automatic planters with a work-rate of 10-20ha per day. The machines are pulled by tractor with an additional operator loading bags of rhizome into the hopper periodically to achieve the higher rate. Micro-propagation produces a large number of small plants which are then planted, after the last spring frost but early enough to allow for good establishment, using a semi-automated cellular vegetable planter. This is a relatively costly method.

Weed control is essential at establishment and in the following spring. A mature crop should suppress any weed growth. So far in the UK no serious pathogens and pests have been encountered. Fertilizer requirement is low; a small amount (perhaps 40kg/ha N, 40kg/ha P and 40kg/ha K) is applied in the first year; little if any is needed subsequently as the leaf mulch supplies nutrients.

Each spring the crop produces new shoots, usually in April, which grow into strong erect stems up to 4 metres in height by late August. They resemble bamboo canes and contain solid pith. The plants senesce in the autumn, nutrients pass down into the rhizomes and a deep leaf litter forms. All foliage dies after the first frost and the stems desiccate to 50% moisture content during winter. The leafless canes are harvested between January and April, when the crop begins to shoot again. The robust rhizome network provides a platform for harvesting machinery; frosty conditions also help.

The harvest method depends on end use. For energy the crop is cut with a mower conditioner and then baled into 5-600kg Heston bales. These are stored outside before being taken to the power station. For other end uses a modified maize harvester can be used. New machinery is being developed to make operations more efficient and cheaper.

In the UK the likely yield of a mature crop should be 12-14 oven dried tonnes (odt)/ha/year. In the year after establishment 50 to 60% of the full yield is obtained. The price for energy crops ranges mainly between £25 to £40/odt. Horse bedding can retail for as much as £100/tonne in bulk to £240/tonne, de-dusted in 20kg bags.

Currently there are 10,000ha of miscanthus in England and the area is expanding. Initially much of the crop was used for propagation material but now it is being planted for both energy and fibre end uses. In East Anglia 5,000ha are being used by the Ely power plant, which burns both straw and miscanthus. A number of other biomass projects, supported by the DTI, are in train. Small on-farm boilers, to produce heat and energy, have been developed which also offer potential for miscanthus; it is estimated that 20ha of miscanthus would provide all the energy necessary for an average farm and could be valued at £75/tonne.

Establishment costs approximately £2,500/ha, including some £2,000 for the plants (rhizomes); a planting grant of £920/ha has been referred to above.

Acknowledgement: Dr Paul Carver, *Bical*.

D. Liquid Biofuels

Liquid biofuels are road transport fuels produced from plants, including several mainstream farm crops. Biodiesel is produced from oilseed crops such as oilseed rape, soybeans, and palm. As the name suggests it is a replacement for mineral diesel. Bioethanol/biobutanol is a petrol replacement and is produced from starch-based crops including wheat, maize and sugar/fodder beet. A 'second generation' of biofuels is being researched. This includes cellulosic ethanol and biomass-to-liquid (BtL). There are presently three cellulosic ethanol plants in the EU (Sweden, Spain and Denmark), with BtL demonstration plants operating in Sweden and Germany.

Road traffic emissions account for 22% of UK Green House Gas (GHG) emissions. The Government has provided a major push to this sector with the introduction of the Renewable Transport Fuel Obligation (ReTFO). This requires that by 2010, 5% of road transport fuel sold through a forecourt must come from renewable sources. GHG emissions from biofuels can be 70% lower than from fossil fuels. In addition, there has been a 20ppl reduction in duty for biodiesel since July 2002 and on bioethanol since January 2005. These financial incentives, coupled with the ReTFO are essential to the economics of the sector as biofuels cost more than fuel produced from crude oil.

A 5% biodiesel blend, with 95% fossil diesel, can be used with no engine modifications and meets the vehicle manufacturers' warranties. Bioethanol can also be used as a 5% blend in petrol with no engine modifications. With some engine modification up to 85% bioethanol can be used as transport fuel.

To supply 5% of the current road fuel market from biofuels, 0.9 million tonnes of biodiesel, and 1 million tonnes of bioethanol would be required. This is equivalent to 650,000ha oilseed rape (2.2mt) and 420,000ha wheat (3.3mt) (assuming yields of 3.4t/ha and 8t/ha of OSR and wheat respectively and extraction rates of 41% and 30%). A market for some 1 million hectares of agricultural commodity is therefore developing. However, it must be recognised that it unlikely that all the feedstock for the biofuels industry will come from the UK. Many of the projected biofuel plants are to be built at deep water locations with easy access to global commodity markets. It is likely that trade flows will alter; some of the UK's exportable surplus of grain and oilseed rape could become diverted to the biofuels market, and imports could increase. Facilities will predominantly use the cheapest feedstock – likely to be those that command no quality premium from the food industry.

SET-ASIDE

The Provisions

Set-aside is one of the three conditions of claiming the Single Payment (SP), the other two being land occupation (10-month rule) and cross-compliance. If farmers wishing to claim the SP hold set-aside entitlements (either owned or leased in), they are obliged to claim them before they can claim on any other entitlements. To do this, the farmer must manage 1 hectare of 'arable' land according to set-aside regulations for every set-aside entitlement held. Failure to do this will result in penalties being applied to the SP. The only exception to this rule is for farms that are wholly registered as organic or organic conversion. Any set-aside entitlements transferred into an organic holding must be with (organic) land.

Farmers were allocated set-aside entitlements in 2005 by varying methods depending on region: In England, land that was arable status in both 2005 and 2003 was allocated set-aside entitlements at the rate of 8% for lowland areas, and 1.3% for SDA non-Moorland. Note that the definition of arable land has changed since Arable Area Payments (AAP) to include fruit, vegetable, sugar beet, some temporary grass and most horticultural land. This decreased the set-aside percentage from the previous 10% to 8% in lowland areas and 1.3% in SDA-non-moorland areas (SDA = Severely Disadvantaged Areas). In Wales and Scotland, set-aside entitlements were allocated simply as 10% of area claimed under the AAP scheme in the reference period. Those claiming small areas of arable land under the 2005 SPS were not issued with set-aside entitlements (carrying-over the 'small producers' exemption' from the previous AAP scheme). For example, in lowland England, there was an exemption for farmers with less than 19.48 hectares of arable land (122.36 ha in SDA non-moorland areas).

Set-aside entitlements can be freely traded, like all other types of SP entitlement. The requirement to set land aside moves with the entitlement. Therefore, through trading, farmers can end up with a greater or lesser set-aside requirement than their original allocation.

In England, only the regional average component of the SP is paid on set-aside entitlements. In early years of the SP, it is therefore a low value per hectare.

Management Rules

Normally the minimum size of each set-aside block must be 0.1 ha, with a minimum width of 10 metres. However, smaller areas are acceptable provided they are alongside boundaries such as watercourses, hedges, edges of woodland, or Sites of Special Scientific Interest (SSSIs). In these locations, strip width can go down to 6 metres wide and cover a minimum area of 0.05 ha.

Participation in environmental schemes does not normally affect eligibility to site set-aside, as long as the requirements of both set-aside and the environmental scheme can be met.

Set-aside can be either cropped or fallowed. Cropping set-aside can spread overheads and increases farm income. Fallowing set-aside land, whilst it bears a cost without generating an income, may be useful if the farm's optimum cropped area (to suit resources such as management ability, machinery, labour and capital), is smaller than the total area of the farm. It can also be useful if the holding has some unproductive arable land. Cropping and fallowing options have separate regulations although cross-compliance regulations apply throughout:

Crops with no food or animal feed use can be grown on set-aside land without a contract with a buyer/collector. Examples include short rotation coppice and miscanthus. Other crops may be produced on set-aside land on condition they are not used for human or animal consumption. These crops have to be grown under a contract with a buyer/collector. By-products from processing these crops can be used for food or feed such as oilseed rape meal or straw for bedding. The contracts must be submitted to the RPA by the 15th May ahead of harvest but may be amended up to the 31st May. The buyer/collector must submit a deposit to the RPA of €250 per hectare for the area covered in the contract. The entirety of the crop harvested must be delivered to the collector and the crop must be kept separate from other non-set-aside material until an accurate reliable weight is established. A minimum representative yield must be met. These are published on an annual basis, the figures for 2006 are set out below;

Minimum Yields 2006	t/ha		t/ha
Winter '00' Oilseed Rape.	2.36	Spring HOLL Oilseed Rape . .	1.31
Spring '00' Oilseed Rape.	1.31	Winter Linseed	1.29
Winter HEAR Oilseed Rape . .	2.10	Spring Linseed	1.29
Spring HEAR Oilseed Rape . .	1.20	Wheat	4.00
Winter HOLL Oilseed Rape . .	1.90	Barley	3.25

The Energy crop supplement is not available on set-aside land (see page 70).

If set-aside is being fallowed, green cover is required on set-aside land in England, Wales and Northern Ireland by 15th January. This is unless a harvest crop is still in the ground on 1st October. Natural regeneration is permitted; deep cultivation is allowed to remove compacted areas. After 15th January there must (normally) be no attempt to harvest crops remaining in the ground and the land must not be grazed, i.e. all livestock must have been removed. Non-selective, non-residual herbicides may be used in England and Wales after 15th April (1st May in Scotland). Between 15th July and 15th August green cover must either be cut short at least once and the cuttings left on the ground to rot or be destroyed by 31st August (with some exceptions). No commercial activity is allowed to take place on the land without an RPA exemption. Non-lucrative operations can be conducted on the land like fencing as long as cross-compliance conditions are not jeopardised. Other activities are allowed which could be carried out equally well if there was a standing crop on the land such as shooting. Crops may be sown on fallow set-aside from 15th July for harvest or grazing after 15th January (which excludes most horticultural crops).

This is not an exhaustive list of the set-aside regulations and farmers are advised to refer to the set-aside handbook.

A NOTE ON DIVERSIFICATION

While diversification is to be encouraged, wherever feasible, especially to help maintain incomes when the main farm enterprises are falling in profitability, a number of points need stressing. Many new enterprises require a substantial amount of capital; many need new skills (both in production and marketing), which take time, or a particular type of personality, to acquire. The market may be limited; and there is usually a considerable level of risk attached. Nevertheless, there are many ventures to be seen where entrepreneurial skills have achieved notable success. Conversion of surplus farm buildings, for offices, workshops, retail and storage, has been the primary farm diversification activity up to date. A 2006 DEFRA survey found that 46% of farms had diversification activity generating an average income of £10,900 pa. But if letting farm buildings is stripped out, the percentage of diversified farms falls to 19%.

Some 'diversification enterprises' have been included above and there are more in the next section. There are many others, amongst them are;

Alpacas	Sporting Fisheries	Tourism:
Herbs	Game Shooting	Caravans and Camping
Carp and Crayfish	Stalking	Holiday Cottages
Llamas	Clay Pigeon Shooting	Barn Conversions
Quails	Horses:	'Added Value' enterprises:
Snails	Riding School	Yoghurt, ice cream, etc.
	Trekking	Motor Sports
		Adventure Games

Periodic information on some of the above appears quarterly in 'Farm Development Review', published by Easton Press, Rural Support Centre, Easton College, Easton, Norwich, NR9 5DX.

2. GRAZING LIVESTOCK

DAIRY COWS

Holstein Friesians (per Cow)

Performance level (yield (1))........................	Low	Average	High	Very High
Milk Yield per Cow (litres) (2)....................	6000	7000	8000	9000
	£	£	£	£
Milk Value per Cow (3)...............................	1080	1260	1440	1620
Plus Value of Calves (4).............................	45	45	45	45
Plus Value of Cull Cows (5)........................	75	75	75	75
Less Cost or Market Value of Replacements (6, 7)	187	187	187	187
Output...	1013	1193	1373	1553
Concentrate Costs (8)...............................	187	254	324	405
Miscellaneous Variable Costs (10)...................	129	139	149	160
Gross Margin before deducting Forage Variable Costs (inc. Bought Fodder)................	697	800	900	988
(Margin of Milk Value over Concentrates [9])...	893	1006	1116	1215

Gross Margins per Cow & per Hectare (acre) at 4 different stocking rates (11) **are**

Performance level	Low	Average	High	Very High
1. At 1·75 cows per forage hectare (low):				
(0·57 forage hectares (1·4 acres) per cow)				
Forage V.C. & Bulk Feeds per Cow (11)	80	80	80	80
Gross Margin per Cow	617	720	819	909
Gross Margin per Forage Hectare	1080	1260	1434	1590
Gross Margin per Forage Acre	437	510	580	643
2. At 2 cows per forage hectare (average):				
(0·5 forage hectares (1·25 acres) per cow)				
Forage V.C. & Bulk Feeds per Cow (11)	**95**	**95**	**95**	**95**
Gross Margin per Cow	**602**	**705**	**804**	**894**
Gross Margin per Forage Hectare	**1204**	**1410**	**1608**	**1788**
Gross Margin per Forage Acre	**487**	**570**	**650**	**723**
3. At 2·25 cows per forage hectare (high):				
(0·45 forage hectares (1·1 acres) per cow)				
Forage V.C. & Bulk Feeds per Cow (11)	105	105	105	105
Gross Margin per Cow	592	695	794	884
Gross Margin per Forage Hectare	1332	1564	1787	1989
Gross Margin per Forage Acre	539	633	723	804
4. At 2·5 cows per forage hectare (very high):				
(0·4 forage hectares (1 acre) per cow)				
Forage V.C. & Bulk Feeds per Cow (11)	120	120	120	120
Gross Margin per Cow	577	680	779	869
Gross Margin per Forage Hectare	1443	1700	1948	2172
Gross Margin per Forage Acre	583	688	788	878

1. Performance level refers primarily to milk yield, although increases in this are usually (though not necessarily) associated with higher gross margins. Some increase in concentrate feeding (kg/litre) has been assumed as yield rises: see further note 8, page 79.

2. *Yield.* The yield referred to is litres produced during a year divided by the average number of cows and calved heifers in the herd. The average yield given (7,000 litres) is an estimated national figure for sizeable herds of black and white cows in 2007. Note average yields for *costed* herds are invariably above national averages; they are sure to exceed 7,500 litres in 2007, with the 10% highest yielding exceeding 9,000. The same is true of 'recorded herds', i.e. those in Milk Recording Schemes, where the average yield is well over 1,000 litres above the national average. The average yield for organic milk producers is around 6,000 litres.

3. *Milk Price.* This is assumed (as an average for the 2007 calendar year) to be 18.00p per litre, after deducting transport costs. It incorporates all adjustments: for milk composition, hygiene and seasonality. This is an average for all milk marketing groups, after bonuses etc., assuming an average-sized herd. Variable transport charges according to the amount collected mean that smaller herds will achieve a lower average price.

The average price received by individual producers depends on seasonality of production and compositional quality. Output and Gross Margin per cow are changed approximately as follows by each 0·25p per litre difference in price at each performance level:

Low	Average	High	Very High
±£15	±£17.50	±£2019	±£22.50

Seasonality Price Adjustments. These are diverse between the various dairy companies. An increasing number of companies no longer operate conventional seasonal adjustments but instead have payment systems that encourage a level monthly production, with a range of deductions and bonuses related to the individual producer's spring and autumn deliveries. The average adjustments for a selection of companies still operating conventional adjustments were as follows in 2006/07:

April	May	June	July	Aug	Sept	Oct	Nov	Dec	Jan– Mar
–2	–3	–2	+1.25	+2	+2	+1.25	+0.5	+0.5	0.00

Some companies also offer a premium for a level delivery option if supplies in a calendar month are within 10% of an agreed daily volume; the premium is typically 0·2 ppl. The trend towards new production profile payments is continuing, with more and more co-ops and companies introducing them, along with more individual pricing mechanisms.

Compositional Quality Payments

Constituent values vary widely between buyers and months. As an example, the average values for three large co-ops were, in June 2006:

Butterfat: between 1.455p and 2.520p per litre per 1 per cent; average 1.651p.

Protein: between 2.000 and 2.620p per litre per 1 per cent; average 2.310p.

The *standard litre* price is typically 4·1% butterfat and 3·3% protein.

Breeds and average milk composition by breed are as follows (England and Wales, MMB recorded herds, 2-year averages, 1999/00 and 2000/01):

	Cows %*	Butterfat %	Protein %
Holstein Friesian........................	94·1	3·905	3·26
Ayrshire..................................	1·9	4·005	3·33
Dairy Shorthorn.........................	0·6	3·86	3·29
Jersey.....................................	1·7	5·365	3·86
Guernsey.................................	1·4	4·68	3·56
All Breeds...............................		3·93	3·27

* 1988/9; no later data known. Holstein Friesians probably around 96% in 2006/7.

Within Breed Quality Variation. For Holstein Friesians the range can easily be as follows, without going to extremes: between 3.5 and 4.1 for butterfat and from 3.1 to 3.4 for protein. The difference in value between these two levels combined is around 2p per litre.

Hygiene Price Adjustments. These vary widely between the different dairy companies. A mid-2006 example is as follows:

A. *Bactoscan (bacteria measure)*

Band	Bactoscan Reading	Price Adjustment (ppl)
A+	0- 50,000	+0.5
A	51-100,000	nil
B	101-250,000	− 1
C1*	Over 250,000	− 6
C2**	Over 250,000	−10

*1st month. **2nd and any subsequent months.

B. *Somatic Cell Count (Mastitis)*

Band	Count	Price Adjustment (ppl)
1+	0-200,000	+ 0.3
1	201-250,000	nil
2	251-300,000	− 0.5
3	301-400,000	− 2
4*	Over 400,000	− 6
5**	Over 400,000	−10

*1st month. **2nd and any subsequent months.

Some milk buyers no longer pay a premium for the top hygiene bands – they expect their suppliers to deliver top quality milk in order to receive the standard litre price.

C. *Antibiotics.*

The price of all milk in a consignment that fails an antibiotics test ranges from 1-5p/litre.

Organic milk: While 29.5p/litre was the typical contract price pre 2001 increasing supply since then has exceeded increasing demand, lowering the average price to approximately 22ppl. However, a better supply and demand position in 2006/2007 could increase this to 24-25p/litre

4. *Value of Calves.* Average annual value per cow of purebred and beef cross heifer and bull calves of all qualities, at 10-20 days old, allowing for mortality and an average calving index of 385 days.

5. *Value of Cull Cows.* £300 allowing for casualties; 25% per annum replacement rate.

6. *Cost of Replacements* (N.B. average in 2007). £750 per down-calving heifer (purchase price or market value (mainly home-reared)); 25% per annum replacement rate.

7. *Herd Depreciation*: thus averages £112 per cow per year, i.e., 25 per cent of £450 (i.e., £750-£300).

Net Replacement Cost = £67 per cow per year, i.e., herd depreciation (£112) less value of calves (£45).

Bull. AI is assumed in the tables; bull depreciation would be approx. £350 a year (£2,500 purchase price less £750 cull value, 5-year herd life); tight calving pattern: 60 cows per bull, well spread calving pattern: 100; 10 to 20 tonnes silage, 0·75 tonnes concentrates a year.

8. *Concentrate Costs.*

Amounts:	*Performance level*	*Low*	*Average*	*High*	*Very High*
	kg/litre (approx.)	.25	.285	.325	.36
	tonnes/cow	1.5	2.03	2.6	3.24

Price: taken (for 2007) as £125 per tonne, which is an average of home-mixed rations and purchased compounds of varying nutritive value, averaged throughout the year.

A difference of £5 per tonne has approximately the following effect on margin over concentrates and gross margin per cow, on the assumptions made regarding the quantity fed at each performance level:

Low	Average	High	Very High
±£7.5	±£10	±£13	±£16

Seasonality. Typically, specialist spring calving herds (60% or more calvings between January and May), compared with autumn calving herds (60% or more calvings between August and December), use 0.09 kg per litre/550 kg (£69) per cow per year less concentrates. See further note 12 below.

Typical Monthly Variation in Concentrate Feeding (kg per litre, 7,000 litre herd)

Winter		Summer	
October	0.32	April	0.29
November	0.35	May	0.18
December	0.35	June	0.18
January	0.35	July	0.24
February	0.35	August	0.26
March	0.32	September	0.29
Average winter: 0.34		Average summer: 0.24	
	Average whole year: 0.29		

The actual distribution on any individual farm will obviously vary according to such factors as seasonality of calving, level of milk yield, grazing productivity during the summer, the quantity and quality of bulk feeds in the winter, and turnout and housing dates. The March figure in particular will be affected by type of soil and seasonal rainfall.

Yield with no concentrates and good quality silage: approximately 4000 litres for spring calvers.

9. Margin over Concentrates and Concentrates per litre

The emphasis in the initial tables should be laid on the differences between the margin of milk value over concentrates per cow; the same large variation can occur with widely differing combinations of milk yield and quantity of concentrates fed.

In the following table, at each yield level figures are given for (a) margin of milk value over concentrates per cow (£) and (b) concentrates per litre (kg) at seven levels of concentrate feeding.

Yield level	Low		Average		High		Very High	
Milk Yield per cow (litres)	6000		7000		8000		9000	
	(a)	(b)	(a)	(b)	(a)	(b)	(a)	(b)
	£	kg	£	kg	£	kg	£	kg
1.00 tonne (£125) concs. per cow	955	0.17	1135	0.14	-	-	-	-
1.50 tonne (£187.5) concs. per cow	892.5	0.25	1072.5	0.21	1252.5	0.19	-	-
2.00 tonne (£250) concs. per cow	830	0.33	1010	0.29	1190	0.25	1370	0.22
2.50 tonne (£312.5) concs. per cow	-	-	947.5	0.36	1127.5	0.31	1307.5	0.28
3.00 tonne (£375) concs. per cow	-	-	-	-	1065	0.38	1245	0.33
3.50 tonne (£437.5) concs. per cow	-	-	-	-	-	-	1182.5	0.39
4.00 tonne (£500) concs. per cow							1120	0.44

On the same assumptions re the other items of output and variable costs as in the tables on page 76 a very high margin over concentrates of £1,350 per cow (in 2007) would give the following results (£):

Stocking rate	Average	High	Very High
Gross Margin per Cow	998	974	953
Gross Margin per Forage Hectare	1996	2191	2382
Gross Margin per Forage Acre	808	887	965

This level of margin over concentrates (£1,350) could be achieved by a range of combinations of yield and concentrate feeding. With the price of milk (18p/l) and concentrates (£125/tonne) assumed the following are examples: 8,500 litres, 1.41tonnes/cow, .17 kg/l; 9,000, 2.16, .24; 9,500, 2.88, .30; 10,000, 3.6, .36.

10. *Miscellaneous Variable Costs (average)*

	£
Bedding*...	20
Vet. and Med...	42
A.I. and Bull Hire...	27
Recording, Consultancy, Consumables, Dairy Stores.................	50
Total...	139

* Straw can vary from 0.4 to 1.5 tonne per cow and from £10 to £50 per tonne (or even more in some areas in exceptional years).

11. *Stocking Rate and Forage Costs.* **The stocking rates given assume that nearly all requirements of bulk foods – both winter and summer – are obtained from the forage area,** i.e. little is bought in. On average about 55 per cent of the forage area (or production) is grazed and 45 per cent conserved. It will be observed that as the stocking density increases, gross margin per cow falls, but gross margin per hectare rises.

The levels of nitrogen are assumed to be as follows: 1.75 cows per forage hectare, 160 kg (128 units/acre), 2.0, 220 (176); 2.25, 275 (220); 2.5, 360 (288). An increase in potash application is also assumed. Seed costs clearly depend on the percentage of permanent pasture, if any, the length of leys, etc. The following variable costs per hectare (fertilizer, seed and sprays) have been assumed for grassland: 1.75 cows per forage hectare, £92.5 (£37/acre); 2.0, £135 (55); 2.25, £172.5 (70); 2.5, £222.5 (90). Forage maize variable costs are higher, averaging £225/ha (£91/acre); it is assumed that part of the conserved forage consists of maize silage.

A small amount of purchased bulk fodder is assumed, increasing with the stocking rate as follows (per cow): low £15, average £20, high £25, very high £30.

An increase in stocking density can be obtained not only by intensifying grassland production, as above, but also by buying in winter bulk fodder (assuming the same level of concentrate feeding in both cases). This will cause the gross margin per cow to fall still further, but will usually result in a higher gross margin per hectare than where all forage is conserved on the farm — at any given level of grassland management.

In the table below four examples are given: two policies at two different stocking rates. (A) and (B) assume the land is used for grazing only, i.e. all winter bulk fodder is purchased. (C) and (D) assume the land provides grazing and half the winter bulk fodder, the other half being bought in. (A) and (C) assume a stocking rate equivalent to 2 cows per hectare where the land provides both grazing and all the winter bulk fodder, which is an average level of stocking. (B) and (D) assume the equivalent of 2.5 cows per hectare where all bulk food is provided both summer and winter, which is a very high level of stocking. It is assumed that the full winter fodder requirement is 2 tonnes of hay (or other equivalent foods), costing £125 per cow if it is all purchased. (Prices vary widely according to the season and part of the country.) Forage variable costs per hectare (acre) are £135 (55) and £222.5 (90) at the average and high levels of stocking respectively.

		Margin of Milk Value over Concentrates			
		Low	Average	High	Very High
		Gross Margin per Forage Hectare (Acre)			
		£	£	£	£
(A)	All winter fodder purchased; average stocking rate.........	1975 (800)	2365 (960)	2750 (1115)	3095 (1250)
(B)	All winter fodder purchased; very high stocking rate.......	2415 (975)	2905 (1175)	3385 (1370)	3815 (1545)
(C)	½ winter fodder purchased; average stocking rate.........	1525 (615)	1805 (730)	2075 (840)	2220 (900)
(D)	½ winter fodder purchased; very high stocking rate......	1850 (750)	2200 (890)	2540 (1030)	2845 (1150)

It must obviously not be forgotten that 'fixed' costs per hectare, e.g. labour and depreciation on buildings, can increase considerably if an increase in stocking density is achieved by keeping more cows, at least when cow numbers outstrip the capacity of existing buildings and labour. Furthermore, husbandry problems such as poaching will multiply, unless zero-grazing is practised — with its further additions to fixed costs and management difficulties. In addition the Nitrate Vulnerable Zone regulations must be abided by.

12. *Seasonality*. Price and concentrate feeding differences according to the seasonality of production have already been outlined in notes 3 and 8.

Under similar levels of management mainly autumn calving herds average up to 1,000 litres more milk/cow/year than mainly spring calving herds but feed around a tonne more concentrates cow/year; spring calving herds should normally only be feeding about 0.15 kg/litre. The average milk price would be expected to be higher for autumn calving herds, but the difference is less than might be supposed and has been steadily reduced with better prices being paid for summer milk.

13. *Quota*. Values are particularly dependent on the levels of farmgate milk prices and national milk production v. quota. For many years the price of unused quota averaged around 35p a litre and leasing 5p to 5.5p. The highest levels reached were 80p and 20p respectively in late 1994/early 1995. In recent years, with low milk prices and production below quota, values fell to very low levels. Levels were higher in 2004: a combination of higher milk production in the 2003/04 milk year and the effects of the Mid-Term Review: around 8p to lease, 14p to buy in mid-summer. However, by midsummer 2005, with no apparent likelihood of annual production exceeding quota, values had fallen below 1p to lease and 5.5p to buy. 2006 and 2007 sees quota prices at an all time low due to a fall in national production

14. *Labour*: see page 148.

15. *Building Costs*: see page 187.

16. *Costs per litre* (Holstein Friesians)

	Average (pence)		'Premium' (pence)	
Concentrates..............................	3.50		3.15	
Forage and Bought Bulk Feed	1.35		1.10	
Vet. & Med................................	0.70		0.60	
Other Variable Costs	1.35		1.05	
Total Variable Costs		6.90		5.90
Labour: direct (milking etc.)	4.15		3.05	
: field/farm work	1.00		0.70	
Power and Machinery....................	2.80		2.20	
Rent/Rental Value	1.50		1.15	
General Overheads	1.05		0.90	
Total Fixed Costs		10.50		8.00
Net Replacement Cost		0.96		0.80
Total (excl. Quota Leasing/Purchase)		18.36		14.70

Notes on the above

With regard to the average costs the variable costs per litre are derived from the data (and therefore the assumptions made) in the main per cow cost table on page 76. The labour cost is as on page 148. The average fixed costs are as for the medium-sized farm data on page 173, with adjustments made to allow for the greater use of resources by dairy cows compared with followers (and possibly cereals). The 'premium' figures are as estimated for the average of the most profitable 10% of herds, with lower than average costs per cow (except for concentrates) and yields of 8,500 litres or more per cow and an above average stocking rate.

Labour includes farmer and any unpaid family labour.

Power and machinery cover all machinery and equipment costs, including the use of farm vehicles, etc.

General overheads similarly relate to the whole farm, including property repairs.

Where the dairy is part of a farm with other enterprises on a significant scale most of the fixed costs per cow and therefore per litre are difficult to determine.

The net replacement cost is herd depreciation less the value of calves.

As said in the table, the cost of additional quota, whether leasing charges or the annual cost of purchased quota, is not included.

Note too that neither interest on capital nor any management charge have been included.

If leasing or buying extra quota is being considered it is of course not the average but the marginal cost of producing the extra milk that needs to be considered. This will depend largely on whether the extra milk is being obtained through increasing yield per cow or by keeping more cows (or a combination of the two).

Channel Island Breeds

Performance level (yield)	Low	High	Average	Very High
Milk Yield per Cow (litres)	4150	4850	5550	6250
	£	£	£	£
Milk Value per Cow	954.5	1115.5	1276.5	1437.5
Concentrate Costs per Cow	166	224	284	351
Margin of Milk Value over Concentrates per Cow	789	892	993	1087
Herd Depreciation less Value of Calves	65	65	65	65
Miscellaneous Variable Costs	129	139	149	160
Gross Margin per Cow before deducting Forage Variable Costs	595	688	779	862
Forage Variable Costs/Bought Fodder	80	80	80	80
Gross Margin per Cow	515	608	699	782
Gross Margin per Forage Hectare (2.4 cows per ha: 0.42 ha/cow)	1235	1458	1676	1876
Gross Margin per Forage Acre (1.05 acres/cow)	500	590	679	759

1. *Yield.* Average of Jerseys and Guernseys. See Note 2 for Holstein Friesians (page 77). Guernseys average some 300 litres more than Jerseys (i.e. giving an average of approximately 4,700 for Jerseys, 5,000 for Guernseys) but Jerseys achieve a higher average price of above 2p per litre. Note that the average for Channel Island costed herds should not be compared with the average national (Pocketbook) figure for Holstein Friesians; costed herd yield averages are invariably well above national averages; (i.e. they will well exceed 5,250 litres for Guernseys and 5,000 for Jerseys in 2007).

2. *Milk Price.* This has been assumed to be 23.00p per litre (average of Jerseys and Guernseys), i.e. 5p above Holstein Friesian milk; (23.25p Jersey milk, 21.00p Guernsey). Some dairy companies pay a premium in addition to the higher price obtained through the higher compositional quality for Channel Island milk; this varies both between companies.

3. *Concentrate Costs.*

Amounts: Performance level	Low	Average	High	Very High
kg/litre	.32	.37	.41	.45
tonnes/cow	1.33	1.795	2.275	2.81

   Price: taken (for 2007) as £125 per tonne.

4. Net Annual Replacement Value. (i.e. Value of Calves less Herd Depreciation) were calculated as follows:

	£ per cow in herd
Cost of replacements: 25% of herd per year @ £480	120
LESS Value of culls: 25 per cent of herd per year @ £160 (allowing for casualties)*	40
Herd Depreciation	80
Annual Value of Calves**	15
Net Annual Replacement Cost	65

* Cull cow prices for Guernseys are about £40 higher than for Jerseys.

** Allowing for calving index of 390 days and calf mortality; mixture of pure bred calves and beef crosses. Guernsey calves, especially crosses, fetch more than Jersey calves, averaging perhaps £10 more per head — but substantially more for some Guernsey beef crosses.

5. *Miscellaneous Variable Costs.* See Note 10 for Holstein Friesians (page 80).

6. *Stocking Rate.* See, in general, Note 11 for Holstein Friesians (page 80). The effect of varying the stocking rate on gross margin per forage hectare is as follows:

GM/Cow before deducting Forage V.Cs.

Cows per Forage Hectare	Forage Hectares (Acres) per cow	Low £594		Average £687		High £779		Very High £861		Forage V.Cs per cow (inc Bought Fodder)
		Gross Margin £ per Forage Ha (Acre)								£
2.1	0.48 (1.18)	1108	448	1303	528	1494	605	1668	675	67
2.4	**0.42 (1.03)**	**1235**	**500**	**1458**	**590**	**1678**	**679**	**1876**	**759**	**80**
2.7	0.37 (0.92)	1368	554	1619	655	1866	755	2088	846	88
3.0	0.33 (0.82)	1484	601	1763	714	2037	825	2285	925	100

A small amount of purchased bulk fodder is assumed, increasing with the stocking rate as follows (per cow): low £12, average £16, high £20 very high £24.

At the average stocking rate given above for combined Channel Island breeds (2.4 cows per forage ha) the average figure for Jerseys would be approximately 2.55 and that for Guernseys 2.25.

Ayrshires

	Low	Average	High	Very High
Performance level (yield)......................				
Milk Yield per Cow (litres)...................	4900	5725	6550	7375
	£	£	£	£
Milk Value per Cow...........................	892	1042	1192	1342
Concentrate Costs per Cow...................	153	200	254	314
Margin of Milk Value over Concentrates per Cow.........................	739	842	938	1029
Herd Depreciation less Value of Calves....	80	80	80	80
Miscellaneous Variable Costs................	129	139	149	160
Gross Margin per Cow before deducting Forage Variable Costs.........................	530	623	709	789
Forage Variable Costs/Bought Fodder......	85	85	85	85
Gross Margin per Cow.......................	445	538	624	686
Gross Margin per Forage Hectare (2.1 cows per hectare: 0.475 hectares/cow)	934	1130	1311	1441
Gross Margin per Forage Acre (1.175 acres/cow)...............................	378	458	531	584

1. *Yield.* See Note 2 for Holstein Friesians (page 77).

2. *Milk Price.* See in general, note 3 for Holstein Friesians (page 77). The price assumed in the above table is 18.2p per litre. The compositional quality of milk from Ayrshires is higher than for the black and white breeds.

3. *Concentrate Costs.* See notes 8 and 9 for Holstein Friesians (pages 79). In the above table, the levels of feeding per kg (and tonnes per cow) are as follows: low .25 (1.225 tonne), average .275 (1.54), high .30 (1.89), very high .325 (2.275); price £125 per tonne.

4. Net Annual Replacement Value. (i.e. Value of Calves less Herd Depreciation) were calculated as follows:

	£ per cow in herd
Cost of replacements: 25 per cent of herd per year @ £600..	150
Less Value of culls: 25 per cent of herd per year @ £200	
(allowing for casualties and slaughter premium)............	45
Herd Depreciation	105
Annual Value of Calves*.......................................	25
Net Annual Replacement Cost....................................	80

*Allowing for calving index of 385 days and calf mortality; mixture of pure bred calves and beef crosses.

5. *Miscellaneous Variable Costs*. See Note 10 for Holstein Friesians (page 80).

6. *Stocking Rate*. See, in general, Note 11 for Holstein Friesians (page 80).

Shorthorns. The above data could be used for Shorthorns, although one would expect their average yield to be about 5% lower, their cull and calf prices to be higher and their stocking rate to be slightly lower – similar to Holstein Friesians.

DAIRY FOLLOWERS (per Heifer Reared)

A. *Holstein Friesians*

Performance Level.............................	Low	Average	High
	£	£	£
Value of heifer (allowing for culls) (1).....	715	715	715
Less Value of calf (allowing for mortality)	75	75	75
Output...	640	640	640
Variable Costs:			
Concentrate Costs (2)	154	138	122
Miscellaneous Variable Costs (3)..........	103	108	113
Total Variable Costs			
(excluding Forage)............................	257	246	235
Gross Margin per Heifer, before			
deducting Forage Variable Costs...........	383	394	405
Forage Variable Costs (4)....................	65	90	115
Gross Margin per Heifer....................	318	304	290
Forage Hectares (Acres) per Heifer			
reared (5).......................................	0.8 (2)	0.7 (1.75)	0.6 (1.5)
Gross Margin per Forage Hectare (6)...	398	434	483
Gross Margin per Forage Acre...........	159	174	193

B. Channel Island Breeds

Performance Level............................	Low	Average	High
	£	£	£
Value of heifer (allowing for culls) (1)....	440	440	440
Less Value of calf (allowing for mortality)	15	15	15
Output...	425	425	425
Variable Costs:			
Concentrate Costs........................	127.2	113.42	100.7
Miscellaneous Variable Costs.........	92.7	97.85	103
Total Variable Costs (excluding Forage)	220	211	204
Gross Margin per Heifer, before			
deducting Forage Variable Costs........	205	214	221
Forage Variable Costs.......................	55	75	97
Gross Margin per Heifer..................	150	139	124
Forage Hectares (Acres) per Heifer			
Reared.......................................	0.675 (1.7)	0.575 (1.4)	0.5 (1.2)
Gross Margin per Forage Hectare......	222	241	249
Gross Margin per Forage Acre...........	88	99	104

N.B. On average, Channel Island heifers calve about three months younger than Holstein Friesians.

C. Ayrshires

Performance Level............................	Low	Average	High
	£	£	£
Value of heifer (allowing for culls) (1)....	570	570	570
Less Value of calf (allowing for mortality)	40	40	40
Output...	530	530	530
Variable Costs:			
Concentrate Costs........................	138	123	110
Miscellaneous Variable Costs...........	95	100	105
Total Variable Costs (excluding Forage)	233	223	215
Gross Margin per Heifer, before			
deducting Forage Variable Costs........	297	307	315
Forage Variable Costs.......................	61	88	110
Gross Margin per Heifer..................	236	219	205
Forage Hectares (Acres) per Heifer			
Reared.......................................	0·75 (1·85)	0·675 (1·65)	0·575 (1·425)
Gross Margin per Forage Hectare.........	315	325	355
Gross Margin per Forage Acre...........	127	132	144

1. The heifer values are based on the purchase price of down-calving heifers, allowing for culls. Most heifers are home-reared. If heifers are reared for sale, the price of whole batches are likely to be lower than the values given in the tables, by perhaps 10 or 15 per cent. On the other hand the purchaser will often take the batch a few months before the average expected calving date, thus reducing feed and area requirements for the rearer.

2. The lower levels of concentrate costs are the combined result of more economical feeding, lower cost per tonne and a lower average calving age. (Other things being equal, however, including the overall level of management, a lower calving age requires higher levels of feeding.) Average (Holstein Friesians) = £43 to 3 months plus 250 kg calf concentrates @ £137.50/tonne and 500 kg @ £115/tonne.

3. Miscellaneous variable costs include bedding (£25): straw requirements average approx. 1 tonne per heifer reared, but are variable, depending on time of year and age

when calved, as well as system of housing and extent of outwintering. Vet. and med. approximately £35 per heifer reared.

4. Forage variable costs. Grass for both grazing and conservation, at £75, £115 and £165/ha respectively (low, average and high) plus a small amount of bought and bulk food (£5, £10, £15 a head).

5. With an average calving age of 2 years 4 months, a 'replacement unit' (i.e. calf + yearling + heifer) equals about 1·25 livestock units. The three stocking rates given above are equivalent to approximately 0·64, 0·56 and 0·48 forage hectares (1·6,1·4,1·2 acres) respectively per Holstein Friesian cow.

6. Much higher gross margin figures per hectare can be combined by intensive grazing methods, particularly if combined with winter feeding systems which involve little dependence on home-produced hay or silage (cf. Note 11, last three paragraphs, page 80).

7. Contract Rearing: see page 104-105.

8. Labour: see page 148.

Self-Contained Dairy Herd: Cows and Followers

At average annual replacement rates (25% of the milking herd), nearly one-third of a replacement unit is required for each cow in the herd, i.e. roughly one calf, yearling and heifer for every three cows (including calved heifers), allowing for mortality and culling. At average stocking rates for both this means more than 1 hectare devoted to followers for every 3 hectares for cows. Since surplus youngstock are often reared and frequently the stocking rate is less intensive the ratio often exceeds 1:2 in practice. 1: 2·75 is about the minimum where all replacement heifers are reared, unless their winter feeding is based largely on straw and purchased supplements, or unless there is a combination of long average herd life and early calving, i.e. at 2 years old or just over.

Gross Margin per Forage Hectare (Acre) (£) for the Whole Herd (i.e., Cows and Followers Combined); (at four levels of performance, including four commensurate levels of stocking rate, for the dairy cows; and three levels of performance, including different stocking rates, for the followers) are as follows, assuming a 2:1 land use ratio (dairy cow area: followers area); (Holstein Friesians only):

				G.M. per Forage Hectare (Acre)							
				Dairy Cows							
				Low		Average		High		Very High	
				£		£		£		£	
G.M. per				1080	(437)	1410	(581)	1787	(723)	2172	(879)
Forage	Low	398	(159)	853	(345)	1073	(434)	1324	(536)	1581	(640)
Hectare (acre)	Ave.	434	(174)	865	(350)	1085	(439)	1336	(541)	1593	(645)
Followers	High	483	(193)	881	(357)	1101	(446)	1352	(547)	1609	(651)

As an example, the above table indicates that at the average level of performance and stocking rate for both cows and followers, the whole dairy gross margin per hectare (acre) figure falls to £1085 (439) compared with £1410 (570) for the dairy cows alone, a reduction of 23%. If more than the assumed (minimum) number of dairy followers are kept and the ratio is 1·5:1 (i.e. 40% of the dairy herd forage area is devoted to followers rather than a third) the whole forage area figure (on the assumption again of average performance) falls to £1020 (413), which is a reduction of 28% compared with cows only. However, the requirements per hectare for labour, machinery and buildings are of course less for heifer rearing than for dairy cows and there are other benefits from/reasons for home-rearing. The higher the value of replacement dairy heifers and cows the less the discrepancy between the gross margins of dairy cows alone and the self-contained herd.

Note that for a combined, self-contained enterprise budget for the dairy herd and followers there are the following differences:

Fewer calves for sale (as the required number of heifer calves are retained).

No replacement heifers/cows are purchased. (Thus high prices for replacement heifers reduces the gross margin of the milking herd and raises that of the dairy followers, but they have no effect on the gross margin of the combined, fully self-contained dairy herd breeding all its own replacements [assuming no surplus stock are reared]).

Value of any culled or surplus heifers are included.

Variable costs of replacements are added to those for the cows (on the basis of approximately one in-calf heifer entering the herd each year per 3·5 cows and calved heifers [which allows for mortality and culling]).

BEEF

The Single Payment Effect

From January 2005 subsidies were decoupled from production in the UK. The beef sector has been particularly dependent on subsidies. For beef farmers, even the most efficient, will find it difficult to make a positive net margin without subsidies; especially those in suckler production. Of course the Single Payment (SP) can still be used to subsidise production and the reality is that many will need to rely on the SP for some time. Producers should use the next few years of relatively high support to move their businesses to lower unit costs of production. This could be by simplifying systems which, are often too complex. Payments will continue even if production ceases (as long as cross compliance rules are met), although for many beef producers in England payments will reduce substantially over the next few years.

Unless producers can cut their unit costs of production, beef numbers are bound to fall as time goes on. Margins could of course be maintained if end prices rise significantly and/or the cost of calves and stores fall. Calf and store prices have reduced but this obviously has an effect on other enterprises. Finished cattle prices have been moving steadily in the right direction coupled with cheaper feed costs. However, the ready availability of imports is bound to restrict end price rises.

Finished Cattle Prices

Finished cattle prices in the first half of 2006 have been similar to the previous year but unlike last year when prices deteriorated during the traditional summer peak, prices this year appear to be firming. The relaxation of the Over Thirty Month Scheme Rules (OTMS) to allow older cattle back in to the food chain was a major boost to the industry. Initial fears that prices would weaken due to an increase of beef on the market were eased by orderly marketing of cattle and subsequently by the lifting of the export ban on British beef. The new market for older and cull cows, has settled at an average of 50 to 70p/kg lw with some good beef bred animals receiving considerably more With a strong EU and world demand for British beef following the lifting of the ban a weakening of prices is not expected, but it will take time to build up new markets again, so albeit an upward trend, it is expected to move slowly. A summer (July) peak of 114p/kg lw and an autumn (October) trough of 100p/kg lw are assumed i.e. a yearly average of approximately 200p/kg dw. The prices assumed in the subsequent tables relate either to the 2007 calendar year or 2007/08 as appropriate (e.g. the latter is used for winter finished beef).

Hill Farm Allowances

Hill Farm Allowance Payments (which continue for one more year at least) can be found on page 102.

Calf Prices

Highly variable. It is the balance between three (or four) factors: calf (or store) prices, finished cattle prices and feedingstuff prices (and in some cases stocking rate), that will mainly determine the levels of the gross margin and profit for the different beef systems included in the following pages. Small differences in each factor can cause large differences in the margins.

Calf prices dropped sharply in late 2004 and early 2005 (especially Holstein Friesians) once they became ineligible for subsidy. A further fall in prices was seen in the latter part of 2005 and the first three months of 2006. Prices for calves have subsequently firmed a little, probably due to the resumption in calf exports following the export ban on British beef being lifted and an increase in finished cattle prices. Continental cross calves did not drop as much as black and whites and heifers not by as much as bull calves. Again, a reflection of the change in subsidy regime and the strong demand for cattle. There continues to be a much smaller differential between bull and heifer calves following decoupling.

The values below assumed for 2007 relate to black and white bulls or beef cross calves of all qualities in all markets, less than three weeks old.

	Bulls	Heifers
Holstein Friesians........	25	-
Hereford cross	75	45
Continental cross	135	90

A. Calf Rearing

Early Weaning – Bucket Rearing (per calf)

	3 months	6 months
Value of Calf	190	255
Less Calf (1)	104	104
Output	86	151
Variable Costs:		
Milk Substitute and Concentrates (2)	43	85
Miscellaneous Variable Costs (3)	20	30
Hay (4)	1	8
Total Variable Costs	64	123
Gross Margin per Calf reared	**22**	**28**

1. £100 per calf (Holstein Friesian/Continental beef cross bull calves, 1-2 weeks old; 4 per cent mortality assumed, mainly in first 3 weeks. Value of pure Holstein Friesian bull calf £80 or so less; sale value at 3 or 6 months old correspondingly less).

2. Milk substitute: 15 kg @ £1200/tonne = £18.00. Calf concentrates: to 3 months, 160 kg @ £155/tonne = £24.80; to 6 months, additional 290kg @ £145/tonne = £42.05 Calves fed less well, i.e. with lower concentrate costs, will fetch proportionally lower market prices, probably resulting in a lower gross margin.

3. Misc. Variable Costs include vet. and med.: 8 (3 months), 11 (6 months); bedding: 3 (3 months), 7 (6 months); plus ear tags etc.

4. Hay: 10 kg to 3 months, 200 kg to 6 months. Variable costs assume made on farm; double the cost if purchased.

5. Weights: at start, 45 to 50 kg; at 3 months, 115 kg; at 6 months, 210 kg. Contract rearing charge (both 0 to 3 months and 0 to 6 months): £9 per week. Direct labour cost: approximately £19 per head to 3 months, £32 per head to 6 months.

   Labour requirements (all beef systems): see page 149.

Veal Calves

Information on veal calf rearing can be found on page 98.

B. Suckler Cows

Single Suckling (per cow): Lowland

System	Spring Calving		Autumn Calving	
Performance Level (1)	Average	High	Average	High
	£	£	£	£
Value of Calf (2)	307	330	358	400
Calf Sales/Valuation. per Cow (3)	276	304	322	368
Less Cow and Bull Depreciation and Calf Purchases (4)	47	47	53	53
Output	229	257	269	315
Variable Costs:				
Concentrate Costs (cow and calf) . . .	28	21	38	32
Miscellaneous Variable Costs (5) . . .	50	44	60	52
Total Variable Costs (excluding forage).	78	65	98	84
Gross Margin per cow, before deducting Forage Variable Costs	151	192	171	231
Forage Variable Costs	57	63	63	68
Purchased Bulk Feed	16	10	16	10
Gross Margin per Cow	**78**	**119**	**92**	**153**
Cows per ha (6)	1.8	2.2	1.65	2.0
Forage Ha (Acres) per Cow	.55	.45	.6	.5
	(1.35)	(1.11)	(1.48)	(1.24)
Gross Margin per Forage Hectare	141	264	153	306
Gross Margin per Forage Acre	58	132	62	123

1. Performance level relates to variations in two factors: weaner calf weight and stocking rate. 'High' refers to the average levels likely to be achieved by the better fifty per cent of producers. It is clearly possible to set still higher 'targets'.

2. Weight of calves (kg) at sale/transfer: spring calving: average 280 (at approximately 7.25 months old), high 295 (slightly older); autumn calving: average 335 (at approximately 10.25 months old), high 365 (11 months old). Price (per live kg): spring calving: average 109.5p, high 112p; autumn calving: 107p, 109.5p. These prices are averages for steers and heifers.

3. Calves reared per 100 cows mated: average 90, high 92.

4. *Assumptions.* Herd life: spring calving, 7 years; autumn calving, 6 years. Purchase price £625, average cull value £390. Calves purchased: average per 100 cows mated: spring calving 2, autumn calving 3; at £100. Bull: purchase price £2,100, cull value £525; (one bull per 35 cows on average; 4-year herd life).

5. *Vet. and med.:* spring calving £20, autumn £23; bedding: spring calving £18, autumn £23; miscellaneous: spring calving £12, autumn £14. Where yarded in winter, straw requirements average 0.5-0.75 tonne per cow for spring calvers and around 0.75 tonne for autumn calvers.

6. The forage area includes both grazing and conserved grass (silage and hay) plus any other forage crops, such as kale. The higher stocking density implies better use of grassland. Higher stocking rates can also be achieved by buying in more of the winter bulk fodder requirements, or by winter feeding largely on arable by-products, including straw. Purchased bulk fodder and/or straw balancer concentrates will reduce gross margin per cow but increase gross margin per hectare.

Headage Payments have been decoupled under the Single Payment Scheme.

Single Suckling (per cow): Upland and Hill

System:	Upland Spring Calving		Upland Autumn Calving		Hill Spring Calving		Hill Autumn Calving	
Performance Level (1)	Ave.	High	Ave.	High	Ave.	High	Ave.	High
	£	£	£	£	£	£	£	£
Value of Calf (2)	297	321	358	400	274	302	348	383
Calf Sales/Valn. per Cow (3)	270	298	326	372	244	275	310	349
Hill Farm Allowances (4)........	8	7	11	9	25	22	27	22
Less Cow and Bull Depreciation. and Calf Purchases (5).........	48	47	54	53	53	52	53	52
Output	230	258	283	328	216	245	284	319
Variable Costs:								
Concentrate Costs (cow & calf)	26	21	46	41	26	23	51	46
Miscellaneous Variable Costs (6)	55	45	65	55	55	45	65	55
Total Variable Costs (excl. forage)	81	66	111	96	81	68	116	101
Gross Margin per cow, before deducting Forage Variable Costs	149	192	172	232	135	177	168	218
Forage Variable Costs	50	56	64	70	50	56	64	70
Purchased Bulk Feed	17	11	13	7	15	8	11	6
Gross Margin per Cow	**82**	**125**	**95**	**155**	**70**	**113**	**93**	**142**
Cows per Forage ha (7, 8)........	1.6	1.9	1.25	1.5	1.0	1.15	0.9	1.1
Forage Ha (Acres) per Cow	.62	.53	.8	.67	1.0	.87	1.1	0.9
	(1.53)	(1.31)	(2.0)	(1.66)	(2.5)	(2.15)	(2.7)	(2.2)
Gross Margin per Forage Ha	132	236	119	231	70	130	85	158
Gross Margin per Forage Acre	54	95	48	93	28	52	34	65

1. Performance level relates to variations in two factors: weaner calf weight and stocking rate. 'High' refers to the average levels likely to be achieved by the better fifty per cent of producers. It is clearly possible to set still higher 'targets'.

2. Weight of calves (kg) at sale/transfer: upland spring calving: average 265 (at approximately 7 months old), high 280 (7.25 months); upland autumn calving: average 335 (at approximately 10.25 months old), high 365 (11 months); hill spring calving: average 250, high 270; hill autumn calving: average 325, high 350. Price (per live kg): upland spring calving: average 112p, high 114.5p; upland autumn calving: average 107p, high 109.5p; hill spring calving: average 109.5p, high 112p; hill autumn calving: average 107p, high 109.5p. These prices are averages for bull and heifer calves.

3. Calves reared per 100 cows mated: upland average 91, high 93; hill: average 89, high 91.

4. *Hill Farm Allowances.* See Page 102. The figures included are based on full rates for England in 2007, assuming DA rates for upland, SDA rates for hill.

5. *Assumptions.* Herd life: spring calving, 7 years; autumn calving and hill, 6 years. Purchase price £600, average cull value £360. Calves purchased: upland average, 3 per 100 cows mated, premium 2, at £95; hill: average 2, premium 1. Bull: purchase price £2,100, cull value £525.

6. *Both upland and hill.* Vet. and med: spring calving £25, autumn £28; bedding: spring calving £17, autumn £20; miscellaneous: spring calving £13, autumn £17. Where yarded in winter, requirements average 0.5-0.75 tonne per cow for spring calvers and around 0.75 tonne for autumn calvers.

7. The forage area includes both grazing and conserved grass (silage and hay) plus any other forage crops, such as kale. The higher stocking density implies better use of grassland. Higher stocking rates can also be achieved by buying in more of the winter bulk fodder requirements, or by winter feeding largely on arable by-products, including straw. Purchased bulk fodder and/or straw balancer concentrates reduce gross margin per cow but increase gross margin per hectare.

8. Forage Hectares (Acres) per cow and Gross Margin per Forage Hectare (Acre) relate to 'in-bye equivalent' (3 hectares of rough grazing are taken as being equal to 1 hectare of in-bye land).

C. Rearing / Finishing Stores

Traditional Finishing of Strong Store Cattle (per head) (1)

System	Summer Finishing		Winter Finishing	
	£		£	
Sales	525	(2)	572	(3)
Less Purchased Store	432	(4)	441	(5)
Output	93		131	
Variable Costs:				
Concentrates	5		45	(6)
Miscellaneous Variable Costs	20		35	(7)
Total Variable Costs (excluding Forage)	25		80	
Gross Margin per Head before deducting				
Forage Variable Costs	68		51	
Forage Variable Costs	30		16	
Gross Margin per Head	**38**		**35**	
No. per ha (acre)	4	(1·6)	10	(4)
Forage Hectares (Acres) per Head	0·25	(0·62)	0·1	(0·25)
Gross Margin per Forage Hectare	152		350	
Gross Margin per Forage Acre	61		140	

1. The financial results of this enterprise are highly dependent on the market margin, i.e. the difference between the price per kg paid for the store and the price per kg obtained for the finished animal. Other important factors are the stocking rate and the degree of dependence on cash-crop by-products and the quality of conserved grass (and hence the quantity of concentrates required in relation to the liveweight gain) in the case of winter finishing.

2. 520 kg @ 101p.

3. 520 kg @ 110p.

4. 400 kg @ 108p.

5. 420 kg @ 105p.

6. 400 kg @ £112tonne.

7. Including straw: average 0.75 tonne per head

BEEF

Finishing/Rearing on Suckler-Bred Stores (per head):

	Winter Finishing		Grass Finishing		Overwintering and Grass Finishing		Grazing and Yard Finishing	
	Average £	High £	Average £	High £	Average £	High £	Average £	High £
Sales	589	610	476	485	519	572	555	610
Less Store (1)	332	329	372	352	327	323	316	297
Output	257	281	104	133	192	249	239	313
Variable Costs:								
Concentrates (2)	75	63	4	3	46	36	53	36
Miscellaneous (3)	48	43	25	23	43	40	42	38
Total Variable Costs (excl. Forage)	123	106	29	26	89	76	95	74
Gross Margin per head before Forage Var. Costs	134	175	75	107	103	173	144	239
Forage Variable Costs	32	26	27	27	38	34	42	42
Purchased Bulk Feed	6	6	-	-	10	8	7	4
Gross Margin per head*	96	143	48	80	55	131	95	193
No. per ha (acre)	9 (3.6)	10 (4)	4 (1.6)	5 (2)	3.75 (1.5)	4.50 (1.8)	4 (1.6)	5 (2)
Gross Margin per Forage Ha*	864	1430	192	400	206	590	380	965
Gross Margin per Forage Acre*	346	572	77	160	82	236	152	386
Weight at start (kg)	310	310	335	320	300	300	285	270
Weight at end (kg)	540	550	445	445	490	530	500	540
Purchase Price (p per kg LW)	107	106	111	111	109	108	111	110
Sale Price (p per kg LW)	109	111	107	109	106	108	111	113
Concentrates per head (kg)	625	600	40	25	390	350	450	350
Silage per head (tonnes)	3.25	3.25	-	-	3.6	3.6	2.1	2.3

All-System Assumptions:

(1) Allowing for mortality at 1%. (2) Concentrate costs per tonne: winter: average £120, high £105; summer: average £105, high £95. (3) Including vet.& med. and bedding.

Additional Note: The gross margin per ha figures must be treated with considerable caution, especially with regard to winter fattening/rearing systems: small variations in land requirements and margins per head cause wide variations in the per ha figures, and capital requirements are considerable. Differences in buying and selling prices per kg can be critical. Very little recent survey data is available on several of these systems.

94

BEEF

Finishing/Rearing on Dairy-Bred Stores (per head):	Winter Finishing Average £	High £	Grass Finishing Average £	High £	Overwintering and Grass Finishing Average £	High £	Grazing and Yard Finishing Average £	High £
Sales	599	621	494	530	505	530	540	605
Less Store (1)	404	390	382	378	321	318	251	260
Output	195	231	112	152	184	212	289	345
Variable Costs:								
Concentrates (2)	61	53	5	4	45	35	72	47
Miscellaneous (3)	48	42	24	23	49	45	43	39
Total Variable Costs (excl. Forage)	109	95	29	27	94	80	115	86
Gross Margin per head before Forage Var. Costs	86	136	83	125	90	132	174	259
Forage Variable Costs	27	27	27	27	44	41	43	44
Purchased Bulk Feed	4	2	-	-	7	5	7	4
Gross Margin per head*	55	107	56	98	39	86	124	211
No. per ha (acre)	7.5 (3)	9 (3.6)	4 (1.6)	5 (2)	3.5 (1.4)	4.25 (1.7)	3.5 (1.4)	4.5 (1.8)
Gross Margin per Forage Ha*	412	963	224	490	136	366	434	950
Gross Margin per Forage Acre*	165	385	90	196	55	146	174	380
Weight at start (kg)	385	375	350	350	300	300	230	240
Weight at end (kg)	560	570	475	495	490	505	500	550
Purchase Price (p per kg LW)	105	104	109	108	107	106	109	108
Sale Price (p per kg LW)	107	109	104	107	103	105	108	110
Concentrates per head (kg)	510	510	50	40	390	350	600	450
Silage per head (tonnes)	3.4	3.4	-	-	3.6	3.6	3.5	4.5

All-System Assumptions:

(1) Allowing for mortality at 1%. (2) Concentrate costs per tonne: winter: average £120, high £105; summer: average £105, high £95. (3) Including vet.& med. and bedding.

Additional Note: The gross margin per ha figures must be treated with considerable caution, especially with regard to winter fattening/rearing systems: small variations in land requirements and margins per head cause wide variations in the per ha figures, and capital requirements are considerable. Differences in buying and selling prices per kg can be critical. Very little recent survey data is available on several of these systems.

D. Intensive Beef

Cereal Beef (per head):

System	Calves Reared On Farm		Reared Calves Purchased	
Performance Level	Average	High	Average	High
	£	£	£	£
Sales (1)	554	589	554	589
Less Calf (2)	113	112	194	192
Output	441	477	360	397
Variable Costs:				
Concentrates (3)	253	246	210	202
Other Feed	4	3	4	3
Miscellaneous (4)	66	61	54	50
Total Variable Costs	323	310	268	255
Gross Margin per Head	**118**	**167**	**92**	**142**

1. Weight at slaughter (kg): average 530, high 550. Price: average 104.5p per live kg, high 107p. All year round production is assumed. Days (on farm) to slaughter: calves reared on farm: 400; reared calves purchased: 320.

2. £110 per beef cross male calf (1 week old, average of all qualities except the poorest) + mortality (average 3, high 1·5 per cent). Reared calves purchased at about 3 months old at £190; average mortality 2, high 1 per cent.

3. £43 calf rearing (to 12 weeks: see page 89) + finishing ration + £3 food to losses. Finishing ration: 17 parts barley @ £68 per tonne (estimated average price, 2007 calendar year), 3 parts concentrate supplement @ £220 per tonne; plus milling and mixing. Total, £100 per tonne.

   Quantity (kg from 12 weeks (115 kg) to slaughter; FCR average 5·0, high 4·6): average 2075, high 2000.

   A difference of £5 per tonne in the cost of barley changes the feed cost by approximately £9 per head.

4. Calves reared on farm (averages): vet. and med. 16, bedding 25, other 25; reared calves purchased: 12, 22, 20 respectively.

5. Recent MLC budget projections suggest that there may be a case for rearing pure Holstein calves as bulls on cereal diets in 2007. The success will depend on the calves being available relatively cheaply (around £25) and the market demand for manufacturing beef remaining strong (180p/kg/dw for a O3 carcase).

Note: Interest on Capital

As examples of the need to be aware of interest paid or forgone on capital invested in beef production, interest on the cost of the calf and variable costs alone, at 6%, are likely to be at least £15 a head for cereal beef and 18-month beef (page 97).

18 Month Beef and Silage Beef (per head produced*):

System Performance Level	18 month Beef		Silage beef	
	Average	High	Average	High
	£	£	£	£
Sales	554	589	554	589
Less Calf	114	112	114	112
Output	442	479	466	504
Variable Costs:				
Concentrates (and milk substitute)...	130	119	178	153
Other Feed	4	4	5	5
Miscellaneous	73	70	68	62
Total Variable Costs (excl. Forage)	207	193	251	220
Gross Margin per Head before deducting Forage Variable Costs	235	286	215	284
Forage Variable Costs	53	53	38	38
Gross Margin per Head	**182**	**233**	**177**	**246**
No. per ha (acre)	3.4 (1.37)	3.8 (1.54)	8 (3.2)	10 (4)
Forage Hectares (Acres) per Head	.29 (.72)	.26 (.65)	0.125 (.31)	0.1 (.25)
Gross Margin per Forage Ha (per year). .	619	885	1416	2460
Gross Margin per Forage Acre (per year)	249	359	566	984

*   *N.B. The variable costs, including feed and forage, the forage area and gross margin per head all relate to the full production period - 18 months or less for silage beef. Nevertheless, the gross margins per forage ha or acre* are *per year. During the winter there will be both the 0-6 month old calves and 12-18 month old cattle on the farm.*

Notes: 18 Month Beef

General: Autumn-born dairy-bred calves, beef crosses.

Slaughter weights (kg): average 520, high 540. Sale price per live kg: average 107p, high 109.5p.

Calf price/value: £110 (1 week old beef cross male calves); mortality: average 4%, high 2%.

Feed: Concentrates (kg; average with high performance in brackets): milk substitute. 15; other: first winter 360 (335), at grass 115 (110), second winter 500 (490). Price of concentrates per tonne: first winter (inc. calf rearing) £120 (£112.50), summer £110 (£102.50); second winter, £112.50 (£105). Silage: 4.5 tonnes (average and high): 0.75 tonne first winter, 3.75 tonnes second. Intensive grazing of fresh leys and good quality silage are needed - especially to achieve the high performance levels.

Other Costs: Miscellaneous (average): vet. and med. £21, bedding £27, other £25.

Notes: Silage Beef

General: Dairy-bred calves (beef crosses) fed indoors on grass silage and concentrates, for slaughter at 14 to 17 months old. Good quality silage is the key to high performance per head (otherwise concentrates per head rise and/or daily liveweight gain falls). High yields of silage per ha raise gross margins per ha.

Slaughter weights (kg): average 540, high 560. Sale price per live kg: average 107.5p, high 110p.

Calf price: £110. Concentrates per head (kg) (from 3 months (£43 to rear)): average, with high performance in brackets: 1200 (1050); price per tonne £112.50 (£105). Silage required: approximately 5.5 tonnes per head.

Other Costs: Miscellaneous (average): vet. and med. £16, bedding £28, other £24.

Note that the gross margin per ha figures must be interpreted with considerable caution: small differences in silage yields can have a large effect and, more important, the working capital and building requirements per ha are extremely high: well above even the high needs of 18 month beef.

VEAL

General points: Veal consumption is very low in the UK: only a small fraction of the per capita consumption in France for example. Continental demand is mainly for white veal, produced in individual veal crates, a system that is illegal in the UK, where the less economic 'welfare system' of groups kept in straw pens is required, producing 'pink veal' at heavier weights. Imported 'white veal' is considerably cheaper.

As very little white veal is now produced in the UK validated economic data is rarely seen. This also applies to 'rose veal' produced at heavier weights, but again mainly on the Continent. Now that calf exports have resumed and, given that some continental countries have retained a headage subsidy payment, it is very unlikely that UK veal systems can make a comeback. *For these reasons the provision of gross margin data has been discontinued.*

SHEEP

A. Lowland Spring Lambing (per Ewe)
(Selling lambs off grass)

Performance level	Low	Average	High
Lambs reared per ewe (put to ram) (1)	1.3	1.45	1.6
Average price per lamb (£) (2)	40.0	41.5	43.0
	£	£	£
Lamb sales	52.0	60.2	68.8
Wool (3)	1.4	1.4	1.4
Cull ewes and rams	6.7	6.7	6.7
Sub-total	60.1	68.3	76.9
Less Ewe and ram replacements	19.3	19.3	19.3
Output	40.8	49.0	57.6
Variable Costs:			
Concentrates (53 kg ewes, 12 kg lambs)		7.5	
Vet. and Med.		4.7	
Miscellaneous and Transport		6.2	
Total Variable Costs (excluding Forage)		18.4	
Gross Margin per Ewe before deducting Forage Variable Costs	22.4	30.6	39.2
Forage Variable Costs (inc. bought forage and keep)	8.4	9.1	9.8
Gross Margin per Ewe	14.0	21.5	29.4
Stocking Rate (Ewes, with lambs, per forage hectare (acre))	8 (3.25)	11 (4.45)	14 (5.65)
Gross Margin per Forage Hectare	112	236	412
Gross Margin per Forage Acre	45	96	166

Notes

1. *Lambs reared per ewe* (x 100 = lambing percentage) is derived as follows (average figures only):
   Lambs born per 100 ewes lambing = 173
   Lambs born per 100 ewes put to ram = 161
   (92% of ewes put to ram bear lambs: 2.5% deaths, 5.5% barren)
   Lamb mortality: 10% (nearly half which are born dead)
   Lambs reared per 100 ewes lambing = 156
   Lambs reared per 100 ewes put to ram = 145

2. *Lamb Prices.* Prices are normally highest in March-May and lowest in August-October. Average prices between June and December were lower in 2005 than in 2004 and are expected to recover towards 2004 values in 2006. Prospects for 2007 are for reasonably strong prices as the ewe flock continues to contract and demand stays firm. The price assumed for lambs sold for slaughter for the 2007 mid-season lamb crop assumes that most of the lambs are sold between mid-June and the end of October which is the usual case. An average market price of 110p/kg lw has been taken, giving £43 per finished lamb at an average weight of 39kglw. The average price given in the above table allows for a proportion (20%) sold or retained in the autumn as store lambs. Low performance is £1.50 a lamb less, high £1.50 more - variations caused by slight differences in weight, time of marketing and proportions sold or retained as stores.

   A difference in price of £2 per lamb (i.e. a difference of approximately 5.10p per kglw for a 39 kglw lamb) causes a difference of £21, £32 and £45 (8, 13, 18) to the low, average and high gross margins per hectare (acre) respectively. Prices of exported lambs are normally above domestic prices.

The *Sheep Annual Premium* has not been paid since 2004, all such payments having been decoupled with CAP reform.

3. *Wool.* The 'wool cheque' (price paid to producers) is based on a rate in the region of 45p/kg in 2006, considerably down on 2005 prices because of low world price prospects. 3kg/head at approximately this price has been assumed for 2007.

4. *Breed* will obviously have a large effect on lambing percentage, rate of liveweight gain (reflected in price per lamb), and amount of wool per ewe.

5. *Stocking Density.* The stocking rates assumed are based on land requirements throughout the year. With a given level of management one would expect higher stocking rates to be associated with a lower gross margin per ewe. The assumption made in the initial table, however, is that management performance is affecting both factors together.

   N.B. The forage variable costs include purchased forage and keep (where appropriate) (£1.2, £1.6 and £1.8 per ewe at the three performance levels respectively).

   High stocking rates are often achieved by substantial use of by-products (*e.g.* autumn or spring grazing of grass grown primarily for seed) and catch crops (*e.g.* rape). Otherwise a stocking rate of 14 per hectare requires a stocking rate of about 22 ewes (with lambs) per hectare in the spring and early summer.

   In an average season for prices and weather, the top few per cent of flocks in the country can achieve gross margins exceeding £500 per hectare (£200 per acre) by a combination of high lambing percentage, high average lamb price and, especially, very high stocking rates.

   Where there are no grazing livestock other than sheep on the farm, some ewes, at the higher stocking rates, are often either agisted (away-wintered) or housed indoors, thus reducing the margin. Agistment costs around 37.50p per week plus transport, *i.e.* approx. £8 per year. Depreciation and Interest on new Housing (1.2 sq. m per ewe) is approximately £6 per ewe per year (10-year life); straw, extra hay and perhaps concentrates will also be required for indoor housing.

   On the other hand, with only 7 or 8 ewes per hectare (2.75 to 3.25/acre) on a lowland farm of reasonable quality with no other grazing livestock, there should be surplus grass available in the late spring or early summer; this could be cut for hay or used for seed production.

6. *Flock Depreciation.* (i.e. Market price of replacements less value of culls). It is assumed above that 20 per cent of the ewe flock is culled each year @ £32 each and that, allowing for 4 per cent mortality, 24 per cent are purchased or home-reared at £70 each. Rams: 1 per 40 ewes, 3-year life, purchased @ £300, sold @ £35. The net cost (flock depreciation) is £12.60 per ewe per year. N.B. Cull ewe prices are approximately £4 per head higher for heavy breeds and £4 lower for light breeds. Cull values tend to be highly variable but have been high of late, partly at least through a strong, consistent demand from the ethnic sector of the population. No other changes in flock valuation are assumed.

7. *Miscellaneous Costs* include lambing and shearing bonus. Contract shearing is approximately £1.05 per head, including rolling (but can be around £1.25 for small flocks); 70-80p/ewe for shearing only in upland flocks. Scanning 40-50p/ewe. Trained sheepdogs average around £400, but top quality dogs for breeding and trialling can cost £1,250.

8. *Prices of Specialised Equipment:*

Troughs (2.75 m)	£50 to £60
Racks (2 to 3 m)	£200 to £225
Foot Baths (3 m)	£100 to £125
Shearer (electric)	£650 to £1050
Lamb Creep and Shelter, skids . .	£625
Netting	80p to £1.50 per metre

9. Fencing: approximately £1.70 per metre + 85p labour.

10. Home-reared tegs (shearlings). Output: value £70 (allowing for culling and mortality) less £41 for the lamb, plus wool = £30. Variable costs (including forage) = £15. Gross margin per head = £15, per forage hectare £300 (£120 per acre).

If the figures for home-reared replacement tegs are included in the figures per ewe, the latter are increased approximately as follows: output by £7.50, gross margin (per ewe) by £4. The stocking rate in terms of ewes per hectare devoted to sheep will be about 15 per cent less and the overall sheep gross margin per hectare will be around £10/ha (£4/acre) higher, on the assumptions made.

11. *Labour*: see page 150.

B. Other Sheep Systems (average performance level only)

System	Early Lambing per ewe	Winter Finishing of Store Lambs per head	Upland Flocks per ewe	Hill Flocks per ewe
Lambs reared per ewe (put to ram)	1.375	-	1.325	11.025
	£	£	£	£
Average price per lamb sold	52.0	48.0	40.0	37.0
Lamb sales	71.5	47.0	53.0	28.7
Wool	1.4	-	1.3	1.0
Hill Farm Allowances	-	-	1.4*	5.8*
Sub-total	72.9	47.0	55.7	35.5
Less Livestock Purchases (net of culls) . .	11.4	35.0	12.7	(+) 3.5
Output	61.5	12.0	43.0	39.0
Variable Costs:				
Concentrates	17.0	1.4	5.8	3.5
	(150 kg)	(12.5 kg)	(50 kg)	(30 kg)
Vet. and Med.	4.4	0.5	3.8	3.0
Miscellaneous and Transport	6.8	2.0	5.6	3.0
Total Variable Costs (excl. Forage)	28.2	3.9	15.2	9.5
Gross Margin per ewe (or head) before deducting Forage Variable Costs	33.3	8.1	27.8	29.5
Forage Variable Costs (inc. bought forage)	8.4	2.3	7.8	5.4
Gross Margin per ewe (or head)	**24.9**	**5.8**	**20.0**	**24.1**
Stocking Rate (No. per Forage Ha [Acre])	14 (5.75)	40 (16)	9.5 (3.85)	-
Gross Margin per Forage Hectare	348	232	190	-
Gross Margin per Forage Acre	143	93	77	-

* *Hill Farm Allowances are assumed at 2006 levels for England (see page 102). The upland figure assumes 'disadvantaged land'. The hill flock stocking rate is inevitably extremely variable: the £5.80/head figure would be with a stocking rate of close to 4.25 ewes/ha (farming under 350ha).*

Notes:

Early Lambing. In this system, 60% of the lambs are sold before the end of May, and the remainder before the end of August. This may be compared with Mid-Season lamb production (see table on page 99), in which about 80% of the lambs are sold between early June and mid-September, and Late lamb production, in which only two-thirds or so of the lambs are sold for slaughter by the end of the normal grazing season, 60% of total lambs being sold for slaughter or as stores in October/November, or the stores are retained on the farm for winter finishing. The gross margin per ewe tends to be slightly higher with the latter system compared with Mid-Season production, provided the proportion of stores is not too high — but more grass is utilised per ewe, making per hectare results similar.

Winter Finishing of Store Lambs. The gross margin per head is particularly variable, being very dependent on the difference between the purchase and sale price of the lambs. Some of the forage variable costs consist of bulk feed and agistment.

Hill Sheep. The flock is assumed to be self-maintained; thus only about 0.75 lambs are sold per ewe per annum and the fleece of the yearling ewes are included in wool sales. Only the rams are purchased, costing approximately £1.50 per ewe per year. Results obviously vary according to the height of the hill and severity of the winter.

Note. The figures for early lambing, upland and hill sheep are largely based on the relative figures for these systems as compared with the lowland spring lambing results obtained from the Meat and Livestock Commission's Flockplan recording and costing service.

Hill Farm Payments

Area payments replaced headage payments (HLCAs) for beef and sheep in the summer of 2000. They are part of the Rural Development Regulation and therefore are additional to the Single Payment. As part of the new Rural Development Programmes for the period 2007 to 2013 (see page 215) the UK administrations have been consulting on changes to the current systems.

In *England* DEFRA has announced that the current system will continue for a further year i.e. for 2007 payments, after which a new scheme is expected to be in place. At the time of writing there has been no announcement on payment rates for 2007, the following rates per hectare applied for the year ending March 2006: £9.39 on moorland and common land, £13.42 on disadvantaged land and £24.82 on severely disadvantaged land. For 2005 these rates were £11.26, £16.10 and £29.78 respectively. Only half these rates are paid between 350 and 700 ha and none over 700 ha per holding. A claimant must have at least 10 ha of LFA land and a stocking density of at least 0.15 LU/ha; if it exceeds 1.4 LU/ha there is an inspection to ensure that the land is not being over-grazed. An additional 10% or 20% is available if certain environmental criteria are satisfied (this no longer includes being registered as organic).

DEFRA has been consulting on four options for the new scheme:

- A scheme based on compensatory allowances (similar to the current HFA)
- A top-up payment for eligible farms participating in an agri-environment scheme
- Upland options within the Environmental Stewardship Scheme
- No specific upland farming support.

In *Wales* (Tir Mynydd) the Welsh Assembly Government has announced that the current scheme will continue for the 2007 and 2008 scheme years, but funding will be approximately one third less than current levels. The rates per hectare in 2006 were £25.50 on disadvantaged land and £37.50 on severely disadvantaged land.. For 2001 to 2004 the rates were £23 and £35 respectively and 2005 £26 and £38. The full rates are paid up to 140 ha, 65% between 140 and 640 ha and 30% over 640 ha. The minimum area is 6ha and the stocking density must be between 0.1 and 1.8 LU/ha. There is a range of enhancements up to 10 or 20%.

In *Scotland* the Less Favoured Area Support Scheme (LFASS) looks set to continue with only minor amendments for the 2007, 2008 and 2009 scheme years. Changes are expected in 2010 following an EU wide review of the Less Favoured Areas. Payments will be based on 2006 LFASS receipts. The payment rates are far more complex. A minimum of 3 ha is required but there are no size differentials: there is a minimum stocking rate of 0.12 LU/ha and a maximum of 1.4 LU/ha (payments are scaled back if the latter is exceeded). Certain environmental conditions have to be met. Payments vary according to three criteria: location, 'grazing category' and enterprise mix (enhancements). The rates in three different locations were as follows in 2006, the first figure being for grazing categories A and B (see below) and the second for C and D: Islands £47.00 and £41.50, Mainland Peripheral £45 and £39.50, Other LFA £39 and £33.50. Payment rates for 2007 are expected to be similar. These payments are increased if suckler cow livestock units exceed a certain percentage of the total: they are raised by 35% if this percentage is between 10% and 50% and by 70% if over 50%. A fraction of the above rates is paid according to the 'grazing capacity' in LU/ha in year 2001, as follows: A. up to 0.19LU/ha, one-sixth; B. 0.2 to 0.39 LU/ha, one third; C 0.4 to 0.59 LU/ha, two thirds; D. 0.6 LU/ha and over, four-fifths. There is a minimum payment of £350.

GRAZING AND REARING CHARGES:
CATTLE AND SHEEP

Grazing charges vary widely according to the quality of the pasture and local supply and demand. The following figures are typical (estimated for 2007):

Summer Grazing (per head per week)

Store Cattle and in-calf heifers over 21 months, dry cows, and fattening bullocks over 18 months	£3.50-£4.50
Heifers and Steers, 12-21 months	£2.50-£3.50
6-12 months Cattle	£2.00-£2.75
Cattle of mixed ages	£2.50-£3.50
Ewes	35p-55p

Winter Grazing (per head per week)

'Strong' Cattle	£2.25-£3.50
Heifers	£2.00-£3.00
Sheep..	35p-55p

Note: the above figures assume the farmer whose land the livestock are on does all the fencing and 'looking after'. Where the owner of the, say, sheep does the fencing, shepherding, etc., the figures may be halved, or be even less depending on local demand.

Grass Keep (per hectare, per acre in brackets)

Most typically around £150-200 (£60-80), with the best £250-300 (£100-120) and poorish quality £85-£100 (£35-40).

These figures are highly variable, especially between one part of the country and another, and between one season and another. The charge can be very high where the pasture is good, the supply scarce and the demand strong. In an average price year poor quality keep may fetch only £75 (30), top quality (fenced and with mains water) more than £300 (120). For top quality grassland, fertilised, well-fenced and watered, with stock seen daily, prices can be even higher for some lots in the west and north-west in years of grass shortage; a top figure as high as £400 (160) is sometimes reported. The average price can exceed £300 (120) in some years in parts of the west and west midlands but can fall below £100 (40) in some eastern and south-eastern counties.

A lowering of these levels following the introduction of the Single Payment Scheme had been expected but experience of 2005 and 2006 has seen only minor reductions in averages let at auction in most parts of the country. On the other hand there is increasing evidence in some localities that grassland subject to environmental schemes is fetching very low or negative rents where the landowner is taking the payment.

Winter Keep (Cattle) (per head per week)

Grazing + 9 kg hay and some straw	£8.00
Full winter keep in yards	£8.50-£10.50
Calf rearing for beef (0 to 12 weeks or 0 to 6 months)..........	£9.00

These rates apply where feed to achieve maintenance plus some growth is supplied plus labour and buildings and bedding where applicable. A typical rental for labour, buildings and a maintenance diet would be £5 per head per week.

Heifer Rearing Charges

Points to clarify in any arrangement are: who pays for transport, who pays the vet. and med. expenses, who bears the losses or pays for replacements, how often are payments made (monthly payments save the rearer interest compared with lump sum payments when the heifer is returned)?

Two possible arrangements are:

1. Farmer X sells calf to Rearer at agreed price; the calf is then Rearer's responsibility and he pays for all expenses and bears any losses. Farmer X has first option on heifers, which he buys back two months before calving. Approximate price: £775above cost of calf for Holstein Friesians. Rearer fetches calf; Farmer X supplies transport for heifer.

2. Farmer X retains ownership of calf. Approximate charges: £35 per month from 10 to 14 days old (£38 if two-year old calving), or £33 per month from 6 months old (£37 if two-year old calving), (£40 per month from 10 to 14 days to 6 months). As Rearer has no interest on capital to bear, he supplies transport and pays for vet. and medical expenses. In the case of losses by accident/chance, the rearer either refunds payments or replaces calf (this means Farmer X and Rearer share a loss averaging approximately £35 each per heifer reared, assuming 10 per cent losses at average 6 months old). In the case of losses by negligence, the rearer both refunds payments and replaces calf. (The NFU can supply model agreements).

Calf and Heifer Rearing for Shorter Periods

Calf, 10 days to 3 months, £112.50 (for food, labour and housing) to £125 (all costs, and rearer bearing losses). Heifers, average from 3 months old to steaming up: approximately £16 per month in summer, £45 in winter.

RED DEER

A. Breeding and Finishing

	Per 100 hinds
Sales:	£
42 stags (15-18 months) : 55kg dw @ £3·20/kg	7390
33 hinds (15-18 months) : 42·5kg dw @ £3·20/kg	4490
8 cull hinds @ £75	600
Average annual value of cull stags	70
Less average annual cost of replacement stags	500
Output.	12050
Variable Costs:	
Concentrates 10·5 tonnes @ £130/tonne	1365
Vet and Med.	825
Miscellaneous	1250
Total Variable Costs	3440
Gross Margin before deducting forage	8610
Forage Variable Costs (5·5 hinds/ha, £115/ha)	2090
Gross Margin (per 100 hinds)	**6520**
Gross Margin per Forage Hectare (18·2 ha)	358
Gross Margin per Forage Acre (45 acres)	145

B. Selling Calves

	Per 100 hinds
Sales:	£
43 stags @ £80 (45 kg lw)	3440
34 hinds @ £62·50 (40 kg lw)	2125
8 cull hinds @ £75	600
Average annual value of cull stags	70
Less average annual cost of replacement stags	500
Output	5735

Variable Costs:	
Concentrates 7 tonnes @ £150/tonne	1050
Vet and Med.	550
Miscellaneous	700
Total Variable Costs	2300
Gross Margin before deducting forage	3435
Forage Variable Costs (6·5 hinds/ha, £105/ha)	1615
Gross Margin (per 100 hinds)	**1820**
Gross Margin per Forage Hectare (15·4 ha)	118
Gross Margin per Forage Acre (38 acres)	48

C. Finishing Stag Calves	Per 200 stags
Sales:	£
195 @ 55kg dw @ £3·20/kg	34320
Less : 200 @ £75	15000
Output	19320
Variable Costs:	
Concentrates 15 tonnes @ £105/tonne	1575
Vet and Med.	900
Miscellaneous	2000
Total Variable Costs	4475
Gross Margin before deducting forage	14845
Forage Variable Costs (11 stags/ha, £105/ha)	1910
Gross Margin (per 200 stags)	**12935**
Gross Margin per Forage Hectare (18·2 ha)	710
Gross Margin per Forage Acre (45 acres)	287

Additional Notes

Lowland assumed.

Hind replacements home-reared in systems A and B.

Herd Life: hinds, 12 years; stags, 7 years. 25 hinds per stag.

Calves reared per 100 hinds: 85.

Purchase price of breeding stock (good quality): hinds £275 plus, yearling hinds £225 plus, stags £500 plus.

The venison prices reflect projected sales for 2006/07 to wholesale buyers. Higher prices will be obtained for direct sales to consumers (e.g. farm shops and farmers' markets) and caterers, but extra costs will normally be incurred.

Capital costs: perimeter fencing, £5/metre; internal fencing, £3/metre; handling yard, pens, scales, crush: £10,000—in existing buildings. Total cost of establishing a 100-hind breeding flock is typically in the order of £50,000, including breeding stock and £12,500 for fencing, housing and handling facilities. Labour: with an experienced stockman: 400 plus head with additional help when yarding.

Sources of further information: *'Introduction to Deer Farming'* (Barony College, Dumfries. Tel: 01387 860251. *British Deer Farmers Association*, The Counting House, Mill Road, Cromford, Derbyshire, DE4 3RQ. Tel. 01629 827037.

Acknowledgement: Russell Marchant, Principal and Chief Executive, Barony College.

HORSES: LIVERY

The horse industry is now reported to be the second biggest employer in the rural economy and is also one of the fastest growing. Although there are other equine enterprises that farm businesses can operate, by far the most common is providing accommodation for horses; i.e. livery. There are many different forms of livery and the charges, therefore, vary widely also. This is apart from the effects of local supply and demand. However, three fairly standard forms are offered on farms:

Grass Livery. Keep at grass, preferably with shelter, water supply and secure area to keep tack and store feed. Some grass livery will provide an exercise arena and off-road riding. Charges average £20-£25 per week; range £15-£35.

DIY Livery. The owner still has full care of the horse but has the facilities of a stable, grazing, and in some cases an all-weather exercise arena. The owner is responsible for mucking out, turning out, grooming, exercising and all vet./med. care and the cost of all feed and bedding. Charges average £25-£30 per week; range £20-£50.

DIY Plus Livery. As the above, except that the yard manager is responsible for certain tasks, such as turning out and feeding. Charges average £35-£40 per week; range £30-£50.

The above are only guidelines. There is a wide variation both within, and between regions. Where more services, such as exercise, are provided by the yard the charges may be fitted to the needs of a particular horse. Full livery charges average £85-£95 per week; with a range between £75-£100. Part livery average £65 per week; range £50-£90.

Other Costs:

Grazing. Variable costs will average some £30 per horse per year. Average stocking rates are 0·8 ha (2 acres) for the first horse and 0·4 ha (1 acre) for each horse after.

Hay. Average price £2·75 per conventional bale (approximately 20 kg); has to be of good quality. Average consumption is one to two bales per horse per week: less in the summer depending on the grass quality/quantity and the work of the horse. Some horses now have haylage: more expensive, dust free and higher fibre and energy/protein levels; less required per head.

Concentrate Feed. Can range from almost nil to 3 to 4 kg per day depending, amongst other factors, on breed, size and intensity of work. Compound feed 25 to 30p per kg.

Bedding. Averages around £5 per stabled horse per week for half the year, i.e. £110-£130 per year. Straw might cost only half as much; however, more expensive, but preferable, alternatives (such as wood shavings, shredded paper and hemp fibre) are now increasingly being used.

Vet. and Med. Averages approximately £150 per horse per year. Some yards include worming of the horse in the livery cost.

Further Notes:

The supply of livery yards appears to be increasing, both from farms diversifying and other yards setting up. Filling a yard is, consequently, getting more difficult. The level of service and facilities expected by customers has increased. There is a trend towards greater professionalism in the running and management of livery yards.

To be successful, a livery enterprise needs higher quality facilities than farm livestock. To the owner, the horse can be anything from a highly trained athlete to a family pet. Horses are expensive: even modest quality horses cost between £1,500 and £3,000. Good customer relations and an effective security system (including burglar and fire alarms) are crucial to success, as is good market research and effective advertising.

A full livery yard will require stables, a secure room to store tack, a vermin-proof hard feed store, storage for hay and bedding, a muck heap and parking provision with room for horse boxes. Planning permission is required for the conversion of an existing building to stabling or the erection of new, purpose-built stables. Permission is also required for construction of an all weather arena used for training and exercising. Hay and straw should be stored away from the stables and down-wind of them to minimise the fire risk. A hard standing area with a water supply and good drainage should be provided for grooming and washing down the horses. Good ventilation in the stables is crucial as horses are prone to respiratory diseases caused by spores and dust. Provision should be made for owners to soak hay in clean water before feeding it, to reduce respiratory problems.

Fences must be sound and must be free of protruding nails, wire etc. Ideally fields should be fenced using post and rail, but this is expensive. Barbed wire should be avoided wherever possible or should be 'protected' with an offset electrified fence. Fields should be divided into smaller paddocks to reduce the possibility of fighting between incompatible horses and to separate mares and geldings. Paddocks may be divided using two or more strands of electrified tape or rope but wire is not advisable as it is not easily visible.

Off-road riding opportunities on the farm are a real asset. The farmer may provide riding trails, a jumping paddock, or a cross country course. An all-weather ménage for exercising horse, possibly with floodlighting, is highly desirable, and some livery yards have horse walkers too. Good facilities can be rented out to individuals or organisations such as pony clubs. It is sometimes possible to link up with nearby farms to increase the length of riding tracks available.

Construction Costs. The cost of conversion of existing buildings will depend on their quality; prefabricated hardwood and steel internal stable partitions can be purchased from upwards of £750 per stable, depending on size and specification. Free standing timber stables cost between £800 and £2,000 (plus base), depending on size and quality. As horses are fairly destructive animals (they both kick and chew) better quality stables will often prove more economic in the long run. All weather arenas (20 metres by 40 metres) cost between £10,000 and £25,000; construction is a specialist job as good drainage is essential; a badly constructed arena is worthless.

Contact*:* Further financial information on horse enterprises, including riding schools and equestrian centres, is available in 'Equine Business Guide', 5th Edition, 2005, edited by Richard Bacon, Warwickshire College; Tel. 01926 318338.

OSTRICHES

The sector has contracted from 250 producers in the early 1990s to less than 100 at present. Few are strictly commercial and the British Domesticated Ostrich Association has only 30 members. There is little, if any demand for breeding stock, and producers must make an income from meat and hides. Although it is estimated that 4,000-5,000 birds are slaughtered annually in the UK, the great majority come from one enterprise whose main interest is in hides.

Ostriches are subject to the Dangerous Wild Animals Act requiring licensing (£45 to £360) and inspection by the Local Authority.

Breeding Stock

Adult breeding stock are normally kept in trios of one male and two females, but pairs and colonies are not unusual. A trio will require about 0.2 ha (0.5 acre) for grazing and room in which to exercise: they must be able to run. (More land will be required if it is not free draining). A stout hedge or smooth wire fence of a minimum of 1.7 metres (5.5 ft) high should surround the enclosure. Adult birds need shelter from wind and rain, and a dry floor on which to sleep. Domesticated ostrich are generally docile and easily handled.

A female from 2-3 years of age lays 30-60 eggs a year (March to October); on average, 75% will be fertile (settable). A female may have a productive life of 20 to 30 years. An experienced producer will aim to hatch and rear at least half the eggs set, but there can be significant losses. A 10% replacement rate is anticipated for breeding stock.

A young fertile trio should cost between £600 and £1,000 for good quality stock. Although there is almost no demand it is unlikely a producer of birds would accept less for breeding stock that the birds would fetch for meat. A good meat bird can be worth £400 or more providing the meat is sold at retail and the hide is of good quality.

Grass and other vegetation can form part of the diet, and specially formulated concentrate, barley, silage and vegetable waste are also fed. Dry matter and silage should be chopped. The birds must be provided with grit when young and small stones (up to 12 to 15mm) for adults, oyster shells, and perhaps vitamin supplement. A breeding ration is fed at 1.5-2.5 kg per day for 180 days a year. A specialist feed can cost up to £200 per tonne but a sheep ration with added minerals is £100-£115 per tonne.

Rearing and Meat Production

In theory, fertile eggs are worth £5-£10 each (infertile eggs can be sold for cooking or crafts for about £3-£5 each.) Incubation lasts 42-45 days. Chicks are reared indoors with access to heat for two to three months and then allowed outside. They are fed starter crumb and then small pellets costing £250 per tonne. A high level of care and expertise is required. Meat birds are grouped according to size rather than age from 12 weeks and kept at 25-35 per hectare (10-14 per acre) up to 6 months and 18 per ha (7.5 per acre) when older.

Birds are slaughtered at 10-16 months at a live weight of 95-110kg, giving 25-35kg of de-boned meat. On-farm slaughtering is permitted under poultry regulations but meat can only be sold locally and the producer will have the added cost of packaging and marketing, which could amount to £1 per kg. The majority of ostriches are processed at one of the very few specialist slaughter facilities, which must have veterinary and meat hygiene inspections. The new EU-wide Slaughter Licence that came into effect on January 2006 means that red meat plants can slaughter ostriches providing they have appropriate de-feathering and chilling facilities. Charges are in the order of £40 per bird if the carcase is returned to the producer or the meat is sold on directly to the wholesaler at £3-£4.5 per kg. For slaughter, butchering and returning the meat vacuum packed to the producer the charge is £80/bird. Transport to the abattoir and return carriage for the meat may add significantly to this sum. The skin is returned, sold on commission or bought directly by the processing company. Birds sold to a slaughterhouse will fetch £100-£150, depending on their condition and skin quality. Meat sold at retail will fetch between £9-£23 per kg.

Ostrich meat sold at wholesale prices does not appear to give producers an adequate return. Individual farmers can exploit local outlets such as farmers' markets or nearby shops but this requires positive marketing initiative.

Ostrich skins can be just as valuable as the meat, but British producers have found it difficult to produce a bird with a highly saleable skin, and quality is all important. A top quality skin can fetch over £100, but in the absence of UK tanning facilities skins are generally exported in a batch at £30-£40 each. Feathers are potentially valuable but no market has been established yet.

Meat Production	per meat bird	per hen
Output:	£	£
Assuming 15 birds produced per hen		
30kg of meat each at £4 per kg.............	120	1,800
Skin at £40	40	600
Output	160	2,400
Variable Costs:		
Feed	90	1,350
Vet and med	1	15
Forage	5	75
Egg + incubation	15	225
Slaughter charge	40	600
Misc. and transport	10	150
Total Variable Costs	161	2,415
Gross Margin	**-1**	**-15**
Farmer Retailing (excluding retailing costs):		
30kg meat at £15 per kg	450	6,750
Slaughtering and butchering charge*	90	1,350
Gross Margin	**360**	**5,400**

* There may also be a carriage charge for return of butchered meat from slaughterhouse.

Fixed Costs

Housing £6; fencing £4; labour: adult birds require about 25 hours a year and chicks and young birds about 4 hours a year. One stockperson might look after 500 meat birds. Two people are needed at times to handle adult stock.

Contact: *British Domesticated Ostrich Association (BDOA),* 33 Eden Grange, Little Corby, Carlisle, CA4 8QU. (Tel.: 01228 562946); www.ostrich.org.uk

SHEEP DAIRYING

	Per Ewe		
Performance Level (yield)	Low	Average	High
Milk Yield (litres)	175	275	350
	£	£	£
Milk Value (1)	140	220	280
Value of Lambs (2)	51	51	51
Cull Ewes (3)	3	3	3
Wool	2	2	2
Output	196	276	336
Variable Costs:			
Concentrates (4)		117	
Miscellaneous (including vet and med)		15	
Forage Variable Costs		15	
Total Variable Costs		147	
Gross Margin per Ewe	49	129	189
Ewes (plus replacements) per ha (acre)		11.25 (4.5)	
Gross Margin per Forage Hectare	551	1451	2126
Gross Margin per Forage Acre	220	581	851

Notes

1. *Price:* 80p per litre at farmgate (range from 75p-90p per litre).

2. *Lambing %:* 175%. Assume a 300 Friesland ewe flock. Retain 60 ewe lambs for flock replacements. Sell 400 finished lambs reared from 2 days old (inc. 12.5% mortality) at £38. If meat-type terminal sires used then cross-bred lamb values increase to £48.

3. *Cull ewes:* 20/25% culled at £15 per head (including mortality).

4. *Concentrates:* Milking ewes: 200 days at 1.5 kg/head/day, 100 days at 0.5 kg/head/day; cost £160/tonne. Ewe lamb replacements and artificially reared finished lambs at £40/head.

5. *Forage costs:* Quality silage: 1 tonne per milking ewe (or hay equivalent). Grazing: early grass in March/April; good grazing on leys or pasture similar for dry stock and lambs.

Additional Points

Fixed Costs per Ewe: Labour £65; Power and Machinery £15; Pproperty £10; Other £10; Total excluding Finance and Rent, £100.

Capital Costs of Equipment: Complete milking unit for 300 ewes (including yokes, bulk tank, dairy equipment, installation): £6,000-£10,000. A small 50 ewe unit can be put together for under £2,500. Any building works would be additional to the above costs.

Acknowledgement: Anthony Hyde, FRICS, FBIAC.

GOAT DAIRYING

		Per Goat	
Performance Level (yield)	Low	Average	High
Milk Yield (litres) (1)	500	800	1200
	£	£	£
Milk Value (2)	137	215	273
Value of Kids (3)	48	48	48
Livestock Depreciation (4)	3	3	3
Output	190	268	326
Variable Costs:			
Concentrates (4)		105	
Forage		15	
Miscellaneous (including vet and med)		15	
Total Variable Costs		135	
Gross Margin per Goat	55	133	191
Stocking Rate: Goats per ha (acre) (zero-grazed system)			
(Equivalent) **Gross Margin** per Forage Hectare...	620	1495	2150
(Equivalent) **Gross Margin** per Forage Acre	250	605	870

Notes

1. *Yield:* Per 300 day lactation, kidding each year. Autumn kidders tend to yield less.

2. *Price:* 40p per litre; seasonal variation from 33p in June to 53p in November. 12.5% solids delivered.

3. *Kid(s):* Prolificacy relates to age, breed, seasonality and feed level. Assumptions: low 140%; average and high 180%. There is very little trade in kids for meat.

4. *Culls and Replacements:* Replacements at £180/head; culls £17.50, average life 6 years. Bucks: 1 per 40-50 does. Does normally mate in autumn; gestation 150 days; young goats can be mated from 6 months.

5. *Concentrates:* Average 0.55 kg concentrate per litre, at £125 per tonne.

6. *Forage:* Average 0.9 kg DM forage per litre at £80 per tonne DM (part purchased, part home-grown). Goats can be grazed but are normally storage fed to avoid problems with worms, fencing, milk taints and pneumonia. Farmers able to produce maize silage will have a better forage conversion ratio.

7. *Miscellaneous:* Bedding £12, vet and med. £24 (includes treatment for out-of-season breeding, vaccination against Johnes and humane disposal of unsaleable kids), sundries £19.

8. *Stocking rate:* Based on home-grown forage.

9. *Labour:* 1 full-time person per 100 goats is a guide, but very dependent on technology employed.

10. *Markets:* There is no government support for goat produce and a strong pound makes imported produce cheap. Some successful businesses have been built on producer processing and retailing. Bulk purchasers of goats milk are few and far between. Herd sizes in the UK range from 50 to 3,000 milking does. Average herd size is growing rapidly as established producers expand with the market at about 15% average annual growth. Prolificacy and technical improvements allow higher annual growth than the market and there is a cycle in milk and stock prices.

Contact: The British Goat Society (Bovey Tracey, Devon (tel. 01626 833168)) registers pedigree animals and publishes a monthly newsletter.

Acknowledgements: The above information originally supplied by *Dr. T. Mottram*, Silsoe Research Institute, Bedford MK45 4HS, amended since by the author.

ANGORA GOATS

	Breeding Does (2)	Subsequent Shearing (2)
Yield of Fibre (kg per year)	14.8	5.45
Price of Fibre (less handling charge) (£ per kg) (3)	3.64	3.48
	£ per Doe	£ per Head
Value of Fibre	53.9	19.0
Value of Kids (1.42 per doe mated) (4)	33.3	-
Value of Cull (5)...........................	3.5	9.4
Less Replacements (5)	9.0	10.0
Output	**81.7**	**18.4**
Variable Costs:		
Concentrates (6)	25.0	5.5
Vet and Med	8.0	0.8
Miscellaneous (7)	10.0	3.2
Total Variable Costs (excl. forage)	**43.0**	**9.5**
Gross Margin per Doe/Head before Forage Costs	38.7	8.9
Forage Variable Costs	8.5	5.5
Gross Margin per Doe/Head	30.2	3.4
Stocking Rate (Does (incl. followers) per ha (acre))	10 (4)	15 (6)
Gross Margin per ha (acre)	302 (122)	51 (21)

Notes

The above figures are for a commercial enterprise. Many UK angora flocks are kept on a semi-commercial or hobby basis, in which case different criteria may apply – does retained longer, mortality rates lower, doe/buck ratio different.

1. Angora goats produce mohair; angora rabbits produce angora; cashgora is produced by angora cross feral goats; cashmere is produced by improved feral goats (valuable 'down' has to be separated from guard hairs; thus, with cashmere production, 'yield of down' must not be confused with 'weight of clip' as percentage down is low and can vary widely). Goat meat is called 'chevon'. UK mohair output is currently around 25 tonnes per year, which indicates a population of between 4,000 and 6,000 animals.

2. The data for Breeding Does include output and inputs for a proportion (4%) of a buck and the doe's progeny. Progeny are sold after 2 clips for breeding or after 3 clips for meat. Stock may be retained for further shearing. This has become more common, as the demand for breeding stock is small, fibre quality has improved and there is little market for meat.

3. Angora goats are usually clipped twice a year. Yield increases over first four clips, but quality decreases. Prices can be volatile, being dependent on fashion and on the world market dominated by South Africa and Texas. Demand and prices are highest for the high quality kid fibre <30 microns in diameter. The following yields and prices have been used:-

   Clip 1: 1.1 kg, £6.5 per kg; clip 2: 2.0 kg, £6.5 per kg; clip 3: 2.5 kg, £3.98 per kg; adult doe: 3.5 kg, adult buck 4.0 kg, £2.78 per kg.

   British Mohair Marketing arranges a collection once a year, in April, and sends the fibre to be cleaned. It is then either returned to the producer or sold. There is a handling charge of 50p per kg of fibre. Membership of BMM costs £30. (Some producers improve their return by processing and using the fibre themselves or selling to local spinners. Commercial processing costs are significant: combing about £1.8 per kg and spinning about £6 per kg).

4. 1.5 kids born alive per doe mated; 2% mortality to each clip. Number of doe kids sold for breeding equal to number of replacements (unless the flock size is changing). Value comprises: 0.17 breeders at £50 each, 1.25 kids for meat at £20 each.

5. Culls. Breeding stock in commercial flocks are culled after six years on average. Doe:buck ratio averages 25:1. Subsequent shearing stock culled after a further 4 clips. Value of all cull stock: £20 each. Depending on quality, the skin can be worth £10 before curing or up to £80 after curing. Replacement costs: does, £50; bucks, £100. Shearing stock, £20 (as transfer from breeding enterprise). Show quality stock command a premium.

6. Concentrates. Price: £135 per tonne on average. Quantities: Kids - 50 kg to clip 2, 15 kg to clip 3; Adults - breeding adults 90 kg per year, shearing 40 kg per year.

7. Veterinary costs can be high. Miscellaneous costs include £1.50 to £2.00 per shearing per head (it may be more) and bedding materials.

8. Angora goats require more management than sheep. Fencing requirements are similar but housing costs rather higher. Margins are particularly sensitive to the value and number of breeding stock sold, yield and value of fibre, kidding percentage and meat values. There is a market for meat from older animals but no market has yet been developed specifically for younger animals. Angoras are probably most successfully run as a subsidiary enterprise on a farm rather than a stand alone operation.

Contact: *British Angora Goat Society*: www.britishangoragoats.org.uk

WILD BOAR

Wild Boar are now being farmed in the UK on more than 60 farms, with a population probably exceeding 2,000 sows. They produce a firm dark meat with a characteristically 'gamey' flavour which is in demand particularly from the hotel and restaurant trade.

Wild Boar come under the Dangerous Wild Animals Act and wild boar farms must be licensed by the Local Authority. There is no uniformity of fee or conditions that have to be met, but typically licences cost £100-£150 and are renewed annually following an inspection of the farm. Enclosures must be secure with strong fencing: a minimum height of at least 1.8m is usually specified and most authorities require 30-80cm below ground plus an additional strand of electric fence inside the main fence. The estimated minimum cost of fencing using approved contractors is from £8 per metre erected plus the hire of a digger. All gates and access areas must be padlocked at all times. However, the Act is under review and there is a recommendation that farmed boar will bee exempt, giving them the same legal status as the domestic pig.

Wild Boar are kept in groups of up to 10 sows with a boar. They are nearly always kept outdoors, often on arable land (as outdoor domestic pigs), although rough land with some natural vegetation, such as scrub, or best of all, woodland, is ideal. Good husbandry requires some basic housing, such as arcs. Large arcs are suitable for a group of gestating sows, or sows running with maturing boarlets. Sows should have access to an individual shelter for farrowing and the first few days of lactation. If good vegetation is available sows may make their own farrowing nest away from the main group with satisfactory results.

Stocking rates vary according to the type of land but about a hectare would be needed for a group of 5 sows and a boar. They will forage actively on suitable terrain but this is unlikely to provide a significant part of their diet. They need to be fed a balanced ration (additive free pig concentrate is suitable but specially formulated feeds are available) with supplementary vegetable material. If a good supply of root crops is available this may replace some concentrate. Wild boar mate and farrow naturally and have few health problems, so little if any intervention is needed. Gilts mature at 18 months. In the wild breeding occurs in the autumn and early winter and the sows farrow from February to March after 4 months gestation. One little per year is the norm. However, most farmed sows maintained at a good nutritional level will give two litters in most years. Young sows produce 2 to 3 boarlets and mature sows 6 to 8. A well-run enterprise should average 7 boarlets per sow per year raised to maturity. Wild boar can live from 12 to 15 years, perhaps more, but in a commercial herd the sows are usually culled at 7 to 8 years old.

The boarlets remain in the family group until they are all weaned together at 8 to 12 weeks (16 at the outside). Although some (usually smaller) producers leave growers to mature in family groups, they are generally separated into grower/finisher groups on rough grass or in open barns. Wild boar will take between 9 and 18 months to reach a slaughter weight of 75-85 kg. This produces a 45-50 kg carcase. They are slaughtered in the same way as pigs. The carcase has more shoulder and less on the hind-quarters than a domestic pig. It can be butchered like a domestic pig or without the skin like venison. The meat from male animals 2 years old or over is too strong, except for sausages, but sows up to 8 years old still have an acceptable carcase and a good cull value. A real problem for some producers is arranging slaughter: abattoirs are currently required to have wild boar specified on their licence and many expect them to be difficult to handle.

Labour requirements are low, owing to the 'hands off' nature of wild boar management. One person might manage a herd of 30-40 sows and fatteners.

In spite of the large and apparently unsatisfied demand for wild boar meat, as with other alternative enterprises, there is no organised marketing system and producers have to develop their own outlets. There are some wholesale butchers and game dealers who will take whole carcass in significant numbers, but many producers organise their own processing into a variety of pre-packed products and arrange their own retailing. Sold at retail the meat commands a considerable margin over the wholesale price, but butchering, packaging and marketing costs have to be considered. Wild boar production can be successful both as a secondary enterprise on a farm or as a stand-alone operation.

Finished boarlets per sow per year	7 (6-9)
Finished carcase weight (over 15 months)	45-50kg
Price per kg deadweight	£3.75 (£3-£4.50)
Depreciation per sow per year (1)	£30
Total Output per Sow	£1,095
Variable Costs:	
Concentrates ....sow (2)	200
.................fatteners (£50 each)	490
Bedding	10
Vet., Med. and Licence	30
Water and electricity	10
Total Variable Costs per Sow	£740
Gross Margin per Sow	£355

1. Cost of sow £400, cull value £200, herd life 7 years, plus share of boar

2. Including share of boar

Capital Costs: Housing and fencing is likely to cost around £4,000 per hectare.

Contact: *The British Wild Boar Association,* PO Box 100, London W6 0ZJ. Tel: 020 8741 7789; www.bwba.co.uk

GRAZING LIVESTOCK UNITS

Dairy cows	1.00	Lowland ewes		0.11
Beef cows (excl. calf)	0.75	Upland ewes		0.08
Heifers in calf (rearing)	0.80	Hill ewes		0.06
Bulls	0.65	Breeding ewe hoggs,		
		½ to 1 year		0.06
Other cattle (excl. intensive beef):		Other sheep, over 1 year		0.08
0-1 year old	0.34	Store lambs, under 1 year		0.04
1-2 years old	0.65	Rams		0.08
2 years old and over	0.80			

Source: as advised by DEFRA for the Farm Business Survey.

Notes

1. Total livestock units on a farm should be calculated by multiplying the above ratios by the *monthly livestock numbers averaged over the whole year*.

2. The ratios are based on feed requirements. Strictly speaking, when calculating stocking density, allowances should also be made for differences in output (e.g. milk yield per cow or liveweight gain per head), breed (e.g. Friesians v. Jerseys), and quantities of non-forage feed consumed.

OTHER LIVESTOCK UNITS

Breeding sows	0.44	Broilers	0.0017
Gilts in pig	0.20	Other table chicken	0.004
Maiden gilts	0.18	Turkeys	0.005
Boars	0.35	Ducks, geese, other poultry	0.003
Other pigs	0.17	Horses	0.80
Cocks, hens, pullets in lay	0.017	Milch goats	0.16
Pullets, 1 week to point of lay	0.003	Other goats	0.11

Source: as advised by DEFRA for the Farm Business Survey.

FORAGE VARIABLE COSTS

£ per hectare (acre) per annum	Grass: Dairying (1)	Grass: Other (1)	Forage Maize (2)	Kale	Fodder Beet
Yield tonnes/ha (tons/acre)	-	-	40 (16)(silage)	45 (18)	80 (32)
Seed	10 (4)	7 (3)	115 (47)	50 (20)	125 (51)
Fertilizer	120 (49)	80 (32)	75 (30)	85 (35)	115 (46)
Sprays	5 (2)	3 (1)	35 (14)	40 (16)	130 (53)
Total	135(55)	90 (36)	225 (91)	175 (71)	370 (150)

	Forage Peas	Forage Rape	Turnips	Stubble Turnips	Swedes
Yield tonnes/ha (tons/acre)	35 (14)	35 (14)	65 (26)	35 (14)	75 (30)
Seed	65 (26)	15 (6)	15 (6)	15 (6)	30 (12)
Fertilizer	40 (16)	65 (26)	80 (33)	70 (28)	80 (33)
Sprays	10 (4)	20 (8)	40 (16)	20 (8)	40 (16)
Total	115 (46)	100 (40)	135 (55)	105 (42)	150 (61)

(1) These are average figures only. Intensively silaged and grazed grass may have much higher fertilizer costs in particular - even as much as £200 (80) for dairying. The seed costs will vary according to the proportion, if any, of permanent pasture and the length of the leys. Fertilizer inputs are often less on permanent pasture too, but this depends largely on the attitude of the farmer/manager, which will also be reflected in the stocking rates and productive levels per animal achieved. The dairying cost covers both cows and followers; the cost for cows alone is likely to be higher.

(2) Contract work on maize: drilling £34 (14); harvesting £80 (32), or £134 (54) to include carting and clamping. The area grown in the United Kingdom was 131,000 ha in 2005.

Standing maize crops are typically sold for between £425 and £525/ha (£170-210/acre) but can be as high as £800/ha (£325/acre) and as low as £250/ha (£100/acre), depending on the potential yield of the crop and local supply and demand. The sale value averages approx. £25/tonne (at 30% dry matter).

Whole Crop Cereals (winter wheat; fermented). Variable costs as for combined crop (see page 16) plus contract harvesting at £150 per ha (£60 per acre). Fresh yield averages 27.5 tonnes per ha (11 tons per acre). Urea treatment (for higher dry matter): add £100 per ha (£40 per acre) for urea prills.

Labour: grass, pages 143; kale, page 144-145; conservation labour, pages 143-145. Conservation machinery, page 143.

Grass Silage and Hay Costs and Value

Estimated average costs (for 2007) of producing and harvesting, on a full costs basis (i.e. including rental value of the land, all labour, share of general overheads, etc.) are: Hay: £90 per tonne; Silage: £25 per tonne.

Approximately half the silage cost is for growing the grass and half for harvesting and storage. The % breakdown of total costs is typically as follows:

Variable Costs:	Fertilizer	Seeds and Sprays	Contract	Sundries
Silage	23	1	10	5
Hay	18	1	2	2

Fixed Costs:	Rent	Labour	Tractors	Deprec. & Reps.	FYM/Lime
Silage	21	10	16	9	5
Hay	25	16	19	12	5

Sale Value of hay and (far less common because of its bulk) silage vary widely according to the region and type of season (supply/demand situation), quality and time of year.

Hay (pick-up baled) has an average ex-farm sale value of £65 to £70 per tonne for seed hay (main range November to May £60 to £75) and £52.50-£57.50 for meadow hay (main range November to May £50 to £65); prices are higher in the west than the east and more after a dry summer (giving low yields of grass) than a wet one. Prices tend to be nearer £80-£90 per tonne for horses. Big bale hay is cheaper, averaging £40 to £45 per tonne, ranging mainly between £30 and £50 per tonne.

Grass silage is typically valued at about £30 a tonne delivered (up to £40 when forage is very short in an area, down as low as £22.50 if it is plentiful), maize silage approx. £25 a tonne.

Relative Costs of Grazing, Conserved Grass, etc.

	Yield DM tonnes/ha (acre)	Cost per tonne DM (£)	MJ per kg DM	Pence per MJ of ME in DM
Grazed Grass	11.1 (4.5)	38.6	11.8	0.33
Kale (direct drilled)	6.9 (2.8)	42.0	11.0	0.38
Forage Turnips (direct drilled)	6.9 (2.8)	38.1	10.2	0.37
Grass Silage	11.1 (4.5)	69.1	10.9	0.63
Big Bale Silage	11.1 (4.5)	74.1	10.9	0.68
Purchased Hay (1)	-	76.5	8.8	0.87
Brewers' Grains (2)	-	90.5	10.0	0.91
Concentrates (3)	-	145	12.8	1.14

(1) at £65 per tonne (2) at £20 per tonne (3) 14% CP, delivered in bulk, £125 per tonne

Notes

1. The above data was reviewed in 2006 by Tony Evans at The Andersons Centre, with a few changes made in the prices of purchased feeds.

2. In interpreting the above figures for use in planning feed use on the individual farm it is important to remember two points: (a) that own land, labour and capital for equipment are required for home-produced fodder but not for purchased feed, and much more storage is required, and (b) the limitation on the consumption of bulk fodder by ruminant livestock - although this very much depends upon its quality/digestibility.

Relative Value of Feeds (based on their energy contents fed to dairy cows)

These values, given in a table in this position in previous editions, are now to be found on page 228.

FODDER CROPS, GRASSES AND CLOVERS
SEED PRICES (2006) AND SEED RATES

Crop	Price	Seed Rate per hectare
Fodder Kale	£8 to £11 per kg	5 to 7 kg
Swedes	£25 per kg	3.0 to 4.0 kg broadcast
	£46 per kg graded	0.6 kg precision drilled
Stubble Turnips	£4.00 to £10 per kg	3.7 kg drilled,
		5.0 kg broadcast
Rape	£1.75 per kg	3.8 kg drilled (7.5 kg broadcast)
Mustard	£1.30 per kg	20 to 25 kg
Rape and Turnips	£17 per hectare	1.25 kg rape
		3.75 kg turnips
Kale, Swede and Turnips	£51 per hectare	1.85 kg kale, 0.5 kg swede,
		1.85 kg turnips
Forage Maize: Silage	£115 to £125 per hectare	110,000 to 115,000 seeds
Forage Maize: zero grazed	£143 to £165 per hectare	130,000 to 150,000 seeds
Arable Silage	£85 per hectare	125 kg oats, 60 kg tares
Tares/Vetch	£1 per kg	100 to 125 kg
Westerwold Ryegrass	£1.50 per kg	35 kg
Italian Ryegrass	£1.20 to £1.60 per kg	33 to 50 kg
Perennial Ryegrass	£1.10 to £1.50 per kg	22 to 33 kg
Hybrid Ryegrass	£1.20 to £1.60 per kg	30 to 40 kg
Cocksfoot	£2.60 per kg	20 to 25 kg
Timothy	£2.80 per kg	7 to 9 kg
Meadow Fescue	£2.60 per kg	11 to 13 kg
Broad Red Clover	£5.50 to £6.00 per kg	18 to 22 kg
Alsike Clover	£4.80 per kg	18 to 22 kg
White Clover	£4.50 to £7.50 per kg	5 kg
Kent Wild White Clover	£7.50 to £9.50 per kg	—
Lucerne	£3.90 per kg	18 to 22 kg
Sainfoin	£2.00 per kg	60 to 90 kg
Forage Rye	£0.60 per kg	180 kg
Rye and Ryegrass	£80 per hectare	125 kg rye
		22 kg Italian Ryegrass
1 year leys	£53 to £75 per hectare	—
2 year leys	£50 to £67 per hectare	—
4-6 year leys	£69 to £82 per hectare	—
Long-term Ley	£80 to £91 per hectare	—
White Clover Ley	£81 to £87 per hectare	—
Red Clover Ley	£69 to £72 per hectare	—
Wye College mixture	£60 per hectare	—
Horse grazing	£50 to £88 per hectare	—
Game Cover mixture	£59 per hectare	—
Set-aside mixture	£53 to £60 per hectare	
Field Margin mixture	£65 to £80 per hectare	
Gallop mixture	£3.00 per kg	100-250 kg

3. PIGS, POULTRY, TROUT, RABBIT

PIGS

1. Breeding and Rearing (to 30 kg liveweight):
per sow per year and per 30 kg pig reared

Performance Level	*Average*		*High*	
	per sow	per pig	per sow	per pig
	£	£	£	£
Weaners: (ave) 21.5 (1) @ £33.00 (3)	710	33.00		
(high) 24.5 (2) @ £33.00 (3)			809	33.00
Less Livestock Depreciation (4)	36	1.66	44	1.78
Output	674	31.34	765	31.22
Variable Costs:				
Food (5)	289	13.45	312	12.74
Miscellaneous (6)	69	3.20	72	2.95
Total Variable Costs.	358	16.65	384	15.69
Gross Margin (per year)	316	14.69	381	15.53

Notes

1. Weaners per sow - average: 9.75 reared per litter, 2.2 litters per year = 21.5 weaners per sow per year. (The average has recovered somewhat since early 2004 after falling in recent years due to the wasting diseases PMWS and PDNS).

2. Weaners per sow - high: 10.53 reared per litter, 2.32 1itters per year = 24.5 weaners per sow per year.

3. Price – assumed pig cycle average. (See note (N.B.) on p. 121). Prices for 30 kg weaners have varied from £10 to £55 during the past decade but have been between £25 and £40 in the last three years.

4. Average livestock depreciation assumes an in-pig gilt purchase price of £135, a cull value per sow of £80 and a 45% replacement rate (i.e. approximately 6 litters per sow life). Sow mortality 5%. Boars (1 per 22.5 sows) purchased at £580 (40% a year replacement), sold at £65. 'High' compared with 'Average': higher gilt and boar purchase prices and slightly fewer sows per boar assumed.

5. Food – 2.15 tonnes per sow: sow 1.25, boar (per sow) 0.05, other feed (per sow) 0.85. Price of feed consumed: £135 per tonne; (average of 60% sow (and boar) feed (at £105) and 40% piglet and rearing feed (at £180), and of home-mixed and purchased compounds). High performance: extra piglet and rearing feed for additional weaners. Piglets weaned at average 3.75 weeks, 7.25kg weight.

6. Average: vet. and med. £39, transport £11, straw and bedding £8, miscellaneous £10. (Electricity and gas [£15] and water [£5] included in fixed costs below).

7. Direct Labour Cost per sow: average £168, good £132; per weaner: average £7.80, good £5.36. See further page 150. Other Fixed Costs: approx. £120.

8. Building Costs: see pages 188-189.

   N.B. Outdoor Breeding: see page 123.

   Acknowledgement: The main data source for the margins within the Pigs section is the *Pig Yearbook* (Meat and Livestock Commission), 2006 and previous years, but the pig and feed price assumptions are entirely the author's responsibility. Small differences in the relationship between these can of course cause large differences in margins. Big variations can occur between farms.   The weaner price is crucial as regards the relative margins between breeding and rearing, and finishing.

2. Feeding (from 30 kg liveweight): per pig

A. Average Performance

	Pork £	Cutter £	Bacon £
Sale Value	59.90	68.90	75.60
Less Weaner Cost*	33.00	33.00	33.00
Mortality charge	1.50	1.65	1.80
Output	25.40	34.25	40.80
Variable Costs:			
Food......................	15.30	19.40	22.90
Miscellaneous	3.50	4.00	4.50
Total Variable Costs	18.80	23.40	27.40
Gross Margin	**6.60**	**10.85**	**13.40**
Liveweight (kg)	76	87	96.1
Deadweight (kg)	56	65	72
Killing out (%)	74	75	75
Price per kg deadweight (p)	107	106	989
Price per kg liveweight (p)	78.8	79.2	73.5
Food Conversion Rate	2.6	2.7	2.8
Food per pig (kg)	120	154	1855
Average Cost of Food per tonne** ..	£120	£126	£135
Food Cost per kg Liveweight Gain ..	33.3p	34.0p	37.9p
Liveweight Gain per day (kg)	0.62	0.65	0.66
Feeding period (weeks, approx.)	11	13	14
Mortality (per cent)	4.5	5.0	4.8
Direct Labour Cost per pig	£3.57	£4.47	£4.30

B. High Performance (same pig price)

Food Conversion Rate	2.4	2.5	2.55
Food per pig (kg)	110	143	172
Food Cost per pig (£5/t less than average)	£13.60	£17.25	£20.40
Food Cost per kg Liveweight Gain ..	29.5p	30.3p	30.9p
Gross Margin per pig	**£8.50**	**£13.15**	**£16.05**
Direct Labour Cost per pig	£3.35	£3.80	£4.25

*   Weaner cost assumes on farm transfer. If purchased (i.e., feeding only) transport and purchasing costs have to be added: these are very variable but average about £1.75 per weaner.

** Average of home-mixed and purchased compounds. There can be big variations in feed costs per tonne between farms, according to whether the food is purchased as compounds or home-mixed, bought in bulk or in bags, size of unit, etc.

Labour: see page 150. Building Costs: see pages 188-189.

Sensitivity Analysis. The effect on gross margins per pig (£) of changes in important variables (other things being equal) are as follows (per porker, cutter and baconer respectively). Price: 5p per kg dw difference: 2.80, 3.25, 3.60. Food Cost/tonne: £10 difference: 1.20, 1.54, 1.85. FCR: 0.1 difference: 0.59, 0.72, 0.82. The effect of differences in the cost per weaner is obvious.

N.B. Pig prices are notoriously difficult to predict. In 1996 average GB prices per kg deadweight were 138p. By 1999 they had fallen to 79p on average. Over the last three years the range has been 96p to 112p, with the average for 2005 being 104p. The level shown above of 105p is an estimate for 2007.

3. Combined Breeding, Rearing, and Feeding: per pig

	Pork £		Cutter £		Bacon £	
Level of Performance*	Average	High	Average	High	Average	High
Sale Value	59.90	59.90	68.90	68.90	75.60	75.60
Sow/boar deprecn.......	1.66	1.78	1.66	1.78	1.66	1.78
Mortality charge	1.50	1.30	1.65	1.50	1.80	1.65
Output	56.74	56.82	65.59	65.62	72.14	72.17
Food	28.75	26.34	32.95	30.00	36.35	33.14
Miscellaneous	6.70	6.45	7.20	6.95	7.70	7.45
Total Variable Costs....	35.45	32.79	40.15	36.95	44.04	40.59
Gross Margin per pig....	**21.29**	**24.03**	**25.44**	**28.67**	**28.10**	**31.58**
Gross Margin per sow...	*458*	*589*	*549*	*703*	*604*	*774*
Labour cost per pig	10.73	8.25	11.62	8.69	12.51	9.14
Labour cost per sow	231	202	250	213	269	224

* Performance levels refer to breeding and rearing differences as on pages 120-121 and, for feeding, differences in food conversion rate, food costs and labour cost only.

4. Further Performance Data

Source: The Meat and Livestock Commission's 'Pig Yearbook 2006' (data for the year ended Sept. 2005).

		Performance Level	
A. Breeding	Average	Top Third*	Top 10%*
Sow replacements (%)	46.2	44.8	54.8
Sow sales and deaths (%)	44.7	41.0	43.4
Sow mortality (%)	4.7	3.4	3.9
Litters per sow per year	2.22	2.27	2.32
Pigs reared per litter	9.61	10.09	10.02
Pigs reared per sow per year	21.5	23.3	24.5
Weight of pigs produced (kg)	7.1	7.2	7.2
Average weaning age (days)	26	26	26
Sow feed per sow per year (tonnes)..	1.34	1.33	1.21
Feed per pig reared (kg)	68	63	54
Sow feed cost per tonne (£)	105	102	95
Sow feed cost per sow per year (£) ..	141	135	114
Feed cost per pig reared (£)	7.24	6.40	5.17
B. Rearing	Average	Top Third**	Top 10%**
Weight of pigs at start (kg).........	7.3	7.1	7.1
Weight of pigs produced (kg)	36.3	36.1	37.8
Mortality (%)	3.4	3.3	2.2
Feed conversion ratio.............	1.70	1.65	1.55
Daily gain (g)	509	515	548
Feed cost per tonne (£)............	183	172	165
Feed cost per kg gain (p)	30.6	27.4	25.6
Feed cost per pig reared (£)	9.16	7.98	7.87

* selected on basis of pigs reared per sow per year.

** selected on basis of feed cost per kg liveweight gain.

C. Feeding	Average	Top Third*	Top 10%*
Weight of pigs at start (kg).........	25.9	30.0	31.7
Weight of pigs produced (kg)	96..9	101.8	103.0
Mortality (%)...................	6.5	5.2	5.3
Feed conversion ratio.............	2.74	2.65	2.70
Daily gain (g)...................	639	707	703
Feed cost per tonne (£)............	120	101	91
Feed cost per kg gain (p)..........	32.8	26.7	25.6
Feed cost per pig reared (£)........	23.3	19.2	17.5
Carcase weight (kg)..............	74.2	75.7	76.1

*   selected on basis of feed costs per kg liveweight gain.

Feed conversion ratio for rearing and feeding combined, from 7.5kg to 85kg liveweight was 2.39 for the year ending Sept 2005.

5. Outdoor v Indoor Performance

A. Breeding	Outdoor	Indoor
Average number sows and gilts	820	406
Sow replacements (%)	45.9	47.1
Sow sales and deaths (%).........	45.2	43.8
Sow mortality (%)	5.6	4.9
Average age at weaning (days)	27	27
Pigs born alive per litter	10.74	11.12
Pigs reared per litter..............	9.61	9.81
Litters per sow per year	2.20	2.25
Pigs reared per sow per year	21.2	22.10
Sow feed per sow per year (tonnes)..	1.42	1.27
Sow feed cost per tonne (£)	110	103
Sow feed cost per sow per year (£) ..	156	130
Feed cost per pig reared (£)	8.10	6.67
B. Rearing		
Weight of pigs at start (kg)	7.2	7.5
Weight of pigs produced (kg)	36.4	36.3
Mortality (%)...................	3.7	3.0
Feed conversion ratio.............	1.64	1.76
Daily gain.....................	505	512
Feed cost per tonne (£)	174	184
Feed cost per kg gained (p)	28.4	32.5
Feed cost per pig reared (£)	8.29	9.90

Stocking Rate for outdoor pigs is mainly between 12 and 25 per hectare (5 and 10 per acre), 20 (8) being the most common. Good drainage is essential. A low rainfall and mild climate are also highly desirable.

In 2003, MLC's Agrosoft puts the cost of establishing a sow herd on a greenfield site at £1,800 per sow place for an indoor unit and about £600 per sow place for an outdoor unit.

Over 35% of the UK breeding sow herd is now kept outdoors. The percentage of outdoor rearing/finishing pigs is in the order of 5%.

Further details can be found in 'Pig Production 2003-04' by Andrew Sheppard, Centre for Rural Research, University of Exeter (address on page 250).

EGG PRODUCTION

(brown egg layers, 52 week laying period)

Level of Performance....	Cages				Free Range	
	Average		High		Average	
	per bird	per doz eggs	per bird	per doz eggs	per bird	per doz eggs
	£	p	£	p	£	p
Egg Returns	10.33	40.0	10.80	40.0	16.50	66.0
Less Livestock Depreciation	2.80	10.8	2.80	10.4	3.00	12.0
Output (per year)	7.53	29.2	8.00	29.6	13.50	54.0
Variable Costs:						
Food	5.31	20.6	5.31	19.7	6.40	25.6
Miscellaneous	1.50	5.8	1.50	5.6	1.45	5.8
Total Variable Costs....	6.81	26.4	6.81	25.3	7.85	31.4
Gross Margin	**0.72**	**2.8**	**1.19**	**4.3**	**5.65**	**22.6**

Notes:

Hen-housed data are used throughout, i.e. the total costs and returns are divided by the number of birds housed at the commencement of the laying period.

A. Cage Production

1. The yields assumed are:

   Average .... 310 (25.83 dozen)

   High .... 324 (27.00 dozen)

2. The average price assumed (for 2007), 40p per dozen, includes all quantity and quality bonuses. Farmer to shop and consumer prices are well above packer to producer levels and normally 35p and 65p per dozen premiums respectively are required.

3. Livestock depreciation—the average point of lay pullet is priced at £2.50 (16/17 weeks old); old hen processors are currently charging between 6.5 and 21.5 pence/bird to take them away.

4. The food price assumed (for 2007) is £125 per tonne. The feed cost is dependent on breed, housing and environmental conditions, quantity purchased and type of ration. Quantity of feed used = 42.5 kg.

5. Direct Labour Costs: average 1.22p per bird, premium 96p. See page 150.

   Housing Costs: see page 189. Deadstock depreciation averages about £1 per caged bird.

B. Free Range Production

1. Egg yields: 300 (25 dozen).

2. Average price: 66p per dozen.

3. Quantity of feed used = 47.4 kg. Price £135 per tonne.

4. Direct Labour Costs: average £3.90 per bird, dependent on automation.

Acknowledgement: The figures in the whole of the poultry section are provided by Tony Warner, *AAW Poultry Consultancy*, Lilleshall, Newport, Shropshire.

REARING PULLETS

(Average per bird reared)

	£
Value of 16/17 weeks old bird	2.50
Less Chicks 1.02 (1) @ 52p (including levy)	0.53
Output	1.97
Variable Costs:	
Food: 6.25 kg @ £125 per tonne	0.78
Miscellaneous (2)	0.71
Total Variable Costs	1.49
Gross Margin	**0.48**

1. Assumes 3 per cent mortality, but 2 per cent allowed in price.

2. Excluding transport (15p), but including full vaccination costs.

   Labour (34p); deadstock depreciation (38p).

TABLE POULTRY

A. **Broilers** (per bird sold at 41 days)	p
Returns: 2.35 kg per bird @ 50.0p per kg lw	117.5
Less Cost of Chick	25.4
Output	92.1
Variable Costs:	
Food: 4.10 kg per bird @ £168 per tonne	68.9
Heat, Light, Miscellaneous	15.1
Total Variable Costs	84.0
Gross Margin	8.1

Capital cost of housing and equipment: £6.25 per broiler space (depreciation cost approximately 5.4p per bird sold). Housing Costs: see page 189.

Labour: 4.6p, excluding catching and cleaning out (4.5p) but includes management; see page 150.

B. **All Year Round Turkey** (per bird sold at 20 weeks, sexed stags)	£
Returns: 14.3 kg @ £1.10 per kg OR*	15.73
Less cost of poult	1.70
Output	14.03
Variable Costs:	
Food: 50 kg @ £175 per tonne	8.75
Miscellaneous	3.95
Total Variable Costs	12.70
Gross Margin	1.33

10% mortality allowed in cost of poult figures.

* Rearing turkeys all the year round now tends to be just in the hands of a few large companies. Cheap imports has led to many smaller operators giving up.

C. *Christmas Turkey* (Traditional Farm Fresh – indoor reared)

	Light	Medium	Heavy
	£	£	£
Returns per bird sold	22.27	25.19	23.03
Less Cost of Poult	3.70	3.70	3.05
Output	18.57	21.49	19.98
Variable Costs:			
Food	4.20	5.45	5.83
Miscellaneous	2.45	2.80	3.25
Total Variable Costs	6.65	8.25	9.08
Gross Margin	**11.92**	**13.24**	**10.90**
Killing Age (weeks)	18	22	22
Live weight (kg)	7.2	8.3	12.0
Oven ready weight (kg)	6.1	6.9	9.8
Food Conversion	3.2	3.7	2.8
Food per bird (kg)	22.7	30.3	33.3
Food cost per tonne	£185	£180	£175

1. 7, 8 and 10% mortality allowed for in cost of poult figures for light, medium and heavy weights respectively.

2. Light and medium = slow growing sexed hens.
   Heavy = stags (as hatched).

3. Price per kilogram:
   Christmas (fresh, eviscerated): hens 330-400p range; stags 210-260p range.

Note: With both turkey enterprises considerable variations will occur between individual strains and because of different production systems and feeding regimes. Free range systems for example will show higher costs and returns. The figures should therefore be used only as rough guidelines.

D. *Roasters (Capons)* (per bird sold at 12 weeks; Christmas – males only)

	£
Returns: 4.8 kg @ £2.60 per kg O.R	12.48
Less Cost of Chick	0.65
Output	11.83
Variable costs:	
Food: 14.3 kg per bird @ £175 per tonne	2.50
Miscellaneous	1.27
Total Variable Costs	3.77
Gross Margin	8.06

10% mortality allowed for in cost of chick figures.

E. Ducks *(Aylesbury Type)* (per bird sold at 7 weeks)

	£
Returns: 2.8 kg @ £4.50 per kg O.R.	12.60
Less Cost of Duckling	1.92
Output	10.68
Variable Costs:	
Food: 9.5 kg per bird @ £197 per tonne	1.82
Miscellaneous	1.72
Total Variable Costs.	3.54
Gross Margin	**7.14**

Heavier ducks of the Pekin type can be grown to 15-16 weeks, when oven-ready weights of 3.5-4.0 kg can be realised.

Day-old costs allow for 10% mortality.

F. Geese (Traditional Farm Fresh – free range and dry plucked)

	£
Returns: 5.0 kg @ £7.50 per kg O.R.	37.50
Less Cost of Gosling	5.90
Output	31.60
Variable Costs:	
Food: 20.0 kg @ £185 per tonne	3.70
Miscellaneous	2.04
Total Variable Costs	5.74
Gross Margin.	**25.86**

Day-old costs allow for 6% mortality.

RAINBOW TROUT

	£ per tonne of fish
Sales: 1 tonne of fish @ £1.50 per kg	1,500
Less 4,000 fingerlings @ 5.5p each	220
Output	1,280
Variable Costs:	
Food: 1 tonne @ £675 per tonne	675
Vet. and med; miscellaneous	125
Water environment costs	20
Total Variable Costs	820
Gross Margin	**460**

Notes

1. Fish growing to 350g from fingerlings at 4.5g.

2. Prices are estimated ex-farm to processor or wholesaler. Higher prices of up to £4.20 per kg can be achieved by selling direct to retailers, caterers and consumers at, say farmers markets, but significant additional costs are associated with such sales.

3. Fingerlings price: varies according to quantity ordered and time of year.

4. Average feeding period, 10 months. Mortality, from fingerling to market size, 15%. Food conversion ratio, 1.0:1. The price for fish food is for a pigmented high oil expanded pellet.

5. Current capital costs for construction of earth pond unit approximately £60 per cubic metre, to include buildings, holding systems and installation of water supply and services, but excluding land.

6. Labour requirement: the basic norm has in the past been 1 man per 50 tonnes of fish produced per annum on a table fish farm, but to remain competitive farmers now need to produce at least 150 tonnes per annum of table fish per man.

Acknowledgement: British Trout Association, The Rural Centre, West Mains, Ingliston, Edinburgh, EH28 8NZ. Tel: 0131472 4080 www.britishtrout.co.uk

MEAT RABBITS

Although the consumption of rabbit meat in the UK is low, at less than 2oz per person per year, most of it is imported. Commercial rabbit production is an intensive livestock enterprise and will probably require planning permission and building regulation approval from the Local Authority.

A meat rabbit unit needs a weather- and vermin-proof building, which is insulated, well-drained and has good ventilation, lighting and a water supply. Housing can be fully environment controlled to give good feed conversion rates and better winter conditions for both stock and personnel, or be natural environment, which has lower capital and running costs and possibly keeps animals healthier. Rabbits are kept in wire cages, usually in one tier, ideally suspended; a single tier system needs 10-12 square feet per cage. Feed hoppers, drinkers and nest boxes are required. Some experimental work to provide less intensive conditions for the animals, possibly with outside access, is in progress, but is at an early stage.

New Zealand White or Californian stock is used. Young does are bought in at 12 weeks and mated at 16-20 weeks. Bucks are bought at 16 weeks and first mated at 20 weeks. A ratio of one buck to 10-20 does is recommended. Gestation is 31 days. Average litter size is 8-9, of which 6-7 should be successfully fattened. Re-mating can be immediately post-partum or up to 6 weeks afterwards; the average is about 21 days. A doe can have a useful life of 10-12 litters over 18 months; less productive animals may be culled sooner. An overall mortality rate of up to 12.5% can be expected.

Young rabbits are weaned at 35-42 days at about 2.5-3 lb and then fed ad-lib until they are ready for marketing at 5.5-6.5lb liveweight at 11-13 weeks. Food conversion rate, including the doe's feed and a share of the buck's is around 4:1. A balanced ration can be obtained for £165 per tonne in bulk but may cost up to £185 per tonne. A doe should produce around 50 meat rabbits each year but experienced producers would aim for 60-70. Health, hygiene and good stockmanship are crucial to the enterprise. One full-time person can look after 250-300 does and their progeny.

There are only a few buyers and processors of meat rabbits in the UK and they do not cover all parts of the country. Hence transport costs may have to be allowed for. The demand for rabbit meat is seasonal - more is eaten in the winter than the summer, which can pose marketing problems. Producers are advised to adjust their production by 15 to 20% in summer to allow for this. An individual producer may develop local markets but this will require initiative. There may be a market for the manure but again this would have to be developed.

Capital Costs	£	No./50 does	£/50 does
Doe at 12 weeks	10	50	500
Buck at 16 weeks	12	3	36
Cage	10	87	870
Drinker	5	87	435
Nest box	4	50	200
Building (new): (10 sq.ft./cage at £3/sq.ft. x 1.75)	52.50/doe		2625

	£/doe/year	£/50 does/year
48 young at 2.6kg at £1.25/kg (1)	156	7800
Depreciation (2)	4.5	225
Output.	151.5	7575
Variable Costs		
Feed (3)	77.5	3875
Vet and Medicine	1.7	85
Bedding	1.8	90
Misc. including electricity	4	200
Total Variable Costs	85	4250
Gross Margin...	**66.5**	**3325**

1. £1.17 to £1.35 depending on delivery and collection

2. Cull value: Does £1.5 over 2 years. Bucks £1.5 over 3 years. Both 10% mortality.

3. Food conversion 4:1 at £165 per tonne including allowance for doe and share of buck.

Acknowledgement: David Blythe, *Woldsway Foods Ltd.* Tel: 01754 890641. www.woldsway.co.uk

IV. LABOUR

1. LABOUR COST

1. Statutory Minimum Wage Rates

The following rates are applicable from 1st October 2006. (As at August, 2006 they were only 'Revised proposals', and not yet confirmed). The minimum weekly rates relate to a 39-hour standard week of normal hours worked on any five days between Monday and Saturday.

A. *Normal Hours (Standard Rates)*

Grade		Weekly Rate	Hourly Rate	Overtime per Hour
		£	£	£
1.	Initial Grade Over 16 years	208.65	5.35	8.03
	Under 16 years	-	2.68	4.02
2.	*Standard Worker*...................	*223.86*	*5.74*	*8.61*
3.	Lead Worker	246.09	6.31	9.47
4.	Craft Grade	264.03	6.77	10.16
5.	Supervisory Grade	280.02	7.18	10.77
6.	Farm Management Grade	302.25	7.75	11.63
	Apprentice: Years 1 & 2	134.16	3.44	5.16
	Advance Apprentice Year 2	168.09	4.31	6.47

Night work rates are £1.14 per hour; standby rates £22.75 per day; dog rates £6.30 per week.

B. *Flexible Working*

Grade		Number of days basic hours worked	Weekly Rate	Hourly Rate	Overtime per Hour
			£	£	£
1.	Initial Grade (16+ only)....	4 to 5	219.18	5.62	8.03
		6	223.08	5.72	8.03
2.	Standard Worker	4 to 5	235.17	6.03	8.61
		6	239.46	6.14	8.61
3.	Lead Worker.............	4 to 5	258.57	6.63	9.47
		6	263.25	6.75	9.47
4.	Craft Grade	4 to 5	277.29	7.11	10.16
		6	282.36	7.24	10.16
5.	Supervisory Grade	4 to 5	294.06	7.54	10.77
		6	299.52	7.68	10.77
6.	Farm Management Grade ...	4 to 5	317.46	8.14	11.63
		6	323.31	8.29	11.63

Notes

1. The new grading structure, comprising six grades instead of the previous five, was introduced in 2005. The Manual Harvest Worker category, introduced in 2003, was abolished. Flexible working rates were set for each of the six new grades. For 2006 the Basic Trainee Grade was renamed the Initial Grade. All age differentials were abolished apart from the under 16 category in the Initial Grade.

2. Part standby duty days are paid at half the rates given above.

3. A deduction up to a maximum £1.50 a week may be made for a house and up to £29.05 a week or £4.15 a day for other accommodation. There are specified provisions for sick pay, paid bereavement leave and paid paternity leave (3 days).

Full details are available from the Agricultural Wages Board for England and Wales (Telephone: 020 7238 5862).

Holiday Pay

Holidays with pay. The number of days holiday that workers are entitled to in a year depends on the number of days worked each week. For those working full-time, 5 days a week, the 2006 Wages Board Order increased holidays from 22 to 23 days per year. There are rules as to timing.

For part-time workers the number of days worked per week is based on the total hours worked over the 12 months ending on the last 5th April.

2. Estimated Average Earnings, Year 2007

Government statistics are no longer available for different categories of worker as listed above; the last year such data was available was 1997. The figure below for all hired men is approximately 39% more than the 1997 average, which is by how much the statutory minimum wage has risen between 1997 and 2006; the retail price index has risen by approximately 26% over that period. The differentials for the listed categories of worker are based on the average differentials for the three years 1995 to 1997 (they differed very little indeed during those years). The same applies to the hours of work.

Type of Worker	Average Total Earnings Annual	Average Total Earnings Per Week	Total Hours Per Week
	£	£	
All Hired Men	19,650	378	47.4
Foremen.........................	23,500	452	47.4
Dairy Herdsmen	23,800	458	52.7
Other Stockmen	19,750	380	46.5
Tractor Drivers	20,900	402	49.4
General Farm Workers	18,250	351	46.7
Horticultural Workers	16,550	318	42.4

3. Typical Annual Labour Cost

Estimated for the 2007 calendar year, based on a Standard Worker.

	Average Annual Cost(1)	Average Weekly Cost	Average Hourly Cost(2)
	£	£	£
Minimum Wage (basic standard and worker rate). .	11,830	227.5	6.74
National Insurance Contribution and Employers Liability Insurance	1,625	31.25	
Minimum Cost	13,455	258.75	7.67
Overtime, average 10 hours per working week @ £8.61 (+ NIC, ELI)	4,400	84.62	
	17,855	343.37	10.17
'Premium' over basic rate average £42.50 per week (+ NIC, ELI)	2,515	48.35	
Total Cost (3,4)	20,370	391.73	11.61

(NIC = National Insurance Contribution; ELI = Employer's Liability Insurance)

1. Estimated average annual cost higher than 2006 AWB rate as figures based on calendar year rather than Oct-Oct AWB year.
2. Hours, excluding overtime, based on 45 weeks (of 39 hours) per year, i.e. statutory holidays (23 days), public holidays (8 days) and illness (4 days), have been deducted.
3. Annual cost (or net value) of cottages, value of perquisites, contribution towards payment of the council tax, etc., would have to be added where appropriate.
4. Total average worker's gross earnings on the above assumptions = £18,625 a year, £358 a week, £9.18 an hour.

4. Assessing Annual Labour Requirements

The regular labour staff required for a farm is sometimes assessed by calculating the total number of Standard Man-Days (Man-Work Units), as given on page 229. The number of days supplied by casual labour is first deducted, then 15% is added for general maintenance work; no allowance is made for management, for which 7.5% may be added if required. It is assumed that 275 Standard Man-Days are provided annually per man, including national average hours of overtime and allowing for holidays and illness; allowance needs to be made for any manual labour supplied by the farmer himself. A full-time dairyperson will average 300 SMD a year, again including overtime. (1 SMD = 8 labour hours a year.)

This is a crude calculation in that it makes no allowance for seasonality and the special circumstances of an individual farm, such as soil type, level of mechanization, and condition and layout of the buildings.

The following sections supply the type of data that should be used in assessing labour requirements.

2. LABOUR HOURS AVAILABLE FOR FIELD WORK

(per man per month)

	Total Ordinary Hours (1)	Adjusted Ordinary Hours (2)	% Workable	Available Ordinary Hours (3)	Available Overtime Hours (4)	**Total Available Hours**	Total Available '8-hour Days' (5)
January	177	148	50	74	28 (61)	**102** (135)	13 (17)
February	160	134	50	67	33 (55)	**100** (122)	12½ (15)
March	172	149	60	89	69 (82)	**158** (171)	20 (21½)
April	161	139	65	90	86	**176**	22
May	171	151	70	106	110	**216**	27
June	170	150	75	112	112	**224**	28
July	177	157	75	118	113	**231**	29
August	169	150	75	112	104	**216**	27
September	172	152	70	106	82 (69)	**188** (195)	23½ (24½)
October	177	153	65	99	63 (83)	**162** (182)	20 (23)
November	172	144	50	72	26 (59)	**98** (131)	12 (16½)
December	161	135	50	67	25 (65)	**92** (132)	11½ (16½)

(1) 40 hour week, less public holidays. No deductions have been made for other holidays because they may be taken at various times of the year.

(2) After deducting (a) for illness (10 per cent Nov. to Feb., 7½% March, April and Oct., 5% May to Sept.), and (b) for contingencies and non-delayable maintenance (½ hour per day).

(3) Adjusted Ordinary Hours x percentage Workable.

(4) Maximum 4 overtime hours per day summer, 3 hours winter, and 12 to 14 hours' work at weekends, according to season. Same adjustments for illness and percentage workable as for ordinary hours. Figures in brackets indicate hours available if headlights used up to limit of overtime stated. The percentage overtime (without headlights) available from weekend work as opposed to evenings = (January to December respectively): 100, 78, 58, 50, 40, 40, 41, 42, 53, 67, 100, 100.

(5) Total available hours ÷ 8.

Notes

(1) These figures relate to medium land. The percentage workability will be higher with light soils and less with particularly heavy soils. On heavy soils, of course, the land may be virtually 100 per cent unworkable between late November and early March (or still later, according to the season), particularly if undrained. A rough estimate of variations in workability according to soil type (compared with the figures in the above table) are as follows. Heavy land — March, October, November: one-third less; April: one-fifth less; September: 10% less; May to August: no difference. Light land — October to April: one-sixth more; May and September: 10% more; June to August: no difference.

(2) When these figures are used for farm planning, it must be remembered that indoor work, e.g. livestock tending or potato riddling, can be continued over the full working-week, i.e. the hours available are the Adjusted Ordinary Hours, plus overtime. Also, some handwork in the field has to continue even in rain, e.g. sprout picking.

(3) To be precise, percentage workability varies according to the particular operation, e.g. compare ploughing and drilling.

(4) Furthermore, some operations are limited by factors other than soil workability, e.g. combine-harvesting by grain moisture content.

(5) Factors touched upon briefly above are discussed fully in Duckham's 'The Farming Year'.

3. SEASONAL LABOUR REQUIREMENTS FOR

CROPS AND GRASS

On the following pages, data on labour requirements for various farm crops and types of livestock are given. Two levels are shown: average and premium. **The average figures relate to the whole range of conditions and farm size, i.e. small and medium-sized farms as well as large; the figures give all farms equal weight. The premium rates do not denote the maximum rates possible, for instance by the use of especially high-powered tractors under ideal conditions, but relate to rates of work estimated to be obtainable over the whole season, averaging good and bad conditions, with the use of wide implements, largish tractors (75 to 90 kW) (100-120 hp) and high capacity equipment in 8 hectare fields and over, where no time is wasted. Most farmers with more than 200 hectares (500 acres) of arable land are likely to achieve at least the premium levels shown. Those with over 400 hectares (1,000 acres) will have still bigger machines and therefore faster work rates, and thus require 15 to 25% less labour than even the premium levels given.**

The rates of work include morning preparation, travelling to fields, and allow for minor breakdowns and other stoppages. They relate broadly to medium and medium-heavy land; some jobs, such as ploughing, may be done more quickly on light soils. Operations such as combine harvesting can obviously vary according to many factors to do with the topography and other natural features of the farm.

The usual times of year when each operation takes place are shown; these relate to lowland conditions in the south-eastern half of Britain. They will obviously vary between seasons, soil types, latitude and altitude. In particular, on light land, land can be ploughed over a longer winter period and a high proportion of cultivations for spring crops may be completed in February in many seasons. All such factors must be allowed for in individual farm planning. Conditions in different seasons will also affect, for instance, the number and type of cultivations required in seedbed preparation. Typical monthly breakdowns of requirements are given for various crops.

To illustrate the type of questions that need to be asked for full details of seasonal labour requirements on the individual farm, 'Critical Questions affecting Timing' are listed for cereals. Similar questions would, of course, need to be asked for other crops.

WINTER CEREALS

Operations	Labour-Hours per hectare		Time of Year
	Average	Premium	
Plough (1).	1.4	1.0	July to October (according to previous crop)
Cultivate (often power harrow).	1.0	0.7	September to October (according to previous crop) (½ Aug if ploughed in July)
Drill (often with power harrows), followed by Roll	1.1	0.7	Mid-September to 3rd week October (according to previous crop and soil)
Apply Fertilizer.	0.3	0.2	
Spray.	0.3	0.2	October-November
Top Dress (three times [2]).	0.9	0.6	March and April
Spray (three or four [2]).	1.0	0.5	Spring/early summer
Combine, Cart Grain, Barn Work	2.5	1.9	Mid-Aug to approx. 10th Sept
Later Barn Work (3).	0.7	0.4	September to June
Total.	**9.2**	**6.2**	
Straw: Bale.	1.3	0.8	Mid-August to end
Cart.	3.5	2.6	September

Typical Monthly Breakdown

Month	Average	Premium	Notes
October	2.4	1.7	Approx. 60% of Ploughing,
November	—	—	Cults., Drill, Harrow
December	—	—	
January	—	—	
February	—	—	
March	0.4	0.2	Part Top Dress
April	0.8	0.5	Part Top Dress, Spraying
May	0.3	0.2	Spraying
June	0.3	0.2	Spraying
July	—	—	
August	1.7	1.3	⅔ of harvesting (4)
	(+2.4 Straw)	(+1.7 Straw)	
September (harvest)	0.9	0.6	⅓ of harvesting (4)
	(+2.4 Straw)	(+1.7 Straw)	
September (prepn. drill)	1.7	1.1	40% of Ploughing, Cults., Drill, Harrow

Notes

1. Some cereal crops are direct drilled or drilled after reduced, or minimal, cultivations, i.e. without traditional ploughing. Direct drilling reduces man-hours per hectare by about 2.5 (average) or 1.8 (premium), and minimal cultivations by about 1.2 (average) and 0.9 (premium).

2. Winter wheat; winter barley will often have one less top dressing and spraying and oats two less.

3. Later barn work excluded from monthly breakdown.

4. Winter wheat (see page 137 for harvest times for winter barley and oats).

SPRING CEREALS

Operations	Labour-Hours per hectare		Time of Year
	Average	Premium	
Plough (1)................	1.4	1.0	July to October (according (according to previous crop and soil type)
Cultivate (often power harrow)..	1.0	0.7	March (½ in second half February on light land)
Apply Fertilizer	0.3	0.2	
Drill (often with power Harrow), plus Roll..........	1.2	0.8	March (½ at end February on light land)
Top Dress (once, some possibly twice)....................	0.4	0.2	
Spray (two or three)	0.7	0.3	May
Combine, Cart Grain, Barn Work	2.4		1.8 Last three-quarters of August (affected by variety as well as season)
Later Barn Work (2)	0.6	0.4	September to June
Total	**8.0**	**5.4**	
Straw: Bale (unmanned sledge)..	1.3	0.8	Mid-August to end
Cart	3.5	2.6	September

Typical Monthly Breakdown

Month	Average	Premium	Notes
October	0.4	0.3	Ploughing. How much in
November	0.8	0.5	October depends on area
December.................	0.2	0.2	W. Wheat, Potatoes, etc.
January....................	—	—	
February..................	—	—	
March	2.4	1.6	All Cults. Drilling, Rolling, (nearly half in February on light land)
April.....................	—	—	
May......................	1.1	0.6	Spray and Top dress
June......................	—	—	
July	—	—	
August(3).................	2.4	1.8	Harvesting
	(+2.6 Straw)	(+1.8 Straw)	
September	—	—	
	(+2.2 Straw)	(+1.6 Straw)	

Notes

1. See note 1 on page 135.

2. Later barn work excluded.

3. Spring barley; spring wheat and oats partly September (see page 137).

In a *normal* (i.e. neither early or late) *season*:

WINTER WHEAT

Drilling mid-September to 3rd week October.
Harvesting mid-August to approx. 10th September.

WINTER BARLEY

As for winter wheat, except that:

Ploughing unlikely to start before cereal harvest, as usually follows a cereal crop.
Harvesting some weeks earlier: mid July to approx. 10th August.

WINTER OATS

As for winter wheat, except that:

Drilling usually first full half of October.
Harvesting earlier (first half of August).

SPRING BARLEY

Drilling end of February to end of March or early April.
Harvesting last half/¾ of August.

SPRING WHEAT

As for spring barley, except that:

Drilling is on average one or two weeks earlier (should be finished in March) — lose more if late than barley.

Harvesting, on average, is two weeks later: last week of August/first half of September (two-thirds in September).

SPRING OATS

As for spring barley, except that:

Drilling is usually a little earlier.

Harvesting is later than spring barley, earlier than spring wheat: end of August/beginning of September.

Critical Questions affecting Timing (Autumn-sown Cereals)

1. Previous crops (affects time available and need for ploughing and cultivations).
2. Will the crop be ploughed traditionally, chisel ploughed, minimally cultivated, or direct drilled?
3. Earliest and latest drilling date, by choice.
4. Effect on yield if drilling is delayed.
5. Autumn weed control?
6. In the spring: (a) whether crop is rolled, and when,
   (b) whether crop is harrowed, and when,
   (c) time of top dressings,
   (d) number of spray applications.
7. (a) Average period for harvesting.
   (b) Earliest dates for starting and finishing harvest, and latest dates for starting and finishing harvest, ignoring extreme seasons (one year in ten).

Critical Questions affecting Timing (Spring-sown Cereals)

1. Previous crops.
2. Will the crop be ploughed traditionally, chisel ploughed, minimally cultivated, or direct drilled?
3. Months when winter ploughing is possible, on average. (Where relevant).
4. Is spring ploughing satisfactory? (Where relevant).
5. Average period of cultivations and drilling.
6. Earliest dates for starting and finishing spring cultivations/drilling and latest dates for starting and finishing cultivations/drilling, ignoring extreme seasons (1 year in 10).
7. Effect on yield if drilling is delayed.
8. Is the crop rolled (a) within a few days of drilling or (b) later?
9. (a) Average period of harvesting.

   (b) Earliest dates for starting and finishing harvest, and latest dates for starting and finishing harvest, ignoring extreme seasons (one year in ten).

MAINCROP POTATOES

Operations	Labour-Hours per hectare		Time of Year
	Average	Premium	
Plough	1.4	1.0	September to December
Cultivating, Ridging, Destoning/			
Clod sep. (as required)	6.5	5.0	March, early April
Plant and Apply Fertilizer (1)	4.5	3.5	Last quarter of March, first
Apply Herbicide	0.3	0.2	three-quarters of April
Spray for Blight (av. 4 times)	1.2	0.9	July, first half August
Burn off Haulm	0.3	0.2	End September, early October
Harvest, Cart, Clamp (2)	15.0	10.0	End September, October
Work on Indoor Clamp	4.8	3.2	November
Riddle, Bag, Load	40.0	30.0	October to May
Total	**74.0**	**54.0**	

(1) Automatic planter. Hand-fed planters: approx. 12 hours plus 8 that could be casual labour.

(2) Mechanical harvester, excluding up to 25 hours for picking off on harvester—usually casual labour. None may be needed on clod- and stone-free soils. Hand harvesting: additional approx. 80 hours of casual labour.

Typical Monthly Breakdown

Month	Average	Premium	Notes
October	12.2	8.2	80% of harvest, ½ burn off
November	5.9	4.0	Clamp work and ¾ plough
December	0.3	0.2	¼ plough
January	—	—	
February	—	—	
March	7.8	6.0	All fert., ½ cults.,¼ plant
April	3.5	2.7	½ cults., ¾ plant
May.	—	—	
June.	—	—	
July	0.9	0.7	3 blight sprays
August	0.3	0.2	1 blight spray
September	3.1	2.0	20% harvest, ½ burn off

Note: These figures exclude casual labour and riddling.

EARLY POTATOES

Operations	Labour-Hours per hectare		Time of Year
	Average	Premium	
Plough	1.4 (1)	1.0(1)	September to December
Cultivating, etc	6.5(1)	5.0(1)	Late February, early March
Plant and Apply Fertilizer	4.5(1)	3.5(1)	Late February, early March
Apply Herbicide	0.3(1)	0.2(1)	1st half March (some in February on light land or in early season)
Further Spraying	0.3(1)	0.2(1)	
After-Cultivation/Spray	0.3(1)	0.2(1)	April, early May
Harvest, bag, load	30.0(1)	25.0(2)	2nd week June onwards. All June or till mid-July

(1) Excluding 80 hours picking—usually casuals.

(2) Excluding 60 hours picking—usually casuals.

SECOND EARLY POTATOES

Operations	Labour-Hours per hectare		Time of Year
	Average	Premium	
Plough	1.4 (1)	1.0(1)	September to December
Cultivating, etc	6.5(1)	5.0(1)	March
Plant and Apply Fertilizer.	4.5(1)	3.5(1)	March
Apply Herbicide	0.3(1)	0.2(1)	Half 2nd half March, half 1st half April
Further Spraying	0.9(1)	0.7(1)	End April, May, early June
Harvest	15.0(1)	10.0(2)	Mid-July to end August

(1) Spinner or elevator-digger, excluding picking and riddling—usually casual labour.

(2) Mechanical harvester, excluding picking off on harvester and riddling—usually casual labour.

SUGAR BEET

Operations	Labour-Hours per hectare		Time of Year
	Average	Premium	
Plough	1.4	1.0	September to December
Seedbed Cults	3.2	2.2	Mainly March (some early April. Some late February in good seasons)
Load, Cart, Apply Fertilizer	0.7	0.4	
Drill (and Flat Roll)	1.8	1.1	Between mid-March and mid-April
Spray (herbicide: pre- and post-emergence)	0.6	0.3	Late March/April
Spray (x 2).................	0.6	0.3	May/June
Spray (aphis)	0.3	0.2	July
Harvest (machine)...........	14.0	9.0	End September, October, November
Load	3.4	2.5	End September to early January
Total	**26.0**	**17.0**	

Typical Monthly Breakdown

Month	Average	Premium	Notes
October	7.2	4.6	45% harvest; + loading
November	8.2	5.3	45% harvest; ¾ ploughing; + loading
December	1.0	0.8	¼ ploughing; + loading
January	0.5	0.4	Loading
February	—	—	
March	3.8	2.3	Fert., most cults., some drilling
April	2.5	1.7	Some cults., most of drilling
May.................	0.3	0.2	Spray
June	0.3	0.15	Spray
July.................	0.2	0.15	Spray
August	—	—	
September............	2.0	1.4	10% harvesting; + loading

VINING PEAS

Operations	Labour-Hours per hectare		Time of Year
	Average	Premium	
Plough	1.4	1.0	September to December
Cults., Fert. and Drill	2.3	1.6	Mid-Feb. to April
Post Drilling and Spraying	1.5	0.8	
Harvesting	20.0	15.0	July and early August
Total	**25.2**	**18.4**	

Note

Drilling is staggered in small areas through the season, ranging from early varieties to late varieties.

DRIED PEAS

Month	Labour-Hours per hectare		Notes
	Average	Premium	
October	1.4	1.0	
November	0.9	0.6	Stubble cult., Plough
December	0.2	0.2	
January	—	—	
February	0.2	0.1	Cult. x 2, harrow; drill & fert.
March	3.0	2.0	(80% March); light harrow and
April	0.6	0.4	roll; and spray
May	2.5	1.2	
June	0.2	0.2	Scare pigeons; spray
July	2.1	1.3	Possible spray desiccant; combine
August	2.4	1.5	and cart, dry
September	1.0	0.5	Stubble cult.

Assumes direct combining.

FIELD BEANS

A. Winter Beans

Operations	Labour-Hours per hectare		Time of Year
	Average	Premium	
Broadcast Seed	0.6	0.4	
Apply Fertilizer	0.3	0.2	
Plough	1.4	1.0	September/October
Power Harrow	1.0	0.8	
Spray (pre-emergence)	0.3	0.15	
Spraying (two or three times)	0.8	0.35	Spring
Combine and cart and barnwork	3.3	2.7	August

B. Spring Beans

Operations	Labour-Hours per hectare		Time of Year
	Average	Premium	
Plough	1.4	1.0	September to December
Cultivate (often power harrow) . .	1.0	0.7	
Apply Fertilizer	0.3	0.2	
Drill, Roll	1.2	0.8	End Feb, early March
Spray (two or three times)	0.8	0.4	
Combine and cart and barnwork	3.3	2.7	September

OILSEED RAPE

(Autumn Sown)

Month	Labour-Hours per hectare		Notes
	Average	Premium	
October			
November	0.6	0.3	Spray herbicide and
December			insecticide if necessary
January	—	—	
February	—	—	
March			
April	0.8	0.4	Top dress twice
May	—	—	
June	—	—	Windrow (1st half July);
July	2.8	2.0	combine (½ 1st half July
August	2.5	1.7	1st half Aug.); straw, dry
August	1.8	1.1	Cults. (x 2), spray, drill, fert.;
September	3.1	1.8	harrow, roll, barn work (0.5)

HERBAGE SEED

A. Undersown

Operations	Labour-Hours per hectare		Time of Year
	Average	Premium	
Undersow	0.6	0.4	March, April
Roll	(0.6	0.4)	Straight after drilling
	0.4	0.3	September
	0.4	0.3	Late February, March
Harvest (by Combine): Mow....	1.4	0.9	3 to 4 days before combining
Combine and Cart	4.5	3.5	*Ital. Ryegrasses and Early Perennials: late July.*
			Intermed. Perennials: late July/early August.
			Late Perennials/White Clover: mid-August
	6.0	4.5	Meadow Fescue: early July
	7.0	5.0	Cocksfoot: early July
	10.0	7.0	Timothy: mid-August
			Red Clover: late September

B. Direct Drilled in Autumn

Operations	Labour-Hours per hectare		Time of Year
	Average	Premium	
Plough	1.4	1.0	
Seedbed Cults	2.2	1.6	Depends on previous crop—
Load, Cart, Apply Fertilizer	0.3	0.2	Usually July or August
Drill (with harrows behind).	0.8	0.6	As early as previous crop allows. This may be up to mid-Sept for ryegrass without detriment to the yield.
Roll (soon after drilling). .... cocksfoot	0.6	0.4	Meadow fescue and
			are best sown no later than July and it is risky to sow Timothy much later than this.

GRASS

A. Production

Operations	Labour-Hours per hectare		Time of Year
	Average	Premium	
Plough	1.4	1.0	Autumn drilling: may not
Seedbed Cults	2.2	1.6	
Load, Cart, Apply Fertilizer	0.3	0.2	
Drill*....................	0.7	0.5	Mid-March to mid-April (1) or end July to mid-Sept.
Roll	0.6	0.4	Soon after drilling
Load, Cart, Apply Fertiliser*: (three lots)	0.9	0.6	March to mid-August (2)
Top*	1.3	0.8	Mid-June to mid-July; if grazed only.

Notes

1. Spring drilling may continue to mid-May to enable extra cleaning cultivations or the application of farmyard manure.

2. P. and K. may be applied in September—especially on undersown ley in year sown.

* Only these operations apply where the seeds are undersown in a spring cereal crop soon after drilling. One extra harrowing and rolling is needed if undersown in an autumn-sown cereal crop.

B. Conservation

Operations	Labour-Hours per hectare		Time of Year
	Average	Premium	
Plough	1.4	1.0	Autumn drilling: may not
Hay (5.5 tonnes per hectare)			
Mow	1.2	0.9	
Turn, etc	2.6	1.9	Two-thirds June, one-third
Bale	1.3	0.9	July
Cart	6.0	4.5	
Total per hectare	11.1	8.2	
Total per tonne	2.0	1.5	
Silage (17 tonnes per hectare)			
Mow	1.2	0.9	
Turn, etc	0.7	0.5	Two-thirds May, one-third
Load	2.3	1.7	June
Cart	3.0	2.3	
Clamp	2.3	1.7	
Total per hectare	9.5	7.1	
Total per tonne	0.56	0.42	

Specialized Equipment Prices for Grass Conservation: see page 153.

Typical Monthly Breakdown

A. Production (figures averaged over the life of the ley)

	1-year ley undersown in spring		3-year ley undersown in autumn (1)		1-year ley drilled		3-year ley drilled	
	Ave.	Prem.	Ave.	Prem.	Ave.	Prem.	Ave.	Prem.
March	0.9	0.5	0.7	0.5	0.6	0.3	0.6	0.3
April......	0.9	0.5	0.7	0.5	0.6	0.3	0.6	0.3
May	0.6	0.3	0.6	0.3	0.6	0.3	0.6	0.3
June	0.6	0.3	0.6	0.3	0.6	0.3	0.6	0.3
July	0.6	0.3	0.6	0.3	0.6	0.3	0.6	0.3
August	0.3	0.2	0.3	0.2	5.0	3.4	1.9	1.4
September ..	0.6	0.3	0.3	0.2	3.2	2.2	1.4	1.0

Note

1. On land ploughed after a cereal crop, drilled early August to mid-September.

	1-year ley drilled in autumn (1)		3-year ley drilled in spring		Permanent Pasture	
	Ave.	Prem.	Ave.	Prem.	Ave.	Prem.
March	3.0	2.1	1.4	1.0	0.6	0.3
April	1.8	1.2	0.9	0.7	0.6	0.3
May	0.3	0.3	0.6	0.3	0.6	0.3
June	0.6	0.3	0.6	0.3	0.6	0.3
July...........	0.6	0.3	0.6	0.3	0.6	0.3
August	0.3	0.2	0.2	0.2	0.3	0.2
September	—	—	—	0.2	0.2	0.2
October........	0.9	0.5	0.6	0.3	—	—
November......	1.4	1.0	1.0	0.3	—	—
December	0.7	0.5	0.6	0.2	—	—

B. Conservation

	Hay per hectare		Hay per tonne		Silage per hectare		Silage per tonne	
	Av.	Prem.	Av.	Prem.	Av.	Prem.	Av.	Prem.
May.........	—	—	—	—	6.3	4.7	0.37	0.28
June.........	7.4	5.6	1.3	1.0	3.2	2.4	0.19	0.14
July	3.7	2.6	0.7	0.5	—	—	—	—

KALE

(Growing only)

A. Production

Operations	Labour-Hours per hectare		Time of Year
	Average	Premium	
Plough	1.4	1.0	September onwards
Seedbed Cults	2.2	1.6	March, April, early May
Fertilizer	0.3	0.2	April, early May
Drill	1.3	1.0	May
Roll	0.6	0.4	Straight after drilling
Spray (weedkiller)	0.3	0.2	6 weeks after drilling

B. Catch Crop

Kale may be drilled up to the first week of July; the crop will be smaller but either an early bite or silage crop may have been taken from a ley earlier in the year, or the ground may have been fallowed and thoroughly cleaned during the spring and early summer. The smaller crop is also easier to graze using an electric fence.

The above operations will still apply although the times of the year will obviously be different, but there may be an additional three or so rotavations and two or three heavy cultivations if fallowed for the first half of the year or ploughed after an early bite. This means approximately an extra 10 (average) or 8 (premium) man-hours per hectare in April, May, June.

FIELD SCALE VEGETABLES

(Labour hours per hectare unless otherwise stated)

Cabbage Transplanting	Hand 150-160. Spring cabbage, Sept.-Oct.; summer, April; autumn, May-June Machine (3.5 gang). Spring cabbage 75, summer 85, autumn 100. Pulling and dipping plants. 20 per hectare transplanted.
Cabbage Harvesting	Early spring cabbage, 210, Feb.-April; hearted spring, 250, April-June; summer, 220, June-July; autumn, 220, Oct.-Dec.
Brussels Sprouts Transplanting	45 (machine) to 55 (hand), May-June.
Brussels Sprouts Picking	320-400: picked over 3-5 times, maximum approx. 3 hectares per picker per season. Early sprouts, Aug.-Dec.; late, Nov.-Mar.
Peas Hand Pulling	475-525 (150 per tonne). Early, June; maincrop, July-Aug.
Runner Beans (Picked)	Harvesting. 625 (175 per tonne), July-Sept.
Runner Beans (Stick)	Harvesting. 675, July-Sept.
Runner Beans (Stick)	Erecting Canes and String. 100-150, May-June.
Carrot Harvesting.	Elevator-digger: 260 (1 man + 12 casuals, 20 hours per hectare). Earlies, July-Aug.; maincrop, Sept.-Feb. Harvester: 30 (3 men, 10 hours per hectare). Riddle and Grade: (1° per tonne), Dec.-Feb.
Beetroot Harvest and Clamp.	25, Oct.-Dec. 12-15 man-hours per tonne to wash and pack.

Source: The Farm as a Business, Aids to Management, Section 6: Labour and Machinery (M.A.F.F.). (N.B. This data is now very dated, but it is still the latest known to the author.)

4. LABOUR FOR FIELDWORK

Gang Sizes and Rates of Work

Basic information on Rates of Work is given on pages 156-158, where both 'average' and 'premium' rates for many operations are listed.

The following data relate to rates of work with gangs of different sizes. The rates of work are averages for good and bad conditions throughout the season, including preparation time and travelling to the field, and assume an 8-hour day, unless otherwise stated. Obviously these rates can be exceeded by overtime work in the evenings.

Combine Harvesting

Gang size can vary from 1 to 4 men per combine (excluding straw baling) according to the number of men available, size and type of combine, distance from grain store, crop yield, type of grain drier, and degree of automation in the grain store. The main possibilities are:

1 man: all jobs (trailer in field)
2 men: 1 combining, 1 carting and attending to grain store
3 men: 1 combining, 2 carting and attending to grain store
3 men: 1 combining, 1 carting, 1 attending to grain store
4 men: 1 combining, 2 carting, 1 attending to grain store

Three men is most typical, although two is quite feasible with a fully automated grain store with in-bin or floor drying, unless transport times are excessive owing to distance or lack of good connecting roads. Four men is most usual with two combines, but an extra man may be needed with a continuous drier.

Except in the case of the small area cereal producer operating on his own, the rate of work will normally depend on the speed of the combine, sufficient tractors and trailers being provided to ensure that combining does not have to stop because of their absence.

Assuming a 9-hour combining day, typical rates of work are:

Size of combine (metres cut)	No. of Men	Ha/day
3 to 4.2	1	4.5 to 7.75
	2 or 3	6 to 10
4.25 to 5.4	2 or 3	8 to 12
5.5 and over.	3 or 4	10 to 15

Straw Carting

2 men, 1 or 2 tractors and trailers 'traditional system'	2.5 to 3.25 ha a day
3 men, 1 to 3 tractors and trailers	3.25 ha a day
1 man, 1 tractor with front and rear carriers	2.5 ha a day
2 men, flat 8/10 accumulator mechanised system	10 to 15 ha a day
2 or 3 men, big bale system	8 to 15 ha a day

Potato Planting

Hand planting (chitted seed) 3 men, 16 women	2 ha a day
Hand planting (unchitted seed) 2 men, 12 women	2 ha a day
(women working a 6-hour day only)	
2-row planter (chitted seed) 3 workers	1 ha a day
3-row planter (chitted seed) 4 or 5 workers	1.75 ha a day
2-row planter (unchitted seed) 3 workers	1.5 ha a day
3-row planter (unchitted seed) 4 workers	2.25 ha a day
2-row automatic planter (unchitted seed) 1 worker	2.5 ha a day

(part-time help loading and carting seed additional; this may be
full time if fertilizer is applied with an attachment to the planter)

Potato Harvesting

Hand harvesting (piecework) 3 to 5 men, 10 to 15 women	0.65 to 0.85 ha a day
(women working a 6-hour day only)	
Machine harvesting (1-row) 4 men, 3 women	0.65 to 0.9 ha a day
Machine harvesting (2-row) 5 men, 3 women	1 to 1.5 ha a day
(lower end of range for heavy land, upper end for light land	
and good work organization)	

Potato Riddling

3 to 5 workers	10 to 15 tonnes a day

Sugar Beet Harvesting (1-row)

Gang can vary from 1 to 5 (1 or 2 on harvester, 2 or 3 carting, 1 at clamp) but is
usually 3 or 4.

3 or 4 men	0.9 ha a day
2 men	0.8 ha a day
1 man	0.7 ha a day
(add 20% for light loams and silts)	

Vining Peas

Drilling (2 men)	7 to 10 ha a day
2.5-3 m. cutter (1 man)	2 ha a day
Pea pod picker, and carting, 5 or 6 men	0.4 ha a day
(large-scale growers: two 12 hour shifts worked per day)	

Carting Hay Bales

2 men, 1 or 2 tractors and trailers	7 to 9 tonnes a day
3 men, 1 to 3 tractors and trailers	9 to 14 tonnes a day

Silage-Making with Forage Harvester (excl. mowing but inc. clamping; 15 tonne/ha crop)

1 man gang (1)	1.25 ha a day
2 man gang (1,3)	2.25 ha a day
3 man gang (1,3)	3.5 ha a day
4 man gang (2,3)	4.5 ha a day
(1) trailers towed behind, in line	
(2) trailers towed alongside	
(3) man with buckrake at clamp full-time	

Farmyard Manure Spreading

1 man: front loader and mechanical spreader	28 tonnes a day
4 men: front loader and 3 mechanical spreaders	90 tonnes a day

5. LABOUR FOR LIVESTOCK

DAIRY COWS

Herd size (no. of cows)	60	80	100
			or more
	hours per cow per month		
January..	3.3	2.9	2.5
February..	3.3	2.9	2.5
March..	3.3	2.9	2.5
April..	3.0	2.7	2.4
May...	2.7	2.4	2.2
June...	2.7	2.4	2.1
July...	2.7	2.4	2.1
August...	2.7	2.4	2.1
September.......................................	2.7	2.4	2.2
October..	3.0	2.8	2.4
November.......................................	3.3	2.9	2.5
December.......................................	3.3	2.9	2.5
Total per cow per year........................	36	32	28
Total hours per year...........................	2160	2560	2800
Total hours per week..........................	42	49	54
Total cost per annum	£21,120	£25,250	£28,350*
Total cost per week............................	£406	£486	£545*
Total cost per cow per annum............	**£352**	**£316**	**£284***
Cost per litre: 6000 litres/cow.................	5.87p	5.27p	4.73p
Cost per litre: 6500 litres/cow.................	5.42p	4.86p	4.37p
Cost per litre: 6650 litres/cow.................	5.29p	4.75p	4.27p
Cost per litre: 7000 litres/cow.................	5.03p	4.51p	4.06p
Cost per litre: 7500 litres/cow.................	4.69p	4.21p	3.79p
Cost per litre: 8000 litres/cow.................	4.40p	3.95p	3.55p
Cost per litre: 8500 litres/cow.................	4.14p	3.72p	3.34p
Cost per litre: 9000 litres/cow.................	3.91p	3.51p	3.16p

*   For more than 100 cows per man (i.e. without additional help) the cost per week per additional cow is likely to be in the order of £2 per week (approx. £100 per annum), with the cost per cow per annum falling by around £1. Labour hours per cow will fall very little.

Note

These *costs* (note, not *earnings*) are *estimates for 2007* and are based on the average number of *direct* hours of work per cow for different herd sizes obtained from University costings; they do not include fieldwork, such as hay and silage making. The costs include craftsman addition and any other premiums paid, overtime, national insurance payments, and holidays with pay. They also include the cost of relief milking, including during annual holidays.

Earnings. The average earnings of all 'dairy herdsmen' in 2007 are estimated to be approximately £23,800 a year (£458 for an average 53-hour week).

DAIRY FOLLOWERS AND BEEF

Note

No recent survey work has been published on labour requirements for beef animals and dairy followers. The following data can therefore only be taken as 'best estimates'. They are for average performance under average conditions, excluding fieldwork (see page 230, note 5). Substantial variations can occur from farm to farm, e.g. through economies of scale with widely differing herd sizes.

A. Calves (per head, early weaning)

Age Group	Labour hours per month	
	Average	Premium
0-3 months..	2.3	1.6
3-6 months..	0.9	0.6
(av. 0-6 months......................................	1.6	1.1)
6-12 months, yarded.................................	1.1	0.8
6-12 months, summer grazed......................	0.3	0.2
(av. 0-12 months, during winter (1)..............	1.3	0.9)
(av. 0-12 months, during summer (1)..............	0.9	0.6)

Note

1. Assuming 6 to 12-month olds yarded in winter and grazed in summer, and calvings or calf purchases fairly evenly spaced throughout the year.

B. Stores (per head)

Yearling, yarded....................................	1.0	0.7
2 year olds and over, yarded......................	1.4	0.8
Outwintered store.................................	0.7	0.5
12 months and over, summer grazed...........	0.2	0.1

C. Dairy Followers

(Per 'replacement unit', i.e. calf + yearling + in-calf heifer.) (1)		
During winter...	2.9	2.0
During summer.......................................	1.2	0.8

Note

1. Assuming calvings fairly evenly spaced throughout the year and heifers calving at 2 to 2.5 years old.

D. Beef Finishing (per head)

Yarded..	1.9	1.3
Summer Grazed....................................	0.2	0.1
Intensive Beef (0-12 months).....................	1.35	1.0

E. Suckler Herds (per cow)

Single suckling (av. whole year).................	0.9	0.6
Multiple suckling (av. whole year)..............	2.9	2.1

SHEEP
(per ewe)

	Labour hours per month	
	Average	Premium (4)
January	0.3	0.2
February	0.3	0.2
March	1.0 (1)	0.7
April	0.4	0.25
May	0.3	0.2
June	0.4 (2)	0.3
July	0.2	0.15
August	0.2	0.15
September	0.25	0.15
October	0.25	0.15
November	0.2	0.15
December	0.2	0.15
Total	4.0 (3)	2.75

1. Assuming mainly March lambing.
2. 0.3 if shearing is by contract.
3. A full-time shepherd, i.e. one who did no other work on the farm, would have to have a flock of at least 600 ewes for the average 4 hours per ewe per year to be achieved, assuming full-time assistance during lambing time.
4. In a national survey conducted in 1999 the average annual requirement for flocks exceeding 500 ewes was 2.9 hours.

PIGS

Age Group	Labour hours per month	
	Average	Premium
Breeding and Rearing, per sow (Average 140 sows per worker, Premium 175)	1.6	1.25
Feeding only, per 10 pigs No. at a time, per worker: Average 1,300 per man, Premium 1,750 No. per year, per worker: Average: 6,250 porkers, 5,000 cutters, 4,750 baconers Premium: 7,750 porkers, 6,250 cutters, 6,000 baconers	1.7	1.25
Breeding, Rearing and Feeding, per sow(with progeny)		
Porkers, average 90 sows per worker, premium 110	2.4	2.0
Cutters, average 80-85 sows per worker, premium 100-105	2.6	2.1
Baconers, average 75-80 sows per worker, premium 95-100	2.8	2.2

POULTRY
(large scale, automated)

	Labour hours per month
Laying hens: battery cages (18,000 per full-time worker)	1.1 per 100
free range	4 per 100
Broilers: 32,500 at a time per full-time worker* (225,000 a year)	1.0 per 100

* N.B. additional help needed for catching and cleaning out (included in labour hours per month)

V. MACHINERY

1. AGRICULTURAL MACHINERY PRICES

(Estimated Spring 2007 prices for new machinery, net of discounts and ex. V.A.T.)

1. *Tractors*

(a) *Two-Wheel Drive* £

35-41 kW (47-55 hp)	13,500-15,500
43-49 kW (57-66 hp)	16,000-19,000
50-56 kW (67-75 hp)	17,000-21,500
57-66 kW (76-89 hp)	19,500-23,500
67-75 kW (90-100 hp)	21,500-25,500

(b) *Four- Wheel Drive*

43-50 kW (57-67 hp)	15,500-22,600
56-65 kW (75-87 hp)	21,500-26,500
66-75 kW (88-100 hp)	23,500-31,000
76-90 kW (101-120 hp)	31,000-39,000
94-105 kW (125-140 hp)	36,000-45,000
115-134 kW (154-180 hp)	45,000-54,500
140-165 kW (187-220 hp)	52,500-58,000
170-200 kW (228-268 hp)	67,000-77,000

(c) *High Road Speed*

15-130 kW (155-175 hp)	49,000-60,000
140-165 kW (188-221 hp)	60,000-70,000

(d) *Crawlers*

175-225 kW (230-300 hp) rubber track	108,000-118,000
225-300 kW (340-400 hp) rubber track	124,000-144,000
336-410 kW (450-550 hp) rubber track	150,000-165,000

2. *Cultivating Equipment*

(a) *Ploughs*

	Fixed width	Variable width	
		Mechanical Adjustment	Hydraulic Adjustment
Reversible:			
3-furrow	5,800-6,500	6,300-8,000	—
4-furrow	6,700-7,500	7,400-10,000	10,000-13,000
5-furrow	7,600-8,500	8,600-11,400	11,700-15,000
6-furrow		11,000-14,100	13,300-16,500
6-furrow (semi-mounted)		13,000-15,000	14,500-17,500
7-furrow (semi-mounted)		14,000-16,000	15,500-19,500
8-furrow (semi-mounted)		18,000-20,000	18,500-22,500
9-furrow (semi-mounted)			21,500-26,000

(b) *Furrow Presses* £

1.6-1.8 m double row	2,300-2,700
2.0-2.4 m double row	2,600-3,600
2.6-3.0 m double row	3,400-5,000
3.2-3.6 m double row	5,000-6,200
3.8-4.0 m double row	6,000-7,000
Front Press Arm – hydraulic	1,100-1,200

(c) *Front Presses (excluding linkage)*

1.5 m single row	1,800-2,000
3.0 m single row	2,700-3,800
4.0 m single row — hydraulic folding	4,000-5,000

(d) *Front Press Linkage*
1.5 to 2.0 tonne 1,500-1,800
3.5 to 5.5 tonne 2,000-2,600

(e) *Other Cultivating Equipment*
Sub Soiler 2-3 leg.. 2,000-2,500
Soil Looseners   (3 m)... 4,600-5,600
                         (4 m).. 7,200-8,200
Vibrating Compaction Breaker   (2-2.5m)............. 5,000-6,000
                                      (3 m)................... 7,200-8,200
Straw Incorporating Disc Cultivator   (2.5-3 m)............ 5,800-6,800
Stubble Cultivator   (3 m):....................................... 4,000-4,600
(heavy duty)   (4 m): hydraulic folding.......... 7,200-8,200
                         (6 m): hydraulic folding.......... 10,500-12,500
Spring-tine Cultivator   (3-4 m): 1,700-2,400
                         (5-6 m): hydraulic folding....... 4,600-5,600
Combination Harrows   (2.5-4 m)................................ 3,500-5,500
                         (5-6 m): hydraulic folding....... 9,300-10,000
Levelling Harrows   (2.5-4.2 m)............................. 1,200-2,000
                         (3.7-6.1 m): hydraulic folding   3,100-4,600
Disc Harrows   (2.7-3.6 m): trailed 9,300-10,300
                         (4.25-6.25 m): trailed, folding   16,500-24,000
Harrows (5-6 m): light-medium, hydraulic folding 2,000-2,400
Rotovator   (up to 100 kW tractor) 5,500-6,500
                         (150 kW tractor)..................... 9,000-10,000
Power Harrow (with crumbler roller)
                         (2.5-3 m)................................ 5,000-5,700
                         (3.5-4m)................................. 7,000-8,300
                         (5-6m): folding........................ 15,500-17,500
Roller Packer for power harrow   (2.5-4 m)............ 1,000-1,400
                                      (5-6 m) 1,700-2,400
Rolls: triple gang, hydraulic folding   (6 m)................. 5,500-6,500
       five gang,   "   "   (12m) 13,300-14,400

3. *Fertilizer Distributors, Seed Drills, Sprayers*
    (a) *Fertilizer Distributors*
    Mounted Spinners
                    (500-750 litre)... 1,200-1,700
                    (700-1,200 litre): twin disc, hydraulic control1 1,800-2,300
                    (1,300-1,700 litre): twin disc, hydraulic control 3,000-3,300
                    (1,650-2,300 litre): twin disc, electronic control....... 5,000-5,500
                    (3,200 litre): twin disc, electronic control 6,500-6,700
                    Bag lifter (850-1,000kg)... 1,200-1,500
    (b) *Seed Drills*
    Grain: mounted   3 m, gravity fed, 25 row.......... 5,000-6,200
                             3-4 m, pneumatic, 24-32 row.. 10,300-12,500
                             6 m, pneumatic, 48 row 20,500-24,000
    (c) *Combined Cultivator and Pneumatic Drill*
                             3-4 m, 24-32 row.................... 14,500-17,500
                             6 m, 48 row 29,000-33,000
    (d) *Combined Power Harrow and Pneumatic Drill*
                             3-4 m, 24-32 row.................... 15,500-20,700
                             6 m, 48 row 36,000-41,000
    (e) *Direct Drill*
    6m, 32 chisel openers 51,000-57,000

152

(f)   *Sprayers*

Mounted, 400 litre tank, 6 m boom	1,600-1,900
Mounted, 600-800 litre tank, 12 m boom	3,000-3,400
Mounted, 1,000-1,300 litre tank, 20-24 m hydraulic boom..	12,400-15,500
Mounted, Air Assisted, 1,000 litre tank, 18 m boom	17,500-20,600
Trailed, Air Assisted, 2,500-3,000 litre tank, 24 m boom	31,000-36,000
Trailed, 2,500-3,000 litre tank 18-24 m boom	23,000-26,000
Trailed, 3,000-3,500 litre tank 24-30 m boom	27,000-31,000
Self-propelled, 24-36 m boom, 4-wheel drive	60,000-72,000

4. Grass Conservation and Handling Equipment

(a)   *Silage Equipment*

Forage Harvester: trailed, precision chop	20,000-26,000
Self-propelled (3 m pick-up 210-280 kW)	100,000-113,000
Maize attachment, 4-6 row	20,000-26,000
Silage Trailer, 5-6 tonne	3,000-3,800
Silage Trailer, 10 tonne, tandem axle	5,500-6,500
Buckrake (push off)	1,600-1,800

(b)   *Haymaking Equipment*

Mower (1.6-1.8 m, 2 drum)	1,900-2,500
Mower (2.0-2.4 m, 5-6 disc)	3,400-3,900
Mower (disc) Conditioner, mounted (2.4-3.2 m)	7,000-8,000
Mower (disc) Conditioner, trailed (2.8-3.2 m)	11,000-12,000
Tedder (5-7 m, 4-6 rotors)	3,500-5,500
Windrower, (3.9-4.2 m)	3,300-3,800
Balers and Bale Handling: see 5(c) and (d) below	

(c)   *Silage Handling Equipment*

Silage shear bucket (1-1.2 m)	1,800-2,600
Silage grab	1,300-1,700
Big Bale Silage Feeder, mounted	5,000-6,500
Diet-feeder Wagon (8-14 m)	17,500-21,500
Clamp Silage Mixer (12-18m³)	16,500-21,500

5. Grain and Straw Harvesting and Handling Equipment

(a)   *Combines*

Engine size kW (hp)	Cutterbar width metres (feet)	
128-148 (170-199)	4.0-5.0 (13-16)	67,000-77,000
149-185 (200-249)	4.2-5.5 (14-18)	83,000-93,000
186-223 (250-299)	5.5-6.1 (18-20)	90,000-113,000
223-298 (300-399)	6.1-7.6 (20-25)	124,000-155,000
Over 300 (400)		155,000-180,000
	(For self-levelling models add 7,000-8,500)	

(b)   *Yield monitoring/mapping*   *6,500-7,500*

(c)   *Pick-up Balers (twine tying)*

Small rectangular bales	8,000-9,000
Small rectangular bales, heavy duty models	10,000-12,000
Big round bales, twine tying	14,000-15,000
Big round bales, twine tying and net wrap	14,000-17,000
High density rectangular bales	55,000-60,000

(d) Bale Wrappers

Big Bale Wrapper: mounted/trailed	8,000-9,000
Big Square Bale Wrapper: mounted	12,000-13,000
Combined Baler and Wrapper	33,000-39,000
Bale Trailers, 5-8 tonne	2,500-3,300
Accumulator, flat 8, mechanical	1,700-2,200
Loader, flat 8	700-900
Big Bale Spike	175-250
Big Bale Handler	500-700
Big Bale Shredder, silage or straw	5,000-6,000

(e) Drying, Handling, Food Processing Equipment

Grain driers and Grain storage: see pages 171 and 189	
Cleaner/grader, 10-20 tonnes/hour	7,500-10,700
Grain augers 100 mm, 3.3-7.3 m	450-600
Grain augers 150 mm, 6-8.5 m, with trolley	1,500-1,800
Grain conveyors, (25-50t/hour)	1,200-1,500 + 100-120 per m
Specific gravity separator, (5-10t/hour)	12,000-14,000
Bucket elevator, (25-50t/hour)	1,650-2,200 + 140-170 per m
Hammer mill, 7.5-15 kW	2,700-3,000
Roller mill, 4-5.5 kW	2,300-2,700
Mixer, 750-1000 kg	3,000-3,500
Mill and mixer, 1,000-1,300kg, 3.7-5.5 kW	5,000-6,000
Grain weigher, 25 tonne/hour	1,500-1,800

6. Potato, Sugar Beet and Vegetable Machinery

(a) Potato Machinery

Stone separator, 1.6 m		33,000-38,000
Bedformer, 2 row		3,000-3,300
Bed cultivator, 1.7-1.8 m		6,300-6,700
Planter:	2 row mounted	8,000-10,000
	3 row mounted	13,500-15,500
	4 row mounted	25,000-28,000
Haulm pulveriser:	2 row	5,000-5,700
	2 row cross conveyor	7,700-8,700
Elevator-Digger,	2 row	5,000-5,700
Harvesters (trailed):	1 row, 2-3 tonne bunker	30,000-36,000
	2 row, elevator manned/unmanned	55,000-65,000
	2 row, 6 tonne bunker	70,000-83,000
Store loader (heavy duty)		18,700-22,000
Flat belt conveyor, 3-8 m		1,800-3,000
Soil elevator (rubber belt)		5,500-6,000
Self-unloading hopper, 3-5 tonnes		6,000-7,000
Clod separator		7,000-7,500
Sizer, 5-30 tonnes/hour		5,000-9,500
Sponge drier, 0.9-1.2m		6,700-10,000
Barrel washer, 8-10 tonnes/hour		10,500-12,000
Roller inspection table, 1.2 x 2.4 m		3,000-3,500
Weigher, automatic, 8-10 tonnes/hour		4,000-5,000
Box tipper with cross conveyor		12,000-13,000
Box filer, automatic		10,000-11,500
Bag stitcher (hand held)		800-1,000
Complete out of store grading line:	20 tonnes/hour	30,000-37,000
	30 tonnes/hour	66,000-72,000
Box filler	30 tonnes/hour	11,000-13,500

(b) *Sugar Beet Machinery*

Precision Drill:	6 row (pneumatic)	8,000-9,500
	12 row-18 row (pneumatic)..................	16,000-25,000
Hoe:	6 row-12 row (heavy duty)..................	5,000-10,000
Harvesters:	Trailed, 2 row, tanker............................	50,000-55,000
	Trailed, 3 row, tanker............................	60,000-65,000
	Trailed, 4 row, tanker............................	70,000-75,000

Self-propelled, 6 row (including power unit), 18 tonne tank 240,000-270,000
Cleaner-loader, with engine, 1-3 tonnes per minute 20,000-23,000
Fodder beet harvester 5,500-6,000

(c) *Vegetable Machinery*

Onion windrower..		7,500-8,500
Root crop digger: 1 webb		5,000-5,500
2 webbs...		6,000-7,000
Top lifting vegetable harvester: single row, bunker...........		40,000-45,000
twin row, bunker/elevator		70,000-85,000
four row, elevator............		90,000-105,000
four row, self-propelled ...		240,000-260,000
Leek harvester (mounted)..		15,000-25,000

7. General

Trailer, 4 tonne tipping...	1,700-2,000
Trailer, 5-6 tonne tipping; grain/silage....................	2,500-3,000/3,000-3,500
Trailer, 10 tonne tipping, tandem axle; grain/silage	4,500-5,000/5,500-6,000
F.Y.M. Spreaders, (4-6 m^2)	3,000-3,500
F.Y.M. Spreaders, (6-8 m^2)	4,000-5,000
Loaders, front mounted	3,500-4,000
Pallet loader, self levelling (1,000-1,600 kg)........................	4,000-5,000
Materials Handler, telescopic boom (2.5-3.0 tonne).............	32,000-38,000
Skid steer loader (500-600 kg)	13,000-15,000

Slurry Stores (metal), including base for 120 day storage period for:

100 cows	£220 per cow
200 cows	£200 per cow
400 cows	£175 per cow
Vacuum Tankers (5,000-6,000 litre).....................................	4,000-4,500
Low Ground Pressure Tankers (9,000-11,000 litre)	8,500-10,000
Slurry pump	3,000-3,500
Cattle crush..	800-1,000
Cattle crush with weigher...	1,500-1,600
Cattle trailer (twin-axle)	1,800-2,200
Yard scrapers	500-600
Rotary brush (2-2.5 m)	1,400-1,800
Grassland roll, ballastable (2.5-3 m)....................................	800-1,000
Pasture topper (2.0-3.0 m)...	1,800-2,500
Hedger: hydraulic angling; flail head...................................	9,500-11,000
Ditcher: fully slewing...	7,000-8,000
Carrier box..	400-500
Post hole digger/driver	1,000-1,200/1,600-2,000
Saw bench..	1,500-1,600
Log splitter..	650-750

2. TYPICAL CONTRACTORS' CHARGES, AVERAGE FARMERS' COSTS, AND RATES OR WORK FOR VARIOUS FARM OPERATIONS

Contractors' charges vary widely according to many factors: those given below are estimates for 2007. Farmer-contractors often charge less, since their overheads and machinery fixed costs are largely covered by their own farming operations, but the service may not always be so complete, including specialist advice.

Farmers' own costs (which include the value of the farmers' own manual labour) vary even more widely; those given below (estimated for Spring 2007) are averages in every respect — covering different types of soil, size of farm, and so on; they are based on accounting cost procedures in that labour, tractor and machinery fuel, repairs and depreciation are included — but no allowance has been added for general farm overheads, interest on capital, supervision/management or under-occupied labour during slack times. They assume four-wheel drive 75-90 kW (100-120 hp) tractors for ploughing, heavy cultivation and other work with a high power requirement. Four-wheel drive 55-65 kW (75-87 hp) tractors are assumed to be used for most other operations. The figures should not be used for partial budgeting.

For a typical set of farm operations, excluding harvesting, the breakdown of the farmers' costs averages very approximately one third each for labour, tractors and implements/machines. The larger the farm, the lower the labour element and the higher the machine element, and vice versa.

The contract charges and average farmers' costs are put side-by-side for tabular convenience, not to facilitate comparisons. Apart from the fact that contractors' charges must cover expenses omitted from the farmers' cost, the advisability or otherwise of hiring a contractor for a particular job depends on many factors, varying widely according to farm circumstances; furthermore, there are advantages and disadvantages not reflected in a cost comparison alone.

Machinery rings. Prices charged by farmers offering services through machinery rings are extremely variable but are generally between average farmers' costs and contractors' charges. There are exceptions, which mainly relate to relatively expensive items of machinery (e.g. precision drills, destoners and combine harvesters), where the charges for services offered through machinery rings are close to and often less than average farmers' costs.

Four-wheel drive 120-150 kW (150-200 hp) tractors are assumed where appropriate to achieve the 'Premium' rates of work (which will be achieved on most farms with more than 200 hectares (500 acres) of arable land); obviously, still larger wheeled tractors and crawlers could achieve still faster rates of work, particularly on light land. The rates of work include preparation, travelling to and from the fields and allow for minor breakdowns and other stoppages. See further page 134, first paragraph.

All charges and costs below are per hectare unless otherwise stated.

Operation	Contract	Average Farmer's	Rate of Work (Ha per 8 Hr day)	
		Cost	Average	Premium
	£	£		
Cultivations				
Ploughing (light/heavy soils)	42.00-48.00	38.50-49.00	5-6½	7½-9
with furrow press	Extra £5.00	40.50-54.00	4½-6¾	7-8½
Deep Ploughing (over 300 mm)	52.00-62.00	67.00-84.00	3-3¾	5-6½
Rotavating	57.00-65.00	73.00	4½	6

156

Operation	Contract	Average Farmer's Cost	Rate of Work (Ha per 8 Hr day)	
			Average	Premium
	£	£		
			(ploughed land)	
		109.00 (grass)	3	4
Subsoiling	49.00	39.00	6	10
Stubble Cultivating	27.00	21.00	12	16
Heavy Disc Cultivating	33.00	30.30	10	15
Disc Harrowing	23.00	15.50	12	16
Power Harrowing	40.00	29.00	10	15
Spring tine Harrowing	23.00	16.00	12	18
Seedbed Harrowing	18.00	13.20	12	20
Rolling (flat 3-4 tonne)	23.00	22.50	6	10
(ring, set of 3, 6 m)	14.20	12.00	15	25
Fertilizer Distributing (including loading and carting):				
Broadcast (125-375 kg/ha)	8.50-11.50 (fert. in field)	6.20	30	60
Broadcast (500-750 kg/ha)	—	10.00	22.5	45
Broadcast (1,000-1,250 kg/ha).	—	14.75	15	30
Pneumatic (125-375 kg/ha)	—	14.00	25	40
Drilling:				
Cereals : conventional	27.00	20.50	14	18
Cereals : combi-drilling	42.00	36.20	10	14
Grass (broadcast)	18.50	15.30	11	15
Roots/Maize	38.00	62.00	3½ (4 row)	5 (6 row)
Sugar Beet—precision drill	38.00	36.40	6 (6 row)	10 (12 row)
Destoning potato land	214.00	180.00	3.25	4
Potato Planting automatic	—	122.00	2½ (2 row)	3½
Potato Ridging	35.50-45.50	29.00	5½	7
Spraying (excl. materials):				
(extra £1-£2 for < 20ha)	11.00-15.00			
Low Volume (up to 175 l/ha)	—	7.75	35	75
Medium Vol. (200-300 l/ha)	—	9.00	30	60
High Volume (over 800 l/ha)	—	16.25	25	50
Tractor Hoeing Sugar Beet	—	36.50	5	8
Combine Harvesting:				
Combine Harvesting Cereals:			(hectares per hour)	
100 ha/year		102.00	¾-1	1-1¾
200 ha/year	75.00	73.00	1	1½
300 ha/year		66.00	1½	2
Carting to barn add	30/hr	15.00		
Straw Chopper incorporated	4.00			
Straw chopping (sep. operation).	40.00			
Oilseed rape (direct)		as cereals + 10%	⅔-1	¾-1¼
Beans	79.00	as cereals + 10%	⅔-1	¾-1¼

Operation	Contract	Average Farmer's Cost	Rate of Work (Ha per 8 Hr day)	
	£	£	Average	Premium
Peas		as cereals	¾-1	1-1½
Windrowing Oilseed Rape	43.00	—	1.2	1.4
Pick-up Baling (incl. string)	26p per bale	20.0p per bale	0.8 per hour	1.25 per hour
Big Baling (round)	1.60-1.81 per 80x70 cm bale	1.80 per bale	—	—
Crop Drying (inc. intake and pre-cleaning) (per tonne)				
Cereals:				
by 6 per cent	13.50	9.90	—	—
by 10 per cent	17.75	12.50	—	—
Oilseed Rape:				
by 5 per cent	18.75	12.00	—	—
by 10 per cent	24.00	15.60	—	—
Cleaning without drying (£/t)	8.50	—	—	—
Mobile Seed Cleaning (cereals) (per tonne) (inc. chemicals)	65-100	—	—	—
Grain Storage (per tonne per week)	32p	(see page 171)	—	—
Handling into store (per tonne)	£1.50	£1.20		
Handling out of store (per tonne)	£1.50	£1.20		
Potato Harvesting	£63/hour (2-row unmanned)	—	0.75	2
Sugar Beet Complete Harvesting	185	170	3.5	4.5
	(excl. carting)			
	215	215		
	(excl. carting)			
Grass Mowing/Topping				
(inc. Set-aside)	24.00	21.50	8	12
Swath Turning/Tedding	13.00	14.75	11	15
Forage Harvesting:				
First cut	55.00	—	—	—
Other cuts	45.00	—	—	—
Forage harvesting, carting and ensiling grass				
First cut	110.00	—	—	—
Other cuts	95.00	—	—	—
carting and ensiling maize 25-30 tonnes/ha	135	—	—	—
F.Y.M.: Tractor and Spreader	30.00 per hour	—	—	—
F.Y.M.: Tractor and Loader	26.50 per hour	—	—	—
Lime Spreading	3.00 per tonne	—	—	—

Operation	Contract	Average Farmer's Cost	Rate of Work (Ha per 8 Hr day)	
			Average	Premium
	£	£		
Hedge Cutting	20.00 per hour			
Tractor Hire (inc. driver and fuel):				
2 wheel drive, 56 kW (75 h.p.)	135	—	—	—
2 wheel drive, 75 kW (100 h.p.)	145	—	—	—
4 wheel drive, 75 kW (100 h.p.)	165	—	—	—
4 wheel drive, 112 kW (150 h.p.)	175	—	—	—
Trailer (with driver and tractor)	24.00 per hour	17.00 per hour	—	—

Acknowledgement. The above estimates for contractors' charges are based in part on information supplied by the National Association of Agricultural Contractors.

Contract Charge for All Operations (Cereals and Combinable Break Crops, 'stubble to stubble' i.e. up to and including Combine Harvesting and Carting the Grain to Store): £220 to £270/ha (£90-110/acre). Variations depend upon such factors as distance away, area contracted, size of fields, type of terrain, quality of soil and level of inputs (as affecting weight of crop to be harvested and carted). The charge is most typically £222 to £235/ha (£90-£95/acre).

Management Agreements. The above contract charge can be as low as £200/ha (£80/acre) where a proportion of the profit is also taken by the contractor or a neighbouring farmer after payment of a prior charge to the landowner. This was usually between £220 and £270/ha (£90-£100/acre) in 1995-8, but is now likely to average £200 to £210/ha (£80-£85/acre) owing to the fall in farm profitability. The percentage share of total gross margin less these two deductions has been typically 70%-80% to the contractor and 20%-30% to the landowner. These figures and percentages are expected to fall following CAP reform.

One sometimes sees farmers' total power and machinery costs compared with stubble to stubble contractors' charges. It has of course to be remembered that the former include many cost items not included in the latter, e.g. the cost of farm vehicles, fixed plant such as grain stores and general farm maintenance.

Total Cultivations cost typically £70/ha (£28/acre) on light land, £100/ha (£40/acre) on heavy land.

Haulage Costs
Great Britain average costs per tonne in 2004 and 2005 are summarised as follows:

	2004	2005
10 miles	£4.05	£4.29
20 miles	£4.52	£4.77
40 miles	£5.47	£5.74
60 miles	£6.42	£6.71
100 miles	£8.31	£8.65
150 miles	£10.68	£11.08

(Home-Grown Cereals Authority).

3. TRACTOR HOURS

(per annum)

A. Crops

	per hectare	
	Average	Premium
Cereals	9	7
Straw Harvesting	3.5	2.5
Potatoes	25	15
Sugar Beet	20	12
Vining Peas	20	12
Dried Peas	10	8
Field Beans	9	7
Oilseed Rape	9	7
Herbage Seeds:		
1 year undersown or 3 year direct drilled	7	5
1 year direct drilled	11	8
Hops (machine picked)	125	—
Kale (grazed)	8	6
Turnips/Swedes: folded/lifted	12/35	10/25
Mangolds	50	35
Fallow	12	7
Ley Establishment:		
Undersown	2	1
Direct Seed	7	4
Making Hay	12	8
Making Silage:		
1st Cut	12	8
2nd Cut	9	6
Grazing:		
Temporary Grass	3	2.5
Permanent Grass	2	1.5

B. Livestock

	per head Average
Dairy Cows	6
Other Cattle over 2 years	5
Other Cattle 1-2 years	4
Other Cattle ½-1 year	2.25
Calves 0-½ year	2.25
Yarded bullocks	3
Sheep, per ewe	1.25
Store sheep	0.8
Sows	1.75
Other pigs over 2 months	1
Laying Birds	0.04

1. For livestock, annual requirements are the per head requirements above multiplied by average numbers during the year (i.e. average numbers at end of each month).

2. As with labour, the number of tractors required by a farm depends more on the seasonal requirements and number required at any one time than on total annual tractor hours. These can be calculated from the seasonal labour data provided earlier in this book. The soil type and size/power of tractors purchased are obviously other relevant factors.

Tractor Power Requirements		hp/acre		hp/ha		kW/ha	
		av.	prem.	av.	prem.	av.	prem.
Combinable crops:	heavy land	.75	.65	1.85	1.5	1.4	1.1
	light land	.5	.45	1.25	1	0.95	0.75
Mixed cropping:	heavy land	1	.75	2.5	1.85	1.85	1.4
	light land	.7	.5	1.75	1.25	1.3	1.95

The average size of tractors purchased in 2005 was 94kw (126hp), a 1.2% fall on the previous year but still the second highest year. The number of units sold at 13,300 was 11% lower than in 2004. (Agricultural Engineers Association).

4. TRACTOR COSTS

(Estimates for Spring 2007)

	Two-Wheel Drive 43-49 kW (56-66 h.p.) £18,000		Four-Wheel Drive 56-65kW (75-85 h.p.) £25,000	
Initial Cost..............................	per year £	per hour £	per year £	per hour £
Depreciation............................	1,080	2.16	1,562	3.12
Insurance................................	227	0.45	285	0.57
Repairs and Maintenance..............	720	1.44	1,000	2.00
Fuel and Oil.............................	1,576	3.15	2,514	5.03
Total.....................................	3,603	7.21	5,362	10.72

	Four-Wheel Drive			
	76-90 kW (101-120 h.p.) £38,000		115-134 kW (154-180 h.p.) £50,000	
Initial Cost..............................	per year £	per hour £	per year £	per hour £
Depreciation............................	2,470	4.94	3,500	7.00
Insurance................................	391	0.78	478	0.96
Repairs and Maintenance..............	1,520	3.04	2,000	4.00
Fuel and Oil.............................	3,481	6.96	4,835	9.67
Total.....................................	7,863	15.73	10,813	21.63

	Crawlers			
	60 kW (80 h.p.) £22,000		200 kW (266 h.p.) £112,000	
Initial Cost..............................	per year £	per hour £	per year £	per hour £
Depreciation............................	1,540	3.08	7,840	15.68
Insurance................................	248	0.50	986	1.96
Repairs and Maintenance..............	880	1.76	4,480	8.96
Fuel and Oil.............................	2,476	4.95	8,250	16.50
Total.....................................	5,144	10.29	21,558	43.12

Depreciation is based on the assumption that small two-wheel drive tractors are sold for 40% of their original value after ten years and that small, medium and large four-wheel drive tractors (including crawlers) are sold for 37.5, 35 and 30% respectively of their original value after ten years. Annual repair costs have been calculated at 4% of initial cost for all tractors. No interest on capital has been included. Fuel has been charged at 39 pence per litre.

The hourly figures are based on a use of 500 hours a year. A greater annual use than this will mean higher annual costs but possibly lower hourly costs. On large arable farms in particular, many tractors do over 750 hours a year, or even 1,000 in some cases. Early replacement at a given annual use will increase depreciation costs per hour but should reduce repair costs. The hourly figures are averages for all types of work: heavy operations such as ploughing obviously have a higher cost than light work.

5. ESTIMATING ANNUAL MACHINERY COSTS

Annual machinery costs consist of depreciation, repairs, fuel and oil, contract charges, and vehicle tax and insurance. These can be budgeted in three ways, assuming there is no available information on past machinery costs on the farm:

(a) Per hectare, by looking up an average figure for the district, according to the size and type of farm. Approximate levels are shown in the tables of whole farm fixed costs (pages 175-178). This is obviously a very rough and ready measure.

(b) Per standard tractor hour. The crop area and livestock numbers can be multiplied by the appropriate standard (average) tractor hours per hectare and per head as given on page 162. The total can then be multiplied by the machinery cost per standard tractor hour as calculated from farm surveys. The following average figures (estimated for 2006/07) are based on 2001-2004 levels in South-East England.

Farm Type	Cost per Standard Tractor Hour
Mainly Sheep/Cattle, over 100 ha............................	£10.00
Sheep/Cattle and Arable, over 100 ha	£14.00
Mainly Sheep/Cattle, under 100 ha	£15.00
Mainly Dairying, under 60 ha..............................	£18.00
Mainly Dairying, over 120 ha.............................	£18.00
Mainly Arable, over 200 ha	£18.00
Dairying and Arable..	£18.00
Sheep/Cattle and Arable, under 100 ha.....................	£18.00
Mainly Dairying, 60-120 ha	£18.00
Mainly Arable, 100-200 ha................................	£21.00
Mainly Arable, under 100 ha..............................	£32.50

Premium levels are about 15 per cent lower.

The capital element of leasing (but not the interest) is included in depreciation.

The percentage composition of the total cost (based on Cambridge, Reading and Wye Farm Business Survey data) varies with size and type of farm but averages approximately:

Depreciation	Repairs	Fuel/Elec.	Contract	VTI*
35.5	22.5	17.5	20	5

*Vehicle tax and insurance.

This method may be used as a check on the per hectare calculation.

(N.B. The standard tractor hour is used only as a convenient measure of machinery input. The costs incorporate not only tractor costs but all other power and machinery expenses, including field machinery and implements, fixed equipment, landrovers, vans, use of farm car, etc.)

(c) Fully detailed calculation, costing and depreciating each machine in turn, including tractors, estimating repairs and fuel costs for each, and adding the charges for any contract work. The following tables give, for different types of machine, estimated life, annual depreciation, and estimated repairs according to annual use.

1. Estimated Useful Life (years) of Power Operated Machinery in relation to normal use

Equipment	Annual Use (hours)				
	25	50	100	200	300
Group 1:					
Ploughs, Cultivators, Toothed harrows, Hoes, Rolls, Ridgers, Potato planting attachments, Grain cleaners……………..	12+	12+	12+	12	10
Group 2:					
Disc harrows, Corn drills, Grain drying machines, Food grinders and mixers……	12+	12+	12	10	8
Group 3:					
Combine harvesters, Pick-up balers, Rotary cultivators, Hydraulic loaders……	12+	12+	12	9	7
Group 4:					
Mowers, Forage harvesters, Swath turners, Side-delivery rakes, Tedders, Hedge cutting machines, Semi-automatic potato planters and transplanters, Unit root drills, Mechanical root thinners……	12+	12	11	8	6
Group 5:					
Fertilizer distributors, Combine drills, Farmyard manure spreaders, Elevator Potato diggers, Spraying machines, Pea cutter windrowers………………	10	10	9	8	7
Miscellaneous:					
Beet harvesters………………………	11	10	9	6	5
Potato harvesters……………………	—	8	7	5	—
Milking machinery…………………	—	—	—	12	10

	Annual Use (hours)					
	500	750	1,000	1,500	2,000	2,500
Tractors…………	12+	12	10	7	6	5
Electric motors…	12+	12+	12+	12+	12	12

2. Depreciation: Average annual fall in value

(per cent of new price)

Frequency of renewal. Years	Complex. High Depreciation Rate e.g. potato harvesters, mobile pea viners, etc.	Established machines with many moving parts, e.g. tractors, combines, balers, forage harvesters	Simple equipment with few moving parts, e.g. ploughs, trailers
	%	%	%
1	40	30	20
2	27½	20	15
3	20*	16*	12½
4	17½†	14½	11½
5	15‡	13†	10½*
6	13½	12	9½
7	12	11	9
8	11	10‡	8½†
9	(10)	9½	8
10	(9½)	8½	7½‡

* Typical frequency of renewal with heavy use.

† Typical frequency of renewal with average use.

‡Typical frequency of renewal with light use.

Tractors. For the results of a recent study giving variations in tractor depreciation according to size and annual use as well as age when sold see P. Wilson and S. Davis, 'Estimating Depreciation in Tractors in the UK (etc)', 'Farm Management', Vol. 10, No. 4, Winter 1998/99, pp. 183-193.

3. Net Purchases and Closing Value of Farm Machinery in the Eastern Counties, 2004/05

£ per ha (% of total in brackets)

Type of Farm	Mainly Cereals	Mixed Cropping	Mixed Farms
Tractors	34 (46)	44 (35)	23 (26)
Vehicles	9 (12)	26 (21)	11 (12)
Harvesters	7 (10)	16 (13)	18 (20)
Other Equipment	24 (32)	40 (31)	37 (42)
Total	74 (100)	126 (100)	89 (100)
Total 2003/2004	88	137	87
Total 2002/2003	67	74	101
Closing Value (2004/2005)..........	411	587	360

Source: Report on Farming in the Eastern Counties of England, 2004/2005. University of Cambridge, Rural Business Unit, 2006.

4. Depreciation: Percentage rates

A. Straight-Line

Trade-in, Second-hand or Scrap Value as % of New Price

Years Retained	5%	10%	20%	25%	33%	40%	50%	60%
3	—	—	—	—	—	20	16%	13%
4	—	—	—	—	17	15	12%	—
5	—	—	—	15	13%	12	—	—
6	—	—	13%	12%	11	10	—	—
8	—	11	10	9%	—	—	—	—
10	9%	9	8	—	—	—	—	—
12	8	7%	—	—	—	—	—	—
15	6%	—	—	—	—	—	—	—

Example: If a machine costing £10,000 is retained for 8 years, at the end of which the trade-in value is 20% of the new price (i.e. £2,000), the average depreciation per annum has been £8,000 over 8 years = £1,000 (i.e. 10% of the new price).

B. Diminishing Balances

Trade-in, Second-hand or Scrap Value as % of New Price

Years Retained	5%	10%	20%	25%	33%	40%	50%	60%
3	—	—	—	—	—	26	21	16
4	—	—	—	—	24	20	16	—
5	—	—	—	24	20	17	—	—
6	—	—	23	20	17	14	—	—
8	—	25	18	16	—	—	—	—
10	25	20	15	—	—	—	—	—
12	22	17	—	—	—	—	—	—
15	18	—	—	—	—	—	—	—

Example: If a machine costing £10,000 is retained for 4 years, at the end of which the trade-in value is 40% of the new replacement price, the annual depreciation on the diminishing balances method is: Year 1, £2,000 (i.e. 20% of £10,000); Year 2, £1,600 (i.e. 20% of £8,000 [the written-down value]); Year 3, £1,280 (i.e. 20% of £6,400); Year 4, £1,024 (20% of £5,120). The total written-down value at the end of Year 4 is therefore £4,096 (i.e. £10,000 less the total depreciation of £5,904). This is approximately 41% of the new price. (Taking the percentages in the above table to decimal places would give the trade-in prices stated more precisely).

Note. The trade-in value taken for purposes of the calculation must exclude any 'disguised' discount on the price of the new machine.

Calculations of data collected as part of the Farm Management Survey in 1982/83 found the following to be the best estimates of the real diminishing balance rates of depreciation for machines sold during that year: (source: S. Cunningham, University of Exeter, Agricultural Economics Unit, 1987):

Tractors	15%	Potato harvesters	21%
Combine harvesters	15%	Forage harvesters	21%
Balers	18%	Beet harvesters	23%

For other machinery and equipment an average rate of 15% is suggested (author).

Tax Allowances on Machinery. See page 210.

5. Estimated Annual Cost of spares and repairs as a percentage of purchase price* at various levels of use

	Approximate Annual Use (hours)				Additional use per 100 hours
	500	750	1,000	1,500	ADD
	%	%	%	%	%
Tractors...	5.0	6.7	8.0	10.5	0.5

	Approximate Annual Use (hours)				Additional use per 100 hours
	50	100	150	200	ADD
Harvesting Machinery:	%	%	%	%	%
Combine Harvesters, self-propelled and engine-driven.........................	1.5	2.5	3.5	4.5	2.0
Combine Harvesters, p.t.o. driven, metered-chop forage harvesters, pick-up balers, potato harvesters, sugar beet harvesters.....................	3.0	5.0	6.0	7.0	2.0
Other Implements and Machines:					
Group 1					
Ploughs, Cultivators, Toothed harrows, Hoes, Elevator potato diggers......................................	4.5	8.0	11.0	14.0	6.0
Group 2:					
Rotary cultivators, Mowers, Pea cutter-windrowers..................	4.0	7.0	9.5	12.0	5.0
Group 3:					
Disc harrows, Fertilizer distributors, Farmyard manure spreaders, Combine drills, Potato planters with fertilizer attachment, Sprayers, Hedge-cutting machines..	3.0	5.5	7.5	9.5	4.0
Group 4:					
Swath turners, Tedders, Side-delivery rakes, Unit drills, Flail forage harvesters, Semi-automatic potato planters and transplanters, Down-the-row thinners.............................	2.5	4.5	6.5	8.5	4.0
Group 5:					
Corn drills, Milking machines, Hydraulic loaders, Potato planting Attachments............................	2.0	4.0	5.5	7.0	3.0
Group 6:					
Grain driers, Grain cleaners, Rolls, Hammer mills, Feed mixers Threshers...................................	1.5	2.0	2.5	3.0	0.5

* When it is known that a high purchase price is due to high quality and durability or a low price corresponds to a high rate of wear and tear, adjustments to the figures should be made.

6. IRRIGATION COSTS

(Estimated for 2007)

A. Capital Costs
(before any grant)

1. Pumps (delivering from 20 to 200 cubic metres per hour from a surface water source, all with portable suction and delivery fittings)

Tractor pto shaft driven c/w monitoring equipment	£2,700-5,200
Diesel engine driven c/w monitoring equipment	£4,800-20,000
Electric motor driven (c/w switch gear)	£2,500-36,000
Optional remote/wireless monitoring controls	£2,000-5,200

2. Pipelines (averages per m)

    Portable: (excl. valve take offs) 50mm, £2.50; 75 mm, £3.00; 100 mm, £4.50; 125 mm, £5.50; 150 mm, £7.75; (incl. valve take offs) 75 mm, £4.75; 100 mm, £6.00; 125 mm, £7.00; 150mm, £10.00.

    Permanent Underground P.V.C. pipe 12.5 bar rating (supply and laying) per metre: 75 mm, £4.50; 100 mm, £5.50; 150/160 mm, £7.75; 200 mm, £11.00; 250mm, £15.00. Hydrants: 100 mm x 100 mm, £200; 150 mm x 125 mm, £240.

3. Application Systems

    (a) Traditional portable hand move sprinkler systems
    75mm dia. Sprinkler line assemblies:

1 move/day/six day cycle	£750/ha
2 moves/day/six day cycle	£400/ha
3 moves/day/six day cycle	£275/ha

    (b) Solid set sprinkler lines – semi-permanent systems
    63mm dia. pipework assemblies at

18m x 18m triangulated spacings	£1,300/ha
As above but infra-red automated hand-held controls	£1,500/ha

    (c) Drip irrigation systems

16.5mm non-recoverable tape (excluding header mains, control valves and filtration equipment)	£350/ha

    (d) Hose reel systems using rain guns (average cost per machine)

		Manual controls	Electric Controls
Small	6-15m3/hr	£4,000	–
Medium	20-40m3/hr	£10,000	£11,000
Large	40-80m3/hr	£14,000	£15,000

    (e) Hose reel systems using irrigation booms (average cost per unit)

Small including	20m boom	£7,200
Medium including	40/50m boom	£13,500
Large including	70/80m boom	£27,000

    (f) Pivot and linear systems

Small pivot	200m radius (12.5ha)	£1,300/ha full circle
Large pivot	600m radius (113ha)	£775/ha full circle
Linear machine (dependent on length)		£1,500-2,100/ha

4. *Total*

   If no source works are needed, as with water from a river, or pond, total capital costs are likely to vary between £1,000 and £2,000 per hectare requiring irrigation at regular intervals, depending on the levels of sophistication and automation of the system installed.

B. *Water Sources*

An abstraction licence is required if more than 20m³ of water per day are taken from surface or underground sources. Abstraction charges vary widely, depending on the region, season and whether or not the source is supported by Environment Agency operations. Winter abstraction charges typically range from £2 to £3 per 1000m³ and summer rates from £15 to £30 per 1000m³ for sources that are not supported by the Environment Agency operations. Abstraction charges during the summer can be up to £90 per 1000m³ in areas where supplies are supported by Environment Agency operations. A charge of £3 per 1000m³ equals 75p per 25mm hectare whilst a charge of £25 per 1000m³ would cost £6.25 per hectare per 25mm application. Mains water at 80p per m³ would cost £200 per application of 25mm per hectare.

New time limited abstraction licences are difficult to obtain, especially for summer abstraction. Hence there is an increasing trend towards constructing reservoirs that can be used to store water abstracted during the winter months. The cost of clay-lined reservoirs varies widely but would typically be of the order of £1 per m³ of water stored. The cost of storing 4546m³ (1 million gallons) could easily be £4,000. This price could double if the reservoir is lined and fenced.

Because of licensing restrictions new boreholes are seldom installed and would typically cost from £160 to £250 per metre depth. The prices of specialist submerged pumping installations vary depending on the level of sophistication and could add between £600 and £900 per hectare to capital costs.

Charges for 2006/7 are: Application charge £135, advertising administration charge £100

Region	2006/7 Standard Unit Charges (£/1000m³)
Anglian	23.35
Midlands	13.28
Northumbria	24.27
Yorkshire	10.33
North West	12.34
Southern	17.36
South West including Wessex	19.06
Thames	12.39
EA Wales	12.18

Note: South West and Wessex regions have now been merged

C. *Overall Operating Costs*

Because of variations in individual farm circumstances in terms of source works and the irrigation system used the overall cost of applying 25mm per hectare can range widely, from £60 to £120. Very sophisticated systems distributing mains water over intensive specialist crops could be much more expensive.

Note:

The (approximate) imperial equivalents for metric values commonly used in irrigation are as follows:

1 cubic metre = 1,000 litres = 220 gallons.

A pump capacity of 100 cubic metres per hour is equivalent to 22,000 gallons per hour (366 gallons per minute).

In terms of water storage 1,000 cubic metres (1 million litres) is equivalent to 220,000 gallons (1 million gallons = 4,546 cubic metres).

1,000 cubic metres is sufficient to apply 25 millimetres of water over 4 hectares, which is approximately equivalent to applying 1 inch over 10 acres.

---

7. FIELD DRAINAGE

(Estimated for 2007)

1. Installation (costs per metre of excavating a trench, supplying and laying the pipe and backfilling with soil).

		£ per metre
Plastic pipes:	60mm diameter	1.50—1.80
	80mm diameter	1.75—2.25
	100mm diameter	2.60—2.80
	125mm diameter	3.50—3.75
	150mm diameter	4.00—4.50
	300mm diameter	9.50—10.50

The above rates apply to schemes of 5 hectares or more; smaller areas and patching up work can cost up to 50% more.

Supplying and laying permeable backfill to within 375mm of ground level will add between £2.40 and £3.00 per metre to costs.

Digging new open ditches (1.8m top width, 0.9m depth) costs £1.75-£2.25 per metre compared with improving existing ditches at £1.25 to £1.75 per metre.

Subsoiling or mole draining will cost in the region of £50-£65 per hectare.

2. *Total*

Costs per hectare for complete schemes will vary depending on the distance between laterals, soil type, size of area to be drained, region of the country and the time of year when the work is to be undertaken. The cost of a scheme with 20m spacing between laterals and using permeable backfill will typically be in the range £2,250 to £2,750 per hectare (£900-£1,100 per acre). Backfilling with soil, rather than with permeable material such as washed gravel, may reduce the cost by almost half but is only possible on certain types of soil. Equally, certain soil types which are particularly suitable for mole drainage may permit spacing between laterals to be increased to 40m or even 80m in some instances. Where this is possible costs will be reduced proportionately.

Grant aid is no longer available for field drainage.

8. GRAIN DRYING AND STORAGE COSTS

(Estimated for 2007)

A. Drying

Capital Costs: vary widely according to type and capacity of drier; assuming 125 to 150 hours of use per season and continuous flow driers with a rated capacity of 12 to 41 tonnes per hour at 5% extraction, a typical range from £38 per tonne dried annually for the smaller capacity driers falling to £23 for the higher throughput machines.

Annual fixed costs: depreciation and interest £2.50 to £5.50 per tonne.

Running costs: fuel and repairs, £3.75 to £5.50 per tonne (6 per cent moisture extraction) for oil-fired driers or where little heat is used in ventilated plants; £5.70 to £7.40 for electrically-heated driers. Little labour is required for modern automatic driers unless grain has to be passed over the drier several times.

Total operating costs: average £6.00 to £11.00 per tonne (6 per cent) for cereals; costs for oilseed rape are likely to be £2 to £3 per tonne higher when drying in ventilated bins, because of higher labour requirements.

B. Storage

Capital Costs: from approximately £75 per tonne (on-floor storage in a purpose-built building) to over £215 per tonne for an elaborate plant, including pit, elevator, conveyors, ventilated storage bins etc. in a new building.

Typical costs are given on page 189.

Depreciation and Interest: £175 per tonne depreciated over 20 years, with 6 per cent interest, equals £15.25 per annum; over 15 years, at 8 per cent interest, £20.45. (In highly mechanized bulk plants, part of this may be charged against harvesting and drying rather than entirely against storage).

Fuel and Repairs: £2.20 per tonne.

Extra Drying: Additional drying costs will be borne if storage necessitates further moisture reduction. Average £3.00 per tonne where own drier, £4.50 if dried on contract, for an additional 4% moisture extraction.

Loss of Weight: the value of the weight of grain lost should be considered as an additional cost of storage if storage requires extra drying. 2% = £1.30 to £1.60 per tonne.

Interest on Grain Stored: from 32p (£65 per tonne grain, at 6%) to 53p (£80 per tonne grain, at 8%) per month.

Contract Storage: typically £1.25 per tonne per month with a handling charge of around £1.50 per tonne for loading into store and out of store.

VI. OTHER FIXED COST DATA

1. WHOLE FARM FIXED COSTS

The following are a *broad indication* of the levels of fixed costs (£) per hectare (acre) for various types and sizes of farm, estimated for 2007, *including the value of unpaid family manual labour*, including that of the farmer and his wife.

All of these costs can of course vary widely according to many factors, especially the intensity of farming, e.g. the number of cows per 100 farm hectares on the mainly dairying and dairying and arable farms, or the hectares of intensive crops such as potatoes, sugar beet and vegetables per 100 farm hectares on the mixed cropping farms.

Furthermore, *the figures provided are only averages. 'Premium' farms of the same level of intensity can have labour, machinery and general overhead costs at least 20% lower.* However, the most profitable farms are often more intensive and therefore have higher fixed costs associated with the great intensity — but with substantially higher total farm gross margins; it is the net amount (TGM-TFC) that matters.

Regarding the under 75 or 100 hectare figures, it needs to be noted that these relate only to full-time holdings and do not include very intensive holdings occupying very small areas.

Regional survey results can be obtained from reports published annually by the agricultural economics departments of certain Universities and Colleges. These are listed on page 5.

The term 'fixed costs' is used here as it is in gross margin analysis and planning: a full explanation of the differences between fixed and variable costs in this context is given on pages 1 and 2. N*ote that all casual labour and contract work have been included under fixed costs.* In calculating enterprise gross margins on the individual farm these costs are normally allocated as variable costs if they are specific to a particular enterprise and vary approximately in proportion to its size, i.e. are approximately constant per hectare of a particular crop or per head of livestock. Otherwise they are included as fixed costs. In both cases, however, they could be regarded as substitutes for regular labour and/or the farmer's own machinery — which are both items of fixed cost. It is therefore simpler if both are included, fully, as fixed costs. If one is comparing results from accounts set out on a gross margin basis, and some or all of the casual labour and contract work have been included as variable costs (especially on cropping farms, e.g. for potato harvesting using casual labour or a contractor's machine), the necessary adjustments need to be made in making the comparisons.

Notes

Unpaid Labour. Refers to the value of unpaid family manual labour, including that of the farmer and his wife.

Depreciation. This is based on the 'historic' (i.e. original) cost of machinery, not on the current (i.e. replacement) cost. Although the latter is a truer reflection of the real loss of value of machinery (as is apparent when replacement becomes necessary), virtually all farm accounts use the historic cost method. Hence the use of the latter facilitates efficiency comparisons. It should, however, be noted that depreciation is based on current costs in the University/College reports listed on the previous page; on average this increases the figure by about 10%. Both this item and Repairs include vehicles.

Leasing Charges: The capital element, but not the interest, is included in depreciation; the proportion paid as interest varies according to the rate of interest paid and the length of the leasing period, but is typically 10 to 15%.

Rental Value. Estimated rent for owner-occupied land, based on actual rents of farms of similar type and size (established tenancies; i.e. not new / farm business tenancies). 'Landlord-type' expenses average about 40% of the estimated rent.

General Overheads include general farm maintenance and repairs, office expenses, water, insurance, fees, subscriptions, etc. 'Farm maintenance', i.e. repairs to property (buildings, roads, etc.), averages approximately one-quarter of total general farm overhead expenses.

In making comparisons with fixed costs taken from farm accounts it is important to note that in the figures below unpaid manual labour and a rental value for owner-occupied land are included. Very low 'target' figures given in press articles often omit these items and can therefore be misleading; usually, too, they relate only to large, very well appointed farms. Note too that the figures given below do not include management, whether paid or unpaid, nor interest on capital - again whether paid or unpaid. The margin after deducting the fixed costs below from the total gross margin plus any other farm receipts represents the total return to the management supplied and the capital utilised.

Labour, machinery and buildings are the main items of 'fixed' costs subject to change with major alterations in farm policy. Each has a separate section in this book.

Mainly Dairying

	Under 75 ha (Under 185 acres)		75-125 ha (185-310 acres)		Over 125 ha (Over 310 acres)	
Regular Labour (paid).......	75	(30)	130	(53)	185	(75)
Regular Labour (unpaid).....	575	(233)	350	(141)	185	(75)
Casual Labour.............	20	(8)	20	(8)	20	(8)
Total Labour	**670**	**(271)**	**500**	**(202)**	**390**	**(158)**
Machinery Depreciation.....	95	(38.5)	95	(38.5)	95	(38.5)
Machinery Repairs..........	70	(28)	70	(28)	70	(28)
Fuel, Elec., Oil.............	70	(28)	65	(26)	60	(24)
Contract..................	100	(41)	92.5	(37.5)	90	(36.5)
Vehicle Tax and Insurance ...	15	(6)	12.5	(5)	10	(4)
Total Power and Machinery	**350**	**(141)**	**335**	**(135)**	**325**	**(131)**
Rent/Rental Value..........	190	(77)	180	(73)	175	(71)
General Overhead Expenses..	170	(69)	140	(57)	130	(53)
**Total Fixed Costs..........	**1380**	**(558)**	**1155**	**(467)**	**1020**	**(413)**

Dairying and Arable

	Under 100 ha (Under 250 acres)		100-200 ha (250-500 acres)		Over 200 ha (Over 500 acres)	
Regular Labour (paid).......	225	(91)	240	(97)	230	(93)
Regular Labour (unpaid).....	225	(91)	150	(61)	65	(26)
Casual Labour.............	25	(10)	20	(8)	5	(2)
Total Labour	**475**	**(192)**	**425**	**(172)**	**300**	**(121)**
Machinery Depreciation.....	110	(45)	100	(41)	95	(39)
Machinery Repairs..........	70	(28)	60	(24)	55	(22)
Fuel, Elec., Oil.............	60	(24)	55	(22)	50	(20)
Contract..................	72.5	(29)	85	(34)	62.5	(25)
Vehicle Tax and Insurance ...	12.5	(5)	10	(4)	7.5	(3)
Total Power and Machinery	**325**	**(131)**	**310**	**(125)**	**270**	**(109)**
Rent/Rental Value..........	175	(71)	165	(67)	160	(65)
General Overhead Expenses..	130	(53)	125	(51)	115	(47)
**Total Fixed Costs..........	**1105**	**(447)**	**1025**	**(415)**	**845**	**(342)**

	Under 100 ha (Under 250 acres)		100-200 ha (250-500 acres)		Over 200 ha (Over 500 acres)	
Regular Labour (paid).......	90	(36)	65	(26)	85	(34)
Regular Labour (unpaid).....	165	(67)	100	(41)	40	(16)
Casual Labour............	15	(6)	10	(4)	10	(4)
Total Labour............	**270**	**(109)**	**175**	**(71)**	**135**	**(54)**
Machinery Depreciation.....	100	(41)	75	(31)	65	(27)
Machinery Repairs.........	45	(18)	40	(16)	40	(16)
Fuel, Elec., Oil............	42.5	(17)	37.5	(15)	37.5	(15)
Contract.................	60	(24)	47.5	(19)	25	(10)
Vehicle Tax and Insurance...	12.5	(5)	10	(4)	7.5	(3)
Total Power and Machinery	**260**	**(105)**	**210**	**(85)**	**175**	**(71)**
Rent/Rental Value.........	150	(61)	145	(59)	140	(57)
General Overhead Expenses..	120	(49)	90	(36)	70	(28)
Total Fixed Costs.........	**800**	**(324)**	**620**	**(251)**	**520**	**(210)**

With combinable break crops.

	Under 100 ha (Under 250 acres)		100-200 ha (250-500 acres)		Over 200 ha (Over 500 acres)	
Regular Labour (paid).......	75	(30)	110	(44.5)	145	(59)
Regular Labour (unpaid).....	215	(87)	100	(40.5)	35	(14)
Casual Labour............	5	(2)	10	(4)	10	(4)
Total Labour............	**295**	**(119)**	**220**	**(89)**	**190**	**(77)**
Machinery Depreciation.....	110	(45)	100	(41)	95	(39)
Machinery Repairs.........	60	(24)	60	(24)	57.5	(23)
Fuel, Elec., Oil............	50	(20)	47.5	(19)	42.5	(17)
Contract.................	55	(22)	65	(26)	60	(24)
Vehicle Tax and Insurance...	15	(6)	12.5	(5)	10	(4)
Total Power and Machinery	**290**	**(117)**	**285**	**(115)**	**265**	**(107)**
Rent/Rental Value.........	170	(69)	165	(67)	160	(65)
General Overhead Expenses..	125	(51)	95	(39)	75	(30)
Total Fixed Costs.........	**880**	**(356)**	**765**	**(310)**	**690**	**(279)**

With potatoes and/or sugar beet and/or field vegetables; grade 1 or 2 land.

Large-Scale Arable Farms (over 400 ha (1,000 acres))

There is no conclusive evidence from tables for different sizes of farm published in Cambridge University's Farm Business Survey in the Eastern Counties that total labour and machinery costs per hectare are on average significantly lower on arable farmers exceeding 400 ha (1,000 acres) than the average figures given above for such farms over 200ha (500 acres).

However, the lowest cost large-scale cereals and combinable crop farms average around £235/ha (£95/acre) for paid labour and machinery, which is the sort of figure at which farm management companies would be budgeting.

Mainly Sheep/Cattle (lowland)

	Under 100 ha (Under 250 acres)		100-200 ha (250-500 acres)		Over 200 ha (Over 500 acres)	
Regular Labour (paid).......	35	(14)	40	(16)	50	(20)
Regular Labour (unpaid).....	300	(122)	185	(75)	130	(53)
Casual Labour.............	15	(6)	10	(4)	10	(4)
Total Labour	**350**	**(142)**	**240**	**(97)**	**190**	**(77)**
Machinery Depreciation	65	(27)	60	(24)	55	(22)
Machinery Repairs..........	40	(16)	35	(14)	30	(12)
Fuel, Elec., Oil.............	45	(18)	35	(14)	30	(12)
Contract..................	40	(16)	35	(14)	32.5	(13)
Vehicle Tax and Insurance ...	10	(4)	10	(4)	7.5	(3)
Total Power and Machinery	**200**	**(81)**	**175**	**(70)**	**155**	**(62)**
Rent/Rental Value..........	125	(51)	120	(49)	110	(45)
General Overhead Expenses..	125	(50)	90	(36)	70	(28)
Total Fixed Costs..........	**800**	**(324)**	**625**	**(252)**	**525**	**(212)**

Sheep/Cattle and Arable

	Under 100 ha (Under 250 acres)		100-200 ha (250-500 acres)		Over 200 ha (Over 500 acres)	
Regular Labour (paid).......	30	(12)	45	(18)	85	(35)
Regular Labour (unpaid).....	255	(103)	130	(53)	60	(24)
Casual Labour.............	15	(6)	10	(4)	10	(4)
Total Labour	**300**	**(121)**	**185**	**(75)**	**155**	**(63)**
Machinery Depreciation	65	(26)	62.5	(25)	57.5	(23)
Machinery Repairs..........	32.5	(13)	32.5	(13)	30	(12)
Fuel, Elec., Oil.............	35	(15)	32.5	(13)	27.5	(11)
Contract..................	40	(16)	27.5	(11)	22.5	(9)
Vehicle Tax and Insurance ...	12.5	(5)	10	(4)	7.5	(3)
Total Power and Machinery	**185**	**(68)**	**165**	**(66)**	**145**	**(58)**
Rent/Rental Value..........	140	(57)	135	(55)	130	(53)
General Overhead Expenses..	105	(43)	80	(32)	70	(28)
Total Fixed Costs..........	**730**	**(296)**	**565**	**(228)**	**500**	**(202)**

Arable and Pigs/Poultry*

	Under 100 ha (Under 250 acres)		100-200 ha (250-500 acres)		Over 200 ha (Over 500 acres)	
Regular Labour (paid)	360	(146)	205	(83)	205	(83)
Regular Labour (unpaid)	205	(83)	95	(38)	25	(10)
Casual Labour	10	(4)	10	(4)	10	(4)
Total Labour	**575**	**(233)**	**310**	**(125)**	**240**	**(97)**
Machinery Depreciation	130	(53)	110	(45)	100	(41)
Machinery Repairs	90	(36)	75	(30)	65	(26)
Fuel, Elec., Oil	80	(33)	72.5	(29)	60	(24)
Contract	75	(30)	75	(30)	75	(30)
Vehicle Tax and Insurance	15	(6)	12.5	(5)	10	(4)
Total Power and Machinery	**390**	**(158)**	**345**	**(139)**	**310**	**(125)**
Rent/Rental Value	190	(76)	180	(73)	175	(71)
General Overhead Expenses	175	(71)	155	(63)	135	(55)
Total Fixed Costs	**1330**	**(538)**	**990**	**(400)**	**860**	**(348)**

The number of pigs in relation to the total farm area varies widely, and so, therefore, can these per hectare (per acre) figures.

Livestock Rearing

	Upland (per adjusted		Hill hectare (acre))*	
Regular Labour (paid)	70	(28.5)	40	(16)
Regular Labour (unpaid)	100	(40.5)	70	(29)
Casual Labour	10	(4)	5	(2)
Total Labour	**180**	**(73)**	**115**	**(47)**
Machinery Depreciation	60	(24)	42.5	(17)
Machinery Repairs	25	(10)	15	(6)
Fuel, Elec., Oil	22.5	(9)	20	(8)
Contract	22.5	(9)	10	(4)
Vehicle Tax and Insurance	5	(2)	2.5	(1)
Total Power and Machinery	**135**	**(54)**	**90**	**(36)**
Rent/Rental Value	100	(40.5)	50	(20)
General Overhead Expenses	75	(30.5)	45	(18)
Total Fixed Costs	**490**	**(198)**	**300**	**(121)**

Divisors to give the actual area figure = upland 1.33, hill 2.2.

Horticultural Holdings

See page 51.

2. RENTS

Unless otherwise stated the figures in this section relate to farms let with a combination of crops, grass and rough grazing in England; they include housing and buildings, as available.

It has to be borne in mind that rough grazing, including upland, is included in the figures given below. Some farms are likely to be let at below competitive rates, for various reasons. **The average rent for lowland, excluding woodland and rough grazing, for farms under full agricultural tenancies is likely to be approximately £150 per ha, £60 per acre, in 2007.** Rents for land are tending to fall, but this is being offset by higher rents for housing and buildings so that overall per hectare rents are stable. The levels on large mixed arable farms (i.e. including potatoes, sugar beet and/or vegetables) on very good soil, or well-equipped dairy farms, will tend to average £160 to £210 per ha, £65 to £85 per acre. Rents on moderate, below average, quality farms, particularly with full repairing and insuring leases, are likely to average £110 to £120 per ha, £45 to £50 per acre. Some future rents, at least, are likely to be affected by the Single Payment Scheme provisions which started in 2005; it is, however, too early as yet to speculate; the situation will vary from farm to farm and differ between the different regions/countries of the UK. The tenant is the only person who can claim the single farm payment, except in some seasonal agreements where the landlord may be able to claim.

Farm Business Tenancy rents will remain higher than those above for traditional tenancies, although significantly lower on average than those initially offered when such tenancies first became available, in 1996, at a relatively prosperous time. Farmers who already own land, with little or no mortgage, can afford to offer a higher figure than bidders with no other farm. £200/ha (£80/acre) for cereals land of reasonable quality was still common in 2006 in east and south-east England.

The following data all relate to 2004. The figures are rounded to the nearest 50p/ha or 25p/acre.

Average Rent by Type of Agreement:	£/ha (acre)
Full Agricultural Tenancies........................	110 (44.50)
Farm Business Tenancies for 1 year and over	143 (58.00)
Seasonal Lets of less than one year..................	113 (45.75)

Average Rent by Farm Type: (£ per ha [acre])	Full Agricultural Tenancies		Farm Business Tenancies* All Agreements
	Land Only	**Other**	
Cereal..................	129.00 (52.25)	123.50 (50.00)	160.00 (64.75)
General Cropping.........	134.00 (54.25)	141.50 (57.25)	205.00 (83.00)
Dairy	117.00 (47.25)	131.50 (53.25)	176.50 (71.50)
Cattle and Sheep (Lowland).	102.00 (41.25)	115.50 (46.75)	98.00 (39.75)
Cattle and Sheep (LFA)....	26.00 (10.50)	35.00 (14.25)	47.00 (19.00)
All	101.50 (41.00)	112.00 (45.50)	143.50 (58.00)

* for a year and over

Source of Data

DEFRA (Farming Statistics): Tenanted Land Survey - England, 2004. The survey's results were based on approximately 7,500 agreements, covering 9% of all tenanted land in England by area. There was no Tenanted Land Survey published for 2005; there will be for 2006.

3. LAND PRICES

Sale Value of Farmland, England and Wales (£ per hectare (acre))

(1) Auction Sales (with Vacant Possession only):
Oxford Institute/Savills(1) series, 1937-2000

Year	Current Prices		Real Values(2)		Index (3)	Year	Current Prices		Real Values(2)		Index (3)
1937-9	0	(24)	2030	(822)	33	1982	4557	(1844)	8373	(3389)	136
1945	111	(45)	2246	(909)	37	1983	5145	(2082)	9041	(3659)	147
1955	198	(80)	3274	(1325)	53	1984	4888	(1978)	8180	(3310)	133
1960	198	(80)	2643	(1070)	43	1985	4781	(1935)	7542	(3052)	123
1965	304	(123)	3608	(1460)	59	1986	4193	(1697)	6398	(2589)	104
1970	581	(235)	5857	(2370)	95	1987	4944	(2001)	7242	(2931)	118
1971	605	(245)	4872	(1972)	79	1988	6716	(2718)	9376	(3794)	153
1971	647	(262)	4761	(1927)	77	1989	6558	(2654)	8493	(3437)	138
1972	1473	(596)	9603	(3886)	156	1990	6346	(2568)	7505	(3037)	122
1973	1871	(757)	11793	(4773)	192	1991	6007	(2431)	6708	(2715)	109
1974	1572	(636)	8529	(3452)	139	1992	5441	(2202)	5859	(2371)	95
1975	1332	(539)	5817	(2354)	95	1993	5456	(2208)	5783	(2340)	94
1976	1814	(734)	6798	(2751)	111	1994	5028	(2035)	5204	(2106)	85
1977	2449	(991)	7922	(3206)	129	1995	6140	(2484)	6140	(2485)	100
1988	3279	(1327)	9794	(3964)	160	1996	8797	(3560)	8591	(3477)	140
1979	4371	(1769)	11513	(4659)	188	1997	8065	(3263)	7636	(3090)	124
1980	4265	(1726)	9521	(3853)	155	1998	7250	(2934)	6637	(2686)	108
1981	4272	(1729)	8525	(3450)	139	1999	13920	(5634)	12565	(5085)	205
						2000	7895	(3196)	7125	(2885)	116

(1) Savills after 1988. (2) At 1995 general price levels. (3) Real Values, 1995 = 100.

From 1970, figures were based on sales reports in the Estates Gazette and the Farmers Weekly, plus some unpublished sales, with a minimum size of 10 hectares

The series was discontinued after 2000.

(2) Current Agricultural Prices (CALP and CALP/RICS) series *(vacant possession only)*

Covers sales of 5 ha and above but excludes land sold for development or forestry, gifts, inheritances and compulsory purchases. Includes sales of bare land as well as land with dwellings, buildings, etc. Calculated by dividing the total value of sales by total area sold.

CALP series (England only) data collected jointly by ADAS (Agricultural Development and Advisory Service) AMC (Agricultural Mortgage Corporation) and CLA (then Country Landowners Association) and were published by the AMC until 1993. A CALP/RICS Farmland Price Index (England and Wales) began in 1995.

(i) *CALP Annual Figures*

	Average price (A)	Average price (B): in 1995 £	Index (of B) (1995 = 100)
1978	3160 (1280)	9438 (3820)	176
1979	4140 (1675)	10497 (4248)	196
1980	3975 (1610)	8874 (3591)	166
1981	3940 (1595)	7863 (3182)	147
1982	4125 (1670)	7579 (3067)	142
1983	4630 (1875)	8288 (3354)	155
1984	4555 (1845)	7622 (3085)	142
1985	4340 (1755)	6846 (2771)	128
1986	3675 (1485)	5608 (2270)	105
1987	3780 (1530)	5537 (2241)	103
1988	5350 (2165)	7469 (3023)	139
1989	5595 (2265)	7245 (2932)	135
1990	4440 (1795)	5251 (2125)	98
1991	4145 (1675)	4629 (1873)	86
1992	3658 (1480)	3939 (1594)	74
1993	3608 (1460)	3824 (1548)	71
1994	5085 (2060)	5263 (2130)	98
1995	5355 (2170)	5355 (2170)	100
1996	6940 (2810)	6778 (2743)	127
1997	7295 (2955)	6907 (2795)	129
1998	7055 (2855)	6459 (2613)	121

Series discontinued: superseded by (ii) below

(ii) *CALP/RICS Farmland Price Index**

	2001	2002	2003	2004	2005
Jan. – Mar.	7273 (2943)	7906 (3200)	7817 (3163)	9526 (3855)	9099 (3682)
Apr. – Jun.	7967 (3224)	7579 (3067)	7910 (3201)	9255 (3745)	8834 (3575)
Jul. – Sept.	7169 (2901)	7694 (3114)	7629 (3087)	10670 (4318)	10053 (4068)
Oct. – Dec.	7327 (2965)	6390 (2586)	8367 (3386)	9828 (3977)	9494 (3842)

* Average prices weighted to remove the effect of exceptional sales.

Sales of vacant possession land in England and Wales, excluding residential value where more than 50% of total sale price; value of milk quota excluded. Calculated by dividing total value of sales by total area sold. Figures for the most recent quarters are subject to revision as further information becomes available. Also, the reliability of these figures as true reflections of price trends is limited by the small amounts of land being sold in recent years. **A more realistic figure is £6,800/ha (2,750/acre) for prime arable land (including buildings, but excluding houses and cottages) in mid-2006.**

(iii) **FPD Savills Farmland Value Survey** *(vacant possession, lowland, excluding houses)*

	March	June	September	December
1993	2995 (1212)	3145 (1272)	3290 (1332)	3440 (1393)
1994	3500 (1417)	3565 (1442)	3625 (1467)	3685 (1491)
1995	3960 (1603)	4240 (1715)	4520 (1829)	4800 (1942)
1996	5035 (2037)	5265 (2131)	5310 (2149)	5355 (2167)
1997	5405 (2187)	5450 (2206)	5390 (2181)	5325 (2155)
1998	5155 (2086)	5035 (2038)	4860 (1967)	4755 (1925)
1999	4740 (1918)	4775 (1932)	4780 (1934)	4705 (1904)
2000	4575 (1852)	4560 (1846)	4445 (1799)	4405 (1782)
2001	4360 (1765)	4360 (1764)	4365 (1766)	4360 (1765)
2002	N/A	4370 (1769)	N/A	4325 (1751)
2003	N/A	4330 (1752)	N/A	4440 (1797)
2004	N/A	4845 (1961)	—	5145 (2083)
2005	N/A	5410 (2190)	N/A	5780 (2339)
2006	N/A	6030 (2440)*	—	—

This series includes farm buildings but not houses or cottages. A static portfolio of nine types of equipped VP land in 25 regions in Britain is valued quarterly by a panel of expert agricultural valuers, taking into account local transactions and any special circumstances.

* Prime arable 7250 (2935); arable 6480 (2622); poor arable 4620 (1870); dairy 6360 (2574); pasture 5150 (2084); poorer pasture 3960 (1602).

(3) *Inland Revenue Returns (England only; Oct.-Sept. 30 years)*

	Vacant Possession		Tenanted	
Year(1)	Farms(2)	Bare Land	Farms(2)	Bare Land
1980/1	3568 (1444)	3325 (1346)	2334 (945)	2354 (953)
1981/2	3503 (1418)	3281 (1328)	2644 (1070)	1340 (542)
1982/3	3766 (1524)	3525 (1427)	2549 (1032)	2210 (894)
1983/4	3761 (1522)	3835 (1552)	2389 (967)	2511 (1016)
1984/5	4258 (1723)	3466 (1403)	2879 (1165)	2310 (935)
1985/6	4055 (1641)	3477 (1407)	2192 (887)	2217 (897)
1986/7	3703 (1499)	3023 (1223)	2141 (866)	1777 (719)
1987/8	3750 (1518)	3140 (1271)	2252 (911)	2476 (1002)
1988/9	4739 (1918)	3521 (1425)	3178 (1286)(3)	1929 (781)
1989/90	5355 (2167)	4080 (1651)	2143 (867)	2093 (847)
1990/91	5515 (2231)	3750 (1517)	2090 (846)	2505 (1014)
1991/92	5015 (2030)	3370 (1363)	2505 (1015)	1465 (592)
1992/93	4405 (1785)	3120 (1265)	1680 (680)	2045 (830)(3)
1993/94	4319 (1748)	3235 (1309)	2102 (851)	1116 (452)
1994/95	4661 (1886)	3608 (1460)	1860 (753)	1720 (696)
1995/96	5058 (2047)	3936 (1593)	2605 (1054)	1490 (603)
1996/97	6224 (2519)	4548 (1841)	4513 (1826)	2623 (1062)

Series discontinued: see (4) below.

1. There was invariably a delay between the dates when a price was agreed and when it was notified to the Inland Revenue and thus included in the above figures; this time-lag was thought to average about 9 months.

2. Farms = Land and Buildings, including the farmhouse.

3. High figure caused by a few untypically high-priced transactions.

The above figures related to all sales of agricultural properties of 5 ha and over except those for development and other non-agricultural purposes. They included any sales at prices below ruling open market value (as between members of a family), sales where the vendor retains certain (e.g. sporting) rights, sales in which the farmhouse represented a substantial part of the total value, and sales of land which may, in the purchaser's view, have had an element of development value.

Vacant Possession Premium

On the basis of the Inland Revenue Returns above the average price of tenanted land as a percentage of vacant possession land in the five years 1992/93 to 1996/97 was 50% for whole farms and 49% for bare land. In individual years the figure varied from 38% to 73% for whole farms and from 35% to 65% for bare land. A sudden jump (for whole farms) from a previous high of around 50% to 72.5% in 1996/97 could have been attributed to the introduction of farm business tenancies in 1995. For later figures, see (4) B below.

(4) Valuation Office Agency Transactions (England only)

This relatively new series, issued now by DEFRA, uses the same basic data source as the Inland Revenue Returns series above, which it has replaced, but the sales are now analysed on the basis of the time period when the transactions actually take place, not when validated by the Inland Revenue on average nine months later. Hence there is no longer a time-lag. Some restrictions and technical adjustments mean that the new series is not strictly comparable with the old one. The figures are subject to revision for up to three years as late returns are received, but the later revisions are expected to be minor. The 2002 to 2004 figures below are therefore denoted as provisional estimates. (Number of sales: 1999, 3,437; 2000, 3,227; 2001, 2,603; 2002, 3,025; 2003, 2,442; 2004, 1504).

A. By Property Type	Land and Dwellings	Land and Buildings	Land only
1993	4,532 (1,834)	3,315 (1,342)	3,297 (1,334)
1994	5,257 (2,127)	3,918 (1,586)	3,565 (1,443)
1995	5,557 (2,249)	5,125 (2,074)	4,177 (1,690)
1996	7,111 (2,878)	5,596 (2,265)	5,333 (2,158)
1997	7,698 (3,155)	6,565 (2,657)	5,528 (2,237)
1998	7,076 (2,864)	6,294 (2,547)	5,414 (2,191)
1999	9,754 (3,947)	6,217 (2,516)	5,282 (2,138)
2000	10,488 (4,244)	6,922 (2,801)	5,603 (2,268)
2001	11,411 (4,618)	6,466 (2,617)	5,674 (2,296)
2002	10,471 (4,237)	6,568 (2,658)	5,469 (2,213)
2003	11,829 (4,787)	6,758 (2,735)	5,342 (2162)
2004	9,269 (3,751)	7,455 (3017)	6,260 (2533)

B. By Tenure	Vacant Possession	Tenanted
1993	3,829 (1,550)	1,855 (751)
1994	4,323 (1,750)	2,069 (837)
1995	4,946 (2,002)	2,566 (1,038)
1996	6,132 (2,482)	3,227 (1,306)
1997	6,579 (2,662)	3,504 (1,418)
1998	6,191 (2,505)	3,652 (1,478)
1999	6,631 (2,684)	8,391 (3,396)*
2000	7,112 (2,878)	3,996 (1,605)
2001	7,353 (2,976)	13,581 (5,496)*
2002	6,948 (2,812)	3,169 (1,282)
2003	7,244 (2932)	3,995 (1,617)
2004	7,296 (2953)	7,539 (3,051)

* Tenanted figures in 1999 and 2001 affected by a small number of high value sales.

C. By Size Group

C. By Size Group	5-49.9 ha	50-99.9 ha	100 ha and over	All sales*
1993	4,487 (1,816)	3,808 (1,541)	2,944 (1,191)	3,791 (1,534)
1994	5,138 (2,079)	4,272 (1,729)	3,145 (1,273)	4,229 (1,711)
1995	5,933 (2,401)	4,902 (1,984)	3,555 (1,439)	4,788 (1,938)
1996	6,962 (2,817)	5,737 (2,322)	5,161 (2,089)	6,058 (2,452)
1997	7,259 (2,938)	6,118 (2,476)	5,578 (2,257)	6,448 (2,609)
1998	7,126 (2,884)	6,326 (2,560)	4,873 (1,972)	6,134 (2,482)
1999	7,349 (2,974)	5,866 (2,374)	5,975 (2,418)	6,673 (2,701)
2000	7,531 (3,048)	6,686 (2,706)	6,298 (2,549)	7,082 (2,866)
2001	8,357 (3,382)	6,878 (2,783)	5,825 (2,357)	7,406 (2,997)
2002	8,072 (3,276)	6,580 (2,663)	5,010 (2,027)	6,917 (2,799)
2003	8,731 (3,533)	6,508 (2,634)	4,958 (2,006)	7,132 (2886)
2004	8,919 (3,609)	7,002 (2,834)	4,787 (1,937)	7,312 (2,959)

* All sales, 2005: 1st quarter 8,665 (3,507), 2nd 8,809 (3,565)

D. By Land Class*

D. By Land Class*	Grade 1 and 2	Grade 3	Grade 4	All sales*
1995	5,144 (2,082)	5,473 (2,215)	2,677 (1,083)	3,397 (1,375)
1996	6,798 (2,751)	6,396 (2,588)	3,700 (1,497)	4,474 (1,811)
1997	7,348 (2,974)	7,217 (2,921)	3,135 (1,269)	3,738 (1,513)
1998	6,974 (2,822)	6,569 (2,658)	4,066 (1,645)	3,384 (1,369)
1999	7,354 (2,976)	7,313 (2,960)	4,043 (1,636)	2,576 (1,042)
2000	6,948 (2,812)	7,589 (3,071)	5,266 (2,131)	5,029 (2,035)
2001	7,072 (2,862)	7,904 (3,199)	5,297 (2,144)	5,271 (2,133)
2002	6,696 (2,710)	7,614 (3,081)	4,818 (1,950)	4,158 (1,683)
2003	7,044 (2,851)	7,704 (3,118)	6,141 (2,485)	3,557 (1,439)
2004	7,369 (2,982)	8,397 (3,398)	4,857 (1,966)	4,007 (1,622)

* predominant grade of land. % total area, England and Wales: Grade 1, 2.3%; 2, 16.9%; 3, 54.7% (a 19.3, b 35.4); 4, 15.0%; 5, 11.1%.

E. By Region (all sales)

E. By Region (all sales)	2002	2003	2004
North East	4,282 (1,733)	3,364 (1,361)	2,645 (1,070)
North West	6,329 (2,561)	7,709 (3,120)	6,460 (2,614)
Yorkshire and Humber	5,530 (2,238)	6,198 (2,508)	5,515 (2,232)
East Midlands	6,786 (2,746)	7,341 (2,971)	7,852 (3,178)
West Midlands	7,288 (2,949)	6,670 (2,699)	8,102 (3,279)
East of England	7,357 (2,977)	6,756 (2,734)	6,543 (2,648)
South East	9,082 (3,675)	9,131 (3,695)	9,999 (4,046)
South West	7,962 (3,222)	9,092 (3,679)	8,879 (3,593)

Sale Value of Forests and Woodlands

(1) General

The figures in this section relate to planted land sold (over 25 hectares) so that values include the value of the property (land) and the timber. The market has been buoyant in recent years with strong demand and increasing areas sold.. In the forest sector average prices were up 22% in the year to September 2005 compared to 2004, and so the 5 year average values given below will tend to understate the current market and the expectation for 2007. Timber prices have been improving, but by a much smaller margin than the rise in forest values.

(2) Forests

For forests the figures are for the UK and are predominantly upland with at least 50% coniferous content. Values vary with many factors and only size of block and age are recorded here, but yield class is also important.

Forests (approximate 5 year average values): young (1-10 years) £1,200/ha (£485/acre); mid-rotation (11-20 years) £1,100/ha (£445/acre); semi-mature (21-30 years) £1,800/ha (£730/acre); mature (over 30 years) £2,000/ha (£800/acre); mature (over 40 years), 3 year average £2,750/ha (£1,110/acre).

Variations with forest size (approx): below 50 ha, £2,400/ha (£975/acre); 51-100 ha, £2,100/ha (£850/acre); over 100 ha, £1,600/ha (£650/acre).

(3) Woodlands

For woodlands the data relates to England and Wales in 2004 – the series is now discontinued.

Average price range of good quality established lowland woodland: £1500-2000/ha (£600-800/acre): average price approx. £1,825/ha (£740/acre) in 2004; £1,600 (£650/acre) in 2003. However, 'small woodlands' usually fetch far more, averaging over £4,000/ha (£1,600/acre) for a 10 to 25 ha wood up to over £8,000/ha (£3,200/acre) for a 2 ha (5 acre) wood; the average was nearly £7,400/ha (£3,000/acre) in England and Wales in 2004 (£10,300 (£4,170) in South East England).

Source: Tilhill and FPD Savills.

4. BUILDINGS

A. Building Costs

Building costs are notoriously variable. Many factors influence a contractor's price, including distance from his yard, size of contract, site access, site conditions, complexity of work, familiarity with the type of work and his current work load. There will also be differences in efficiency and standard of work between contractors and, as is often the case with farm buildings, the absence of detailed specification by the client may mean that different contractors will not have quoted for identical buildings. The number of extras that are found to be required after a contract has been agreed will also vary.

The costs given below can only be taken as an approximate guide. They refer to new buildings, erected by contractor on a clear level site and exclude VAT and any grants that may be available.

Sources of Further Information

The costs below are based on information gathered by SAC Buildings Design Services, Aberdeen, cross-checked with other sources to ensure general applicability. *The figures were provided in 2005/06; hence average costs in 2007 could be 5% or so higher.* More detailed information is available in the following publications. The books and journals giving general building cost information generally assume knowledge of how to take off quantities for building work.

Specialised Information on Farm Building Costs

Farm Building Cost Guide 2005/2006 published annually by Building Design Services.

Standard Costs Part 1: Specifications; Part 2: Costs. Published by DEFRA and the Agricultural Departments in Scotland, Wales and Northern Ireland. Used when claiming government grants on a standard-cost basis.

General Building Cost Information

Books are produced by a number of publishers with annual or more frequent new editions and updates. Examples are Laxton's Building Price Book, Spon's Architects' and Builders' Price Book, and Wessex Comprehensive Building Price Book. Regularly updated cost information is also given in several professional and trade journals.

1. Constituent Parts

Frame, Roof and Foundations *per m2 floor area*

1. Open-sided timber framed pole barn with round pole uprights on concrete bases, sawn timber rafters and purlins, high-tensile galvanised steel cladding to roof and gable ends above eaves, hardcore floor, eaves height 4.8 m, 9 m span, no side cladding, rainwater drainage to soakaways. £50

2. Open-sided steel portal-framed building with fibre-cement or plastic coated steel cladding to roof and gables above eaves, hardcore floor, eaves height 4.8 m, no side cladding, rainwater drainage to soakaways.

9 m span	£100
13.2 m span	£85
18 m span	£80

    Cost breakdown of 2 above

3.

Materials:	portal frame and purlins	26%
	foundations	3%
	roofing	16%
	rainwater and drainage	3%
	hardcore and blinding	2%
	Total Materials	50%
Erection:	portal frame and purlins	19%
	foundations	2%
	roofing	19%
	rainwater and drainage	5%
	hardcore and blinding	5%
	Total Erection	50%

Roof cladding

per m²

1. Natural grey fibre-cement, 146 mm corrugations fixed with drive screws

Materials	£7.80	
Fixing	£14.80	
Total		£22.60

2. Extra for coloured sheet   £1.80
3. Deduct for translucent sheets   £0.10
4. Deduct for PVC-coated steel   £4.50
5. Deduct for high-tensile corrugated galvanised steel sheeting   £8.00
6. PVC 150 mm half-round gutter on fascia brackets, including stop-ends and outlets   £20.00
7. PVC 100 mm rainwater pipe with fixings, swanneck and shoe   £39.00

per m run

8. Fibre-cement close-fitting ridge   £33.25
9. Fibre-cement ventilating ridge   £36.00

Walls and Cladding

per m²

1. Concrete blockwork, fair faced and pointed both sides
   - 150 mm thick   £39.00
   - 215 mm thick   £55.50
   - 215 mm thick hollow blocks   £58.00
   - 215 mm thick hollow blocks, filled and reinforced   £70.00
2. Extra for rendering or roughcast to blockwork on one side   £18.50
3. Vertical spaced boarding 21x 145 mm with 19 mm gaps including horizontal rails, all pressure treated   £22.50
4. Fibre-cement vertical cladding, including rails   £35.00
5. Corrugated high-tensile steel side cladding, including rails   £28.00
6. Wall element: 215 mm thick blockwork, including strip foundation (base 750 mm below ground level), 2.5 m height above ground level   £142 per m run

Floors

per m²

1. Concrete floor 100 mm thick, Gen 3 mix, on 150 mm hardcore, including excavation: £28.90

    Breakdown:
    - (a) excavate, level and compact — £2.60
    - (b) hardcore — £4.10
    - (c) blinding — £1.90
    - (d) damp-proof membrane — £1.60
    - (e) premixed concrete spread and compacted — £15.50
    - (f) float finish — £3.30

2. Extra to above for
    - (a) 150 mm instead of 100 mm — £4.80
    - (b) laying concrete to falls — £1.35
    - (c) broom or textured finish — £1.60
    - (d) Carborundum dust non-slip finish — £2.80
    - (e) insulating concrete — £8.20

3. Reinforced concrete slatted floors for cattle
    - (a) cattle loading — £62.00
    - (b) tractor loading — £68.50

4. Reinforced concrete slats for pigs — £45.00

5. Insulating floor, including excavation and base
    - (a) 27 mm expanded polystyrene, 38 mm screed — £40.00
    - (b) insulating concrete with lightweight aggregate — £32.00
    - (c) as (b) with 20 mm screed — £40.00

6. Form channel in concrete — £3.50 per m run

7. Excavate for cast 1 m3 in-situ concrete bases for stanchions — £101 each

Services and Fittings

per m²

1. Drainage: 100 mm PVC pipe laid in trench, including 750 mm deep excavation and backfill — £20.50 per m run

    Breakdown:
    - (a) excavate and backfill — £13.00
    - (b) 100 mm PVC pipe laid — £7.50

    Extras:
    - (c) add to (a) for 1 m deep — £3.00
    - (d) add to (b) for 150 mm pipe — £5.20

2. Excavate soakaway and fill with stones — £91.00 each

3. Trap and grid top, 100 mm PVC — £16.00 each

4. Yard gully with heavy duty road grating 400 x 300 mm — £150 each

5. Inspection chamber 900 mm deep, 450 x 600 mm opening and medium duty cast iron cover — £320 each

6. Above-ground vitreous enamel slurry tank on concrete base, 1000 m³ — £32,000 each

7. Reception pit, 20 m³ — £3.200 each

8. Slurry channel beneath (not including) slats, 1.8 m deep, 3m wide — £360 per m run

9. Lighting: 1.5 m 60W single fluorescent unit, including wiring and switch — £110 each

    Extras:
    - (a) PVC conduit — £70
    - (b) screwed steel conduit — £90

10.	Power: 13A switched outlet	£70 each
11.	Diagonal feed fence, fixed, including posts (painted)	£68 per m run
12.	Tombstone feed fence, fixed, including posts (painted)	£82 per m run
13.	Feed bunker	£48 per m run
14.	Hay rack, wall fixing	£52 per m run
15.	Cubicle division, galvanised, fixed in place	£70 each
16.	Fencing: three-rail timber with posts, all pressure treated	£17.00 per m run

17. Gate, 3 m wide, galvanised steel, including posts set in concrete
    (a) medium duty   £165 each
    (b) heavy duty   £225 each
    Deduct for painted instead of galvanised finish   £35

2. Complete Buildings

Fully Covered and Enclosed Barn

Portal frame, 18 m span, 6 m bays, 6 m to eaves, 3 m high blockwork walls with sheet cladding above, 6 m sliding doors at either end, 150mm thick concrete floor — £150 per m^2 floor area

Cows and Cattle Housing

1.	Covered strawed yard, enclosed with ventilated cladding, concrete floor, pens only, with 4.0 m^2 per head floor area	£600 per head
2.	Extra to 1 for 4.0 m wide double-sided feeding passage, barrier and troughs	£250 per head
3.	Kennel building	£350 per head
4.	Portal framed building with cubicles	£1,000 per head
5.	Extra to 4 for feed stance, feeding passage, barriers and troughs	£500 per head
6.	Extra to 4 for slatting of cubicle passages	£500 per head
7.	Covered collecting yard, 1.1 m^2 per cow	£170 per head
8.	Milking parlour building, example: 5.5 x 11.5 m for 8/16 parlour	£12,500

9. Parlour equipment, herringbone parlours:
    (a) low level, 1 stall per point   £3,050 per point
    (b) pipeline   £2,850 per point
    (c) extra for meter and auto cluster removal   £1,800 per point
    (d) auto feed dispenser   £750 per point

10.	Dairy building	£190 per m^2 floor area
11.	Bulk tank and washer	£5.50 per litre
12.	Loose box, 16 m^2 floor area laid to falls, rendered walls	£285 per m^2 floor area
13.	Bull pen and open run	£9,000
14.	Cattle crush and 20 m race	£3,600
15.	Slatted floor cattle building for 120 growing cattle (1.7 m^2 pen space per head) with drive-through feed passage/troughs	£750 per head

Silage
		per tonne stored
1.	Timber panel clamp on concrete base with effluent tank	£50
2.	Precast concrete panel clamp with effluent tank	£65
3.	Glass-lined forage tower and unloader	£175

Waste Storage
		per m³ stored
1.	Lined lagoon with safety fence	£28
2.	Glass-lined steel slurry silo	
	small (400 m³)	£42
	medium (1,200 m³)	£34
	large (3,600 m³)	£32
3.	GRP below-ground effluent tank, encased in concrete	
	small (12 m³)	£370
	large (36 m³)	£320

Sheep Housing

1. Penning, troughs, feed barriers and drinkers installed in suitable existing building — **£25 per ewe**

2. Purpose-built sheep shed with 1.35 m² pen space per ewe concentrate troughs, feed passage and barrier for forage feeding — **£150 per ewe**

   Extras:
   (a) softwood slatted floor panels, materials only — **£6.00 per m²**
   (b) slatted panels as (a), made up, plus supports — **£20.00 per m²**

Pig Housing

per sow and litter

1. Farrowing and rearing
   (a) Prefabricated farrowing pens with crates, side creep areas, part-slatted floors, including foundations, electrical and plumbing work — **£2,050**

   (b) Steel-framed farrowing house with insulated blockwork walls, part-slatted pens with side creeps in rooms of eight with off main passage — **£2,600 per weaner**

   (c) Flat-deck rearing house 3-6 weeks with fully perforated floors to pens, 0.25 m² per pig pen area — **£110 per weaner**

   (d) Prefabricated verandah house including foundations, electrical and plumbing work, 0.3m² per pig internal lying area — **£85 per weaner**

2. Finishing

   per baconer

   (a) Prefabricated fattening house with part-slatted floors, trough feeding — **£195**

   (b) Prefabricated fattening house with part-slatted floors, floor fed — **£175**

   (c) Steel framed building with insulated blockwork walls, part-slatted floors, trough fed — **£245**

   (d) Automatic feeding systems for items (a), (b) and (c) above:
   dry-feed system with ad-lib hoppers — **£5.25**
   dry on-floor feeding — **£10**
   wet feeding — **£16.50**

3.	Dry sows and boars	*per sow*
	(a) Yards with floor feeding	£290
	(b) Sow cubicle system	£480
	(c) Yards with electronic feeders	£780
	(d) Yards with individual feeders	£875
	(e) Two-yard system with flat-rate feeding	£900
	(f) Boar pens as part of sow house	£2,150 each

4. Complete pig unit

Building costs calculated on basis of three-week weaning, 23 pigs per sow per year to bacon, excl. external slurry or dung storage, feed storage and handling/weighing facilities:

(a) Breeding and rearing only	£1,350 per sow
(b) Breeding with progeny to bacon	£2,500 per sow

Poultry Housing and Equipment — *per bird*

1.	Intensive enriched cages with automatic feeding and egg collection; (new traditional cages were banned from 1st January 2003;only enriched cages complete with nest box, perches and scratching area are now allowed)	£17.00-£18.50
2.	Perchery/barn	£15.50-£19.50
3.	Free Range: new sites stocked at 9 birds per m²,	£16.75-£24.75
	existing sites stocked at 11.7 birds per m²	£14.50-£20.50
	smaller mobile units will cost	£22.00 plus
4.	Broiler Breeders, deep litter, 0.167 m² per bird	£21.60
5.	Pullets (cage and floor reared)	£9.50
6.	Broilers, deep litter, 0.05 m² per bird	£5.90-£6.20
7.	Turkeys, 20,000 pole barn fattening unit (cost varies with size of unit and degree of automation)	£14.75-£21.00

(N.B. Source of Poultry Housing costs: as for poultry, see page 126)

Grain Storage and Drying — *per tonne stored*

1.	Intake pit, conveyor, elevator, overhead conveyor and catwalk, storage bins within existing building	£150
	extra for low volume ventilation of bins	£61
2.	As 1 in new building	£230
3.	Portable grain walling for on-floor storage in existing building	£35
4.	On floor grain storage in purpose-built building	£90
	Extras:	
	(a) low volume ventilation	£6.50-£7.00
	(b) on-floor drying with above-ground main duct and laterals	£92.50
	(c) add to (b) for below-ground laterals	£10.50
5.	Sealed towers for moist grain, including loading and unloading equipment	£120-£145

Potato Storage — *per tonne stored*

1.	Pallet-box store with recirculation fans	£160
	Pallet boxes, 1 tonne	£50
2.	Bulk store, building only	£145
	Ventilation system: fans, main duct, below-floor lateral ducts	£32

Roads and Fences

	per m length
3.2 m wide hardcore road with drainage ditches using locally excavated material	£22
using imported hardcore (£6.15/m³)	£33
extra for bitumen macadam surfacing, two coats	£35
Traditional 7-wire stock fence	£4.20
High tensile 7-wire stock fence	£3.50

Construction Equipment Hire

	hourly rate, with driver
Excavator	£18-£22
Tipping lorry	£27.50
10-tonne crane	£30

	weekly rate
Concrete mixer, 100 litre (5/3)	£35
Compressor and heavy breaker	£100

B. Standard Costs

Standard costs are published by the Scottish Executive on the basis of the cost of farm or casual labour and new materials. They do not include an allowance for overheads and profit: in most cases building contractors would add 15-30% to cover them. Standard costs are therefore usually lower, sometimes by a larger percentage than this, particularly where the labour content of the item is high. The following examples are based on standard costs issued in 2002. Farm buildings costs generally will have risen by about 13% between that year and 2006. Crown copyright material is reproduced from 'Standard Costs' with permission of the Controller of HMSO and the Queen's Printer for Scotland.

	per m² floor area
Open-sided framed building with cladding to roof and gable peaks only, hardcore floor, rainwater drainage to soakaways:	
9 x 18 m	£35
13.2 x 24m	£32.50

	per m² wall or roof
Corrugated cladding to roof or walls, including supports (purlins or rails):	
fibre cement sheeting	£16.80
extra for coloured sheeting	£0.80
extra for PVC coated steel instead of fibre cement	£0.60
deduct for metallic coated (e.g. galvanised) steel	£4.90
Spaced boarding	£18.80
Wall element, concrete blockwork 190-324 mm thick with strip foundation (base 750 mm below ground level) and 2.5 mm height above ground level	£92 per m run
Extra for rendering blockwork on one side	£6.50 per m²
Concrete floor, 100 mm thick, including excavation, hardcore and waterproof membrane	£11.50 per m²
Concrete floor, 150 mm thick as above	£15.50 per m²
Reinforced concrete slats for cattle (supports not included)	£47.50 per m²
Yard gully with heavy grating	£251 each

Drainage pipes, 100 mm, jointed in UPVC, clayware or spun concrete including 900 mm trench and backfill	£10.70 per m run	
Drainage pipes 150 mm as above	£19.00 per m run	
Tank for water, effluent etc., 20 m³	£2,966 each	
Gate, 3 m wide, steel, including posts concreted in: light duty cattle yard type	£106.40 each £141.90 each	

	per m² floor area
Fully covered enclosed building with concrete floor, and rainwater drainage to soakaways	
10 x 18 m	£72.50
15 x 24 m	£54.60

C. Storage Requirements

Bulk (cubic metres (feet) per tonne):

Beans		1.2	(43)
Wheat, peas		1.3	(46)
Barley, rye, oilseed rape, linseed, fodder beet		1.4	(50)
Oats		1.9	(68)
Potatoes		1.6	(57)
Dry bulb onions		2.0	(71)
Concentrates:	meal	2.0	(71)
	cubes	1.6	(57)
Grass silage:	18% DM	1.3	(46)
	30% DM	1.6	(57)
Maize silage		1.3	(46)
Silage: large round bales		2.5	(88)
Wheat straw ⎤		13.0	(464)
Barley straw ⎬ small bales		11.5	(411)
Hay ⎦		6.0	(214)
Wheat straw ⎤		20.0	(714)
Barley straw ⎬ large round bales		18.0	(643)
Hay ⎦		8.0	(286)
Brewers' grains		0.9	(32)

(With straw and hay the storage requirement clearly depends on the packing density; the above are simply typical averages).

Boxes (floor area in square metres (feet) per tonne):

Potatoes:	0.5 tonne boxes, 5 boxes high	0.52	(5.6)
	1.0 tonne boxes, 4 boxes high	0.52	(5.6)
	1.0 tonne boxes, 5 boxes high	0.45	(4.8)

Bags (floor area in square metres (feet) per tonne):

Feedingstuffs:	2 bags high	1.6	(17)
Fertilizer:	6 bags high	1.1	(12)
	10 bags high	0.7	(8)

VII. CAPITAL, TAXATION AND GRANTS

1. CAPITAL

(i) *Tenant's Capital consists of:*

    (a) *Machinery.* Costs of new machinery are given on pages 151-155. Written-down values in 2007 are likely to be averaging about £500 per hectare (£200 per acre) taking all farm types together.

    (b) *Breeding Livestock.* Over all types of farm the 2007 average is estimated to be about £450 per hectare (£180 per acre), but the figure varies from zero to over £1,250 (£505) for a small, intensive dairy farm. Approximate average market values (£) of various categories of breeding livestock (of mixed ages in the case of adult stock) are as follows (actual value will vary according to average age and weight, quality and breed):

Holstein Friesian Dairy Cows (inc. dry cows): 700.

Channel Island Dairy Cows (inc. dry cows): 450.

Other Dairy Cows (inc. dry cows): 575.

Beef Cows: 550.

	Dairy Followers		
Other Cattle:	Holstein Friesians	Ayrshires and C.I. Breeds	Beef Cattle
In-calf heifers	725	500	600
Over 2 years.	525	375	500
1-2 years.	435	305	400
6-12 months.	330	220	300
Under 6 months.	180	110	200
Ewes: 60. Rams 275.			
Sows and In-pig Gilts: 110. Boars 500.			

    (c) *Working Capital.* This is the capital needed to finance the production cycle, the length of which varies considerably between different crop and livestock enterprises and different combinations of these enterprises. Because of this, no generalizations are possible, but it can include the cost of purchased fattening stock, feed, seed, fertilizers, regular labour, machinery running costs, general overhead costs, rent and living expenses. This capital may be only £100 per hectare (£40 per acre) or so on an all-dairying farm but £400 or more per hectare (£160 per acre) on an all-cereals farm where the crop is stored until the spring. The average is likely to be about £300 per hectare (£120 per acre) in 2007.

(ii) *Return on Capital*

    (a) *Tenant's capital.* For all lowland farms (excluding intensive pig and poultry units, fruit and glasshouse production), total tenant's capital will average about £1,300 per hectare (£525 per acre) in 2007 (for range, see table on page 194). If the average U.K. management and investment income in year 2007 were, say, £75 per hectare (£30 per acre), the average return on tenant's capital would be 5.8%. 'Premium' levels (the average of the top 50% of farms) would be likely to be some 50% higher (i.e. close to 9%), with the levels achieved for mixed cropping on the very best soils and top dairy farms at least double the average. Note that no charge has been included for management (but that a rental value for owner-occupied land and the value of the unpaid labour of the farmer and wife have been deducted).

(b) *Landlord's Capital* (i.e. land, buildings, roads, etc.). With farms in 2007 averaging, say, £6,800 per hectare (£2,750 per acre), with vacant possession (assuming no special amenity or house value), an average lowland rent of, say, £150 per hectare (£60 per acre) (see p. 177), and assuming ownership expenses at £60 per hectare (£24 per acre), the (net) return (which is £90 per hectare (£36 per acre)) averages close to 1.3%. If land is taken at its tenanted value, with a vacant possession premium of say one-third, the return increases to 2%. If farm business tenancy rents were paid, at say 33% above the average level for established tenants (i.e. £200/ha [£80/acre]), the return would average 2% with land at the vacant possession price assumed and 3% with land at the tenanted value assumed. Full repairing and insurance leases clearly raise the returns above these levels. Above average quality farms acquire higher rents but also obviously command higher prices than the average levels quoted above.

(c) *Total Owner-Occupier's Capital* (i.e. land plus 'tenant's' capital). The combined (net) return on the above assumptions (£165 per hectare, or £66 per acre) on total capital, (£8,100 per hectare, or £3,280 per acre), with land at its vacant possession value, averages 2.03%. This increases to 2.83% if land is taken at its tenanted value and this is two-thirds the vacant possession value. If higher rent levels are assumed (given the same farming return), the overall return remains the same, the distribution simply being reallocated in favour of the land ownership share at the expense of the farming share. 'Premium' farming returns (as defined above), assuming the same capital requirements, raise the returns to 2.5% with land at the vacant possession price and 3.5% with tenanted land values.

(iii) Average Tenant's Capital per hectare (per acre in brackets) for Different Farm Types, as estimated for 2007, are as follows:

Farm Type Group	Average No. Hectares	Livestock	Crops, Cultivns., Stores	Machinery and Equipment*	Total Tenant's Capital	
		£	£	£	£	£
Mainly Dairying:						
under 75 ha..........	40	1250	150	800	2200	(890)
75 to 125 ha.........	100	1050	175	675	1900	(770)
Over 125 ha.........	150	900	200	525	1625	(660)
Mainly Arable:						
under 100 ha.........	60	100	375	575	1050	(425)
100 to 200 ha.......	150	100	350	475	925	(375)
over 200 ha..........	350	75	375	425	875	(355)
Dairy and Arable:						
under 100 ha.........	70	725	250	575	1550	(625)
100 to 200 ha........	150	650	275	550	1475	(595)
over 200 ha..........	350	475	325	525	1325	(535)
Mainly Sheep/Cattle:						
under 100 ha.....	65	550	150	350	1050	(425)
over 100 ha..........	175	525	125	325	975	(395)
Sheep/Cattle and Arable:						
under 100 ha.........	70	600	175	350	1125	(455)
100 to 200 ha........	150	550	200	325	1175	(435)
over 200 ha..........	300	500	250	300	1050	(425)
Dairy, Sheep/Cattle and Arable:	275	450	250	475	1175	(475)
Intensive Arable:						
Fruit...................	90	0	3250	1250	4500	(1820)
Field Vegetables....	60	0	450	2200	2650	(1075)
Mainly Pigs Poultry:						
(per £1000 output).	—	200	75	200	475	

* Based on current (i.e. replacement) costs.

Note: The above (deliberately rounded) data are based on Farm Business Survey results compiled annually by University/Colleges centres (as listed on page 5), where actual figures for previous years can be found. None includes the value of milk quota on farms with dairying, even though a case can be made for this on the grounds of opportunity cost; obviously the cost of additional quota must be included when budgeting for, and calculating the return on capital of, introducing or expanding a dairy herd — whether by increasing yield per cow or the number of cows or both.

(iv) *Return on Capital to Individual Enterprises* on a mixed farm is virtually impossible to ascertain, except perhaps for a full-time pig or poultry enterprise, nor would it be of very much use even if it could be determined. It would require the arbitrary allocation both of costs and capital inputs that are common to several, in some cases all, of the enterprises on the farm.

What is relevant and important is the extra (net) return from an enterprise either to be introduced or expanded, as calculated by a partial budget, related to the extra (net) capital needed. The 'net' in brackets relates, as regards return, to the addition to gross margins less any addition to (or plus any reduction in) 'fixed' costs, bearing in mind that another enterprise may have to be deleted or reduced in size; and, as regards capital, to the fact that deletion or reduction of another enterprise may release capital.

In most cases of 'marginal' substitution, it is differences in the value of breeding livestock and differences in variable costs that are particularly relevant, but the timing of both inputs and sales are also obviously very important.

(v) *'Marginal' Capital Requirements* for small changes in crop areas or livestock numbers can be estimated as follows:

Crops: variable costs till sale.

Dairy Cows and Egg Production: value of the cow* or hens, plus one month's food.

Other Breeding Livestock: average value of stock*, plus variable costs to sale of the progeny (e.g. lambs)—or their transfer to another enterprise (*e.g.* weaners to the pig fattening enterprise). Rearing Breeding Livestock (*e.g.* heifers, tegs, gilts, pullets): cost of the calf, lamb, weaner or chick, plus variable costs till they produce their first progeny/eggs.

Fattening Livestock and Production of Stores: cost of stock, plus variable costs till sale.

* Value of breeding stock, including dairy cows: either the average value over their entire breeding or milk producing life (see table on page 194) or their value when they first produce progeny can be taken. The latter will give the lower return on (marginal) capital and is thus the severer test.

Home-reared stock: where stock to be used for milk or egg production, breeding or fattening are home-reared, there are two possibilities:

(i) either they can be valued at variable costs of production when they are transferred from the rearing to the 'productive' enterprise; in this case the return on (marginal) capital will be estimated over the combined rearing and 'productive' enterprise.

(ii) or they can be valued at market value at point of transfer. This is the procedure if one wishes to work out a return on (marginal) capital for the rearing and the 'productive' enterprises separately.

(vi) Return on 'Marginal' Capital. This is sometimes expressed as the gross margin less fuel and repair costs of the enterprise expanded as a percentage of the 'marginal', or extra, capital. However, two points have to be remembered:

(i) If another enterprise has had to be reduced in size to enable the enterprise under consideration to be expanded, the capital released and the gross margin forfeited by reducing the size of the first enterprise must be brought into the calculation in estimating the net result of the change.

(ii) All the above statements on 'marginal' capital refer to small changes. If the change is large enough to cause changes in labour, machinery or building requirements the capital changes brought about may be considerably greater.

(vii) Return on Investments in Medium-Term and Long-Term Capital. Rate of Return and the Discounted Yield.

Example: If £5,000 investment results in an annual net return of £500 (after deducting depreciation, but ignoring interest payments):

$$\textit{Rate of Return on Initial } \text{Capital} = \frac{500}{5,000} \text{ x } 100 = 10\%$$

$$\textit{Rate of Return on Average } \text{Capital} = \frac{500}{2,500} \text{ x } 100 = 20\%$$

It is more accurate to calculate the 'Discounted Yield', which is the discount rate that brings the present value of the net cash flows (which means ignoring depreciation) to the value of the investment.

The tables on pages 198 and 199 may be used.

'Short-Cut' Estimates of the Discounted Yield on depreciating assets. The Discounted Yield falls between the simple Rates of Return on Initial and Average Capital. In fact, for investments lasting 5 to 15 years, when the Rate of Return on Initial Capital is 10% and on Average Capital 20%, the Discounted Yield will be almost exactly halfway between, i.e. about 15%. However, this is only so providing the anticipated annual net cash earnings are fairly constant — or fluctuate unpredictably around a fairly constant level.

There are three circumstances when the Discounted Yield will get closer to the Rate of Return on Initial Capital (i.e. the lower per cent return) and further from the Rate of Return on Average Capital:

(a) The longer the life of the investment.

(b) The higher the Rate of Return.

(c) The higher the net cash flow is in the later years of the investment compared with the earlier years.

When the opposite circumstances obtain, the Discounted Yield will be closer to the Rate of Return on Average Capital (i.e. the higher per cent return).

Granted that there are inevitably varying degrees of estimation and uncertainty in calculating future net annual earnings of investments, the following short-cuts might reasonably be used where the annual net cash earnings are expected to be fairly constant — or fluctuate unpredictably (e.g. through weather effects on yields) around a fairly constant level. (W.O. period = write-off period; R.R.I.C. = rate of return on initial capital).

1. Where   (i)   the W.O. period is 5 years or less,

          (ii)   the W.O. period is 6 to 10 years and the R.R.I.C. is 15% or less,

          (iii) the W.O. period is 11 to 20 years and the R.R.I.C. is 10% or less,

calculate the Return on Capital as being approximately midway between the Rates of Return on Initial and Average Capital, i.e. by calculating the Rate of Return on 2/3 of the original investment.

For example, following the earlier example (page 192):

$$\frac{500}{3,333} \text{ x } 100 = 15\%.$$

2. Where (i) the W.O. period is 6 to 10 years and the R.R.I.C. exceeds 15%,

(ii) the W.O. period is 11 to 20 years and the R.R.I.C. is between 10% and 25%,

(iii) the W.O. period exceeds 20 years and the R.R.I.C. is 10% or less calculate the Return on Capital on 80% of the original investment.

For example, again following the earlier example:

$$\frac{500}{4,000} \quad \text{x } 100 = 12^\circ\%.$$

3. Where (i) the W.O. period is 11 to 20 years and the R.R.I.C. exceeds 25%,

(ii) the W.O. period exceeds 20 years and the R.R.I.C. exceeds 10%, take the Return on Capital to be the R.R.I.C.

In borderline cases, use method 1 rather than 2, or 2 rather than 3 if there is a tendency for the cash flow to be higher in the earlier years, e.g. because of tax allowances on machinery. Take 2 rather than 1, and 3 rather than 2, if the likelihood is that the cash flow will be lower in earlier years and increase in later years.

However, where the annual cash flow is expected to vary (apart from unpredictable fluctuations) it is safer to make the full D.C.F. calculation. This is particularly so where the variation is both up and down and where further periodic investments are to be made during the life of the project.

Discounting Table A

Discount Factors for Calculating the Present Value of Future (irregular) Cash Flows

Year								Percentage									
	3%	4%	5%	6%	7%	8%	9%	10%	11%	12%	13%	14%	15%	16%	18%	20%	25%
1	0.971	0.962	0.952	0.943	0.935	0.926	0.917	0.909	0.901	0.893	0.885	0.877	0.870	0.862	0.847	0.833	0.800
2	0.943	0.925	0.907	0.890	0.873	0.857	0.842	0.826	0.812	0.797	0.783	0.769	0.756	0.743	0.718	0.694	0.640
3	0.915	0.889	0.864	0.840	0.816	0.794	0.772	0.751	0.731	0.712	0.693	0.675	0.658	0.641	0.609	0.579	0.512
4	0.888	0.855	0.823	0.792	0.763	0.735	0.708	0.683	0.659	0.636	0.613	0.592	0.572	0.552	0.516	0.482	0.410
5	0.863	0.822	0.784	0.747	0.713	0.681	0.650	0.621	0.593	0.567	0.543	0.519	0.497	0.476	0.437	0.402	0.328
6	0.837	0.790	0.746	0.705	0.666	0.630	0.596	0.564	0.535	0.507	0.480	0.456	0.432	0.410	0.370	0.335	0.262
7	0.813	0.760	0.711	0.665	0.623	0.583	0.547	0.513	0.482	0.452	0.425	0.400	0.376	0.354	0.314	0.279	0.210
8	0.789	0.731	0.677	0.627	0.582	0.540	0.502	0.467	0.434	0.404	0.376	0.351	0.327	0.305	0.266	0.233	0.168
9	0.766	0.703	0.645	0.592	0.544	0.500	0.460	0.424	0.391	0.361	0.333	0.308	0.284	0.263	0.225	0.194	0.134
10	0.744	0.676	0.614	0.558	0.508	0.463	0.422	0.386	0.352	0.322	0.295	0.270	0.247	0.227	0.191	0.162	0.107
11	0.722	0.650	0.585	0.527	0.475	0.429	0.388	0.350	0.317	0.287	0.261	0.237	0.215	0.195	0.162	0.135	0.086
12	0.701	0.625	0.557	0.497	0.444	0.397	0.356	0.319	0.286	0.257	0.231	0.208	0.187	0.168	0.137	0.112	0.069
13	0.681	0.601	0.530	0.469	0.415	0.368	0.326	0.290	0.258	0.229	0.204	0.182	0.163	0.145	0.116	0.093	0.055
14	0.661	0.577	0.505	0.442	0.388	0.340	0.299	0.263	0.232	0.205	0.181	0.160	0.141	0.125	0.098	0.078	0.044
15	0.642	0.555	0.481	0.417	0.362	0.315	0.275	0.239	0.209	0.183	0.160	0.140	0.123	0.108	0.084	0.065	0.035
20	0.554	0.456	0.377	0.312	0.258	0.215	0.178	0.149	0.124	0.104	0.087	0.073	0.061	0.051	0.037	0.026	0.012
25	0.478	0.375	0.295	0.233	0.184	0.146	0.116	0.092	0.074	0.059	0.047	0.038	0.030	0.024	0.016	0.010	0.004
30	0.412	0.308	0.231	0.174	0.131	0.099	0.075	0.057	0.044	0.033	0.026	0.020	0.015	0.012	0.007	0.004	0.001

Example: The Present Value of £500 received 10 years from now, at 12 per cent discount rate of interest = 500 x 0.322 = £161.

Conversely, £161 invested now, at 12 per cent compound interest, will be worth £500 in 10 years' time.

Discounting Table B

Discount Factors for Calculating the Present Value of Future Annuity (i.e. Constant Annual Cash Fow) Receivable in Years 1 to n inclusive.

Year	3%	4%	5%	6%	7%	8%	9%	10%	11%	12%	13%	14%	15%	16%	18%	20%	25%
1	0.971	0.962	0.952	0.943	0.935	0.926	0.917	0.909	0.901	0.893	0.885	0.877	0.870	0.862	0.847	0.833	0.800
2	1.913	1.886	1.859	1.833	1.808	1.783	1.759	1.736	1.713	1.690	1.668	1.647	1.626	1.605	1.566	1.528	1.440
3	2.829	2.775	2.723	2.673	2.624	2.577	2.531	2.487	2.444	2.402	2.361	2.322	2.283	2.246	2.174	2.106	1.952
4	3.717	3.630	3.546	3.465	3.387	3.312	3.240	3.170	3.102	3.037	2.974	2.914	2.855	2.798	2.690	2.589	2.362
5	4.580	4.452	4.329	4.212	4.100	3.993	3.890	3.791	3.696	3.605	3.517	3.433	3.352	3.274	3.127	2.991	2.689
6	5.417	5.242	5.076	4.917	4.767	4.623	4.486	4.355	4.231	4.111	3.998	3.889	3.784	3.685	3.498	3.326	2.951
7	6.230	6.002	5.786	5.582	5.389	5.206	5.033	4.868	4.712	4.564	4.423	4.288	4.160	4.039	3.812	3.605	3.161
8	7.020	6.733	6.463	6.210	5.971	5.747	5.535	5.335	5.146	4.968	4.799	4.639	4.487	4.344	4.078	3.837	3.329
9	7.786	7.435	7.108	6.802	6.515	6.247	5.995	5.759	5.537	5.328	5.132	4.946	4.772	4.607	4.303	4.031	3.463
10	8.530	8.111	7.722	7.360	7.024	6.710	6.418	6.145	5.889	5.650	5.426	5.216	5.019	4.833	4.494	4.192	3.570
11	9.253	8.760	8.306	7.887	7.499	7.139	6.805	6.495	6.207	5.938	5.687	5.453	5.234	5.029	4.656	4.327	3.656
12	9.954	9.385	8.863	8.384	7.943	7.536	7.161	6.814	6.492	6.194	5.918	5.660	5.421	5.197	4.793	4.439	3.725
13	10.635	9.986	9.394	8.853	8.358	7.904	7.487	7.103	6.750	6.424	6.122	5.842	5.583	5.342	4.910	4.533	3.780
14	11.296	10.563	9.899	9.295	8.745	8.244	7.786	7.367	6.982	6.628	6.302	6.002	5.724	5.468	5.008	4.611	3.824
15	11.938	11.118	10.380	9.712	9.108	8.559	8.061	7.606	7.191	6.811	6.462	6.142	5.847	5.575	5.092	4.675	3.859
20	14.877	13.590	12.462	11.470	10.594	9.818	9.129	8.514	7.963	7.469	7.025	6.623	6.259	5.929	5.353	4.870	3.954
25	17.413	15.662	14.094	12.783	11.654	10.675	9.823	9.077	8.422	7.843	7.330	6.873	6.464	6.097	5.467	4.948	3.985
30	19.600	17.292	15.372	13.765	12.409	11.258	10.274	9.427	8.694	8.055	7.496	7.003	6.566	6.177	5.517	4.979	3.995

Percentage

Example: The Present Value of £500 a year for the next 10 years, at 12 per cent discount rate of interest = 500 x 5.650 = £2,825. This is the same answer that would be obtained by multiplying 500 by each discount factor (at 12 per cent) in Table A for each year from 1 to 10, and adding together the ten resulting figures.

To obtain the Discounted Yield of a constant annual net cash flow, divide this into the original investment and look up the resulting figure in the table above, against the number of years. Example: an investment of £1,000 is estimated to produce £80 a year additional profit over 10 years (before charging interest). Add £100 depreciation a year = £180 annual net cash flow. 1000 ÷ 180 = 5.56. This equals just over 12 per cent (the 10 years/12 per cent figure being 5.650).

Compounding Table A

The Future Money Value of £1 after n Years

Year	Rate of Intrest																
	3%	4%	5%	6%	7%	8%	9%	10%	11%	12%	13%	14%	15%	16%	18%	20%	25%
1	1.03	1.04	1.05	1.06	1.07	1.08	1.09	1.10	1.11	1.12	1.13	1.14	1.15	1.16	1.18	1.20	1.25
2	1.06	1.08	1.10	1.12	1.14	1.17	1.19	1.21	1.23	1.25	1.28	1.30	1.32	1.35	1.39	1.44	1.56
3	1.09	1.12	1.16	1.19	1.23	1.26	1.30	1.33	1.37	1.40	1.44	1.48	1.52	1.56	1.64	1.73	1.95
4	1.13	1.17	1.22	1.26	1.31	1.36	1.41	1.46	1.52	1.57	1.63	1.69	1.75	1.81	1.94	2.07	2.44
5	1.16	1.22	1.28	1.34	1.40	1.47	1.54	1.61	1.69	1.76	1.84	1.93	2.01	2.10	2.29	2.49	3.05
6	1.19	1.27	1.34	1.42	1.50	1.59	1.68	1.77	1.87	1.97	2.08	2.19	2.31	2.44	2.70	2.99	3.81
7	1.23	1.32	1.41	1.50	1.61	1.71	1.83	1.95	2.08	2.21	2.35	2.50	2.66	2.83	3.19	3.58	4.77
8	1.27	1.37	1.48	1.59	1.72	1.85	1.99	2.14	2.30	2.48	2.66	2.85	3.06	3.28	3.76	4.30	5.96
9	1.30	1.42	1.55	1.69	1.84	2.00	2.17	2.36	2.56	2.77	3.00	3.25	3.52	3.80	4.44	5.16	7.45
10	1.34	1.48	1.63	1.79	1.97	2.16	2.37	2.59	2.84	3.11	3.39	3.71	4.05	4.41	5.23	6.19	9.31
11	1.38	1.54	1.71	1.90	2.10	2.33	2.58	2.85	3.15	3.48	3.84	4.23	4.65	5.12	6.18	7.43	11.64
12	1.43	1.60	1.80	2.01	2.25	2.52	2.81	3.14	3.50	3.90	4.33	4.82	5.35	5.94	7.29	8.92	14.55
13	1.47	1.67	1.89	2.13	2.41	2.72	3.07	3.45	3.88	4.36	4.90	5.49	6.15	6.89	8.60	10.70	18.19
14	1.51	1.73	1.98	2.26	2.58	2.94	3.34	3.80	4.31	4.89	5.53	6.26	7.08	7.99	10.15	12.84	22.74
15	1.56	1.80	2.08	2.40	2.76	3.17	3.64	4.18	4.78	5.47	6.25	7.14	8.14	9.27	11.97	15.41	28.42
20	1.81	2.19	2.65	3.21	3.87	4.66	5.60	6.73	8.06	9.65	11.52	13.74	16.37	19.46	27.39	38.34	86.74
25	2.09	2.67	3.39	4.29	5.43	6.85	8.62	10.83	13.59	17.00	21.23	26.46	32.92	40.87	62.67	95.40	264.7
30	2.43	3.24	4.32	5.74	7.61	10.06	13.27	17.45	22.89	29.96	39.12	50.95	66.21	85.85	143.4	237.4	807.8

Compounding Table B

*The Future Money Value of £1 after n Years**

Rate of Intrest

Year	3%	4%	5%	6%	7%	8%	9%	10%	11%	12%	13%	14%	15%	16%	18%	20%	25%
1	1.03	1.04	1.05	1.06	1.07	1.08	1.09	1.10	1.11	1.12	1.13	1.14	1.15	1.16	1.18	1.20	1.25
2	2.09	2.12	2.15	2.18	2.21	2.25	2.28	2.31	2.34	2.37	2.41	2.44	2.47	2.51	2.57	2.64	2.81
3	3.18	3.25	3.31	3.37	3.44	3.51	3.57	3.64	3.71	3.78	3.85	3.92	3.99	4.07	4.22	4.37	4.77
4	4.31	4.42	4.53	4.64	4.75	4.87	4.98	5.11	5.23	5.35	5.48	5.61	5.74	5.88	6.15	6.44	7.21
5	5.47	5.63	5.80	5.98	6.15	6.34	6.52	6.72	6.91	7.12	7.32	7.54	7.75	7.98	8.44	8.93	10.26
6	6.66	6.90	7.14	7.39	7.65	7.92	8.20	8.49	8.78	9.09	9.40	9.73	10.07	10.41	11.14	11.92	14.07
7	7.89	8.21	8.55	8.90	9.26	9.64	10.03	10.44	10.86	11.30	11.76	12.23	12.73	13.24	14.33	15.50	18.84
8	9.16	9.58	10.03	10.49	10.98	11.49	12.02	12.58	13.16	13.78	14.42	15.09	15.79	16.52	18.09	19.80	24.80
9	10.46	11.01	11.58	12.18	12.82	13.49	14.19	14.94	15.72	16.55	17.42	18.34	19.30	20.32	22.52	24.96	32.25
10	11.81	12.49	13.21	13.97	14.78	15.65	16.56	17.53	18.56	19.65	20.81	22.04	23.35	24.73	27.76	31.15	41.57
11	13.19	14.03	14.92	15.87	16.89	17.98	19.14	20.38	21.71	23.13	24.65	26.27	28.00	29.85	33.93	38.58	53.21
12	14.62	15.63	16.71	17.88	19.14	20.50	21.95	23.52	25.21	27.03	28.98	31.09	33.35	35.79	41.22	47.50	67.76
13	16.09	17.29	18.60	20.02	21.55	23.21	25.02	26.97	29.09	31.39	33.88	36.58	39.50	42.67	49.82	58.20	85.95
14	17.60	19.02	20.58	22.28	24.13	26.15	28.36	30.77	33.41	36.28	39.42	42.84	46.58	50.66	59.97	71.04	108.7
15	19.16	20.82	22.66	24.67	26.89	29.32	32.00	34.95	38.19	41.75	45.67	49.98	54.72	59.93	71.94	86.44	137.1
20	27.68	30.97	34.72	38.99	43.87	49.42	55.76	63.00	71.27	80.70	91.47	103.8	117.8	133.8	173.0	224.0	428.7
25	37.55	43.31	50.11	58.16	67.68	78.95	92.32	108.2	127.0	149.3	175.8	207.3	244.7	289.1	404.3	566.4	1318
30	49.00	58.33	69.76	83.80	101.1	122.3	148.6	180.9	220.9	270.3	331.3	406.7	500.0	615.2	933.3	1418	4034

* Payments made at the beginning of each year.

Amortisation Table

Annual Charge to write off £1,000

							Rate of Interest									
Write-off Period (Years)	3	4	5	6	7	8	9	10	11	12	13	14	15	16	18	20
5	218	225	231	237	244	250	257	264	271	277	284	291	298	305	320	334
6	185	191	197	203	210	216	223	230	236	243	250	257	264	271	286	301
7	161	167	173	179	186	192	199	205	212	219	226	233	240	248	262	277
8	142	149	155	161	167	174	181	187	194	201	208	216	223	230	245	261
9	128	134	141	147	153	160	167	174	181	188	195	202	210	217	232	248
10	117	123	130	136	142	149	156	163	170	177	184	192	199	207	223	239
11	108	114	120	127	133	140	147	154	161	168	176	183	191	199	215	231
12	100	107	113	119	125	133	140	147	154	161	169	177	184	192	209	225
13	94	100	106	113	120	127	134	141	148	156	163	171	179	187	204	221
14	89	95	101	108	114	121	128	136	143	151	159	167	175	183	200	217
15	84	90	96	103	110	117	124	131	139	147	155	163	171	179	196	214
16	80	86	92	99	106	113	120	128	136	143	151	160	168	176	194	211
17	76	82	89	95	102	110	117	125	132	140	149	157	165	174	191	209
18	73	79	86	92	99	107	114	122	130	138	146	155	163	172	190	208
19	70	76	83	90	97	104	112	120	128	136	144	153	161	170	188	206
20	67	74	80	87	94	102	110	117	126	134	142	151	160	169	187	205
25	57	64	71	78	86	94	102	110	119	127	136	145	155	164	183	202
30	51	58	65	73	81	89	97	106	115	124	133	143	152	162	181	201
40	43	51	58	66	75	84	93	102	112	122	131	141	151	160	180	200

Example: £3,000 is borrowed to erect a building. The annual charge to service interest and capital repayment on the £3,000, repayable over 10 years at 12%, is 3 x £177 = £531. Where the write-off period of the building (10 years) is equal to the repayment period of the loan, then the average annual depreciation and interest will also equal £531.

The proportion of the total annual charge representing the average amount of capital repaid per annum can be readily determined by dividing the sum borrowed by the number of years of the loan: (in the above example this is £3,000 ÷ 10 = £300/year). The remainder is clearly the average amount of interest paid per annum: (in the above example, £531 - £300 = £231/year). The year to year variations between the two items (i.e. capital repaid and interest) are shown in the tables on pages 196 to 198, which demonstrate the way in which the capital repayment part increases and the interest part decreases over time.

Sinking Fund Table

The annual sum required to be set aside at the end of

Rate of Interest

No. of Years	3	4	5	6	7	8	9	10	11	12	13	14	15	16	18	20
5	188	185	181	177	174	170	167	164	161	157	154	151	148	145	140	134
6	155	151	147	143	140	136	133	130	126	123	120	117	114	111	106	101
7	131	127	123	119	116	112	109	105	102	99	96	93	90	88	82	77
8	112	109	105	101	97	94	91	87	84	81	78	76	73	70	65	61
9	98	94	91	87	83	80	77	74	71	68	65	62	60	57	52	48
10	87	83	80	76	72	69	66	63	60	57	54	52	49	47	43	39
11	78	74	70	67	63	60	57	54	51	48	46	43	41	39	35	31
12	70	67	63	59	56	53	50	47	44	41	39	37	34	32	29	25
13	64	60	56	53	50	47	44	41	38	36	33	31	29	27	24	21
14	59	55	51	48	44	41	38	36	33	31	29	27	25	23	20	17
15	54	50	46	43	40	37	34	31	29	27	25	23	21	19	16	14
16	50	46	42	39	36	33	30	28	26	23	21	20	18	16	14	11
17	46	42	39	35	32	30	27	25	22	20	19	17	15	14	11	9
18	43	39	36	32	29	27	24	22	20	18	16	15	13	12	10	8
19	40	36	33	30	27	24	22	20	18	16	14	13	11	10	8	6
20	37	34	30	27	24	22	20	17	16	14	12	11	10	9	7	5
25	27	24	21	18	16	14	12	10	9	7	6	5	5	4	3	2
30	21	18	15	13	11	9	7	6	5	4	3	3	2	2	1	1
40	13	11	8	6	5	4	3	2	2	1	1	1	1	—	—	—

MORTGAGE REPAYMENT DATA

Items per £1,000 invested where I = Interest, P = Principal repaid, L = Loan outstanding

Loan through	4%			5%			6%			8%			10%			12%		
	I	P	L	I	P	L	I	P	L	I	P	L	I	P	L	I	P	L
5 years																		
1	40	185	815	50	181	819	60	177	823	80	170	830	100	164	836	120	157	834
2	33	192	623	41	190	629	49	188	635	66	184	645	84	180	656	101	175	670
3	25	200	424	31	200	424	38	199	435	52	199	447	66	198	458	80	197	469
4	17	208	216	21	210	220	26	211	224	36	215	232	46	218	240	56	221	248
5	9	216	0	11	220	0	13	224	0	19	232	0	24	240	0	30	248	0
10 years																		
1	40	83	917	50	80	920	60	76	924	80	69	931	100	63	939	120	57	934
2	37	87	830	46	83	837	55	80	844	75	75	856	94	69	868	113	64	879
3	33	90	740	42	88	749	51	85	758	69	81	776	87	76	792	106	71	808
4	30	94	646	37	92	657	46	90	668	62	87	689	79	84	709	97	80	728
5	26	97	549	33	97	561	40	96	572	55	94	595	71	92	617	87	90	638
6	22	101	448	28	101	459	34	102	471	48	101	494	62	101	516	77	100	538
7	18	105	342	23	107	353	28	108	363	39	110	384	52	111	405	65	112	425
8	14	110	233	18	112	241	22	114	249	31	118	266	40	122	282	51	126	299
9	9	114	119	12	117	123	15	121	128	21	128	138	28	134	148	36	141	158
10	5	119	0	6	123	0	8	128	0	11	138	0	15	148	0	19	158	0

MORTGAGE REPAYMENT DATA (continued)

Loan through	4%			5%			6%			8%			10%			12%		
5 years	I	P	L	I	P	L	I	P	L	I	P	L	I	P	L	I	P	L
1	40	34	966	50	30	970	60	27	973	80	22	978	100	17	983	120	14	986
5	34	39	818	43	37	833	53	34	847	72	30	872	92	26	893	112	22	912
10	26	48	597	33	47	620	41	46	642	58	44	683	76	41	722	95	38	756
15	15	58	328	20	60	347	26	61	367	38	64	407	51	66	445	66	68	483
20	3	71	0	4	76	0	5	82	0	8	94	0	11	107	0	14	120	0
25 years																		
1	40	24	976	50	21	979	60	18	982	80	14	986	100	10	990	120	7	993
5	36	28	870	45	25	884	55	23	897	75	19	920	95	15	938	116	12	952
10	30	34	712	38	33	736	47	31	760	66	27	802	86	24	838	107	21	868
15	22	42	519	29	41	548	37	41	576	54	40	629	72	39	677	91	37	720
20	13	51	285	18	53	307	23	55	330	35	59	374	48	62	418	63	65	460
25	2	62	0	3	68	0	4	74	0	7	87	0	10	100	0	14	114	0

MORTGAGE REPAYMENT DATA (continued)

Loan through	6%			8%			10%			12%			14%			16%		
	I	P	L	I	P	L	I	P	L	I	P	L	I	P	L	I	P	L
5 years																		
1	60	13	987	80	9	991	100	6	994	120	4	996	140	3	997	160	2	998
5	57	16	929	77	12	948	97	9	963	118	7	974	138	5	986	158	3	987
10	51	21	833	71	18	872	92	14	903	113	11	927	134	9	951	155	7	960
15	44	29	706	63	26	760	83	23	807	104	20	846	126	17	890	147	15	903
20	34	38	535	51	38	596	69	37	652	88	36	701	108	35	751	130	32	782
25	21	51	306	33	56	355	46	60	402	61	63	488	83	60	494	95	66	530
30	4	69	0	7	82	0	10	96	0	13	111	0	16	127	0	22	140	0
40 years																		
1	60	6	994	80	4	996	100	2	998	120	1	999	140	1	999	160	0	1000
5	58	8	964	79	5	977	99	3	986	119	2	992	139	2	995	160	1	997
10	56	11	915	76	8	944	97	5	964	118	4	977	138	3	989	159	2	991
15	52	15	850	73	11	895	94	9	928	115	6	951	136	5	973	157	3	978
20	47	20	762	67	17	823	88	14	871	110	11	906	130	11	942	153	7	951
25	40	26	645	59	24	718	80	22	778	102	20	826	123	18	874	145	15	894
30	31	35	489	48	36	563	66	36	628	86	35	685	109	32	742	129	31	775
35	20	47	280	31	53	335	45	58	388	60	61	437	85	56	487	95	66	525
40	4	63	0	6	78	0	9	93	0	13	108	0	18	123	0	22	138	0

Note—All figures rounded to nearest £.

Rates of Interest: Further Points

(i) *Rate of Interest on Bank Loans.* Typically 2.25% to 2.5% above Base Rate. Main range is 1.5% above to 3.5% above. Extremes are likely to be 1% above (minimum) and 5% above (maximum).

(ii) *Annual Percentage Rate (APR).* This is the effective rate of interest calculated on an annual basis and should be used when seeking to make a true comparison between interest charges on money borrowed from different sources. The APR allows for the fact that when interest is applied to accounts at half yearly, quarterly or monthly intervals an element of compounding will arise. For example, £100 borrowed for one year at a quoted annual nominal interest rate of 6% (e.g. 2% over base rate of 4%) with interest charged quarterly, will lead to an accumulated interest charge of £6.136 (i.e., giving an APR of just under 6.14%). The higher the annual nominal interest rate and the more frequently the interest charges are applied to the account, the more pronounced the compounding element becomes. For example, an annual nominal interest rate of 10% produces an APR of 10.25% with half yearly charging, 10.38% with quarterly charging and 10.47% with monthly charging and with a nominal rate as high as 20% the rates become 21%, 21.6% and 21.9% respectively.

In the case of some loans and hire purchase agreements, interest charges may be quoted as a flat rate on the original amount borrowed. The APR will be considerably greater than the flat rate if the loan is repaid by equal periodic instalments, comprising part capital and part interest, so that the borrowing is completely repaid by the end of the agreed term. For example, the APR for a loan at a flat rate of interest of 8% repaid by monthly instalments over 5 years will be 15%. The shorter the repayment period, and the more frequent the payments, the higher is the APR compared with the flat rate.

(iii) *The Real Rate of Interest.* When preparing simple profit and loss budgets to estimate the worthwhileness of an investment in a fixed asset (machinery, buildings, land), it is usual to price inputs and outputs at present-day values even when most costs and returns are expected to rise due to inflation over the life of the investment. Where this real terms approach is adopted a more realistic estimate of the effect on profitability can be gained by basing charges for capital on the real rate of interest rather than the APR. The real rate of interest is the APR adjusted for the annual rate at which prices relevant to the investment are expected to increase. A crude estimate of the real rate of interest can be obtained by simply subtracting the expected rate of price increase from the APR; for example, if the APR were 8% and the expected rate of inflation 3%, the real rate of interest would be $8 - 3 = 5\%$.

Financial Ratios

1. *Common Ratios*

The following ratios are often quoted as rough guidelines:

		% of Gross Output
Variable Costs		30-35%
Labour	15-17½%	
Machinery	15-17½%	35-40%
Sundry Fixed Costs	5%	
Rent & Interest		15%
Margin*		15%

* to cover drawings, tax, capital repayments, reinvestments

It has to be borne in mind, however, that these are indeed only rough guidelines and need to be considered with great care. Values vary, for example, with type of farming and size of farm. Furthermore, it is often unclear how certain items are being measured, especially whether unpaid manual labour of the farmer and family has been included or whether a rental value has been allowed for owner-occupied land.

2. *Farm Survey Ratios*

The following are rounded averages based on farm surveys in recent years on a large sample of all types of farm, assuming a Management and Investment Income (see page 229) of 10% of Total Output is made. It is to be noted that Total Output includes the market value of any production retained for use/consumption on the farm (e.g. cereals for feed or seed), Unpaid Labour (value of manual labour supplied by the farmer and spouse) is included. Rent includes the rental value of owner-occupied land and Interest charges are not included in the costs. Casual labour and all Contract work are included in fixed costs. Obviously, costs are a lower proportion and the margin a higher proportion in profitable years, and vice-versa in low profit years. Obviously, too, within years the more profitable farms have lower percentage costs, leaving higher percentage margins and vice-versa.

	% Total Output	% Total Gross Margin	% Total Fixed Costs
Variable Costs:			
(excl. casual labour and contract work)	32.5		
Fixed Costs:			
Labour: Paid (inc. casuals) }	20	30	33
Labour: Unpaid }			
Power & Machinery			
(inc. contract work)	20	30	33
Labour & Machinery	40	60	66
Rent/Rental Value	12.5	19	21
General Overheads	7.5	11	13
Total Fixed Costs	60	90	100
Margin	**7.5**	**10**	-

Total Gross Margin = 67.5% of Total Output

3. *Lending Criteria*

Another set of standards widely used by lending and leasing institutions looks at total Finance Charges (rent, interest, leasing charges, etc.), as a percentage of Gross Output and Gross Margin;

Finance as a % of Gross Output	Finance as a % of Gross Margin	Lending Criteria
0-10%	0-15%	Normally very safe
11-15%	16-22.5%	Common range, should be safe
16-20%	23-29%	Care required
20% plus	30% plus	Potentially dangerous

As lenders will be well aware, however, these ratios too must be regarded with caution and in conjunction with the farm's level of net worth (% equity) and its trend in recent years, recent trends in its profitability and the potential borrower's record of expenditure both on and off the farm, together with his or her character and potential. Also, of course, some enterprises / types of farming are more risky than others.

2. TAXATION

Note: no responsibility can be taken for any errors or omissions in the information presented in this section or for any action taken on the basis of the information provided. Professional advice should always be sought before taking any decision that may affect your tax position.

1. Income Tax

A. *Rates of Income Tax (2006-07)*

	Income Band	Dividends	Interest	Other Income
Starting rate	Up to £2,150	10	10	10
Basic rate	£2,151 to £33,300	10	20	22
Higher rate	Over £33,300	32.5	40	40

B. *Allowances and Reliefs (2006-07)*

(i) *Personal Allowance*: £5,035 (£7,280 if aged 65 to 74 and £7,420 if aged over 75 on 5th April 2004).

(ii) *Married Couple's Allowance*: abolished from 5th April 2000 except for couples where at least one spouse is 65 or more on that date.

(iii) *Personal Pension Schemes.* Tax relief is obtainable for contributions to a pension. The rules on maximum contributions have been simplified; there is an annual allowance of £215,000 (for 2006-2007) and a lifetime allowance of £1,500,000. Maximum contributions under the simplified Stakeholder Pension rules are £3,600 per year.

2. Private Company Taxation

A. *Rates of Corporation Tax (2006-07)*

Profits are chargeable to Corporation Tax in 2006-2007 at the following rates (the Starting rate of 0% was removed from 1st April 2006):

	Profits band	per cent tax
Small companies' rate	Up to £2,150	19
Upper marginal rate	£2,151 to £33,300	32.75
Main companies' rate	Over £33,300	30

B. *Company Taxation - Other Issues*

(i) *Capital Gains*: Capital gains of companies are charged at the appropriate rate of Corporation Tax.

(ii) *Quotas*: Milk quota purchased by a company after 1st April 2002 will attract corporation tax relief at the rate of depreciation selected in the accounting policies of the company or 4% per year if not depreciated in the accounts of the company.

(iii) *Distributions*: For example, dividends are not deductible in arriving at the amount of Corporation Tax profit. However, the recipient of distributions will be credited with a tax payment of 10% of distributions received, which will be deemed to discharge the liability of lower (10%) and basic rate (22%) taxpayers; however, higher rate taxpayers will have to pay additional tax of 25% of the net dividend; dividends are treated as the top slice of income.

(iv) *Losses*: Restricted carry back to one year with effect from 2nd July 1997.

3. Agricultural Businesses: Other Items

A. *Assessing Self-Employed Profits*

Since 1997-98 self-employed people have been assessed for tax in any tax year on the basis of the profits recorded in the annual accounts which end in that tax year, i.e. on a 'current year basis'.

B. *Livestock*

Dairy cows or breeding livestock may be treated on the herd basis or on a trading stock basis;

(i) *Herd basis:* valuation changes are not included in the trading account, nor are additions to the herd, but sales from the herd and replacements are. On the sale of all or a substantial proportion (normally taken as 20% or more) of the herd, no tax is paid on any profit over the original cost price, nor is there any relief for loss.

(ii) *Trading stock basis:* purchases, sales and valuation changes are all included in the trading account. Under this method stock should be valued at the lower of cost (or cost of production) and net realisable value. Where animals are home-produced and it is not possible to ascertain actual costs from farm records the 'deemed' cost may be used. This is 60% of market value for cattle and 75% for sheep and pigs.

C. *Stock Valuation: Crops*

Crops should generally be valued at the cost of production (or net realisable value, if lower). However, the deemed cost method allows 75% of market value to be used.

D. *Allowances for Capital Expenditure*

(i) *Machinery and Plant* (whether new or second hand). An annual writing down allowance of 25% is available on a reducing balance basis. However, small and medium-sized businesses are eligible to claim a first year allowance of 50%. The writing down allowances will normally be calculated on a "pool" basis. However, where it is expected that a machine will be sold within five years of acquisition and realise less than its written-down value for tax it will be possible for the taxpayer to elect to have allowances calculated separately for each machine. This system will enable balancing allowances to be claimed when a machine is sold for less than its written-down value. If at the end of five years the machine has not been sold its tax written-down value will be transferred to the main machinery pool. Motor cars costing more than £12,000 are included in a separate 'pool' in the year of purchase, on which a 25% writing down allowance is available. The allowance is restricted to a maximum of £3,000 for motor cars with a written-down value of more than £12,000. Special rules apply where a motor car is only partly used for business purposes. There is a 100% first year allowance for new cars with emissions of less than 120gm/km CO_2.

(ii) *Machinery Leasing.* Tax allowances for rental payments on financial leases are spread to reflect the commercial depreciation of the asset. This may mean that full tax relief for rental payments may not be gained in the years in which the payments are made.

(iii) *Buildings.* Farm buildings, fencing, drainage and other improvements (including up to one-third of farmhouses) qualify for a writing-down allowance of 4% annually, given equally over 25 years. These annual allowances are normally available to succeeding owners during the 25 year period. Balancing allowances can now be claimed where buildings are demolished and also on the transfer of the land, but only with the new owner's consent.

E. Losses

Losses can normally be set off against other income in the year in which they are incurred and in the prior year. If other income is insufficient in the year when the loss occurs and in the prior year, any unrelieved losses can be carried forward and set off against future profits from farming. Special rules apply to prevent abuse of loss relief provisions by 'hobby' farmers who are not running their farms on a commercial basis with a view to producing a profit: normally losses are disallowed against other income after 5 consecutive years of loss.

Trading losses may be set against capital gains.

F. Profit Averaging

This relief is to enable farmers, other than companies, to average their taxable profits over two consecutive years. Where the difference between the profits of two consecutive years is 30% or more of the higher profits, the total profits for the two years are equally divided between the two years. Marginal relief is available where the difference is less than 30% but more than 25% of the higher profits. Profit for the purposes of tax averaging calculations is after the deduction of capital allowances. There is a two year limit in which to make the claim.

4. Capital Gains Tax

A. Application and Rates

Applies to capital gains made by an individual. Capital gains accruing to companies are chargeable to Corporation Tax. A capital gain is the difference between the acquisition value and the sale price. The first £8,800 of capital gains realised by an individual in a tax year are free of tax. Capital gains in excess of £8,800 are treated as the top slice of income and are charged to tax at 10%, 20% or 40%.

Exempt assets include a principal private residence (e.g. farm house, if non-exclusive business occupation applies) if occupied as such, normal life assurance policies, animals and tangible movable properly (i.e. chattels) disposed of for £6,000 or less.

Capital Gains Tax is chargeable only on the disposal (including gifts) of assets. Capital Gains Tax is not payable on death.

Payment of Capital Gains Tax is due on 31st January following the tax year of disposal on the self-assessment return.

B. Reliefs

(i) *Losses:* Should a transaction produce a loss, this may be set against any long term chargeable gains arising in the same year or, if these are insufficient, those accruing in subsequent years. Losses brought forward will be used only to the extent necessary to reduce untaxed gains for the year to £8,800. Indexation allowances (for inflation) may not be utilised to create or increase a capital loss. Losses brought forward are set against any gains before applying tapering relief, so that claims need to be made very carefully.

Where a trading loss can be set against other income in the same or prior year for income tax purposes, any unused loss can be set against capital gains for those years.

(ii) *Improvements:* Spending that has increased the value of the asset can be offset against any gain. In the case of agricultural property, allowance would be made for any capital expenditure undertaken to improve the property, even though the expenditure may have obtained a buildings allowance referred to at 3(d) above.

(iii) *Indexation and Tapering:* An indexation allowance for inflation applies to periods of ownership between 31st March 1982 and 1st April 1998 for individuals; for companies indexation carries on past 1st April 1998. The acquisition value of the asset (or its value at 31st March 1982, if it was owned prior to that date) is indexed-up for changes in the Retail Price Index. For assets owned on 31st March, 1982 and disposed of subsequently, providing an appropriate election is made (within two years), only the gain attributable to the period after that date is taxable, i.e. the chargeable gain is the gain from a valuation at 31st March, 1982 to the date of disposal.

Tapering relief was introduced in 1998 to replace the indexation allowance and applies to periods of ownership after 5th April 1998. The taper reduces the amount of the gain that is liable to tax according to the length of the period of ownership and it is more generous for business assets than for non-business assets. The operation of the taper is illustrated below.

Number of complete years of ownership after 5th April 1998	Percentage of gain chargeable to tax	
	Business assets	Non-business assets
0	100%	100%
1	50%	100%
2	25%	100%
3	25%	95%
4	25%	90%
5	25%	85%
6	25%	80%
7	25%	75%
8	25%	70%
9	25%	65%
10	25%	60%

(iv) *Rollover*: Payment of tax may be deferred on gains accruing from the sale of business assets (including land and buildings occupied and used for trade purposes, fixed plant and machinery, milk quotas, and from the sale of shares in a family business) if part or all of the proceeds are spent on acquiring new assets liable to the tax. The tax is deferred by deducting the gain from the acquisition price of the new asset. Normally it can only be done if the new asset is acquired within 12 months before and 3 years after the disposal of the old assets. Disposal and acquisition dates for Capital Gains purposes are almost always contract, not completion, dates.

(v) *Holdover:* Payments of tax may be deferred where disposal is by gift. This relief only applies to gifts of business assets, land which qualifies for agricultural property relief at either the 100% or 50% rate under Inheritance Tax (see next section) and gifts which lead to an immediate charge to Inheritance Tax (e.g. gifts into a discretionary trust). The amount of the chargeable gain which would normally have accrued to the donor will be held over; the value at which the donee is deemed to acquire the asset will be its market value reduced by the amount of the donor's chargeable gain held over. The held over gain is netted down by any time apportionment, indexation allowance, or any retirement relief available to the donor, but not tapering relief. Where deferral is not available payment of tax by interest bearing annual instalments over 10 years will be allowed for gifts of land, controlling share holdings and minority share holdings in unquoted companies.

5. Inheritance Tax

A. *Application and Rates*

This tax, which replaced Capital Transfer Tax, is charged on lifetime gifts and transfers on death.

Slice of Chargeable Transfer	Rate per cent
£1- 285,000	0%
Over 285,000	40%

Outright gifts to individuals are exempt from tax at the time of the gift. If the donor lives for a further seven years then the transfer is fully exempt. Gifts into accumulation and maintenance trusts and interest in possession trusts no longer receive special treatment - all other gifts will be taxed at half the above rates at the time of the transfer.

Tax is charged on the value of an individual's estate at death plus the value of all gifts made within seven years of death. Allowance is made for any tax paid on lifetime gifts included in the value of the estate on death. Relief is given for outright gifts made more than three years before death according to the following scale:

Years between gift and death	Percentage of the full charge to tax
0-3	100
3-4	80
4-5	60
5-6	40
6-7	20

Exemptions include: transfers between husband and wife; the first £3,000 of gift made by a donor in the income tax year and separately up to £250 per year to any number of persons; gifts made out of income which form part of normal expenditure; marriage gifts within limits of £5,000 for a parent, £2,500 for a lineal ancestor and £1,000 for other donors.

B. Reliefs

(i) *Agricultural Property Relief (APR):* Relief may be available for agricultural land. Subject to a general rule that the agricultural land must have been occupied by the transferor (or by his controlled company) for two years, or owned by the transferor for 7 years and occupied for agricultural purposes by someone else before any relief is granted, the relief is at two different rates. If the basis of valuation is vacant possession, the taxable value of the land is reduced by 100%. If the basis of valuation is tenanted value, the taxable value of the land is reduced by 50% of that tenanted value. Ownership and occupation periods normally include prior periods of ownership or occupation by husbands and wives. From 1st September 1995 100% relief applies to new lettings of agricultural land as Farm Business Tenancies.

(ii) *Business Property Relief (BPR):* Relief is also available in respect to 'business property' transferred during lifetime or on death. The relief extends to the business assets of a proprietor and the interest of a partner or controlling shareholder of a company in the business capital. The value of such property, providing certain tests are satisfied (e.g. it has been owned by the transferor for two years preceding transfer), is reduced by 100%. Where a partner or controlling shareholder owns assets (e.g. land) that the business uses, the value will be reduced by 50%. Shareholdings in unquoted companies receive a 100% reduction in market value.

Lifetime gifts of property eligible for Agricultural and Business Property Relief have to be retained (or replaced by similar property) until the death of the donor (or earlier death of the donee) if those reliefs are to be available when the tax (or additional tax) becomes payable subsequent to the donor's death

In the case of the transfer of property eligible for APR and BPR, the tax can be paid by annual instalments over ten years free of interest.

6. Stamp Taxes

A. Stamp Duty

Stamp Duty is charged at 0.5% on the transfer of shares and securities.

B. Stamp Duty Land Tax

Stamp duty land tax is charged on the transfer of an interest in land, including leases. The tax is levies on a percentage of the sale value of the property;

Residential property	Rate	Non-residential and mixed use	Rate
Value up to £60,000	nil	Value up to £150,000	nil
£60,000 to £250,000	1%	£150,000 to £250,000	1%
£250,000 to £500,000	3%	£250,000 to £500,000	3%
Over £500,000	4%	Over £500,000	4%

Special rules apply to land in disadvantaged areas. Leases are taxed according to the net present value of the rent payable.

7. Value Added Tax

Agricultural businesses with a turnover of taxable goods and services in excess of £61,000 per annum (from 1st April 2006) are required to register for VAT. Businesses with a turnover below this limit may apply for voluntary registration. The standard rate of VAT is 17.5%. Most agricultural products are zero rated for VAT purposes. VAT has to be paid on certain inputs. Registered businesses are eligible to reclaim the tax paid where the goods or services purchased have been used in the production of zero-rated supplies.

A flat rate scheme is available to farmers as an alternative to registering for VAT. Farmers under the flat rate scheme do not have to submit tax returns and consequently cannot reclaim tax. They can, however, charge (and keep) a flat rate addition of 4% when they sell to VAT registered customers goods and services which qualify. This addition is not VAT but acts as compensation for losing input tax on purchases. The local VAT office may refuse to issue a certificate to participate in the flat rate scheme if this would mean the farmer would recover substantially (£3,000) more than through the normal system.

On 25 April 2002 a new flat rate scheme was introduced for small businesses generally and is an alternative that farmers can use if they have taxable supplies of no more than £150,000 and a total business income of no more than £187,500. This scheme operates in a different way to the flat rate scheme for farmers in that a business charges the normal rate of VAT on sales. However, the VAT which the business has to remit to Customs and Excise is calculated by multiplying the value of gross sales by a rate specified for each particular trade sector. The rate for agriculture is 6% except for businesses supplying agricultural services, when the rate is 7.5%.

8. National Insurance Contributions (2006-07)

Class 1 (not contracted out).

Employee's weekly earnings	Employee	Employer
£97.00 or less	Nil	Nil
£9.01 to £645.00	11%	12.8%
Over £645.00	1%	12.8%

Class 2.

Self-employed flat rate (exception if earnings below £4,215 a year)	£2.05 a week

Class 3.

Non-employed (voluntary) flat rate	£7.15 a week

Class 4.

Self-employed. On profits or gains between £4,745 and £31,720	8%
over £31,720	1%

3. GRANTS

Grant aid and a number of other support measures for rural areas in England are now predominantly provided under the umbrella of the England Rural Development Programme (ERDP) that was launched in the autumn of 2000. The ERDP comprises a package of schemes which reflect the switch in support away from agricultural production to more general support for the rural economy through measures designed to encourage business diversification and adding value to farm produce, and to protection of the environment. Following devolution separate support arrangements apply in Wales and Scotland.

A new EU Rural Development Regulation has been agreed by Member States for the years 2007 to 2013. Each of the UK agricultural departments will be producing new Rural Development Programmes for this period. DEFRA has completed its first consultation, to determine the objectives of the new England Rural Development Programme (ERDP). There will be further consultations through out the year, to determine the design of any new schemes. As a result, the schemes summarised below may change after 2006. Although, the new Environmental Stewardship Scheme (ESS) and the new English Woodland Grant Scheme are likely to continue with only minor changes, but support for Hill farming and the 'Project Based' grants look set to change.

1. Land Based Schemes

A. *Environmentally Sensitive Areas (ESAs)*

The first ESAs were designated in 1987. Currently there are 22 designated areas in England, covering some 10% of its agricultural land. Within these areas farmers were offered annual payments if they entered into 10 year agreements to manage their land, buildings, walls and other features in ways which will conserve the traditional environment. These agreements have now been superseded by the introduction of the Environmental Stewardship Scheme (ESS) (see 1 D below). No more agreements are being offered, existing agreements will continue until the end of their term. Agreement holders will then be offered the option to enter land into the ESS.

Land which is subject to an ESA agreement will qualify for the Single Payment (SP) as long as scheme rules are adhered to.

B. *Countryside Stewardship Scheme (CSS)*

Once the flagship scheme offering both capital grants and annual payments as incentives to improve the natural beauty and diversity of the countryside. But now, similar to the ESA scheme, it is closed to new applicants following the introduction of the Environmental Stewardship Scheme (ESS). Acceptance into the CSS was competitive and priority was given to proposals offering the best potential for environmental improvement and public benefit. Participants were usually required to enter a 10 year agreement. The following landscape types and features were targeted for support: chalk and limestone grassland, lowland heath, waterside land and coastal land, upland, historic features (orchards, parkland, buildings), old meadows, pastures and orchards, field boundaries (including stonewalls, hedgerows, ditches and dykes), field margins, community forests and countryside around towns, new public access.

Existing Agreements will continue until the end of their term at which point it may be possible to enter the land into the ESS. Land in the CSS is eligible for payment under the Single Payment Scheme as long as scheme rules are followed. Payments are reviewed regularly and can go up or down. Rates are currently under review following the introduction of the Single Payment Scheme (SPS), but are expected to remain largely at current levels.

C. Organic Farming Scheme

This scheme is now closed to new applications in England. Current Agreements will continue until the end of their term. An outline of this scheme, which still operates in Wales, can be found on page 54. A new scheme for organic farmers in England, the Organic Entry Level Scheme (OELS), has been introduced as part of Environmental Stewardship Scheme (ESS) (see 1 D below).

D. Environmental Stewardship Scheme(ESS)

The Environmental Stewardship Scheme was launched in 2005 to replace the Environmental Sensitive Areas, Countryside Stewardship and Organic Farming schemes. The scheme comprises three elements:-

- Entry Level Stewardship (ELS)
- Organic Entry Level Stewardship (OELS)
- Higher Level Stewardship (HLS)

(i) *Entry Level Stewardship (ELS):* This is intended to encourage a large number of farmers across a wide area to adopt simple environmental management practices such as hedgerow management, stone wall maintenance, low input grassland, buffer strips and arable options. The scheme is non-competitive and open to all as long as scheme requirements are met. Points are awarded for each management option adopted. There is a large range of management options including hedgerow management, one side 11 points/100m, both sides 22 points/100m; 2m, 4m, 6m buffer strips attracting 10, 20 and 30 points /100m respectively; overwintered stubbles gain 120 points/ha and beetle banks 580 points/ha. Applicants have to achieve a minimum number of 30 points per hectare (8 points per ha for parcels of LFA land over 15 hectares) to be accepted into ELS. An annual payment of £30 per hectare will be made (£8 per hectare for parcels of land over 15ha within the LFA). ELS agreements will last for five years.

(ii) *Organic Entry Level Stewardship (OELS)*: Is open to all organic farmers with land which is registered as organic or in conversion and not currently receiving aid under the Organic Farming Scheme (see 1 C above). OELS has similar options to those under ELS and participants will receive annual payments of £30 per hectare for carrying out the organic options on the organic land plus an additional £30 per hectare for farming the land organically. There will also be an option to apply for organic conversion with a payment of £600 per ha per year for top fruit orchards and £175 for improved land. To participate in this latter option land must not already have been converted to full organic production and applicants must have registered the land with an organic inspection body. OELS agreements will last five years.

(iii) *Higher Level Stewardship (HLS):* Is targeted towards achieving significant environmental benefits in high priority areas with the objectives being wildlife conservation, protecting historic environments, maintaining and enhancing landscape quality, encouraging public access and resource protection. Applicants have to produce a Farm Environment Plan (FEP) and will usually have to participate in ELS. Only applications that give the best value in meeting the scheme aims will be accepted. Payment will depend on the management options adopted. HLS agreements will normally be for ten years with a break clause after five years.

E. Woodland Schemes

Following a review of the woodland schemes available in England, the Woodland Grant Scheme (WGS) and the Farm Woodland Premium Scheme (FWPS) are now closed for new applications. A new scheme, the English Woodland Grant Scheme (EWGS) is being introduced in England. In Wales the Better Woodlands for Wales scheme opened in April 2006. An outline of these schemes can be found on pages 68.

F. Energy Crops Scheme

This scheme, operates in England and aims to increase the area devoted to energy crops by providing support for establishing Short Rotation Coppice (SRC) (either willow or poplar) and Miscanthus (Elephant Grass), and for setting up producer groups. In order to be eligible for the scheme a minimum total area of three hectares must be planted (although this can comprise of a number of smaller plots), and a contract, or letter of intent, from a crop end user is required. Normally the land being planted must be within a reasonable distance to the end use site - 25 miles radius for large-scale projects and 10 miles for small-scale projects.

Rates of grant for establishment depend on the energy crop being planted and the land type:

	£ per hectare
SRC Standard Rate	1,000
SRC Enhanced Rate	1,600
Miscanthus	920

The *enhanced rate* for SRC applies to land that has previously been claimed as forage area for the purposes of IACS and for which livestock premia has been paid. The SRC standard rate applies to other land. It is not possible to claim payments under the Energy Crops Scheme and payments under the Countryside Stewardship Scheme or the Farm Woodland Schemes. Land in the ECS can count towards the area to calculate your points target and associated payment under Entry Level Stewardship. But ELS options must not be located within parcels covered by the ECS agreement. It is possible to enter into boundary options on boundaries surrounding land within an ECS agreement. It may be possible to validate set-aside entitlements on land planted to energy crops under the Single Payment Scheme

Grant aid of up to 50% (maximum £200,000) is available towards the cost of setting up groups producing SRC. Eligible expenditure includes legal costs, accommodation, office equipment, recruitment cost and harvesting machinery. See page 70.

G. Hill Farm Allowance Scheme

This scheme provides support for beef and sheep farming in the Less Favoured Areas. See page 102.

2. Project Based Schemes

All the existing Project Based Schemes in England closed to new applications on 30th June 2006. Consultations are currently under way as to what funding (if any) should succeed these as part of the Rural Development Programme for 2007 to 2013 (refer to the beginning of section 'Grants' for more details). Below is an outline of what was previously on offer.

A. Rural Enterprise Scheme

This scheme operated in England and aimed to support more sustainable, diversified and enterprising rural economies and communities. It was open to farmers and other rural businesses and community groups. Grants were available for such projects as:

- Setting up farm relief and farm management services
- Marketing quality agricultural produce
- Basic services for the rural economy and population
- Renovation & development of villages and conservation of the rural heritage
- Diversification of agricultural activities and activities close to agriculture
- Agricultural water resource management
- Improvement of infrastructure connected with the development of agriculture
- Protection of the environment in connection with agriculture, forestry and landscape conservation as well as with the improvement of animal welfare
- Encouraging tourist and craft activities

Rates of support were in three bands:

1. Projects with minimum economic return to the applicant:- 50-100% of eligible costs
2. Where the primary objective of the project is to generate an economic return to the applicant:- 30-50% of eligible costs
3. Where the project generates a substantial annual return (in excess of 25% of total capital):- 15-30% of eligible costs.

The maximum rate of support for diversification into alternative agricultural activities is limited to 40% (50% in LFAs) of eligible costs. Although there is no maximum or minimum project size the maximum grant that any agricultural holding can receive under the ERDP is £500,000.

Grant aid to support farm improvement and diversification in Wales is provided by the Farm Improvement and Farm Enterprise Grant schemes.

B. Processing and Marketing Grant Scheme

This scheme operated in England and is still available in Wales. It provides capital grants on a competitive basis to individuals and groups of producers achieve added value for agricultural products and to enhance market opportunities. Aid was available, at the rate of 30% of eligible costs, on investments over £70,000 in England and £40,000 in Wales. The maximum grant for any one project is £1.2 million. Items eligible for grant aid include the cost of buildings (new and refurbishments) and new equipment. Consultants' and architects' fees may also be eligible.

C. Vocational Training Scheme

This scheme operated in England. Payments were made for vocational training of farmers and other persons engaged in farming and forestry. Assistance was provided either to an individual or a group of individuals or businesses. Training must have been vocational and fall within a number of specified areas which included:

- Information and communication technology
- Business and marketing skills
- Conservation and environment skills
- Diversification opportunities
- Resource management
- Technical skills in agriculture, horticulture and forestry
- On-farm food production and processing skills.

Up to 75% of eligible costs were funded. There was a minimum project size of 20 days training e.g. one person for 20 days or 20 people for one day.

A fast-track Vocational Training Scheme was made available for individual trainee applications only with no minimum number of days per application.

3. Other Grants

A number of other grants are available which fall outside the umbrella of the England Rural Development Programme.

A. Fresh Fruit and Vegetable Aid Scheme

Producer organisations recognised under the European Commission Regulation 2200/96 may apply for a contribution towards an operation fund which the organisation has set up to finance a planned programme to improve performance in marketing, produce quality and environmental considerations. The contribution from the European Commission will be a maximum of 4.1% of the producer organisation's marketed production or 50% of eligible expenditure under the planned programme, whichever is the least. Further details are available from the Rural Payments Agency; (see www.rpa.gov.uk).

B. Agricultural Development Scheme

This scheme provides assistance to help farmers and growers in England improve their competitiveness through better marketing. Marketing includes all aspects of preparing a product for the market but excludes advertising. The maximum grant is £0.5m and the maximum grant rate is 50% of eligible expenditure incurred in a project for which assistance is sought. Eligible items include salaries of key staff, depreciation on new items of equipment (but not the capital cost of the equipment itself), and various other costs including overheads, consumable materials, consultancy fees, project management costs, travel and training. Projects should normally be completed within three years and have lasting benefits and an industry wide effect. The scheme is competitive and only the best applications in terms of value for money will be aided.

C. Farm Business Advice

Three days of free farm business advice was available to farmers in England who spent at least 75% of their time on their core farming activities. This service ended on 31st March 2005. A new Farm Business Advice Service (FBAS) – 'Knowing your options' was launched in September 2005. Its aim is to provide farmers with advice on the implications of the Single Payment Scheme. The scheme is being run regionally through the Regional Development Agencies (RDAs). More information on how to access this scheme can be found on the DEFRA website at www.defra.gov.uk. It is expected to be available until 31st March 2007.

D. Redundant Buildings Scheme

Grant aid towards the cost of converting redundant farm buildings may be available from Regional Rural Development Agencies depending on the funding priorities in particular regions. Projects eligible for assistance include the conversion of redundant buildings for office, craft, manufacturing and retail purposes; and tourism and leisure use. Conversion to residential accommodation will not be supported. Aid is usually up to 25% of eligible costs. The minimum grant is £2,500 and the maximum £60,000.

Environment Schemes Payments, 2005 (provisional)		£m	Single Payment
England:	Environmentally Sensitive Areas	66.1	
	Countryside Stewardship	114.9	
	Organic Conversion	3.3	
	Hill Farm Allowance	35.0	
	Other	37.8	
	Total	257.1	1532.6
Wales:	Environmentally Sensitive Areas	2.1	
	Tir Mynydd	35.5	
	Tir Cymen and Tir Gofal	23.8	
	Other	4.0	
	Total	65.4	218.9
Scotland:	Environmentally Sensitive Areas	7.0	
	Countryside Premium & Rural Stewardship	10.4	
	Less Favoured Area Support	61.0	
	Other	6.7	
	Total	85.1	396.4
N. Ireland:	Environmentally Sensitive Areas	3.5	
	Countryside Management Scheme	2.9	
	Less Favoured Area Compensatory Allowances	21.9	
	Other	0.4	
	Total	28.7	227.2
UK:	Total	436.3	2375.1

Source: DEFRA, SEERAD, DARD, WAGDEPC. Agriculture in the UK 2005.

VIII. MISCELLANEOUS DATA

1. CONSERVATION COSTS

Note: Costs can vary quite widely, depending on geographical location and the type and size of the job.

(N.B. Abbreviations. DEFRA: Department of Environment, Food and Rural Affairs; CA: Countryside Agency; FC: Forestry Commission; EN: English Nature; BTCV: British Trust for Conservation Volunteers).

Hedge Cutting. From £200 per day at an average of 3 miles per day.

Hedge Laying. Contract labour, £8-£10 a metre (excluding stakes, bindings, burning debris), or £8.50 per hour. Contractor, 15 metres/day; BTCV, 5 metres/day per person. Nov./March. Every 8 to 20 years. Grant aid: CA, DEFRA, EN. Lantra quotes £1.50 a metre plus 60p a metre for stakers and pleachers, 40 metres a day.

Hedge Planting. Transplants av. £35/100; netlon guards av. 45-50p; canes av. 10p; fencing (labour and materials): stock proof £3.50/metre, rabbit proof up to £4/metre. Overall, £1.80/metre unguarded and unfenced, £6.50/metre guarded and fenced. Contract labour: planting up to £2/metre, fencing up to £2.50/metre. Contractor 100-150 metres/day; BTCV 20 metres/day. Pref Oct./March. Above includes repair. Grant aid: CA, DEFRA, EN.

Hedge Coppicing. By hand: 2 men and a chain saw, £7/metre plus burning debris. Contractor: tractor mounted saw, driver and 2 men, 13 metres/ hour, £30/hour. Grant aid: CA, DEFRA.

Dry Stone Walling. Cost of stone approximately £80/tonne. Cost of building wall £60-£80 per square metre. Grant aid: CA, DEFRA.

Amenity Tree Planting; (half acre block or less). Transplants av. 75p; shelter plus stake and tie av. £1; stake av. 50p; whip av. 70p. (50p-£1); rabbit spiral guard 30p; netlon guard av. 50p (but 15p in a 50 m roll); cane av. 10p. Trees per man day: farmer 200, contractor 400; (large-scale, 33 man days/ha). Nov.-April. Grant aid: CA, DEFRA.

Shelter Belts. Per 100 metre length: 100 large species (oak, lime, etc.) £45; 66 medium species (cherry, birch, etc.) £38; 100 shrubs, £30; 166 tree stakes, shelters and ties, £250; (site preparation, weed control, labour and fencing extra). DEFRA standard costs £637.50/ha; windbreaks £33.85/ha. Grant aid: CA, DEFRA.

Woodland Establishment. Conifers £150/1000. To supply and plant oak or beech transplants in tubes £1.50-£3.25 each, dependent on shelter size. Rabbit fencing £3.80/metre. Contract labour: conifers at 2m (inc. trees) £1,500/ha; broadleaves at 3m (inc. trees) £900/ha; forest transplants (not inc. trees) £270/1000. 12.5 days/ha (contractor). Nov.-April. (Above not inc. maintenance). Grant aid: FC, CA, DEFRA.

Forestry: General. Contract labour: chain sawing £8/hr., brush cutting £7.15/hr., extracting timber/pulp £4-£10/tonne, chemical spot weeding 5p-7p/tree, rhododendron control £600-£800/acre.

Pond Construction. Butyl lining (0.75mm) £5/m^2; other lining £3/m^2. Contract labour: 150 Komatsu £25/hr.; bulldozer D6 LGP £40/hr, 13t 360° excavator £38/hr, Flailmowers from £16/hr. Autumn (dry ground conditions). Grant aid: DEFRA, CA (discretionary), EN (possibly).

Pond Maintenance. Hymac £40/hr.; Backhoe £20-22/hr. 5m^2/day (BTCV); 100 m^2/day (contractor). Timing: probably winter; time depends on ground condition and species whose life cycles may be disturbed. Every 5 to 50 years. Grant aid: CA, EN.

Ditch Maintenance. Backhoe excavator £15/hr; 13 tonne 360° excavator £38/hr.; labour £10/hr. Preferably in winter. Every 3 to 7 years on rotation. Grant aid: DEFRA (improvement plan), EN (conservation interest).

Pollarding and Tree Surgery. Pollard: £40-£60/stool; surgery: £150/ tree. Pollarding: 2 or 3 trees/day. Surgery: 2 days/tree. Winter. Pollard every 20-40 years. Grant aid: CA (discretionary).

Establishment of Wildlife Grassland Meadow. £150-£250/ha for ground preparation, depending on weed burden; costs may be higher if follows set-aside or exceptional weed burden. Seed costs very variable, but as a guide: local provenance grass and wildflower seed, £45/kg; basic long season wildflower mix, £30 per 100g (250g/ha); neutral grassland stewardship mix, approx. £85/ha (at 20kg/ha).

Reducing Pesticide Drift. Use of appropriate spray nozzles: tilt jets £22-£25 for 6; lo-drift nozzles £15 for 6.

Permanent Grass Margins at Field Edges. To provide wildlife benefits and help control pernicious weeds, reducing herbicides at the field edge. A sterile strip provides virtually no wildlife benefit and the initial establishment costs may be offset by savings in maintenance costs in future years. Costs per 100 metres as follows. Establishment: 2m grass margins, £3.50-£5; 6m grass margins, £10.50-£15; beetle banks, £3-£4. Maintenance: 2m margins, 50p to 60p; 6m margins, £1.50-£1.80.

Fertilizer Losses at Field Boundaries. For a 12m spread pattern, at 150 kg/ ha, loss is approx. 30p per 100m per application, or £3 for a 6 ha field (450 x 150m). Loss avoided by driving further away from the field boundary/using a tilting hopper mechanism/using an appropriate border disc or deflector, costing £90.

Grant Aid. A summary of 'Grants for Landscape Conservation' is available from the CA, FC, DEFRA and EN. Countryside Agency grants are usually available through local authorities.

Acknowledgement. Above information supplied by *Farming and Wildlife Advisory Group* (FWAG). Sources: County FWAG personnel, BTCV, local authorities.

2. FERTILISER PRICES

A. *Compounds*

Analysis			Price Per Tonne
N	**P₂O₅**	**K₂O**	**£**
0	24	24	134
0	18	36	140
0	20	30	136
0	30	15	133
0	30	20	139
5	24	24	156
8	24	24	163
10	24	24 (B)	155
10	10	30 (B)	145
12	15	20 (B)	148
13	13	20	149
15	15	20	159
15	19	19 (B)	158
17	17	17 (B)	163
20	5	15 (B)	148
20	10	10 (B)	142
20	8	12 (B)	158
24	4	4 (B)	139
25	5	5 (B)	148
25	0	16	150

B. *Straights*

Type	Price per tonne £
Ammonium Nitrate: UK (34.5% N.)	156
Ammonium Nitrate: Imported (34.5% N.) SP4/5	146
Sulphate of Ammonia (21% N.)	124
Urea (46% N.): granular/ prills	160
Liquid Nitrogen (28% N)	99
Triple Superphosphate (47% P₂O₅)	148
Muriate of Potash (Granular) (60% K₂O)	145

Average price (p) per kg:			
N	:	45	(UK AN)
P₂O₅	:	31	(triple supers).
K2 O	:	24	(muriate).

The prices above are for fertilizer delivered in 500kg bags; delivery in bulk averages £6.50/tonne less; delivery in 50kg bags and pallets £7 to £10/tonne more; collection of bags by farmers £5 to £8/tonne less. They are approximate average prices in August, 2006; they vary according to area and bargaining power. (B) stands for blended; prices for granular (where available) average around £8/tonne more. They assume delivery in 25 tonne loads; add approximately £2/tonne for 10 tonne loads, £4 for 6-9 tonne loads, £6 for 4-5 tonne loads.

3. MANURIAL VALUE OF SLURRY AND FARMYARD MANURE

1.	Composition (% by weight)	N	P_2O_5	K_2O
	Undiluted Slurry			
	(faeces plus urine, or droppings):			
	Cow	0.5	0.2	0.5
	Pig	0.6	0.2	0.2
	Poultry	1.7	1.4	0.7
	Farmyard Manure:			
	Cattle	0.5	0.4	0.6
	Pig	0.6	0.6	0.4
	Poultry	1.8	1.8	1.2

2.	Available Nutrients (kg)			
	Undiluted Slurry (per $10m^3$*):			
	Cow	35	11	58
	Pig	42	11	23
	Poultry	118	82	82

(* = 10 tonnes; 10,000 litres)

	Farmyard Manure (per 10 tonnes):			
	Cattle	17	20	46
	Pig	20	31	31
	Poultry	110	92	92

3. Amount per head

(faeces plus urine, or droppings)	litres per day		kg per year (1)	
		N	P_2O_5	K_2O
1 dairy cow	40	51	16	84
1 pig (dry meal fed)	4.5	6.8	1.8	3.7
100 laying hens	13	55	39	39

(1) housed all year and no losses.

4. AGROCHEMICAL COSTS (2006)

Only the names of the active ingredients are given below, with their principal use. These materials should only be applied in accordance with the manufacturers' recommendations. Application rates can vary and there are differences between the prices of various proprietary brands. The list is not intended to be exhaustive and there is no implied criticism of materials omitted. Note, the variation in costs per hectare is primarily because of varying application rates rather than price variation between suppliers.

Crop	Function		Material	Approx. cost £/ha per application
Cereals	Herbicides	General	MCPA	3.50-8.00
			Mecoprop-P	4.25-10.00
			Ioxynil+Bromoxynil	7.50-11.50
			Dicamba +Mecoprop-P + MCPA	14.00-17.50
			Metsulfuron-methyl	12.50
		Undersown Crops	MCPA+MCPB	42.00
		Blackgrass	Isoproturon	7.75-13.00
			Isoproturon + Diflufenican	13.00-21.00
			Clodinafop-propargyl + trifluralin + cloquintocet-mexyl	20.00
		Cleavers	Fluroxypyr	14.00-18.00
			Amidosulfuron	18.00
		Wild Oats	Diclofop-methyl + Fenoxaprop-P-ethyl	20.00-27.50
		Wild Oats & Blackgrass	Clodinafop-propargyl	33.00
			Fenoxaprop-P-ethy	11.50-17.00
	Growth Regulator		Chlormequat	2.00
			Chlormequat + Choline Chloride	2.50
			2-chlorethylphosphonic acid	5.00-10.00
			2-chloroethyl phosphonic acid + Mepiquat Chloride	8.00-16.00
			Trinexapac-ethyl	14.25-17.75
	Fungicides		Azoxystrobin	27.00
			Epoxiconazole	23.00
			Tebuconazole	18.50
			Cyproconazole	12.00
		Seed Dressing	Fuberidazole + Triadimenol + Imidacloprid	15.50-20.00
			Fuberidazole + Triadimenol	9.50-12.50
			Fludioxonil	7.00-9.00
	Aphicide		Cypermethrin	0.75
			Deltamethrin	2.50-3.25
			Pirimicarb	8.00-8.50
	Slug Killer		Metaldehyde	11.50
			Methiocarb	20.00

Crop	Function		Material	Approx. cost £/ha per application
Oilseed Rape	Herbicides		Propyzamide	45.00-54.00
			Trifluralin	5.50
			Metazachlor	26.00-43.50
	Insecticide		Deltamethrin	3.50
			Pirimicarb	8.00-8.50
			Alphacypermethrin	3.00-5.75
	Fungicide		Iprodione + thiophate-methyl	23.00-35.00
			Tebuconazole	9.25-18.50
			Flusilazde + Carbendazim	16.00-20.00
			Metconazole	23.00
Potatoes	Herbicides:		Metribuzin	14.25-28.50
			Linuron	11.50-22.50
			Paraquat + Diquat	17.50
	Blight Control		Cymoxanil + Mancozeb	8.00
			Cymoxanil + Famoxadone	14.00-20.00
			Fluazinam	10.50
			Mancozeb+Metalaxyl	21.00
	Haulm Dessicant		Diquat	33.00
Sugar Beet	Herbicides:	Pre-emergence	Chloridazon:	
			overall	28.00-66.00
			band spray	9.00-21.00
		Post-emergence	Phenmedipham:	
			low dose	3.00
			band spray	21.00
			Triflusulfron-methyl	19.00
	Insecticide		Oxamyl	29.00-43.00
			Pirimicarb	8.00-8.50
Beans	Herbicide		Bentazone	56.00
	Fungicide		Chlorothalonil	12.00
			Tebuconazole	18.50
			Azoxystobin	27.00
Peas	Herbicide		Bentazone + MCPB + Cyanazine	33.00
Beans & Peas	Insecticide		Pirimicarb	8.00-8.50

Crop	Function	Material	Approx. cost £/ha per application
		Deltamethrin	3.00-4.00
Maize	Herbicide	Prosulfuron + Bromoxynil	23.75
		Nicosulfuron	24.50-37.00
Brassicas	Herbicides	Propachlor	61.00-89.00
		Trifluralin	5.50
Broadleaved Grass weeds and volunteer Crops			
	Cereals	Fluazifop-P-butyl	24.00-36.00
		Propaquizafop	15.00-33.00
		Cycloxydim	19.00-31.00
Grassland	Herbicides	MCPA	7.00-12.00
		MCPA + MCPB	30.00-42.00
General	Weed and Grass Killer		
	General	Paraquat	9.00-24.00
	Prior to Direct Drilling	Paraquat	18.00-33.0
	Couch Grass Control	Glyphosate	5.00-12.00
	Woody Weed Control	Triclopyr	140-210

Note. The above prices are based largely on retail prices paid by farmers (spring 2006) and reflect the discounts available where there are competing products from several manufacturers.

Acknowledgement: Particular thanks to Bartholemews 01243 784 171

5. FEEDINGSTUFF PRICES

£ per tonne

Cattle	Dairy:	High Energy	140 - 165
		Medium Energy	125 - 145
		Low Energy	115 - 130
		Concentrate	210 - 260
	Beef:	Pellets	110 - 135
		Concentrate	195 - 225
	Calf:	Milk Substitute (bags)	1,200 - 1,300
		High Fat (bags)	900 - 925
		Calf Weaner Pellets	150 - 160
		Calf Rearer Nuts	140 - 150
Sheep	Lamb Pellets		130 - 140
	Medium energy sheep		120 - 130
	Sheep/lamb cake		115 - 125
	Ewe cake		125 - 135
Horses	Horse and Pony Pencils		200 - 250
Goats	Goat Nuts		140 - 175
Pigs	Piglet Weaner		175 - 190
	Sow Nuts		135 - 160
	Early Grower Pellets		190 - 225
	Grower/Finisher Pellets		150 - 175
	Sow Concentrate		260 - 275
	Grower Concentrate		270 - 290
Poultry	Chick and Rearer Feeds		120 - 140
	Layers Feeds		115 - 135
	Broiler Feeds		145 - 180
	Turkey Feeds		160 - 220
Straight Feeds	Fishmeal (English; 66/70%)		700 - 800
	Soya Bean Meal (Hipro; 44%)		145 - 175
	Rapeseed Meal (36%)		80 - 110
	Palm Kernel Meal/Cake (17%CP)		65 - 85
	Linseed Cake		170 - 200
	Sunflower Seed Pellets (30/33%)		75 - 100
	Cottonseed Ext. Meal (40/42%)		100 - 155
	Citrus Pulp Nuts/Pellets		90 - 110
	Grass Cubes (16%)		120 - 140
	Wheatfeed		60 - 90
	Maize Gluten		80 - 110
	Molasses (Cane)		100 - 120
	Sugar Beet Pulp (Molassed Nuts/Pellets)		95 - 110
	Brewers' Grains		20 - 30
	Supergrains		30 - 40
	Fodder Beet		20 - 30

Compound feed prices are approximate ranges in August 2006; the range incorporates differences in the ingredients. Straight feed prices are approximate ranges between February 2005 and August 2006.

They are (mainly) delivered prices for hauls more than 10 miles in 20-25 tonne loads. Discounts of £3 to £5/tonne for cash and £3 to £6 for deliveries within 10 miles of the mill at the company's convenience are usually available; they are not allowed for above. The additional farm delivered cost for bags ranges from £17.50 to £27.50 a tonne.

ME requirements for Friesian cows (590kg LW)

Liveweight Change (kg/day)	Maintenance	Milk yield (kg/day)			
		20	25	30	35
−0.5		147	172	196	221
0	62	161	186	210	235
+0.5		178	203	227	252

Source: Broster, W.H. and Alderman, G., Livestock Production Science, 4 (1977).

6. FEEDINGSTUFFS: NUTRITIVE VALUES

Typical Energy and Protein Contents of Some Common Feeds

Type of Feed	Dry Matter Content g/kg	Metab-olizable Energy MJ/kg DM	Crude Protein g/kg DM	Relative Value £/tonne fresh*
Forages:				
Barley Straw	860	7.0	10	32
Grass Silage (typical clamp).	250	10.8	150	17
Hay (typical meadow)	850	8.8	100	45
Maize Silage.	300	11.0	90	19
Pasture (rotational grazed)	180	11.5	160	13
Whole-crop Wheat (fermented)	400	10.5	95	24
Cereals:				
Barley	860	13.2	120	65
Oats	860	12.5	120	62
Wheat	860	13.6	130	68
Maize	880	13.8	90	66
Roots:				
Fodder Beet.	180	12.0	60	11
Potatoes	200	13.3	100	15
Wet By-Products:				
Brewers' Grains	260	11.5	250	21
Pressed Sugar Beet Pulp.	260	12.5	100	15
Straights:				
Cane Molasses	750	12.7	40	48
Distillers Barley Grains	900	12.2	260	77
Distillers Maize Grains	900	14.0	310	90
Distillers Wheat Grains	900	13.5	340	91
Dried Citrus Pulp	900	12.6	70	61
Dried Molassed Sugar Beet Pulp	900	12.5	100	63
Extracted Rapeseed Meal	900	12.0	400	90
Extracted Soyabean Meal	900	13.4	530	109
Extracted Sunflower Meal	900	10.0	390	80
Field Beans	880	13.3	290	83
Lupin Seed Meal	900	14.2	350	95
Maize Gluten Feed	880	12.8	210	73
Palm Kernel Meal	900	11.4	200	68
Wheatfeed.	880	11.3	190	65

* with rolled barley at £65 per tonne and rapemeal at £90 per tonne (delivered)

Acknowledgement: David Peers, ADAS. Based on Nutritive Value of Feed given in Advisory Manual 'Feed into Milk', (ed. C. Thomas, Nottingham University Press 2004).

7. STANDARD OUTPUTS, STANDARD GROSS MARGINS, AND STANDARD MAN DAYS

Crops (per hectare)	Standard Output	Standard Gr. Margin	Standard Man Days
Winter Wheat	620	359	
Spring Wheat	465	264	
Winter Barley	460	248	1.25/2 (2)
Spring Barley	420	235	
Winter Oats	460	279	
Spring Oats	390	245	
Winter Oilseed Rape	487	248	1.25
Spring Oilseed Rape	300	130	1.25
Linseed	240	109	1.25
Field Beans	383	254	1.25
Dried Peas	360	166	1.50
Lupins	395	190	1.50
Vining Peas	1,000	750	3.00
Potatoes	3,738	1,381	10.00 (3)
Sugar Beet	1,378	734	3.00
Herbage Seed	707	321	1.50
Hops	5,227	3,970	7.50
Mangolds (carted)	-	-	25.00
Turnips: folded	-	-	4.00
lifted	-	-	10.00
Kale: cut and carted	-	-	10.00
grazed	-	-	1.50
Hay / Silage: one cut	-	-	2.50
two cuts	-	-	4.00
Grazing only	-	-	0.50
Hay for sale	450	350	2.25
Keep let	175	150	0.75
Bare fallow	-	-	1.25
Set-aside	-	-	0.25
Rough Grazing	-	-	0.20

Livestock (per head) (4, 5)			
Dairy Cows	1200	705	4.25
Bulls	-	-	3.50
Beef Cows (single suckler including calf):			
lowland	249	85	1.40
upland	256	88	1.70
hill	250	81	2.00
Cereal Beef (0-12 months) (6)	441	118	1.50
18-month Beef (6)	442	182	1.50
Grass Silage Beef (6)	466	177	
Other Cattle over 2 years (7)	225	115	1.40
Other Cattle 1-2 years (7)	225	115	1.00
Other Cattle ½-1 years (7)	125	80	1.00

Livestock	Standard Output	Standard Gr. Margin	Standard Man Days
Calves; multiple sucklers – to 6 months add to single sucklers	125	40	0.75
Calves; others to 6 months (6):			
steers	150	25	1.25
heifers	150	25	1.25
Ewes: lowland	49	21.5	0.50
upland	43	20	0.45
hill	39	24.1	0.40
Rams.............................	-	-	0.50
Other sheep over 6 months	36	15	0.30
Sows.............................	674	316	2.50
Boars	-	-	2.00
Other pigs over 6 months	130	40	0.25
Laying Birds: battery cages	8.18	1.72	0.017
free range	14.7	6.94	0.06
Pullets reared (6)	1.93	0.49	0.005
Broilers (6)	1.12	0.23	0.002
Turkeys (6)	17	5	
Capons (6)	10.69	7.23	
Ducks (6)...........................	10.34	7.23	
Geese (6)...........................	30.35	25	

1. Author's estimates for 2007 for average performance under average conditions; the Standard Putputs (S.O.s) and Standard Gross Margins (S.G.M.s) of many of the enterprises have obviously been considerably altered by the Mid-Term Review decoupling. Wide variations can occur from farm to farm. Some of the S.M.D. estimates are based on only limited data — though all that is available; these are subject to substantial variations with scale and production methods.

2. 1.25 if straw ploughed in; 2 if straw harvested. Highly mechanised larger farms will require no more than 0.75 S.M.D./ha of direct labour for cereals and other combinable crops (assuming straw ploughed in).

3. Including casual labour.

4. In calculating the S.O.s and S.G.M.s for livestock, herd depreciation or livestock (e.g. calf) purchases or the value of transfers in have been deducted.

5. Note that for grazing livestock, the S.M.D. per head exclude field work, e.g. grass production and silage making, i.e. the labour for these has to be added to give total labour for these enterprises.

6. For these livestock, S.O., S.G.M. and S.M.D. per annum should be based on numbers produced (sold) during the year. For all other livestock, average numbers on the farm at any one time during the year should be used (i.e. average of numbers at end of each month).

7. 'Other Cattle' can refer to both beef animals and dairy followers (ref. detail on page 149).

For number of Standard Man-Days per worker per year, see page 131; note the addition of 15% to the total of the enterprise S.M.D.s for general maintenance work.

8. FARM RECORDS

The following records should be kept for management purposes:

1. *Basic Whole Farm Financial Position*

1. Cash Analysis Book, fully detailed.

2. Petty Cash Book.

3. Annual Valuation, including physical quantities, with crops in store and livestock at (near) market value, less any variable costs yet to be borne. Fertilizers, seeds, sprays, casual labour or contract work applied to growing crops should be recorded, but 'cultivations' and manurial residues can be ignored for management purposes.

4. Debtors and creditors at the end of the financial year.

2. *Other Financial and Physical Records*

1. Output (quantities and value) of each Crop and Livestock Enterprise for the 'Harvest Year' (or Production Cycle). It may be possible to get information of Sales from a fully detailed cash analysis book (although, for crops, the financial year figures will then have to be allocated between crops from the current harvest and those from the harvest in the previous financial year, in order to check on the accuracy of the opening valuation of crops in store; this is particularly a problem with Michaelmas ending accounts). The following records of Internal Transfers and Consumption will also be required:

   a. Numbers and Market Value of livestock transferred from one livestock category to another, e.g. dairy calves to Dairy Followers or Beef Enterprise, or dairy heifers to Dairy Enterprise.

   b. Quantity and Market Value of Cereals fed on farm and used for seed.

   c. Quantity and Market Value of Milk and other produce consumed by the farmer or his employees, used on the farm (e.g. milk fed to calves), or sold direct.

2. Monthly record of Livestock Numbers; preferably reconciled with the previous month according to births, purchases, deaths, sales and transfers.

3. Costs and Quantities of Concentrate Feed to each category of livestock, including Home-Grown Cereals fed on the farm.

4. Allocation of costs of seed, fertilizer, sprays, casual labour and contract work specific to an enterprise. This is in order to calculate gross margins, where required. It is less essential than the other records listed.

5. Breeding record for cows, including bulling dates, date(s) served, type of bull used, pregnancy testing, estimated calving date, actual calving date, and date when dried off.

6. For each crop, total output and yield per hectare, in both quantity and value. Include each field where the crop has been grown and its approximate yield, where this can be satisfactorily obtained.

7. For each field, keep one page to cover a period of say, ten years. Record on this, each year, crop grown, variety sown, fertilizer used, sprays used, date sown, date(s) harvested, approximate yield (if obtainable), and any other special notes that you feel may have significance for the future.

8. A rotation record. On a single page, if possible, list each field down the side and say, ten years along the top. Colour each field-year space according to the crop grown, e.g. barley yellow, potatoes red, etc.

9. DEFINITION OF FARM MANAGEMENT TERMS

Mainly abstracted from 'Terms and Definitions used in Farm and Horticulture Management', M.A.F.F., 1970.

1. *Valuations and Capital*

Valuations. Valuation is essentially a process of estimation. Thus alternative bases are sometimes possible, according to the purpose intended. The basis should be consistent throughout the period of any series of figures.

(i) Saleable crops in store. At estimated market value less costs still to be incurred, e.g. for storage and marketing. Both may be estimated either at the expected date of sale or at the date of valuation.

(ii) Growing crops. Preferably at variable costs to the date of valuation, although estimated total cost can alternatively be used.

(iii) Saleable crops ready for harvesting but still in the ground. Preferably valued as (i), less estimated harvesting costs, although they can alternatively be treated as (ii).

(iv) Fodder stocks (home-grown). Preferably at variable costs when calculating gross margins. Alternatively at estimated market value (based on hay-equivalent value according to quality). Fodder crops still in the ground, e.g. kale, treated as (ii).

(v) Stocks of purchased materials (including fodder). At cost net of discounts (where known) and subsidies.

(vi) Machinery and equipment. Original cost net of investment grants, less accumulated depreciation to date of valuation.

(vii)Livestock. At current market value, less cost of marketing. Fluctuations in market value expected to be temporary should be ignored.

Tenant's Capital. The estimated total value of capital on the farm, other than land and fixed equipment. There is no easy way of determining this sum precisely and estimates are made in several ways depending on the information available and the purpose for which the estimate is required. One method is to take the average of the opening and closing valuations (at either market value or cost) of livestock, crops, machinery and stores (feed, seed, fertilizers). See also pages 192-193.

Landlord's Capital. Value of the land and fixed equipment (including buildings).

2. *Output Terms*

Revenue (or Income). Receipts adjusted for debtors at the beginning and end of the accounting period. Items such as subsidies, grants, contract receipts and wayleaves are included.

Returns. Revenue adjusted for valuation changes (add closing, deduct opening, valuation).

Gross Output. Returns plus the value of produce consumed in the farmhouse or supplied to workers for which no payment is made, less purchases of livestock, livestock products and other produce bought for resale.

Enterprise Output. The total value of an enterprise, whether sold or retained on the farm. It therefore equals Gross Output of the enterprise plus the market value of any of the products kept on the farm (transfers out). Products transferred from another enterprise to be used in the production of the enterprise whose output is being calculated are deducted at market value (transfers in). Instead of the accounting year the 'harvest year' can be used for crops; valuations are then not relevant.

(Enterprise) Output from Forage. Primarily the sum of the enterprise outputs of grazing livestock, but includes keep let and occasional sales, e.g. of surplus hay,

together with an adjustment for changes in the valuation of stocks of home-grown fodder. However, fortuitous changes in stocks caused by yield variations due to the weather, the severity or length of the winter, or minor changes in livestock numbers or forage area can be either ignored (if small in relation to total annual usage) or included in miscellaneous output.

Adjusted Forage (Enterprise) Output is Output from Forage less rented keep and purchases of bulk fodder.

Net Output. Gross Output less the cost of purchased feed, livestock keep, seed, bulbs and plants.

Standard Output. The average enterprise output per hectare of a crop or per head of livestock calculated from either national or local average price and average yield data.

3. Input Terms

Expenditure. Payments adjusted for creditors at the beginning and end of the accounting period. Capital expenditure is not included.

Costs. Expenditure adjusted for valuation changes (add opening, deduct closing, valuation), with the following adjustments. Add: depreciation on capital expenditure including machinery, any loss made on machinery sales (add to depreciation) and the value of payments in kind to workers if not already included in their earnings. Deduct: purchases of livestock, livestock products and other produce bought for resale, any profit made on machinery (deduct from depreciation), allowance for private use of farm vehicles (deduct from machinery costs), the value of purchased stores used in the farmhouse (e.g. electricity) or sold off the farm (deduct from the relevant item).

Inputs. Costs with the following adjustments, made in order to put all farms on a similar basis for comparative purposes. Add: the value of unpaid family labour, including the manual labour of the farmer and his wife, and, in the case of owner-occupiers, an estimated rental value (based on average rents of similar farms in the area), less any cottage rents received. Deduct: any mortgage payments and other expenses of owner-occupation, interest payments and the cost of paid management. A proportion of the rental value of the farmhouse may also be deducted.

Fixed Costs. See pages 1-2, 172.

Variable Costs. See page 1.

4. Margin Terms

Management and Investment Income. Gross Output less Inputs. It represents the reward to management and the return on tenant's capital invested in the farm, whether borrowed or not. It is mainly used for comparative purposes, all farms having been put on a similar financial basis by the adjustments made to costs in calculating Inputs.

Net Farm Income. Management and Investment Income, less paid management, plus the value of the manual labour of the farmer and his wife. It represents the return to all tenant's type capital and the reward to the farmer for his manual labour and management.

Profit (or Loss). Gross Output less Costs. This represents the surplus or deficit before imputing any notional charges such as rental value or unpaid labour. In the accounts of owner-occupiers it includes any profit accruing from the ownership of land.

Gross Margin. See page 1.

Net Margin. A term sometimes used to denote Gross Margin less direct labour and machinery costs charged to an individual enterprise. This is not, however, nationally accepted terminology.

5. Area Terms

Total Hectares. All hectares comprising the farm.

Hectares. Total hectares less the area of woods, waste land, roads, buildings, etc.

Adjusted Hectares. Hectares reduced by the conversion of rough grazings into the equivalent hectares of average quality grassland. This is the figure often used for lowland farms when calculating 'per hectare' results.

Forage Hectares. Total hectares of forage crops grown, less any hectares exclusively used by pigs or poultry and the area equivalent of any home-grown fodder fed to barley beef. Usually, too, the area of rough grazings is converted to its grassland equivalent (see Adjusted Hectares). Forage crops are all crops, grass and rough grazings grown specifically for grazing livestock, other than catch crops and crops harvested as grain and pulses.

Adjusted Forage Hectares. Forage hectares adjusted as follows. Add area equivalent of keep rented, deduct area equivalent of keep let; deduct the area equivalent of occasional sales of fodder, e.g. surplus hay, and seed cuts (note: hay and seed grown regularly for sale should be regarded as cash crops, not forage crops); add or deduct the area equivalent of planned changes in the valuation of stocks of home-grown fodder (fortuitous changes in stocks resulting from weather conditions may be ignored); convert rough grazings into their grassland equivalent if not already done. The following adjustments also may be made: add the area equivalent of catch crops and of grazing from cash crops of hay or seed: add the area equivalent of purchased fodder.

In calculations such as Gross Margins per Forage Hectare, Adjusted Forage Hectares are usually used. If the area equivalent of purchased fodder has been added the cost of purchased fodder must not be charged as a variable cost: this is probably the best calculation for comparative purposes. Alternatively, when considering all the grazing enterprises taken together, purchased fodder can be deducted as a variable cost and no addition made for its area equivalent.

10. AGRISTATS

Some basic agricultural statistics relating to U.K. agriculture. (All figures are for the U.K. in 2005 unless otherwise stated.)

A. Structure

1. **Agriculture's Economic Contribution** (2005)

   Agriculture's contribution to total economy Gross   £5,238 million
   Value Added (provisional):   0.7%

2. **Agricultural Workforce** (2005)

   (a) *Agriculture's proportion of total workforce in employment:*   2.1%

   (b) *Numbers of Persons Engaged in Agriculture (June) (to nearest '00):*

A: Employed:	Male	Female	Total
Regular Full-time	57,200	10,300	67,500
Regular Part-time*	24,500	17,200	41,700
Seasonal, Casual and Gang	46,400	18,700	65,100
Salaried Managers			15,700
Total Employees			190,000
B: Farmers, Partners Directors and their Spouses			
Full-time			154,400
Part-time*			196,300
Total Farmers, Partners Directors and their Spouses			350,700
Total Labour Force**			540,700

   *   Part-time is 39 hours or less per week in England and Wales, less than 38 in Scotland and less than 30 in Northern Ireland.

   **   Total labour force excludes schoolchildren but includes 'official' trainees.

3. **Livestock Numbers** (June '000 Head)

	2000	2005
Total Cattle and Calves	11,133	10,414
of which Dairy Cows	2,336	2,065
Beef Cows	1,842	1,768
Heifers in Calf	718	639
Total Sheep and Lambs	42,261	35,517
of which Female Breeding Flock	20,447	16,990
Total Pigs	6,482	4,864
of which Female Breeding Flock	610	470
Poultry Broilers	106,050	111,487
Laying Flock	28,686	29,550
Growing Pullets	9,461	10,929
Farmed Deer	36	33
Goats	76	96

4. Crop Areas (June)

	Area ('000 ha) 2000	Area ('000 ha) 2005	% Total Area 2005	% Crops & Grass 2005*
Wheat	2,086	1,868	10.1	16.3
Barley (% winter in brackets)	1,128 (52)	942 (41)	5.1	8.2
Oats	109	91	0.5	0.8
Mixed Corn, Triticale and Rye	25	24	0.1	0.2
Total Cereals (excluding maize)	3,348	2,925	15.8	25.5
Potatoes	166	137	0.7	1.2
Sugar Beet (England and Wales only)	173	148	0.8	1.3
Oilseed Rape (non Set-aside) (% winter in brackets)	332 (90)	519 (94)	2.8	4.5
Peas harvested dry (GB only)	84	45	0.2	0.4
Field Beans (GB only)	124	194	1.0	1.7
Linseed (non Set-aside)	72	45	0.2	0.4
Vegetables & Salad grown in the open	119	121	0.7	1.1
Orchards, Small Fruit and Grapes . . .	38	33	0.2	0.3
Other Horticulture	16	16	0.1	0.1
Maize (excl. Scotland in 2000)	104	131	0.7	1.1
Other Crops	91	129	0.7	1.1
Bare Fallow	37	140	0.8	1.2
Total Tillage	4,702	4,443	31.2	50.3
Temporary Grass (under 5 years old)	1,205	1,193	6.4	10.4
Total Arable	5,907	5,777	34.2	55.2
Permanent Grass (5 years, and over) .	5,584	5,711	30.9	49.7
(Total Grass (excluding Rough Grazing))	(6,789)	(6,904)	37.3	.
Total Tillage & Grass (excl. R.G.) . . .	11,491	11,488	62.1	100.0
Rough Grazing**	5,667	5,590	6.7	.
Set-aside (incl. any in non-food crops)	567	559	3.0	.
Woodland	500	583	3.1	.
Other Land on agricultural holdings .	301	289	1.6	.
Total Agricultural Area***	18,526	18,509	100	.

* Excluding Rough Grazing

** Including 1,232,000 ha of common grazing.

*** Urban land and forest each approximately 2.0 million ha; other non-agricultural land approximately 1.5 million ha; total U.K. land area including inland waters: 24.1 million.

5. Size Structure

(a) *Number and Size Distribution of UK Holdings, 2003* *(latest data):*

Size group (ha)	Total land area			Tillage and grass area		
	No. ('000)	%	% area	No. ('000)	%	% area
0.1 to 19.9	178.8	58.7	5.1	136.4	54.3	7.1
20.0 to 49.9	47.3	15.5	9.1	46.5	48.5	13.7
50.0 to 99.9	36.7	12.0	15.2	35.6	14.2	22.3
100 and over	412.0	13.8	70.6	32.7	13.0	56.9
Total	304.8	100.0	100.0	251.2	100.0	100.0

Average area (ha/[acres]) per holding: 56.6 (140); tillage and grass 45.7 (113).

Size of Business (ESU)	'000 of Holdings	% of holdings	% of total ESU
Under 8	191.9	63.0	3.3
8 to 40	58.0	19.0	14.8
40 to 100	34.2	11.2	27.7
100 to 200	14.8	4.9	25.6
200 and over	6.0	2.0	28.5
Total	304.8	100.0	100.0

Average size of holdings: 26.3. Average size over 8 ESU (which is judged to be the minimum for full-time holdings, which are 37.7% of all holdings) = 67.4 ESU, 124.6 ha (308 acres). ESU = European Size Unit (the number provides a measure of the financial potential of the holding, based on standardised gross margins).

(b) *Number and Size distribution of holdings in England and Wales, 2000*

Size group (ha)	By total land area				By tillage and grass area			
	Holdings		Hectares		Holdings		Hectares	
	'000	%	'0,000	%	'000	%	'0,000	%
Under 10.	62.8	36.0	212	2.0	53.2	33.6	195	2.3
10 to 30	35.2	20.2	646	6.2	33.9	21.4	628	7.3
30 to 50	19.6	11.2	771	7.4	19.9	12.6	779	9.1
50 to 100	27.0	15.5	1,937	18.6	26.6	16.8	1,900	22.2
100 to 200	19.0	10.9	2,641	25.3	17.0	10.7	2,340	27.3
200 to 300.	5.5	3.2	1,342	12.9	4.4	2.8	1,056	12.3
300 to 500	3.7	2.1	1,386	13.3	2.5	1.6	916	10.7
500 to 700.	1.0	0.6	592	5.7	0.6	0.4	344	4.0
700 and over. . . .	0.8	0.5	897	8.6	0.4	0.3	411	4.8
Total	174.6	100	10,425	100	158.5	100	8,570	100

6. *Average Size of Enterprises*

Hectares	1998	2003		1998	2003
Crops and grass	48.7	45.3	Dairy Cows	68	82
Cereals (excl. maize). . .	47.9	52.1	Beef Cows.	27	29
Oilseed Rape	27.9	36.3	Breeding Sheep	241	222
Potatoes	9.1	11.9	Breeding Pigs	77	95
Sugar Beet	20.4	21.8	Fattening Pigs	486	455
			Laying Fowls	1,495	1,205
			Broilers	33,659	39,698

7. *Tenure* (England and Wales, 2000)

Tenure	No. of Holdings	Area owned (%)	Area rented (%)
Wholly owned	119,254 (68.2)	4,969 (47.2)	-
Mainly owned	19,850 (11.4)	1,805 (17.1)	456 (4.3)
Wholly rented	22,643 (13.0)	-	1,826 (17.3)
Mainly rented	13,010 (7.4)	345 (3.3)	1,137 (10.8)
Total	174,757 (100)	7,119 (67.6)	3,419 (32.4)*

N.B. Mixed tenure holdings: mainly owned = over 50% owned;
mainly rented = over 50% rented.

Wholly or mainly owned, 79.6% of holdings; wholly or mainly rented, 20.4%

* N.B. As the above figures for rented land include family arrangements (e.g. farmers, or family farming companies, renting from other members of the family, or family shareholders) the percentage of 'truly' rented land is almost certainly a few percentage points less than the figures given above.

B. Finance

1. *Inputs and Outputs* (2005)

Inputs	£m	Outputs	£m	%
Animal Feed	2,259	Wheat	979	6.9
Seeds	281	Barley	375	2.6
Fertilisers	802	Oats and other cereals. ...	33	0.2
Pesticides	562	Oilseed rape.	263	1.8
Hired Labour	2,027	Potatoes	482	3.4
Consumption of Fixed Capital*	2,658	Sugar beet	263	1.8
Maintenance: materials	708	Fresh vegetables	1,003	7.0
Maintenance: buildings	362	Fruit	369	2.6
Fuels	568	Plants and flowers.	781	5.5
Electricity	224	Cattle	1,328	9.3
Agricultural services.	648	Sheep	654	4.6
Veterinary expenses	274	Pigs.................	673	4.7
Net rent	234	Poultry	1,309	9.2
Interest	530	Milk and milk products ..	2,602	18.2
Other goods and services.	2,362	Eggs	349	2.4
Adjustments	100	Miscellaneous.	2,826	19.8
Total Inputs	14,599	Total Gross Output	14,289	100.0
Total Income From Farming	2,521	Single Payment & subsidies	2,831	
	17,120	Total Gross Output	17,120	
		Total Crops	3,278	22.9
		Total Horticulture.	2,153	15.1
		Total Livestock	4,794	33.6
		Total Livestock Products .	3,000	21.0
		Other	1,064	7.4

* including 670 buildings and 1,216 equipment.

Note. The above layout differs substantially from that published by DEFRA.

2. Income from Farming

(a) *Index of UK Total Income from Farming* in Real Terms (av. 1974-76 = 100)*

Year	Index	Year	Index	Year	Index	Year	Index
1975 ...	93	1983 ...	65	1991 ...	49	1999 ...	39
1976 ...	109	1984 ...	82	1992 ...	64	2000 ...	29
1977 ...	98	1985 ...	44	1993 ...	88	2001 ...	33
1978 ...	86	1986 ...	50	1994 ...	94	2002 ...	42
1979 ...	71	1987 ...	56	1995 ...	108	2003 ...	43
1980 ...	56	1988 ...	52	1996 ...	97	2004 ...	46
1981 ...	64	1989 ...	55	1997 ...	57	2005 ...	41
1982 ...	78	1990 ...	47	1998 ...	39	(provisional)	

* 'TIFF' = business profits plus income to farmers, partners and directors and others with an entrepreneurial interest in the business. It refers only to farming, i.e. diversification incomes and expenditures are excluded. There are no imputed charges (such as a rental value for owned land or value of the farmer's own labour).

(b) *Recent TIFF Values (£ million)*

	Actual	At 2005 Prices
1995 (the 1992-1997 peak)	5,271	6,690
2000 (the lowest recent level)	1,575	1,780
2001	1,847	2,050
2002	2,362	2,570
2003	3,081	3,260
2004	2,767	2,840
2005 (provisional)	2,521	2,521

(c) *Index of UK Farming Income* in Real Terms (av. 1940-69 = 100)*

Year	Index	Year	Index	Year	Index	Year	Index
1940-49	101	1977 ...	98	1987 ...	50	1997 ...	38
1950-59	100	1978 ...	89	1988 ...	34	1998 ...	20
1960-69	99	1979 ...	73	1989 ...	45	1999 ...	20
1970 ...	95	1980 ...	56	1990 ...	43	2000 ...	9
1971 ...	96	1981 ...	66	1991 ...	41	2000 ...	13
1972 ...	110	1982 ...	77	1992 ...	56	2002 ...	22
1973 ...	138	1983 ...	57	1993 ...	79	2003 ...	35
1974 ...	103	1984 ...	86	1994 ...	77	2004 ...	32
1975 ...	98	1985 ...	37	1995 ...	91	2005 ...	20
1976 ...	113	1986 ...	46	1996 ...	80	(provisional)	

* As this figure is no longer produced by DEFRA the figures from 1997 onwards are only approximate. Up to that year a figure for 'Labour: family, partners and director' was deducted from Total Income from Farming (TIFF) to give Farming Income.

3. Indices of UK Net Farm Income in Real Terms by Main Types of Farming
(£s, at 2004/05 prices)

Farm Type	2000/01	2001/02	2002/03	2003/04	2004/05	2005/06
Dairy	15,700	30,500	15,100	15,100	23,700	25,500
Grazing Livestock (LFA)	3,500	6,300	13,700	13,700	13,000	13,000
Grazing L'stock (Lowland)	-200	1,400	7,100	7,300	5,300	3,500
Cereals	7,600	5,400	11,600	34,600	13,600	10,000
General Cropping ...	17,100	15,300	12,400	52,400	26,400	27,500
Specialist Pigs	41,300	21,600	24,900	33,100	25,100	29,500
Specialist Poultry ...	28,900	23,900	88,500	51,500	89,700	71,000
Mixed	8,400	5,700	11,100	23,300	14,800	17,500
ALL TYPES						
(inc. Horticulture)	9,500	14000	14,600	24,700	17,900	17,500

1. In calculating net farm income various adjustments are made to the accounts, e.g. an imputed rent for owned land is deducted but interest payments are not deducted, nor is the value of unpaid labour of the farmer and spouse. Accounting years end of average in February.

2. The 2001/02 figures above exclude farms subjected to foot-and-mouth disease cull.

4. Balance Sheet of UK Agriculture (2005)

			£m	£m
Assets:	Fixed:	Land and buildings	110,176	
		Plant, machinery and vehicles	7,001	
		Breeding livestock	4,072	
	Total Fixed Assets:			*121,249*
	Current	Trading livestock	2,649	
		Crops and stores	1,978	
		Debtors and cash deposits	4,776	
	Total Current Assets:			*9,448*
	Total Assets:			**130,698**
Liabilities:	Long &	Bank loans	2,327	
	Medium-term:	AMC and SASC	1,317	
		Other	1,291	
	Total Long and Medium Term Liabilities			*4,936*
	Short-term	Bank overdrafts	2,913	
		Trade credit	1,373	
		Hire purchase and leasing	850	
		Other	149	
	Total Short-term Liabilities:			*5,287*
	Total Liabilities:			**10,222**
Net Worth:	....			**120,475**

% Equity (Net worth as a % of Total Assets): 92.2%

Total Income from Farming (TIFF) 2004 as a % of a) Net Worth: 2.72%
b) Total Assets: 2.51%
(Note: no charge has been made for farmers' own labour or management)

Bank Lending to Agriculture, Hunting and Forestry (2005 year average): .. *£8,953m*

C. Miscellaneous

1. UK Crop Yields and Prices, 2001-2005 (2005 Provisional)

Average Yields (harvest years) (tonnes per hectare)	2001	2002	2003	2004	2005	Average 2001-05
Wheat	7.1	8.0	7.8	7.8	8.0	7.7
Barley (all)	5.4	5.6	5.9	5.8	5.9	5.7
Winter Barley	5.8	6.3	6.3	6.4	6.5	6.3
Spring Barley	5.1	4.9	5.7	5.3	5.4	5.3
Oats	5.5	6.0	6.2	5.8	5.8	5.9
Oilseed Rape (excl. set-aside)...	2.6	3.5	3.4	3.0	3.3	3.2
Linseed (excl. set-aside)	1.2	1.3	1.7	1.7	1.7	1.5
Field Beans (for stockfeed)	3.5	3.9	3.9	3.7	3.8	3.8
Dried Peas (for stockfeed)	3.5	3.4	3.9	3.5	3.8	3.6
Potatoes (all)	40.2	44.0	40.7	42.5	42.3	41.9
Early Potatoes	12.4	16.4	20.0	17.4	15.1	16.3
Maincrop Potatoes	42.8	46.7	42.9	45.2	45.1	44.7
Sugar Beet (adj. to 16% sugar) ..	47.0	56.5	56.6	58.7	57.3	55.2

Average Prices (calendar years) (£ per tonne)		2001	2002	2003	2004	2005	Average 2001-05
Wheat	milling	82	71	83	86	73	79
	feed	75	63	75	76	66	71
Barley	malting	77	72	82	80	77	78
	feed	67	58	71	70	65	66
Oats	milling	69	57	63	64	70	65
	feed	66	54	61	63	68	62
Oilseed Rape (excl. set-aside)...		144	140	160	163	131	148
Linseed (excl. set-aside)		155	165	170	175	180	169
Field Beans (for stockfeed)		88	73	92	82	84	84
Dried Peas (for stockfeed)		89	76	94	85	87	86
Potatoes (all, inc seed)		111	81	103	117	98	102
Earlies		184	110	132	178	105	142
Maincrop		107	75	99	111	95	97
Sugar Beet (per adjusted tonne) .		31	30	31	31	31	31

2. Self-sufficiency (2005 provisional, [2000 in brackets])

(a) *Total Food*   all food types .... 60.0% *(66.6%)*

indigenous type food .... 73.3% *(80.1%)*

(b) *Individual Products (production as a % of total new supply for use in the UK):*

	2000	2005		2000	2005
Wheat	118	108	Beef and Veal.........	79	74
Barley	137	115	Mutton and Lamb	98	87
Oats	119	100	Pork	92	62
Total Cereals	113	102	Bacon and Ham.......	45	44
Oilseed Rape	83	106	Poultrymeat	89	90
Potatoes	88	82	Butter	64	65
Sugar	71	70	Cheese	63	63
Fresh Vegetables	68	60	Cream	137	138
Fresh Fruit	10	10	Hen Eggs	90	87

3. Food Consumption and Expenditure, UK 2004-05

(a) Food and Drink Consumed Within the Household

Average quantity consumed / expenditure per person per week:

	2001-02 kg per week	2004-05 kg per week	2004-05 £ per week
Milk and Cream (litres)	2.023	1.984	1.56
Cheese	0.112	0.110	0.60
Meat	1.032	1.049	4.94
Fish	0.157	0.158	0.99
Eggs (number)	1.65	1.56	0.18
Fats	0.196	0.182	0.37
Sugars and Preserves	0.147	0.134	0.17
Potatoes	0.907	0.822	1.02
Other Vegetables	1.092	1.106	1.82
Fruit	1.156	1.168	1.67
Bread	0.769	0.695	0.93
All Other Cereals (inc. Pasta & Pizza) .	0.886	0.882	2.83
Beverages (litres)	0.060	0.056	0.42
Soft Drinks (litres)	1.744	1.832	0.81
Alcoholic Drinks (litres)	0.735	0.763	2.66
Confectionery	0.126	0.131	0.84
Other Food.....................	-	-	1.23
Total	-	-	23.05

(b) Food and Drink Consumed Outside the Household

	£ per week
Food and Drink excl. Alcohol	7.72
Alcoholic Drinks	3.54
Total	11.26

(c) Total Food and Drink

	£ per week
Food and Drink excl. Alcohol	28.11
Alcoholic Drinks	6.20
Total	34.31

Sources: Agriculture in the UK: 2005 (DEFRA etc.). All items except for the following:

A5 (part), A7: Other DEFRA etc. Statistics.

B4, Bank Lending: Bank of England, Financial Statistics Division.

C3 and C4: Expenditure and Food Survey, DEFRA.

11. RATE OF INFLATION; PRICE AND COST INDICES

1. *Retail Price Index* (all items)

Year	% increase on year earlier	Index (1970 = 100)	Index (1980 = 100)	Year	% increase on year earlier	Index (1970 = 100)	Index (1990 = 100)
1990	9.5	682	189	1999	1.5	893	247
1991	5.9	722	200	2000	3.0	920	254
1992	3.7	749	207	2001	1.8	937	259
1993	1.6	761	210	2002	1.7	952	263
1994	2.4	779	215	2003	2.9	980	271
1995	3.5	806	223	2004	3.0	1010	279
1996	2.4	825	228	2005	2.8	1040	287
1997	3.1	851	235	2006 (est.).	3.0	1071	296
1998	3.4	880	243	2007 (f'cast)	2.5	1098	303

* Index in 1965: 80; index in 1962: 70. 1970-1994 figures available in earlier editions.

2. *UK Annual Price and Cost Indices, 2001-2005* (2000 = 100)

A. Producer Prices	2001	2002	2003	2004	2005
Feed Wheat	110.6	96.6	105.3	117.6	98.2
Feed Barley	103.3	88.1	104.3	108.3	99.1
All Cereals	107.8	95.0	105.2	114.2	99.1
Oilseed Rape	119.2	121.2	140.3	136.1	112.9
Potatoes (maincrop)	132.5	90.6	106.0	141.6	109.7
Sugar Beet	107.3	114.8	112.1	115.4	116.3
Desert Apples	109.8	111.3	124.6	120.9	116.5
All Fresh Fruit	99.0	113.9	124.2	112.4	120.1
All Fresh Vegetables	113.6	112.7	125.5	113.7	120.2
All Crop Products	112.0	104.0	110.7	115.0	108.4
Milk	113.7	101.0	106.4	109.0	109.0
Cattle	100.8	103.8	106.7	113.4	114.6
Sheep	101.3	118.5	132.5	131.5	122.9
Wool	87.0	96.4	108.4	107.3	99.7
Pigs.	103.6	98.7	109.0	109.3	109.8
Poultry	98.6	97.2	99.4	101.2	100.6
Eggs	104.9	109.5	130.7	135.1	121.1
All Animal Products	105.8	102.7	109.4	112.0	110.4
All Products	108.3	103.3	109.9	113.2	109.6

B. Input Prices					
Seeds	109.2	105.5	116.0	110.3	108.1
Fertilisers	115.8	110.3	119.0	130.5	143.3
Plant Protection Products	96.8	95.8	95.7	100.6	102.9
Energy and Lubricants	96.7	92.4	100.5	108.8	137.4
Animal Feeding Stuffs	107.4	103.5	104.9	111.6	102.9
Maintenance and Repair of Plant . .	104.3	109.4	116.0	122.5	130.3
Machinery and Other Equipment .	97.4	95.7	95.1	96.1	103.8
Buildings	103.3	107.8	112.1	118.1	123.7
General Expenses	102.5	105.5	105.2	114.0	114.6

12. METRIC CONVERSION FACTORS

Metric to Imperial   *Imperial to Metric*

Area

1 hectare (10,000m²) . . . . . 2.471 acres	1 acre . . . . 0.405 ha
	1 square mile . . . . 259 ha
1 square km . . . . 0.386 sq. mile	1 square mile . . . . 2.590 sq. km
1 square m . . . . 1.196 sq. yard	1 square yard . . . . 0.836 sq. m
1 square m . . . . 10.764 sq. feet	1 square foot . . . . 0.093 sq. m

(m = metre, km = kilometre)

Length

1 mm . . . . 0.039 inch	1 inch . . . . 25.4 mm
1 cm . . . . 0.394 inch	1 inch . . . . 2.54 cm
1 m . . . . 3.281 feet	1 foot . . . . 0.305 m
1 m . . . . 1.094 yard	1 yard . . . . 0.914 m
1 km . . . . 0.6214 mile	1 mile . . . . 1.609 km

(mm = millimetre, cm = centimetre)

Volume

1 millilitre . . . . 0.0352 fluid oz	1 fluid oz . . . . 28.413 ml
1 litre . . . . 35.2 fluid oz	1 fluid oz . . . . 0.028 litre
1 litre . . . . 1.76 pints	1 pint . . . . 0.568 litre
1 litre . . . . 0.22 gallon	1 gallon . . . . 4.546 litres

[Milk: 1 litre = 1.03 kg (.971 kg/litre); 1 kg = 1.709 pints, 0.214 gal.; 1 tonne = 213.63 gal; 1 pint = 0.585 kg; 1 gallon = 4.681 kg]

1 cubic m . . . . 35.31 cu feet	1 cubic foot . . . . 0.028 cu m
1 cubic m . . . . 1.307 cu yard	1 cubic yard . . . . 0.765 cu m
1 cubic m . . . . 220 gallons	1 gallon . . . . 0.005 cu m

Weight

1 gram . . . . 0.0353 oz	1 oz . . . . 28.35 gm
1 kg 35.274oz	
1 kg . . . . 2.205 lb	1 lb . . . . 0.454 kg
50 kg . . . . 0.984 cwt	
1 tonne (1,000 kg) . . . . 19.68 cwt	1 cwt . . . . 50.80 kg
1 tonne . . . . 0.984 ton	1 ton . . . . 1.016 tonne

Yields and Rates of Use

1 tonne/ha . . . . .0.398 ton/acre	1 ton/acre . . . . 2.511 tonnes/ha
1 tonne/ha . . . . 7.95 cwt/acre	1 cwt/acre . . . . 0.125 tonne/ha
1 gram/ha . . . . 0.014 oz/acre	1 oz/acre . . . . 70.053 g/ha
1 kg/ha . . . . 0.892 lb/acre	1 lb/acre . . . . 1.121 g/ha
1 kg/ha . . . . 0.008 cwt/acre	1 cwt/acre . . . . 125.5 g/ha
1 kg/ha (fert.) . . . . 0.797 unit/acre	1 unit/acre . . . . 1.255 kg/ha
1 litre/ha . . . . 0.712 pint/acre	1 pint/acre . . . . 1.404 litre/ha
1 litre/ha . . . . 0.089 gal/acre	1 gal/acre . . . . 11.24 litres/ha

Power, Pressure, Temperature

1 Kw . . . . 1.341 hp	1 hp . . . . 0.746 kW
1 kilojoule . . . . 0.948 Btu	1 Btu . . . . 1.055 kilojoule
1 therm . . . . 10,000 Btu	1 Btu . . . . 0.0001 therm
1 lb f ft . . . . 1.356 Nm	1 Nm . . . . 0.738 lb f ft
1 bar . . . . 14.705 lb/sq.in.	1 lb/sq.in. . . . . 0.068 bar
°C to °F . . . . x1.8, +32	°F to °C . . . . -32, ÷1.8

13. USEFUL ADDRESSES AND TELEPHONE NUMBERS*

1. General

ADAS
Headquarters: Woodthorne, Wergs Road, Wolverhampton WV6 8TQ   01902 754190

Advisory Committee on Organic Standards (ACOS)
DEFRA, Area 5F, Ergon House, Horseferry Road, London SW1P 2AL   020 7238 5605

Agricultural Central Trading Ltd. (Act)
90 The Broadway, Chesham, Bucks. HP5 lEG   01494 784931

Agricultural Engineers' Association
Samuelson House, Paxton Road, Orton Centre, Peterborough,
Cambs. PE2 5LT   01733 371381

Agricultural Law Association
6 St. Peters Close, Chislehurst, Kent BR7 6PD   020 8467 0722

Agricultural Industries Confederation (AIC)
Confederation House, East of England Showground, Peterborough,
PE2 6XE   01733 385230

Agricultural Wages Board
Ergon House, Area 3A, Horseferry Road, London SWlP 2AL   020 7238 6523

Association of Independent Crop Consultants
Agriculture Place, Heath Farm, Heath Road East, Petersfield,
Hampshire, GU31 4HT   01730 710095

BBC Radio 4 Farming To-day
The Mail Box, Birmingham B1 1RF   0121 432 8888

British Agricultural and Garden Machinery Association (BAGMA)
1st Floor, Entrance B, Salamander Quay West, Park Lane,
Harefield, Middlesex UB9 6NZ   0870 205 2834

British Association of Seed Producers
Manor House, Woodhall Spa, Lincolnshire, LN10 6PX.   01526 352368

British Cereal Exports
HGCA, Caledonia House, 223 Pentonville Road, London N1 9HY   020 7520 3927

British Crop Protection Council (BCPC)
7 Omni Business Park, Omega Park, Alton, Hampshire GU34 2QD   01420 593200

British Deer Society
Burgate Manor, Fordingbridge, Hampshire SP6 1EF   01425 655434

British Egg Industry Council (BEIC)
2nd Floor, 89 Charterhouse Street, London EC1M 6HR   020 7608 3760

British Grassland Society
PO Box 237, University of Reading, 1 Earley Gate, Berks. RG6 6AR   0118 931 8189

British Institute of Agricultural Consultants (BIAC)
The Estate Office, Torry Hill, Milstead, Sittingbourne,
Kent ME9 0SP   01795 830100

British Pig Association
Trumpington Mews, 40b High Street, Trumpington, Cambs. CB2 2LS   01223 845100

* For a directory of names, addresses and telephone numbers of UK agricultural firms and associations, with over 33,000 listing see Green Pages, 12th Edition, available from 229 Acton Lane, London W4 5DD (tel. 020 8747 8028; fax. 020 8747 8054). Published on CD-Rom, price £65 plus VAT, including post and packing.

British Potato Council
4300 Nash Court, John Smith Drive, Oxford Business Park
South, Oxford OX4 2RT
01865 714455

British Poultry Council
Europoint House, 5 Lavington Street, London SE1 0NZ
020 7202 4760

British Sheep Dairying Association
The Sheep Centre, Malvern, Worcs. WR13 6PH
01684 892661

British Society of Plant Breeders
Woolpack Chambers, Market Street, Ely, Cambs. CB7 4ND
01353 653200

British Sugar
PP Box 26, Oundle Road, Peterborough, Cambs. PE2 9QU
01733 563171

British Veterinary Association
7 Mansfield Street, London WlG 9NQ
020 7636 6541

British Wool Marketing Board
Wool House, Roydsdale Way, Euroway Trading Estate,
Bradford, West Yorkshire BD4 6SE
01274 688666

CAB International
Nosworthy Way, Wallingford, Oxon OX10 8DE
01491 832111

Campaign to Protect Rural England (CPRE)
128 Southwark Street, London SE1 0SW
020 7981 2800

Central Association of Agricultural Valuers (CAAV)
Market Chambers, 35 Market Place, Coleford, Gloucestershire
GL16 8AA
01594 832979

Centre for Agricultural Strategy
University of Reading, P.O. Box 237, Earley Gate, Reading,
Berks. RG6 6AT
0118 931 8152

Country Land and Business Association (CLA)
16 Belgrave Square, London SWlX 8PQ
020 7235 0511

The Countryside Agency
John Dower House, Crescent Place, Cheltenham
Gloucestershire, GL50 3RA
01242 521381
(to be replaced by Natural England from October 2006 - based in Sheffield)

Crop Protection Association UK
4 Lincoln Court, Lincoln Road, Peterborough, Combs PE1 2RP
01733 349225

Dairy Industry Association Ltd.
93 Baker Street, London W1V 6RL
020 7486 7244

Department of Agriculture and Rural Development (DARDNI)
Dundonald House, Upper Newtownards Road, Belfast BT4 3SB
028 9052 0100

Department of Environment, Food and Rural Affairs (DEFRA)
Nobel House, 17 Smith Square, London SW1P 3JR
020 7270 3000

English Heritage
23 Savile Row, London WlS 2ET
020 7973 3000

English Nature
Northminster House, Northminster, Peterborough PE1 lUA
01733 455000
(to be replaced by Natural England from October 2006 - based in Sheffield)

Environment Agency
Rio House, Waterside Drive, Aztec West, Almonsbury, Bristol
BS32 4UD
0870 850 6506

European Commission (London Office)
Jean Monnet House, 8 Storey's Gate, London SW1P 3AT
020 7973 1992

FACE (Farming and Countryside Education)
National Agricultural Centre, Stoneleigh Park, Warks. CV8 2LZ   024 7685 8261

Family Farmers' Association
Osborne Newton, Aveton Gifford, Kingsbridge, Devon TQ7 4PE   01548 852794

Farmers Club
3 Whitehall Court, London SW1A 2EL   020 7930 3751

Farmers Union of Wales
Llys Amaeth, Plas Gogerddon, Aberystwyth, Ceredigion SY23 3BT   01970 820820

Farming and Wildlife Advisory Group (FWAG)
National Agricultural Centre, Stoneleigh Park, Warks. CV8 2RX   024 7669 6699

Food and Drink Federation
Federation House, 6 Catherine Street, London WC2B 5JJ   020 7836 2460

Food from Britain
4th Floor, Manning House, 22 Carlisle Place, London SW1P 1JA   020 7233 5111

Food Standards Agency
Aviation House, 125 Kingsway, London WC2B 6NH   020 7276 8000

Forestry Commission
231 Corstorphine Road, Edinburgh EH12 7AT   0131 334 0303

Grain and Feed Trade Association (GAFTA)
GAFTA House, 6 Chapel Place, Rivington Street, London EC2A 3SH   020 7814 9666

Guild of Agricultural Journalists
Isfield Cottage, Church Road, Crowborough, East Sussex TN6 1BN   01892 611618

Health and Safety Executive (Agriculture Sector)
National Agricultural Centre, Stoneleigh Park, Warks. CV8 2LG   024 7669 8350

Home Grown Cereals Authority
Caledonia House, 223 Pentonville Road, London N1 9NG   020 7520 3926
Price Information Service   020 7520 3972

Horticultural Development Council
Bradbourne House, Tithe Barn, East Malling, Kent ME19 6DZ   01732 848383

Institution of Agricultural Engineers
West End Road, Silsoe, Bedford MK45 4DU   01525 861096

Institute of Agricultural Management
Farm Management Unit, University of Reading, PO Box 236,
Reading RG6 6AT   0118 931 6578

Institute of Agricultural Secretaries and Administrators
National Agricultural Centre, Stoneleigh Park, Warks. CV8 2LZ   024 7669 6592

Institute of Chartered Foresters
7a St. Colme Street, Edinburgh EH3 6AA   0131 225 2705

International Grains Council
1 Canada Square, Canary Wharf, London E14 5AE   020 7513 1122

Land Drainage Contractors Association
National Agricultural Centre, Stoneleigh Park, Warks. CV8 2LG   01327 263264

Land Heritage
Summerhill Farm, Hittisleigh, Devon EX6 6LP   01647 24511

Lands Improvement Holdings plc
1 Buckingham Place, London SW1E 6HR   020 7222 5331

Lantra
Lantra House, National Agricultural Centre, Stoneleigh Park,
Warks. CV8 2LG   024 7669 6996

LEAF (Linking Environment and Farming)
National Agricultural Centre, Stoneleigh Park, Warks. CV8 2LZ   024 7641 3911

London Commodity Exchange (Euronext Liffe)
Cannon Bridge House, 1 Cousin Lane, London EC4R 3XX   020 7623 0444

Meat and Livestock Commission (MLC)
PO Box 44, Winterhill House, Snowdon Drive, Milton Keynes
MK6 1AX   01908 677577

Milk Development Council (MDC)
Stroud Road, Cirencester, Glos GL7 6JN   01285 646500

National Agricultural Centre (NAC)
Stoneleigh Park, Warks. CV8 2LZ   024 7669 6969

National Association of Agricultural Contractors (NAAC)
Samuelson House, Paxton Road, Orton Centre, Peterborough PE2 5LT   01733 362920

National Association of British & Irish Millers (NABIM)
21 Arlington Street, London SW1A 1RN   020 7493 2521

National Beef Association
Mart Centre, Tyne Green, Hexham, NE46 3SG   01434 601005

National Cattle Association (Dairy)
Brick House, Risbury, Leominster, Herefordshire HR6 0NQ   01568 760632

National Dairy Council
164 Shaftesbury Avenue, London WC2H 8HL   020 7395 4030

National Farmers' Retail and Markets Association (FARMA)
The Greenhouse, PO Box 575, Southampton, Hants. SO15 7BZ   0845 458 8420

National Farmers' Union (NFU)
Agriculture House, Stoneleigh Park, Warks. CV8 2LZ   024 7685 8500
London Office, Kings Buildings, 16 Smith Square, London SW1P 3JJ   020 7808 6600

National Non-Food Crops Centre
Innovation Centre, York Science Park, Innovation Way, Heslington,
York YO10 5DG   01904 435182

NFU Scotland
Rural Centre, West Mains, Ingliston, Midlothian EH28 8LT   0131 472 4000

National Federation of Young Farmers Clubs
YFC Centre, National Agricultural Centre, Stoneleigh Park,
Warks. CV8 2LG   024 7685 7200

National Office of Animal Health (NOAH)
3 Crossfield Chambers, Gladbeck Way, Enfield, Middlesex EN2 7HF   020 8367 3131

National Sheep Association
The Sheep Centre, Malvern, Worcs. WR13 6PH   01684 892661

National Trust
36 Queen Anne's Gate, London SW1H 9AS   020 7222 9251

Processed Vegetable Growers' Association Limited (PGVA)
133 Eastgate, Louth, Lincolnshire LN11 9QG   01507 602427

Royal Agricultural Benevolent Institution (RABI)
Shaw House, 27 West Way, Oxford OX2 0QH   01865 724931

Royal Agricultural Society of England (RASE)
National Agricultural Centre, Stoneleigh Park, Warks. CV8 2LZ   024 7669 6969

Royal Association of British Dairy Farmers
Unit 31, Stoneleigh Deer Park, Stareton, Kenilworth, Warks CV8 2LY   0845 458 2711

Royal Forestry Society of England, Wales and N.I.
102 High Street, Tring, Herts. HP23 4AF   01442 822028

Royal Highland and Agricultural Society of Scotland
Ingliston, Edinburgh EH28 8NF   0131 335 6200

Royal Horticultural Society
80 Vincent Square, London SW1P 2PE   020 7834 4333

Royal Institution of Chartered Surveyors (RICS)
12 Great George Street, Parliament Square, London SW1P 3AD   020 7222 7000

Royal Society for the Protection of Birds
The Lodge, Sandy, Bedfordshire SG19 2DL   01767 680551

Royal Welsh Agricultural Society
Llanelwedd, Builth Wells, Powys LD2 3SY   01982 553683

Rural, Agricultural and Allied Workers Trade Group (TGWU)
Transport House, 128 Theobalds Road, Holborn, London WC1X 8TN   020 7611 2500

Rural Development Service (RDS)
Ergon House, 17 Smith Square, London SW1P 3JR   020 7238 5960
(to be replaced by Natural England from October 2006 - based in Sheffield)

Rural Payments Agency
Kings House, 33 Kings Road, Reading RG1 3BU   0118 958 3626

Scottish Executive Environment and Rural Affairs Department (SEERAD)
Pentland House, 47 Robb's Loan, Edinburgh EH14 1TY   0131 556 8400

Tenant Farmers' Association
7 Brewery Court, Theale, Reading, Berks. RG7 5AJ   0118 930 6130

The Stationery Office
The Publications Centre, PO Box 276, London SW8 5DT   0870 600 5522

Ulster Farmers Union
475 Antrim Road, Belfast BT15 3DA   028 9037 0222

United Farmers Trading Agency (UFTA) Ltd.
Hancock House, Smallgate, Beccles, Suffolk NR34 9AE.   01502 717877

Welsh Assembly Government, Agriculture and Rural Affairs Department
Crown Offices, Cathays Park, Cardiff, CF10 3NQ   029 2082 5111

Women's Food and Farming Union
National Agricultural Centre, Stoneleigh Park, Warks. CV8 2LZ   024 7669 3171

2. University Agricultural Economics
(Farm Business Survey work)

ENGLAND AND WALES

Northern: School of Agriculture, Food and Rural Development, University
of Newcastle, Newcastle-upon-Tyne NE1 7RU   0191 222 6902

North Eastern: Rural Business Research Unit, Askham Bryan College, Askham
Bryan, York YO23 3FR   01904 772233

North Western: Centre for Agricultural, Food and Resource Economics, School of
Social Sciences, Dover Street Building,
The University of Manchester, Oxford Road,
Manchester M13 9PL   0161 275 4822
(Farm Business Unit closed in 2005)

East Midlands: Rural Business Research Unit, University of Nottingham,
Sutton Bonington Campus, Loughborough,
Leics. LE12 5RD   0115 951 6070

Eastern:	Rural Business Unit, Centre for Rural Economics Research, 16-21 Silver Street, Cambridge CB3 9EP	01223 337166
South Eastern:	Farm Survey Section, Imperial College London, Wye Campus, Ashford, Kent TN25 5AH	020 7594 2925
Southern:	Department of Agriculture and Food Economics The University of Reading, 4 Earley Gate, Whiteknights, PO Box 237, Reading RG6 6AR	01189 875123
South Western:	Centre for Rural Research, The University of Exeter, Lafrowda House, St. German's Road,Exeter EX4 6TL	01392 263836
Wales:	Institute of Rural Studies, University of Wales, Aberystwyth, Llanbadarn Campus, Aberystwyth, Ceredigion SY23 3AL	01970 622253

SCOTLAND (SAC Farm Business Services)

Scottish Agricultural College
Regional Offices:

North:	SAC Aberdeen, Ferguson Building, Craibstone Estate, Bucksburn, Aberdeen AB21 9YA	01224 711000
East:	SAC Edinburgh, Bush Estate, Penecuik, Midlothian, EH26 0PH	0131 535 3440
West:	SAC Auchincruive, Ayr KA6 5HW	01292 520331

NORTHERN IRELAND (Advisory Services also)

Economics & Statistics Division, DARDNI, Dundonald House, Upper Newtownards Road, Belfast BT4 3SB 028 9052 0100

3. Commercial Banks: Agricultural Departments

Agricultural Mortgage Corporation (AMC)
Charlton Place, Charlton Road, Andover, Hants. SP10 1RE 01264 334747

Bank of Scotland
Agricultural Business, City House, City Road, Chester CH88 3AN 0845 3072852

Barclays Bank
Barclays Bank PLC, 24th Floor, 1 Churchill Place, London, E14 5HP. 0207 116 5515

Clydesdale Bank
AgriBusiness Banking Centre, 10 Fleet Place, London EC4M 7RB 020 7395 5662

Farming and Agricultural Finance Limited (FAF)
PO Box 234, Upminster, Essex RM14 2WS 0800 225567

HSBC Bank
Agriculture Head Office, 51 De Montford Street, Leicester LE1 7BB 0116 281 8328

Lloyds TSB Group
Business Banking Agricultural, PO Box 112, Canons House, Canons Way, Bristol BS99 7LB 0117 943 3114

National Westminster Bank
Agricultural Services, Gogaburn Business House C, PO Box 1000 Edinburgh EH12 1HQ 0131 626 0151

The Royal Bank of Scotland
Agricultural Services, Gogaburn Business House C, PO Box 1000 Edinburgh EH12 1HQ 0131 626 0151

4. Research Organisations

Biotechnology and Biological Sciences Research Council (BBSRC)
Polaris House, North Star Avenue, Swindon, Wilts. SN2 IUH
01793 413200

Babraham Institute
Babraham, Cambridge CB2 4AT
01223 496000

Broom's Barn Research Station
Higham, Bury St. Edmunds, Suffolk IP28 6NP
01284 812200

CEDAR (Centre for Dairy Research)
Arborfield Hall Farm, Reading Road, Arborfield, Reading,
RG2 9HX
0118 976 0964

East Malling Research
East Malling, Kent ME19 6BJ
01732 843833

Elm Farm Research Centre
Hamstead Marshall, Newbury, Berkshire RG15 0HR
01488 658298

Hannah Research Institute
Ayr, Scotland KA6 5HL
01292 674000

Institute for Animal Health
Compton, Newbury, Berks. RG20 7NN
01635 578411

Institute of Food Research
Norwich Research Park, Colney, Norwich NR4 7UA
01603 255000

Institute of Grassland and Environmental Research (IGER)
Aberystwyth Research Centre, Plas Gogerddan, Aberystwyth,
Ceredigion SY23 3EB
01970 823000
North Wyke Research Station, Okehampton, Devon EX20 2SB
01837 883500

Kingshay Farming Trust
Bridge Farm, West Bradley, Glastonbury, Somerset BA6 8LU
01458 851555

Macauley Land Use Research Institute
Craigiebuckler, Aberdeen AB15 8QH
01224 318611

Morley Research Centre
Morley St. Botolph, Wymondham, Norfolk NR18 9DB
01953 713200

NIAB
Huntingdon Road, Cambridge CB3 0LE
01223 342200

Processors and Growers Research Organisation (PGRO)
The Research Station, Great North Road, Thornhaugh,
Peterborough PE8 6HJ
01780 782585

Roslin Institute
Roslin, Midlothian EH25 9PS
0131 527 4200

Rothamsted Research
Harpenden, Hertfordshire AL5 2JQ
01582 763133

Rowett Research Institute
Greenburn Road, Bucksburn, Aberdeen AB21 9SB
01224 712751

Scottish Crop Research Institute (SCRI)
Mylnefield, Invergowrie, Dundee DD2 5DA
01382 562731

The Arable Group (TAG)
Manor Farm, Lower End, Doglingworth, Cirencester, Glos. GL7 7AH
01285 652184

5. National Agricultural Colleges

Cranfield University, Silsoe Campus
Silsoe, Bedford MK45 4DT
01525 863000

Harper Adams University College
Edgmond, Newport, Shropshire TF10 8NB
01952 820280

Institute of Rural Sciences
Llanbadarn Campus, Aberystwyth, Ceredigion SY23 3AL
01970 624471

Royal Agricultural College
Stroud Road, Cirencester, Glos. GL7 6JS
01285 652531

Scottish Agricultural College (student recruitment)
Auchincruive Campus, Ayr KA6 5HW
0800 269453

Shuttleworth College
Old Warden Park, Biggleswade, Beds. SG18 9EA
01767 626222

Writtle College
Lordship Road, Writtle, Chelmsford, Essex CM1 3RR
01245 424200

INDEX